PRENTICE-HALL INTERNATIONAL, INC., *London*
PRENTICE-HALL OF AUSTRALIA, PTY., LTD., *Sydney*
PRENTICE-HALL OF CANADA, LTD., *Toronto*
PRENTICE-HALL OF INDIA (PRIVATE) LTD., *New Delhi*
PRENTICE-HALL OF JAPAN, INC., *Tokyo*

THE FINE AR
OF BASEBAL

THE FINE ART
OF BASEBALL

A complete guide to strategy, skills, and system

LEW WATTS

PRENTICE-HALL, INC., *Englewood Cliffs, New Jersey*

IN MEMORY OF SHERMAN P. YOUNG,
GENTLEMAN, SCHOLAR, AND GREATEST OF COACHES.
DOC YOUNG TAUGHT ME BASEBALL AS A WAY OF LIFE
AND PROVIDED INSPIRATION
THAT WILL SUSTAIN ME FOR A LIFETIME.

PREFACE

This book has but one aim—to be the most complete one yet written on the playing and coaching of baseball.

In endeavoring to accomplish this goal, the author has interpreted the word "complete" as having a two-fold connotation—comprehensive and detailed. This book is comprehensive in that every facet of the game is discussed. It is detailed in that each of these facets is subjected to minute examination.

The section on coaching warrants special attention in that, from the standpoint of both scope and depth of treatment, an attempt has been made to achieve a truly thorough study of the educational aspects of baseball.

Defensive play is approached from both an individual and team standpoint and includes a determined effort to make an exhaustive diagnosis of the pitching game. Offensive baseball is given similar treatment and includes a section that, it is hoped, will provide the reader with a meticulous investigation of batting.

The final section embraces rules interpretation and the analysis of an actual ball game. The latter is intended to demonstrate the practical application of the techniques and tactics presented in the preceding text, using a World Series game, the epitome of professional competition, to do so.

This work is based on the philosophy that baseball is a dynamic game, yet that the basis for a sound approach to it must be founded on the tried and true practices developed and refined by the top performers and strategists in the field. The author is, indeed, fortunate that his playing experience included tenures under an outstanding college coach and nine excellent professional managers, as well as close contact with many accomplished, intelligent ballplayers. The lessons gleaned from this background should, if nothing else, make for a professional approach to the game.

The professional approach to baseball is business-like and precise. In essence, it has reduced correct mechanical moves to the automatic, and proper tactical maneuvers to a matter of percentages. It is the desire of the author to provide the background that will enable coach, player, and fan—at both amateur and professional levels of play—to pursue the game of baseball from a more informed, intelligent, and logical viewpoint, while at the same time furnishing a foundation for creative baseball thinking.

Whereas an authoritative instructional book must deal primarily with the mechanics of play and their tactical use, the mental aspect must not be overlooked. The mental and psychological factors that bear on all phases of baseball are discussed at length herein with the hope that a key to better performance may be uncovered for some aspiring ballplayer or his coach.

The author has attempted his inquiry into baseball in a manner that might be defined as dissection, examination, and reconstruction. This technique consists of stating well-founded theories, breaking them down into their smallest components, investigating the reasoning behind each of these integral parts, and fitting them together in a unified whole. This method is predicated on the belief that the most effective system of teaching baseball begins with the propounding of basic premises and a thorough explanation of just why these are the most efficient means to good performance. When demonstration and application follow, the learning process should be complete. This, of course, is the role of the coach and, in turn, the player. It is hoped that the presentation of this material is such that these interested parties will be stimulated into effective completion of the whole.

If the primary aim of this book is the most complete study and explanation yet made of the fine art of baseball, its corollary objective is to enable the reader—player, coach, or fan—to derive greater benefit and enjoyment from the game. If this is accomplished, in even slight degree, our great game will be richer for it.

ACKNOWLEDGMENTS

The author would like to make acknowledgment to the many people who have helped make this book possible—

To the Office of the Commissioner of Baseball for permission to use material from the Baseball Rules;

To Hillerich and Bradsby Co. for permission to use material from The Louisville Slugger Yearbook of 1955;

To Scholastic Coach Magazine for the use of most of the photographs found herein;

To Coaches John Herbold, William Hatch, and Jack Stallings for additional photographic material;

To George Davis, Athletic Director at Drew University, for his cooperation on some of the photographs found herein;

To my wife Barbara for her photography and for her help in preparing the pictorial material;

To Herman Masin, editor of Scholastic Coach, for his ever available advice and encouragement;

To my ballplaying friends, Danny Mays and Bill George, for their many intelligent ideas on the game;

To Arthur "Dynie" Mansfield of the University of Wisconsin for his work in reading this material and for his helpful suggestions;

To Mary Ann Molloy for her invaluable help in preparing the manuscript;

And, above all, to the late Sherman P. Young who started the thought processes that culminated in this book and who was so helpful in its actual creation.

CONTENTS

CONTENTS

BATTING—THE MENTAL ASPECT, 269

BASE-RUNNING, 287

OFFENSIVE PLAYS, 302

4 ADDENDA

THE FINE ART
OF BASEBALL

1

COACHING

THE ROLE OF THE COACH

The classical tradition of education has always proclaimed the value of athletics in the development of young people as well as its merit in maintaining sound adults. A coach's role is possibly even more important than that of the classroom teacher, since the instruction that he provides includes practical application. He is truly molding the whole man—mental, physical, and spiritual.

Every lasting value to be derived from athletics revolves around playing to win. Even a losing struggle has worth when it is played to the fullest, with victory as the one objective. Certainly, we cannot win them all—but an honest endeavor to do so will give lasting benefit to any participant.

Baseball, perhaps more than any other sport, combines both individual and team effort. The battle between pitcher and batter is an individual one; play in the field is performed by individual players with individual responsibilities—yet each man's own effort must be subordinated to that of the team. It is a wonderful game that teaches youngsters how to win their individual battles within a framework of cooperative enterprise. In baseball the good of the group is always paramount, yet completely dependent upon the individual efforts of each man.

The coach should never lose sight of the fact that his teaching applies to the complete development of his charges—their mental, physical, and spiritual betterment. And how better can he do this than by showing each man just how much he *can* do, thus developing confidence, skill, and a spiritual bond between player and coach?

Obviously the main job of a coach is to organize his squad and to formulate his attack and his defense. Yet, since a squad is made up of human beings, through whom the attack and defense function, the psychological factor cannot be overemphasized. Sound knowledge of skills, strategy, and men is the basis of the successful teaching of baseball. Along with imparting correct techniques and tactics to his men, a coach must build a relationship with each of them that will enable the player, and consequently the team, to capitalize fully on his ability—to rise above the purely mechanical.

A healthy atmosphere of mutual respect demands that the coach make a close study of each player and learn as much as he can about his ability, personality, interests, and idiosyncrasies. This will help the coach to pinpoint the areas in which each individual should try to improve his play; even more important, it will build a squad's confidence in the coach. This is absolutely essential in creating a climate in which both individual and team performance flourish to the fullest possible extent.

Each player should be dealt with honestly and fairly. Favoritism and discrimination are absolutely taboo in building morale. Furthermore, in developing a cohesive unit the lowliest substitute is just as important as the .400 hitter—and he should be made to feel that his role, small though it be, is essential to the over-all success of the team. In truth, he should feel that the success of his team rests directly on him. This, more than any other single factor, will spur him to top performance.

A coach is, to a good extent, a salesman. His job, in this respect, is to sell his players on their own ability as well as on the worthiness of the system of play and teaching that he uses. Unquestionably the greatest factor in successful selling is enthusiasm. The coach must literally radiate enthusiasm and he must kindle and re-kindle it in every man to insure consistent peak performance.

Generally speaking, no offensive play should be made unless the coach has ordered it. It is unfair to burden the player with the responsibility for offensive tactics. The coach should also instruct his defense, especially in a close game. This will not detract from a boy's confidence in himself. On the contrary, it will lend to that confidence when he has faith that his coach can and will come to his aid whenever help is needed. Team morale stays at a high level when the coach does not shirk these responsibilities.

Mistakes definitely should be discussed, with a careful explanation of cause, effect, and proper therapy. But only mental errors should be criticized. Moreover, a coach should give credit for heads-up play. This is the positive approach and is tremendously valuable in building morale.

Serious disciplinary problems which demand a severe reprimand should be handled in private. Serious lapses on the ball field should be discussed at a team meeting but should never give rise to public beratement of a player during the course of a ballgame.

DISCIPLINE

Any discussion of coaching philosophy is replete with the words "morale, cohesiveness, team spirit"—and rightfully so. These are the qualities that lift performance, both individual and collective, above the purely mechanical, and a coach should constantly strive for a high degree of this team character. One of the chief factors contributing to this winning atmosphere is discipline.

Good discipline of a baseball squad does not imply a martinet constantly cracking a whip over his charges. Rather, it presumes the mutual respect of player and coach that is inspired by an air of cooperative helpfulness and arises most effectively from a truly professional approach to the game; it is this aspiring to the best by using the proven methods of experts-at-their-trade that makes scholastic athletics educational.

When Eddie Dyer was managing a good St. Louis Cardinal team I was present during a clubhouse meeting in which his main theme was complimenting his squad on the way in which they were helping each other. Great though the individual performances of such stars as Musial, Slaughter, Marion, and Schoendienst were, it was the cohesive unity, the team spirit of this club that had it in first place.

An atmosphere of togetherness is absolutely essential to the team that would rise above its normal level of play—whether it be for an inning, a game, or a season. Here is the key to molding a collection of individuals into a team—the word "together."

Everything a ball club does should be done together. In this way the essential spirit of unity can best be built. The members of the squad should associate with one another as much as possible, should eat together, talk together, study together, date together, stick together on road trips, dress together in the locker room, and, above all, they should take the field together—as a team.

The members of a baseball squad can take pride in the fact that they belong to something special—an athletic team that should be truly representative of their school.

With this justifiable pride must go the responsibility of wearing it well. Appearance and conduct off the field, as well as on, should be exemplary. This is where discipline—the right kind—takes its roots. The members of a baseball squad should act the part of prideful, skilled gentlemen, worthy representatives of their school and their team.

A coach should insist on neatness off the field—good grooming means clean shaves, trim haircuts, decent clothes—and he should absolutely demand it on the field, where it involves sanitation, protection, practicality, and good common sense.

It is a great privilege to wear a baseball uniform, and a man worthy of it should wear it properly—with no exceptions or deviations. Furthermore, the uniform is not merely decorative, it has a definite purpose—allowing a man freedom of movement within the bounds of protectiveness.

Following are some suggestions on uniforms, equipment, and appearance.

1. All players should dress alike. No extremes will be allowed.
2. No rings or jewelry are to be worn. Nails are to be cut short at all times.
3. Supporters, inner hose, and undershirts should be changed often and kept clean, for sanitary purposes.

4. Stockings should be rolled into a wide, thick band just below the knee joint, for protective purposes. Supporters should be worn over the undershirt to prevent the latter from pulling out; sliding pads are to be worn over shirt and supporter. In this way the uniform will stay in place, where it affords the most protection.

5. Long-sleeved undershirts should be worn in the spring.

6. Jackets are to be worn going to and from the field. They are to be fully buttoned whenever worn.

7. Shoes should fit snugly; cotton inner hose are to be worn. Shoes should be cleaned and polished daily. They are a ballplayer's most important tool. Black shoelaces are to be worn by all players.

8. No oil is to be used on gloves. The slightly shorter wear given by an unoiled glove is more than offset by the fact that a ball hitting the pocket of an un-oiled glove does not become slippery. This point is doubly important for pitchers and catchers.

9. Players are to look neat. They should stick together, especially when taking the field. Finally, everyone but the game pitcher is to run at all times when on the ball field.

Insistence on the above rules, or similar ones, is the first step in building a disciplined, cohesive organization. The second step is to teach properly and in such a way that instructions will be carried out and correct moves made at all times.

Paul Richards is a great disciplinarian and a marvelous manager. It is his theory that during spring training every member of his squad—from the greenest rookie to the most grizzled veteran—must be treated as though he were completely inexperienced. Every mechanical move, every tactical maneuver, every possible play situation must be explained, taught, and practiced until its proper execution becomes almost automatic during a ball game. This method can develop a player who is at once assured, alert, and well-disciplined.

The subtle kind of discipline that results in alert play and correct execution stems from an approach in which the coach must follow these practices:

1. Cover every possible play situation in pre-season practice sessions.

2. Explain as well as demonstrate the correct maneuvers—knowing the purpose for and logic behind every drill helps to prevent their being drudgery.

3. Whenever possible, inject competition into practice sessions.

4. Avoid overly long, tedious drills and practice sessions.

5. Teach your squad to think in correct patterns, along your own carefully devised lines. This can save much anguish and unnecessary hard feeling during games.

6. A coach's performance on the field should be as conscientious, systematic, and well-planned as a teacher's performance in the classroom.

In this way baseball can be made both educational and enjoyable, as it should be.

THE BENCH

A usually neglected factor in building a winning spirit is the bench. So much concentrated effort is devoted to fielding a good nine that the men on the bench are too often neglected—left to twiddle their thumbs, as it were.

On too many occasions reserve players can be seen lolling around in the general vicinity of the bench, indulging in horse-play, or engaged in a slovenly game of catch. This cannot be tolerated if good discipline and team morale are to be achieved.

Baseball is a team game and "team" means every man in uniform. Every member of a squad should be in the ball game at all times—mentally and spiritually. In this way he can perform four valuable functions:

1. He gears himself for the time when he will be in the game.
2. He lends an air of class to his team.
3. He contributes to the morale of his teammates who are playing.
4. He may uncover valuable information about the opponent that will give his team the advantage that can spell victory.

An orderly, alert bench reflects good coaching, the kind that insists on attention to detail and instills in every squad member the belief that he is an integral part of a successful organization. The bench, collectively and as a unit, is literally the tenth man in the lineup.

The coach who seeks to build a hustling bench will insist that substitutes:

1. Keep their attention riveted on the game at all times. Periodic checks help insure this.
2. Lend vocal encouragement to the men on the field.
3. Help them where possible by doing such things as informing the catcher when the runner is stealing ("There he goes!"); informing the pitcher who starts his motion unaware that one of his teammates is out of position; shouting instructions to a player who pursues a fly ball near the bench or home-plate area; and similar acts that are to be expected of the "team man."
4. Act as housekeepers for the bench area. Retrieving a stray ball, glove, etc. may prevent injury to a player whose attention is concentrated on the ball.
5. Attempt to discover opponent's signals, unconventional maneuvers, tell-tale positioning, and pitching "tip-offs."
6. Look for lapses on the part of his own team and report them *to the coach* for correction.
7. Study the opposing batters. This applies to pitchers and catchers, especially the ones due to go into the game next; with these players the practice should be mandatory.

In this way baseball can truly be a team game, as it should be.

SCOUTING

A thorough-going coaching job will prepare every player for any eventuality which may arise on the ball field. Advance knowledge of the time when specific situations will occur would indeed be too good to be true. In absence of it a team should be able to look for the probable, in order to gear itself properly to cope with most of the play situations encountered in a game. It is here that scouting can prove most invaluable.

If the opportunity exists to scout an opponent a coach should, by all means, take advantage of it—along with his catcher and probable starting pitcher, where possible.

In my first year of coaching (at the college level) I was able to scout six of our opponents. We defeated every one of them although at least two of them had superior ball clubs to ours. Undoubtedly the psychological effect of knowing what to expect of our opponents had much to do with this. Also important was the fact that playing strategy could be planned—always an improvement over having to rely strongly on improvisation.

Professional clubs endeavor to compile a complete "book" on their opponents. This is both possible and important in organized baseball where each opponent will be met numerous times during the course of the season. Naturally, the brevity of an interscholastic season plus the year-by-year turnover of personnel make intensive scouting at the school level neither possible nor practical.

When the schedule of the schools involved permits, an attempt should be made to take a look at future opponents in game competition. A cursory inspection of a team's style of play and the individual characteristics of its key players, as well as any apparent flaws in its game, should be the primary targets of a scouting expedition. Here is a brief listing of the more essential points to be covered.

Offense

TEAM

1. Do they bunt, steal, or start the runner—when?
2. Is there a particular type of team strategy? Does the manager favor certain tactics? Do they play for a big inning or go in for a running game?

INDIVIDUAL

1. Who are their pull, opposite-field, and straightaway hitters? Who hits with power?
2. What pitch does each hitter like? Does he have an apparent weakness? Is he a first-ball hitter?
3. Who are their fast men?

Defense

TEAM

1. What are strong and weak points of the defense?
2. How do they look against bunts, or a running game?

INDIVIDUAL

1. What are the strengths and weaknesses of the pitcher(s)? What is his pitching pattern? What are his habits? What does he go to when in the clutch? When behind the hitter? Do base runners upset him? Does he work in a regular cadence with men on base?
2. How does the catcher handle himself? Can and will he throw?
3. How does the outfield throw? Are they fast?
4. How does the second-short duo handle the ball on relays and double steals?

When no opportunity has existed to scout a team there is still one good means of getting advance information: pre-game practice (and, to a certain extent, the early innings of the ball game). The field, the weather, and the opponent's personnel should be taken into consideration.

The field (for a road game)

1. If the field is of skin the ball will skip and bunts will roll more rapidly. If the field is grass the ball will roll more slowly but produce more hops.
2. An outfield fence demands more careful pitching to men who can reach the short parts of it. Outfielders should test the fences for resiliency and angle of bounce; they should also allow for the carom in backing up one another.
3. How far is the backstop from home plate? Can you run on a passed ball?

The weather

1. Wet field: be prepared for a bunting game. Outfielders should charge ground balls. A base runner must begin his slide sooner.
2. Sunny field: who should have glasses? The team should be aware of the possible need to come to the rescue of a man playing a high fly in the sun.
3. Windy day: how will the wind affect the flight of a fly ball, or the action of the pitcher's curve ball?
4. Night game: where are the dark spots on the field? Which players should be made aware of them?

The opponents

OFFENSE. A complete "book" is not needed. In batting practice look for their pull hitters, men who are likely to bunt, those who look weak on the curve ball, those who overstride (pitch them high), those who appear

9

nervous or over-anxious (wait on them), those who are overly muscular (jam them); what pitches do their good hitters hit well in practice—high or low, fast ball or curve?

DEFENSE. How does each of them throw? Does the third baseman seem weak on bunts? In the early innings of a ball game one can gain revealing insights into the opponent's pattern of play. For example, a team that bunts early in the game will surely do so in the late innings.

Individual weaknesses may also reveal themselves. Important here is the possibility of the catcher's signals being picked up by a base coach or the pitcher himself tipping his deliveries. Information of this sort can be passed along to any batter who desires it, and may also be used to guide a team's use of the steal, a move most propitious when a curve or change has been signalled.

THE BATTING ORDER

A team's batting order should be selected along logical, if not scientific, lines. Much thought is given by professional managers to the choice, and even the development, of the right man for each spot in the offensive line-up. Periodic refinements are made according to individual performance, type of ball park, and opposing pitcher. A professional manager, with a large squad of well-trained specialists, playing a long season on a daily basis, can afford this approach. With an entirely different set of circumstances facing them, scholastic coaches *cannot adopt the same methods.* Greater thought and different reasoning should go into the selection of the batting order of an amateur or scholastic team, with its prevalence of weak spots.

In general, a team's best hitters should be at the top of the batting list in order to assure them a maximum number of times at bat. Furthermore, the strength of the first five hitters should build to a high point with number three and then taper off. There is, however, no set formula for selecting the batting order; common-sense rules may guide a coach to the refinements that will give him the most effective offensive line-up possible.

The lead-off man is expected to get on base often, in any way possible. He should have a good eye; be fast of foot and a good base runner; have little or no power, because of the weak hitters he follows in the line-up; and, if the choice is between a lefty or a righty, preference should be given to the right-hand batter.

The number-two hitter has, as his primary requisite, the ability to get a piece of the ball. Ideally, he is left-handed since it is assumed that the lead-off man will get on base often. A left-handed number-two batter will make it easier for the runner to steal; will have a bigger hole to go for with the first baseman holding the bag against the runner; and will be more likely to advance the runner with a batted ball which will, in most cases, go toward right field.

The number-three hitter will probably be the best hitter on the club. As compared to number four, he should be the faster of the two since he will generally have more opportunity to score; if one hits left-handed, the other right, he should be the right-hander. Where two or more factors can go into the selection of a hitter, they should be weighed very carefully, with almost equal consideration given them.

The clean-up man should be one of the two best hitters, with the primary consideration (as opposed to number three) being sheer power.

Number five will generally be the poorest of the big three but he should, nevertheless, hit well, and with power.

Number six is sometimes known as the second lead-off man. Like number one he should have the faculty of getting on base; but he should be the power hitter of the two, since he will have more opportunities to drive in runs. If speed is the determining factor the number-six hitter will be slower than number one. If one of the two is a lefty batter, and the other a righty, the former should fill the number-six slot.

The last three men in the line-up can be taken as a group. At the end of the order, runs should be played for one-at-a-time. Naturally, the hope will be to reach the top of the order with one of the weak sisters on base. Another objective, where possible, is to avoid leading off an inning with one of a team's poorest hitters. For this reason, a more conservative game should be played when the end of the batting order is reached. It would be well to have these men try to work the pitcher for a walk. The extra pitches he may have to throw will also leave him with a little less on the ball for the good hitters. The seventh, eighth, and ninth man to bat should also merely try to get a piece of the ball in hopes of reaching base on an error.

In professional ball the catcher usually bats eighth and the pitcher ninth, not only because they are generally relatively weak hitters, but also because they are not in the line-up every day and their presence elsewhere in the order would disrupt it constantly. In amateur ball, with far fewer and more widely-scattered games this is not necessary and good hitting catchers and pitchers should be spotted where they will bat more often. In the case of a pitcher who is a better hitter than two or three of his teammates, but not outstanding with the stick, it may be best to bat him ninth so as to conserve his strength for the mound. The fact that colleges play nine innings, as opposed to seven for high schools, will also weigh in favor of their having the pitcher bat ninth.

When two or more left-handed batters are in the line-up, the coach should spot them strategically, to help his team's running game. Unless the more conventional considerations weigh very heavily against it, a left-hand batter should be placed behind a man who will reach base often, especially a fast one. For example, a lefty is more desirable in the number-two spot than as lead-off man, and at the end of the order should be placed in the seventh slot rather than the eighth or ninth where he is less likely to come to the plate with men on base. A deviation which may, with some justification, be preferred by a coach is the placing of a good hitter in the seventh spot rather than near the top of the order, where he would come to bat more often. The idea here would be to break up a possible three sure-outs in quick succession. A good-hitting pitcher would fit ideally into this position.

Whatever the lineup, a team must adhere to it carefully during a game lest they lose an out for batting out of order. It is wise, in this respect, to station a scorekeeper on the bench to prevent its happening —and to keep alert for its befalling the opposing ball club.

MANAGER'S DUTIES

A coach's primary responsibility is the mental and physical preparation of his squad and the direction of its play on the field. The many tasks not directly connected with the playing of the game but necessary to the proper conduct of a baseball schedule demand the delegation of authority. Here is encountered the need for a competent nonplaying manager, usually a member of the student body.

A conscientious, efficient manager is a great boon to any coach and, in order to help in attracting the right man, the importance of the job and the prestige which it should carry must be stressed.

Since a topflight manager is a desirable commodity, the process of selection should be a careful one. Willingness to work and a good degree of capability are the main prerequisites in selection. The system of apprenticeship in common use, with perhaps two freshmen, two sophomores, and a junior as assistants to the senior manager, serves as a good means of selection (or elimination) for the top position.

The more competent his manager and the more willing his assistant managers, the less gruelling will be a coach's job. Close supervision of the managerial staff is necessary for the smooth running of the over-all baseball program. Nevertheless, a coach cannot have too many extraneous demands on his time if his primary mission is to be done well. For this reason he must select carefully, inspire constantly, and delineate his manager's duties most explicitly.

Here is a suggested routine for the managerial staff. Times listed are arbitrary and may be altered where needed to conform with school hours.

Practice

1. Keep an inventory of equipment on hand and keep a record of all equipment issued to each player. Keep equipment clean. Get replacements (bats and balls) from coach when needed.
2. Have all equipment on the field at 2:30 daily (1:00 on Saturdays). See that bases are in place.
3. Keep track of equipment in use, especially balls and bats.
4. Keep a fresh supply of water for use by the players.
5. A rotating schedule may be used, but two managers should be present at all times—one on the field, one near the bench.

Game routine (for a 2:30 game)

1. One manager should be assigned to the visiting team upon their arrival.
2. At 1:00 P.M. on game days managers should have all equipment on the field and should be preparing the field for the game.
3. Water and towels should be in each dugout, a game ball should be delivered to the opposing team's coach, a knife for cleaning spikes, and spare shoe laces placed in the home team dugout.
4. Batter's boxes will be marked just prior to the start of the game (during pre-game conference with umpires).
5. All loose equipment should be removed from the playing area.
6. One manager should be prepared to take notes in the dugout during the game. He is to record the coach's comments on each player of both teams as he comes to bat. He should also have the facilities for recording notes on each type pitch and situation for home team pitchers.
7. Towels should be ready for the visiting team after the game.

Road games

1. Submit a complete list of all personnel making the trip to the school office. Each name should be checked off as that man reports to the bus.
2. All necessary equipment should be on the bus fifteen minutes before departure time (check with coaches to make a list of all equipment to be taken on the trip).
3. When arriving at opposing team's field obtain towels (at least three) and water for our bench and arrange all of our equipment at our bench. Obtain towels for use after the game.
4. Have a small travelling bag available for checking the valuables of our players, and be custodian of same.
5. Make a check of all our equipment to see that it is on hand, for the return trip. Unload and store same on our return.

Managers may be delegated the authority for obtaining transportation, handling money, and arranging for rooms and meals on the road. In most cases it is best for the coach or faculty advisor to do so. This will depend to a great extent on the reliability of the manager and the faith of the coach in him.

INJURIES AND THEIR TREATMENT

Proper conditioning of a ball club, even before outdoor work is begun, will preclude the possibility of many injuries, certainly most of those which result from sore muscles and poor coordination. Pre-season training should include lectures by coach and trainer on good health habits, personal hygiene, and injury prevention. It is the responsibility of the coach to see that all injuries are recognized and given proper treatment.

A team physician should be retained by the school. Where feasible he should administer physical check-ups to the squad prior to the start of pre-season work with the additional precaution of insuring that all players have had anti-tetanus innoculations. After this initial phase of his duties as team physician he should serve more in the role of a consultant. He should attend to all apparently serious injuries as well as those that do not respond properly to treatment. He should also instruct and advise the coach and trainer on the handling of minor injuries which may rightfully fall within their province.

In addition to ministering to routine needs of the players and the treatment of minor injuries, the coach and/or trainer must see that good sanitary habits are practiced. Clean showers, well-ventilated dressing quarters, and clean uniforms are necessities to a well-organized ball club and the coach should see that this standard of sanitation is maintained. Where possible, fresh inner hose, undershirts, and jocks should be provided for each player every day. Where economy prevents this, the players should be charged with this responsibility.

Avoiding injuries

There are several precautionary measures which should be taken by all ballplayers. Observance of them will help prevent needless injuries. A coach should instruct his squad to observe the following precautions:

1. Don't wear rings or jewelry, and keep fingernails clipped.
2. Always wear clean underclothes—shirts, socks, and supporter.
3. Shower and change immediately after every game or workout.
4. Stretch and loosen up thoroughly before every game or practice session and condition yourself very gradually early in the season.
5. Never slide unnecessarily, and keep the forward foot in the air when you do slide.

14

6. Avoid indecision in sliding—once you have decided either to slide or stay up, do so.
7. The head-first slide risks injury to the head and face.
8. Advise and warn a player who is chasing a fly ball near the fence, screen, or dugout.
9. Keep all bats in the bat-rack where they cannot cause injury.
10. Never turn your back on a play that is in progress.
11. Don't stand in front of a base when a runner is nearing it. This protects the opposing players; it is a coach's duty to see that his men do not contribute to the unnecessary injury of an opponent.
12. Don't stand behind the batter—if lack of space makes this necessary make sure that you face him.
13. Once you enter the batter's box, always keep your eye on the pitcher.
14. Catch the ball with the fingers slightly bent—never extended.
15. Call all fly balls and obey the call, so as to avoid collisions.
16. Bunt properly—don't hold the bat directly in front of the body and do keep the fingers of the upper hand behind the bat.
17. An injured player is of no help to his team. Don't try to be a hero if incapacitated—report all injuries.

Treating injuries

Certain minor injuries are relatively common and can be treated quite easily and fairly effectively by coach or trainer. If a doctor is available he should be consulted for all injuries and, above all, he should be called on where an ailment persists.

1. *Sprains:* these are serious injuries and should be treated by a physician as soon as possible.
    (a) Ankle—apply ice or ice water immediately (ethyl chloride, where authorized by the team physician); use a pressure bandage; resume normal movements (not heavy exercise) as soon as possible.
    (b) Knee—treat the same as an ankle sprain—but stay off of it.
    (c) Wrist—the same; bandage with alternate circular and longitudinal layers of tape.
    (d) Finger—apply ice, tape it to the next finger for protection.
2. *Charley-horse and muscle bruise*—apply ice at once; then heat (moist heat is preferable to dry), massage and light exercise.
3. *Stone bruise*—apply ice packs; avoid using injured part; protect with a sponge rubber pad.
4. *Pulled thigh muscle*—band of tape one inch above injury and one inch below it.
5. *Shin splint*—heat, massage, and counter-irritant.
6. *Burns*—apply disinfectant, then dusting-powder on a vanishing-cream base; protect with a sponge bandage—don't use petroleum jelly, which keeps it soft.
7. *Blisters*—leave unopened; cover with bandage; if open, treat like a burn.

15

8. *Jock itch*—apply dusting-powder; place a folded handkerchief inside the supporter.
9. *Sore arm*—should not be worked out—heat and rest are the best remedy; rotation of the limb while under a very hot shower is good; massage is very helpful but should be done only by an experienced *"rubber."*
10. *Spike wounds*—cleanse with soap and water; apply disinfectant and bandage; consult physician as soon as possible for advisability of suturing.
11. If the effects of a minor injury persist, a physician should be consulted. Whirlpool baths, infra-red lamps, and diathermy have greatly facilitated the treatment of athletic injuries. But—they are not for use by the neophyte. An experienced trainer or coach, in absence of a doctor, should supervise their usage and administer treatment.

A well-equipped medicine kit should be available whenever a team is on the field. As a minimum it should include:

tape	sulfa-thiazole
gauze	ethyl chloride (with physician's approval)
ace bandages	
band-aids	tincture of green soap
bunion plasters	smelling salts
sponge pads	aspirin
doughnuts (rubber)	antacid tablets
dusting-powder	rubbing alcohol
fungicide	liniment
vanishing-cream	salt tablets
disinfectant	Vitamin C (cold preventative)

CARE OF THE FIELD

It is hoped, if not assumed, that a coach will not have to maintain his own ball field. Yet, he must have a rudimentary knowledge of baseball groundskeeping if he is to supervise his caretaking crew in keeping the field in constant readiness for play.

A well-kept field that is, at all times, as level and dry as possible, and without loose stones, roots, or soft spots not only lends to better play but can contribute greatly to injury prevention.

Here is a basic guide to proper care of a ball field.

1. The grass should be cut weekly and the cut grass left on the field. Cutting should be done before rolling.
2. The field should be watered weekly.
3. The field should be rolled weekly.
4. Fences and screens should be kept in constant good repair.
5. The mound, plate, and base paths should be dragged and tamped daily.

6. Recommended composition of the mound and batter's box is three parts brick dust to one part loam or two and one-half parts clay to one part loam.
7. If the field is too soft add loam.
   If the field is too dry add sand.
8. After rain:
   wet areas can be drained by short lengths of pipe driven into the ground. After draining, the damp area should be leveled off and dry sand or dirt applied. This should be raked in and more added as needed.
   All skin areas should be raked; the diamond dragged; the pitcher's box and plate area tamped as well as raked; and the lines re-marked.
9. Recommended minimum equipment:
   small tarps (5) for mound, plate, and base areas.
   rake
   shovels
   mat (for dragging)
   tamper
   dry sand and dirt
   wheelbarrow

PRACTICE AND CONDITIONING

The aim of any coach should be to prepare his team so well that it will get off to a flying start and build sufficient momentum to carry it successfully through the season. Very often the difference between a good start and a bad one is indoor work.

Gym workouts, in order to be effective, must be purposeful and carefully planned. In fact, indoor practice sessions of a haphazard sort can have a deleterious consequence in two important respects—team discipline can deteriorate to an irretrievably low level and a sore arm or other crippling injury can be sustained by a key man even before the start of the season.

Indoor workouts should be preceded by weekly team meetings, beginning the first week in January. These sessions should cover everything that will be taught to the squad before a condition of game-readiness is achieved, including:

1. Approach to the game and educational philosophy
2. Training and discipline
3. Defensive techniques and tactics
4. Offensive techniques and tactics

5. Rules
6. Future plans—schedule, practice, and training routine

The use of a mimeographed study guide is strongly recommended. If all-inclusive, it can save much valuable time on the practice field merely because material to be covered when actual physical work begins will not be completely unfamiliar to any squad member.

PITCHING READINESS

Since a baseball team's entire operation revolves around its pitching staff, so too should its training period. The section on pitching includes several suggestions on the individual conditioning of pitchers. It would be well to review this material for the edification of the coach who will supervise the over-all training procedure. With this as a guide to conditioning devices, a day-by-day schedule of throwing activity will be outlined. It is assumed that training work of a more general nature will be added to this regimen in an attempt to integrate the preparation of the pitching staff with that of the entire squad. A schedule based on the year 1964 will be used.

Weekly squad meetings are to be held beginning Monday, January 6. The seventh, and last, of these will be held on Monday, February 17, on which date pitchers (and catchers) will start their actual physical work. The entire squad reports on a full-time basis exactly two weeks later, Monday, March 2.

The routine outlined below pertains only to the conditioning of the arm itself. Other activity should be added by the coach.

It is my belief that calisthenics are only incidental to the physical preparation of a baseball squad. Conditioning of the legs by running, and of the arm by throwing, are the most important facets of pre-session workouts—especially for pitchers. For that reason it is recommended that calisthenics be engaged in for only the first two weeks—not in an excessive amount and never in a way that is contrary to baseball's regular muscular actions. Loose muscle exercises are the most effective ones.

Before any physical work is attempted, common-sense precautionary measures should be formulated as mandatory rules for the squad. Suggested ones are as follows:

1. Workouts are to carried out only under the direct supervision of the coach.
2. No throwing is to be done until a player has thoroughly loosened his muscles by stretching exercises.
3. Hard throwing is to be attempted only after a player is fully warmed up.
4. All injuries, including sore arms, are to be reported to the coach immediately.

Pitching schedule

This sequence of arm-conditioning is predicated on a hypothetical opening date of April 7, with the second game scheduled for April 10. It is presumed that Saturday workouts will be held—at least for pitchers—and that indoor sessions will be conducted during inclement weather.

Our routine is designed to prepare two pitchers for starting duty. Until they are definitely selected (by March 1) all pitching candidates should follow this schedule. Relief-men and added starters may be trained at the coach's discretion and along similar lines. Once the entire squad has reported, there should always be a batter in position during these pitching drills. When outdoor work commences this plan may be integrated with batting practice and intra-squad games.

Squad meetings will have been held on Mondays throughout January and up to, and including, February 17. The last of these sessions should be followed by physical work for batterymen, including calisthenics (to be continued for two weeks) and leg-work (running and "pick-ups," which should be continued by the pitchers all season, except on game days).

Pitcher A	Pitcher B
Feb.18(Tu) - 5 minutes throwing	Feb.18(Tu) - 5 minutes throwing
19(W) - 5 " "	19(W) - 5 " "
20(Th) - 5 " "	20(Th) - 5 " "
22(S) - 10 " "	22(S) - 10 " "
24(M) - 10 " "	24(M) - 10 " "
26(W) - 10 " "	26(W) - 10 " "
28(F) - 10 " "	27(Th) - 5 " "
29(S) - 5 " "	29(S) - 15 " "
Mar. 2(M) - 15 " "	Mar. 2(M) - 15 " "
4(W) - 15 " "	4(W) - 15 " "
6(F) - 15 " "	7(S) - 3 innings pitching
9(M) - 3 innings pitching	(51 pitches)
(51 pitches)	10(Tu) - 3 "
11(W) - 3 innings	12(Th) - 3 "
13(F) - 3 "	14(S) - 3 "
16(M) - 3 "	17(Tu) - 5 innings
18(W) - 5 innings	(85 pitches)
(85 pitches)	20(F) - 5 "
21(S) - 5 "	23(M) - 5 "
24(Tu) - 5 "	26(Th) - 5 "
27(F) - 5 "	30(M) - 5 "
30(M) - 6 innings	
(102 pitches)	Apr. 2(Th) - 6 innings
Apr. 3(F) - 7 innings	(102 pitches)
(119 pitches)	6(M) - 7 innings
6(M) - 5 minutes light throwing	(119 pitches)
7(Tu) - GAME	9(Th) - 5 minutes light throwing
	10(F) - GAME

(a) Timed throwing is an over-all figure, representing total throwing.

(b) Innings pitched is in addition to a thorough warm-up.

(c) Part of every workout should be devoted to pitching from a stretch.

(d) A pitcher should always throw for strikes. When the full squad reports and a batter is assigned to a pitcher, his catcher should serve as umpire.

(e) A pitcher should know his own arm and make sure that his coach also does.

THE FULL SQUAD

Pitchers and catchers will have been working for two weeks when the other players report for duty, and should be in a fair state of readiness. Calisthenics on their part are no longer necessary. The rest of the squad should engage in them during the first week of their conditioning period.

The various phases of conditioning a baseball team and the devices for achieving readiness in each of them while the squad is confined to the gymnasium are as follows:

Indoor phase

CALISTHENICS

ERECT—Jumping jack, windmill, trunk twister, knee bends
SITTING—Alternate toe-toucher
PRONE—Stomach rocker, up-and-down (to standing position & back)
SUPINE—Sit-ups, toe-toucher, bicycle

GENERAL EXERCISE

Volley ball is an excellent conditioner and can occupy the entire squad at one time. Furthermore, it adds a competitive element to an otherwise tedious routine.

Pepper games are valuable in that several things are accomplished thereby. Fielding, batting, throwing, and good bodily exercise are being practiced at one time. Several pepper games can be held simultaneously if the ball is hit down one alley with the fielders taking turns—the man who has fielded the ball goes to the end of the line and the others move up, in turn.

LEG CONDITIONERS

RUNNING. Much running should be done by all players. This is doubly necessary for pitchers. Running should be in the form of wind-sprints.

PICK-UPS. This is one of the greatest of conditioning devices, excellent for the legs and good for the entire body. It is done by having one player, stationed about eight feet away, roll a ball to another player—first to one side, then the other, in an arc of about ten feet. The latter must pick up the ball with two hands and return it with an underhand toss. This exercise should be started with about twenty-five pick-ups and increased until fifty is reached on a once-a-day basis. Along with running, it should be continued all season by the pitchers.

Conditioning: Pick-ups for the Pitchers

BATTING

THE STILL HEAD. One of the most important factors in achieving good batting performance is the maintaining of a still head (and level eyes) throughout the entire hitting action. Its accomplishment should be acquired in gradual steps, the first of which is merely swinging a bat. An effective way of checking on head movement is to have a strong light (the sun, when outdoors) behind the hitter. The coach or another player then places his foot on the shadow of the batter's head. A full swing is taken, the object being to take the cut with the "head remaining underfoot." This should be repeated many times, until the head remains consistently still, and should be checked daily throughout the training period and whenever game performance indicates a possible lapse in the practice of this basic.

BATTING TEE. The next step in the acquisition of good batting habits is to swing at a ball—stationary in this case. Indoor use of a batting tee may require the utilization of sponge rubber balls. This gadget, easily constructed, enables a coach to check on the batting form of each player and to apply corrective therapy where needed. Hand position, distribution of weight, stride, swing, follow-through, and the level head are things to be watched, for possible correction.

BATTING PRACTICE. When a coach is satisfied that his players have achieved effective individual hitting form they should progress to regular batting practice.

Sponge rubber balls, fairly similar to a baseball in size, can be used. A pitching machine, if available, should serve as batting practice pitcher. In the absence of one, players can be used—but never a pitcher.

A regular batting cage can be set up with nets. If this is impractical a heavy curtain of asbestos or similar material can be stretched across the gym at the midway point. Balls hit into this drop harmlessly to the floor. Batter, practice pitcher (where used), and three men waiting to hit should be the maximum number in the batting area at one time. The rest of the squad should be engaged in regular practice activity in the other half of the gym.

Where no such equipment is available, one method of batting practice remains—the use of a whiffle ball. This enables players to swing at a moving ball while in no way endangering fixtures or personnel. Furthermore, two groups can engage in batting practice simultaneously, one at either end of the floor, since a whiffle ball travels with little force. No player should throw a whiffle ball; a manager or other non-participant should do the pitching.

BALL-ON-A-STRING. This is a tool which is useful in helping a player learn to cope with the curve ball. Since indoor batting practice pitching will consist of nothing but straight throws it can be valuable as preparation for the breaking balls that will be encountered when outdoor work is begun.

Equipment needed includes a high jump standard, a ten-to-twelve foot length of cord, and a rubber ball. One end of the cord is affixed to the top of the standard, the other to the ball. The batter stands in hitting position, the length of the cord removed from the standard. Another player propels the ball in whip-like fashion. As it nears the batter, he attempts to meet the ball squarely. This provides practice in hitting a ball that is breaking as it nears the plate.

HIP-PIVOT. A good batting swing is given its impetus by a hip-pivot. The hips should begin to rotate into the ball before any other bodily move takes place. Hip action carries the entire body through the swing. For this reason it is wise to begin all phases of batting practice with a hip-turning drill.

BUNTING. This vital phase of batting can be fully perfected indoors. The value of it lies in the fact that, even though confined to a gymnasium the batter can accustom himself to facing live pitching—with a baseball.

A fully equipped catcher should take up his normal position behind the plate. The pitcher should throw from his normal pitching distance. The batter should practice the sacrifice (bunting only a good pitch); the squeeze (bunting the next pitch); and the bunt-for-a-hit. Foul lines should be chalked on the floor and a bunt will be considered a good one when it is in fair territory, near the foul line.

If room is sufficient, infielders should be in position. In this way the men who will handle bunts under game conditions can practice fielding them. It is suggested that throws to the bases be of the "lob" variety.

Even when space is limited the pitcher should be required to capitalize on this opportunity to practice handling bunts.

BASE-RUNNING

Emphasis has already been made of the vital contribution that running can make to the conditioning of a ball club in general, and pitchers in particular. Valuable purpose can be given it by combining it with practice in base-running.

Whether done individually or in groups it should be mandatory that running be performed as though a base runner were tagging up on a fly ball or breaking for the next base on a steal. The two starting positions can be used alternately for wind sprints.

Tagging up: Left foot should be on the bag; weight forward; a full start made just as soon as the ball hits the glove of the coach, who simulates a catch.

Steal: Players should take a lead by backing off the bag; face the pitcher with feet spread and weight evenly distributed on the balls of their feet; a pivot and cross-over step are recommended for the most effective start, same being signalled by a shout of "go" from the coach.

Sliding: Those fields that have a field-house or cage provide outdoor conditions for this phase of practice. Nevertheless, a sliding pit should be used as a precautionary measure against leg injuries.

The intricate technique of correct sliding can be perfected even when no better facilities than a gymnasium floor are available. Indoor sliding practice should be done only at half speed and in stocking feet in order to lessen the possibility of injury. It is further recommended that only a short run be used.

INDIVIDUAL DRILLS

Whereas the primary purpose of indoor workouts is the over-all conditioning of the entire squad and the perfection of skills that pertain to all players, many phases of individual position play can be covered and practiced to a fair degree of perfection. The more of these maneuvers that can be mastered indoors, the more advanced will be a team's state of readiness when it takes to the field.

PITCHER—In addition to arm-conditioning and the handling of bunts, work should be done on covering first base, the pick-off move, and the fielding of ground balls.

CATCHER—The catcher, too, will have practiced fielding bunts. He should also be drilled in shifting, handling low pitches, hiding signs, proper handling of his mitt (bringing the ball toward his belt buckle), cocking his arm, and throwing to a base (where space permits).

FIRST BASEMAN—Added to his work in fielding bunts should be ground balls, feeding the pitcher, correct footwork, holding the runner, and much practice in handling low throws.

SECOND-SHORT—The second baseman and shortstop should be given much work in fielding ground balls. The first few grounders each day should be fielded with the right hand held behind the back, in order to assure correct glove position. Even more time should be devoted to making the double play, with emphasis on feeding the ball properly and learning the several patterns of footwork involved in making the pivot.

THIRD BASEMAN—Fielding ground balls is of importance and the hand-behind-back routine is recommended here. Special stress should be placed on the handling of bunts and slow rollers, initial work each day being performed with a stationary ball.

OUTFIELDERS—Outfielders should be drilled on footwork, hand technique, ground balls, flies (moderately thrown), and their most difficult play—the line drive (thrown).

In any pre-season work, indoors or out, the main concern of the coach should be to keep everyone busy (and interested) at all times with purposeful activity. Where every man undergoes thorough conditioning the squad, when selected, will be at close to playing readiness.

Outdoor phase

Planning a definite timed schedule for pre-season work is difficult since springtime weather is so uncertain in much of the country. Thus, any set routine or, for that matter, any single practice device must be worked into the over-all pre-season schedule as the weather permits. The step-by-step execution of a comprehensive training routine will be possible only when a squad is blessed with an early stretch of good weather. Improvisation, then, is important in the achievement of a condition of game-readiness. Yet a master plan of complete squad training must be used as a guide to each segment of any given workout.

BATTING PRACTICE

The conditioning of a baseball team revolves primarily around the pitching staff, and rightfully so. Yet the major part of any workout centers on batting practice. This, too, is as it should be, since batting is the one activity common to every player. Fortunately, a well-organized batting drill enables every player to practice his individual position play. Conversely, a slovenly hitting session accomplishes little of real value and is the sign of a poorly coached team.

The first step in every session of batting practice should be the dividing of the squad into two teams. This results in two definite assets to both coach and team—(1) an uncluttered field with every player engaged in purposeful activity and (2) more and better practice for each player —batter, pitcher, and those at the various positions.

COROLLARY ACTIVITY. Supernumeraries, if any, should be kept busy at all times and must be given their turns at bat and in the field. While otherwise unoccupied, they should be engaged in warming up pitchers, hitting fungoes (or retrieving for the fungo hitter), and playing pepper. Except for the batter and man on deck, members of the offensive team should busy themselves playing pepper and performing still-head and hip-turning drills. In absence of an adequate managerial staff they should be responsible for retrieving foul balls.

A pitcher is the logical man to back up the batting practice hurler. For safety purposes balls should be rolled to him. This has an ulterior motive—forcing him to exercise with constant bending. The feeder should be stationed at the midway point, between second base and the mound.

DEFENSIVE VALUE. During batting practice, valuable time is available; the coach should capitalize on it by hitting to his infield. Correct position for him during this operation is in the home-plate area close enough so that he is afforded protection by the batting cage, yet far enough removed so that batter and catcher will not be in danger of being hit by a ball returned to him. As in the case of the pitcher, the ball is to be rolled or bounced to the man hitting to the infield or his catcher. As a further precaution this catcher should remain well behind this batter so as to be out of danger from a ball batted from home plate.

A strict adherence to system should be demanded by the coach during batting practice. This can be hazardous, indeed, with several baseballs flying in several directions. The rule for hitting to the infield during batting practice is that "The ball shall be hit to an infielder only after a pitched ball has passed the batter and before it has been returned to the pitcher. Furthermore, the infield ball—not the one used in batting practice—is the only one that is to be thrown to another infielder."

Supernumeraries may be used to hit to the outfield. One engaged in this should be stationed behind first or third in foul territory—preferably one man and a retriever at each of those spots. When two men are so stationed, only one of them should hit to the center fielder, this being decided on before a ball is fungoed, with the man behind third base hitting to right field and the one behind first hitting to left. Whereas the rule need not be adhered to so strictly by this group, wisdom still dictates that a fly ball should be fungoed only after a pitched ball has passed the batter and before it has been returned to the pitcher.

Three general regulations for this area of a batting practice session should be imposed:

(1) Warn any teammate who is in danger of being hit by a thrown or batted ball.
(2) Never turn your back to the plate until a pitched ball has passed the batter or been hit in another direction.
(3) Any man hitting fungoes shall call a player's name before hitting to him.

THE PITCHER AND BATTING PRACTICE

This phase of a pitcher's activity is most valuable in that it affords him an opportunity to work from the mound and face live batters, thereby simulating, to a certain degree, the conditions which will be encountered in game competition.

His work in batting practice should be integrated with his over-all conditioning routine in so far as incidence of throwing and actual time devoted thereto are concerned.

Batting practice is intended primarily for the benefit of the hitter. Only in competitive batting drills should the pitcher go at full speed or endeavor to fool the man at the plate. From the viewpoint of the moundsman his aim should be to perfect his control, with the contingent objective of polishing his footwork and delivery, and of reacting to and fielding batted balls.

Every pitch delivered in a ball game should have a purpose. This also pertains to batting practice. Here the intention should be to throw nothing but hittable strikes. In short, the fewer pitches per batter and the more batters faced in the allotted time (number of pitches when innings are calculated), the greater the benefit that will be derived from batting practice.

A pitcher can further profit from this type of work by close observation of the various batters, as they stand at the plate and as they swing at the ball, with the purpose in mind of discovering any weakness which will properly guide his modus operandi for each hitter. While he will not utilize this knowledge during batting practice, the habit of close observation of the batter will carry over into actual ball games where, in absence of a "book," he may be able to spot tell-tale signs of weakness in a moment's time.

As for general routine: the batting practice pitcher should work from a stretch when the batter is about to bunt and should field the ball just as he would in a game, but without throwing to a base. He should signal his intentions when throwing a curve ball and should not do so until the batter "has his eye on the ball."

A pitcher must not be used for batting practice duty merely because he is a pitcher. His schedule for this work should conform with his over-all conditioning routine. With relatively small pitching staffs other players will have to be assigned this task on occasion, particularly when the actual playing season has been reached.

Non-pitchers who throw batting practice should be selected primarily for their ability to get the ball over the plate. A wildman on the mound wastes precious time and can contribute to a tendency on the part of the batter to go for bad balls.

A coach who is hard-pressed for pitching manpower may resort to a pitching machine. This assures the rapid completion of each round but is not particularly desirable, since the batter should learn to time the pitcher's motion as well as the ball and should accustom himself to facing different angles of delivery.

Once a ball club gets into its actual playing schedule, a different routine will have to be developed for assigning pitchers to batting practice duty. The pattern of this activity will then be an individual matter, dependent on how each pitching arm responds to work and requires rest. For a guide to sensible routines for an individual pitcher the section on pitching should be consulted.

THE BATTER'S PRACTICE

While batting practice is essentially for the benefit of the batter, he must approach it with a businesslike attitude and in full realization that every one of his teammates should reap full value from it. The most good will come from a hitting session that is well organized. Each man should comply with the agenda and the rules for it that are laid down by the coach.

Game conditions should be approached as nearly as possible within the framework of conventional batting practice in two principal respects:

1. The batter should learn his strike-zone by swinging only at good pitches.
2. He should not "take strikes." Being overly choosy, in addition to fostering the habit of passing up good pitches on his part, is harmful to the morale of the pitcher and to the purpose of the entire undertaking, which is to give every man the fullest opportunity to bat within the allotted time. Having the catcher serve as umpire can help make for a snappy batting practice with maximum benefit to all concerned.

A definite batting order should be picked for hitting practice, and followed faithfully. In the case of one of the two teams into which the squad has been divided, this will more than likely be the game line-up. Where a substitute replaces a starter who may be detained or injured he should be inserted in the regular's normal spot so as not to break the day-by-day continuity which builds cohesion.

There are several alternatives in the routine which should be followed, as well as variations which can be profitably inserted once the session is underway. The one condition which common sense dictates is that the course established should provide definite benefit to every player. In batting drills, as in every other phase of baseball practice, moves which will not be used and conditions not to be encountered in a game should not be permitted.

During the early phases of pre-season work more time should be given to bunting, both to perfect skill at it and to help a man get his eye on the ball. In fact, an occasional abbreviated round devoted exclusively to the bunt may well be in order both early in the year and later, should poor bunting show itself as a team weakness.

A thoughtful coach will call for a certain type of bunt at specific times. Such action is in order when he feels that his club's attack may have to include a more than normal use of the squeeze play (here the next pitch must be bunted), or where he has a man who may help the team by occasionally bunting for a hit (here he should indicate whether the ball is to be dragged or pushed and if the batter should try to beat it out).

The routines suggested below may form a basic guide to proper procedure, and the individual coach will adapt them to the needs of his squad.

EARLY SEASON

ROUND 1—
    Two bunts—one down each foul line
    Three swings—all fast balls
ROUND 2—
    One bunt—where the ball is pitched
    Three swings—the last a curve ball
ROUND 3 (time permitting)—
    Two swings—the last a curve ball

INTERMEDIATE

ROUND 1—
    One bunt
    Four swings—the last a curve ball
ROUND 2—
    One bunt
    Three swings—fast ball, curve, and batter's choice
ROUND 3 (time permitting)—
    Two swings—batter's choice, then pitcher's choice

ROUND 1—
    One bunt
    Four swings—two fast balls, curve, and batter's choice
ROUND 2—
    One bunt
    Three swings—fast ball, curve, and pitcher's choice
ROUND 3 (time permitting)—
    Two swings—fast ball and curve

GAME

ROUND 1—
    One bunt
    Four swings—the last a curve
ROUND 2—
    One bunt
    Three swings—two of them curves
ROUND 3 (time permitting)—
    Two swings—both fast balls

EXPLANATORY NOTES

(a) For young ballplayers, unless otherwise noted, bunts should be aimed according to where the ball is pitched.
(b) A particularly good batsman need not be required to bunt, especially on game days.
(c) Catcher should serve as umpire when pitcher has the choice.
(d) Batter should run out his last swing.
(e) A catcher should always be used.
(f) The next pitcher should be warmed up and ready exactly when scheduled to take over.

Variations can add interest and provide benefit by injecting the competitive element into batting practice. Numerous variations may be added to those which are listed here because of their proven worth.

COMPETITIVE. Pitcher tries to retire the batter—as he would in a game. Catcher serves as umpire. As long as the batter "hits safely" he continues to bat.

NEXT PITCH.

1. Batter must hit the ball no matter where it is pitched.
    Pitcher must try to throw a strike.
2. Coach may call this play after pitcher has begun his delivery.
3. Coach may order the ball hit to right field.

In each case a successful effort should be rewarded with an extra swing.

ONE PITCH. Batter must swing at the ball no matter where it is pitched. This is often used when time permits only a last, very rapid round of hitting.

PRACTICE GAME. An attempt is made by all defensive players to retire the batter. Offensive team goes right through its batting order. An umpire calls balls and strikes. Chief difference between this and a game is that the teams do not change sides every three outs.

LONG ROUND. This is an entirely different over-all batting practice routine, in which each hitter takes his full batting workout (for example, two bunts and ten swings) in one time at the plate. Some coaches prefer this method because of the time saved by eliminating frequent changes of batters. Its primary drawbacks are that it makes the simulation of game conditions relatively difficult and that it does not allow the pitcher to face a sufficient number of different batters and vice versa.

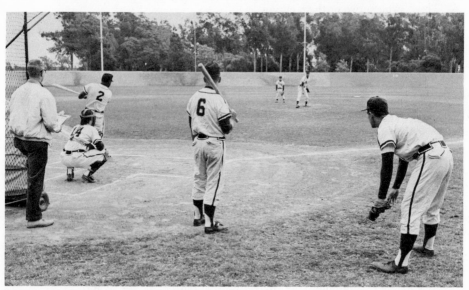

A Well-Organized Batting Practice

Whatever routine is selected, batting practice should be carefully planned and smoothly run if it is to have real value.

Base-running

This is a sadly neglected phase of the game because too much is taken for granted. It should not be assumed that base-running comes naturally to a youngster, that instinct alone will assure his practice of correct method and techniques. The ultimate goal of the offense is to score runs. To facilitate the accomplishment of this objective little should be left to chance. Base-running can be taught and it is the coach's duty to see that his ballplayers learn the proper way to do it by covering the subject completely. His order of instruction should include:

GENERAL

1. The start towards first
2. Rounding the base
3. Taking a lead and getting the jump
4. Going from first to third
5. The steal—straight, delayed, and double steal
6. The squeeze—breaking for the plate correctly
7. The hit-and-run
8. Tagging up—both how and when to do it

SLIDING

1. Bent leg slide—right and left
2. Hook slide—right and left
3. Sliding back to the base
4. Breaking up the double play

A sliding pit should be used to prevent injuries. A good one will be about 12′ x 16′, and 3½′ deep—filled with fine sand topped with sawdust and shavings. It should be raked constantly while in use.

A rope stretched across the front of the pit at a height of 2½′ to 3′, and orders to slide under it, can be of definite help in making a man learn to hit the dirt properly.

BASE-RUNNING SIGNALS

1. When to look for them
2. How to take them when leading off the base
3. What they are

All base-line coaches should use standard signals to indicate to the runner when he should hold up, make a turn, stay on the bag, slide (left, right, or straight in), or keep going.

Team offense

The lessons imparted to each player must be fitted together as a whole to achieve maximum team results from game-to-game individual performance.

31

Through a definite set of offensive plays proper cohesion can be given a team's attack. A coach should make certain that his players understand each offensive maneuver, the philosophy behind it, its strategical use, and their own roles in its effective execution.

Offensive plays are relatively few in number, yet, because every player may be called upon to fulfill one of the roles that each includes, considerable work must be done in perfecting them. Every player should be drilled in each of the various parts.

The basic repertoire of an amateur team should include the sacrifice and the steal—straight and delayed, single and double—as the personnel warrants.

Not essential, yet always desirable in the offensive arsenal, are the squeeze—safe, suicide, and double—and the hit-and-run, with its variations —the bunt-and-run and, more favorable for use by amateur teams, the run-and-hit.

Needless to say, thorough knowledge of offensive signals should be instilled in every member of the squad.

Defense

If thorough knowledge of baseball techniques and tactics is a prerequisite to good coaching, meticulous instruction in every phase of the game is essential in the development of team and player to the maximum of their respective potentials.

Before a team has reached a condition of game-readiness it should have a working knowledge, if not complete mastery, of the following vital defensive plays:

1. Infield depths.
2. The cut-off (including relay assignments).
3. The double play—with runners on first base; first and second; first and third; first, second, and third; and the fake and throw to third.
4. The sacrifice—with runners on first; first and second; first and third; and on second.
5. The squeeze.
6. The hit-and-run.
7. The steal.
8. The double steal.
9. The pick-off play.
10. The run-down.
11. Covering the bases.
12. Backing up the bases.

From an individual standpoint, a team's defense can be considered well prepared when the following points have been thoroughly practiced.

CATCHER—Giving the signal; glove position, catching the ball "toward the belt-buckle"; shifting with the pitch; blocking low throws; removing the mask; catching pop-flies; backing up first; covering third; cocking the arm; the one-step throw to the bases; the pitch-out; the double steal; fielding bunts (and throwing to first); calling the play; and blocking and/or tagging the runner.

PITCHER—Covering first; pick-offs; holding the runner; stepping off the rubber; the double play; playing slowly hit balls; making the play at third at the right time; handling bunts; backing up bases; covering the plate; taking the signal; and the pitch-out.

FIRST BASEMAN—Shifting and stretching; handling low throws; leaving the base to catch the ball; taking a throw from the home plate area; holding and tagging the runner; the pick-off play; handling bunts; the double play to second and back to first; feeding the ball to the pitcher; pop-flies; cut-off and relay; following the runner; and the run-down.

SECOND-SHORT—Base-covering assignments; the steal; the double steal; the bunt; the hit-and-run; the double play; pop-flies; cut-off and relay; the pick-off play; the run-down; and making the play to third.

THIRD BASEMAN—The bunt; slowly hit balls; the cut-off play; steals; the tag; the pick-off from the catcher; pop-flies; and the throw home (and following the runner).

OUTFIELD—The cross-over step; handling ground balls; playing line drives; relays; throwing to bases; backing up the play; calling the play and taking the ball; playing the sun field; using glasses; and playing the fence (where applicable).

The role of the coach in drilling his squad has been presented in the form of a check list. A detailed description of the various maneuvers to be covered, both tactical and mechanical, will be found in appropriate sections of the text.

Infield Practice

Infield practice is the backbone of a team's defensive practice. Except on game days, each period spent on the field should conclude with a spirited infield drill.

Pre-season sessions should see considerable time devoted to combatting the various situations that can arise in a game. The outfielders are to be included in this work, as are live base runners. Game conditions should be duplicated in all respects save that the coach sets up the play he wants practiced and changes it at his discretion. He should call the play, just prior to hitting the ball, and according to game-situation as well as position of base runners; for example (after placing runners at first and third)—"Eighth inning, no outs, we're leading by three runs."

Routine infield drills should be based on game-day procedure. The everyday workout, of course, is not limited in time and a coach may conduct it to accommodate more than just his starting team. Furthermore, he should include practice on pop-flies for each of his infielders and the catcher. Early in the spring, much work should be done on this. When proficiency is achieved less practice is needed but it should be continued throughout the season. The player who is to field it should call for each fly ball, even in practice.

It is game-day infield practice that should most concern a coach, since it reflects the discipline and mood of his ball club. Furthermore, a snappy infield drill can buoy up a team's morale as well as have a definite psychological effect on the opposition.

The following routine has been devised as a logical one, conducive to spirited effort, smart appearance, and good game preparation. It is based on two fundamental principles—no play should be made which will not be encountered in a game; and on all misplays the ball should be returned to the plate for another try.

OUTFIELD ROUND. (Batter should hit hard grounders; cut-off men are in position.)

1. THROW TO SECOND: Hit to left-fielder near the foul line.
                      Hit to center-fielder in left center.
                      Hit to right-fielder near the foul line.
2. THROW TO THIRD: Straight at them.
3. THROW HOME: Straight at them—they should charge the ball.
4. Outfielders then go to deep center field. A pitcher hits to them.

INFIELD. Warm-up round consists of a throw to each man from the catcher.

ROUND 1 To first: ball hit directly at each man (first baseman plays ball to second and takes return throw); first baseman returns ball to catcher who throws to the man who started the play —at his bag; ball returned by way of third; catcher fields ball rolled near third-base line, plays it to first, receives return throw from first baseman.

ROUND 2 To first: ball hit to each man's left; same procedure is followed except that ball for catcher is rolled toward mound.

ROUND 3 Double play: ball hit to left of third baseman and shortstop, to right of second and first baseman, and rolled toward first for the catcher. Return throw routine is the same.

ROUND 4 Double play: ball hit to right of third baseman and shortstop, to left of second and first baseman, and dropped right near the plate for the catcher. Return throw routine is the same.

ROUND 5 To first: ball hit to each man's right; first baseman plays ball to third and receives return throw; catcher plays ball to third on his roller; catcher's throw to shortstop and second baseman is taken in cut-off position and returned home.

ROUND 6 To first: slow roller to each man, who charges the ball, plays it to first (the first baseman throws home), and returns to a position at the edge of the infield grass; there is no throwing by the catcher, nor does he field a roller.

ROUND 7 To home: slow roller to each man who plays the ball to home and returns to his normal position. Throws should be knee-high. No throwing by the catcher.

ROUND 8 A high pop-fly to each man. No throwing.

To save time the batter should use two balls and hit the ball to the next man as the catcher receives the final throw from the previous play. Players should make their moves with snap and precision and with a concentrated effort to make each throw perfect.

GAME PREPARATIONS

DAY BEFORE THE GAME

1. Pitchers throw lightly, do pick-ups, run; shower and dress.
2. Batting practice in the form of a game.
3. Game-day fielding drill; practice relays and cut-offs.
4. Run; shower and dress; brief talk.

DAY OF GAME

A 2:30 starting time is used. Plan A is where facilities are available for both teams to take batting practice simultaneously. Plan B is for fields on which the teams must take turns at batting practice.

A

1:00 Meet in squad room; announce line-up; brief talk.

1:10 Take the field together; warm-up.

1:20 Batting practice for starting line-up and oft-used substitutes; try to use pitcher similar to their starter; our starting pitcher and catcher watch opponents bat.

1:50 Visitor's infield; our squad should watch it, allowing a few minutes for warming up prior to ours.

2:05 Our infield; starting pitcher begins warming up between 2:10 and 2:15, depending on the weather and his arm.

35

2:25　Work on diamond; meet with umpires; squad on the bench; starting catcher should handle last three minutes of pitcher's warm-up; pitcher should allow time to sit down for two or three minutes to dry himself and catch his breath.

B

12:40　Meet in squad room; announce line-up; brief talk.
12:50　Take the field together; warm-up.
1:00　Our batting practice
1:30　Visitor's batting practice; squad on the bench, watching the first 15 minutes of it. Then play pepper and/or catch.
1:55　Visitor's infield; our squad watch last five minutes of it.
2:10　Our infield; same routine for pitcher.
2:25　Same routine.

A copy of the ground rules and line-up should be given to the umpire and the visiting team. Where a field has dugouts the ground rules should be posted in both of them, precluding the need to give the visitors a copy in the home-plate ceremonies.

Those obligations, which a first-rate organization owes its visitors, are detailed in the section on manager's duties. The golden rule demands that these matters be given scrupulous attention.

UMPIRES

The competence of the umpires hired by a coach, and his team's behavior toward any umpire encountered are definite marks of character —individual, team, and school. The coach who tolerates slovenly umpires and home-town decisions when his club is host, or who abuses the arbiters on any occasion, is not worthy of his charge.

Umpiring at all levels of competition has improved tremendously since pre-war days and, as a class, today's men-in-blue are competent, courageous gentlemen of unquestioned integrity. Conference requirements and umpires' associations have made good officiating the rule in today's game. Clinics and lectures by outstanding practitioners have made rule interpretation, knowledge of the game, standards of conduct, umpiring techniques, and, above all, uniformity of officiating, prevalent qualities in our umpires.

The importance of good appearance, bearing, and conduct for players is stressed repeatedly by the outstanding men in the coaching profession. Certainly, then, these attributes, along with technical competence, are imperatives for an umpire.

The finest umpiring I have ever experienced was done by Ed Runge, who worked his rookie year in a Minor League in which I played. The first time he took the field in one of our games one had the feeling that the game was completely under control and that his decisions would be correct and inviolate. There was no arrogance or show behind this, only an air of unmistakable authority and competence. Obviously there was only one place for Ed Runge—the Major Leagues. He is now a veteran in the American League and is considered the best in the business by most of the players in that league.

This is cited merely to show the attitude that a first-rate umpire should inspire and to inform a coach as to the type of official he should seek to hire. True, all umpires cannot be Ed Runges, but men who exude competence and complete impartiality should be sought constantly. They make for well-run ball games and coaches with better dispositions —things which we owe our players.

Dignity and courage should be added to competence and impartiality, as essential qualities in umpires. In short, a coach should engage the services of officials who demonstrate the characteristics he is trying to instill in his own players.

An umpire need not have been an outstanding ballplayer to be sought after as an official, but he should definitely have a feel for the game and the intricacies of position play. An understanding of just what a player must do in a given situation, and the mechanics involved, cannot help but make him a better umpire. It might even be said that sympathy and appreciation of the player's task are requisites for a topflight arbiter.

As for complete integrity in umpires—let a coach merely ask himself if he desires an impartial umpire when his club is the visiting team. Obviously he wants impartiality on the road. Consequently, he is expected to provide it at home. A coach who would look to the "home" type of umpire to assure his team an advantage should not be entrusted with the leadership of young men.

A tried-and-true maxim for salesmen is "win the argument, lose the sale." For a baseball coach the admonishment should be, "Lose the argument, lose the decision anyhow." Not particularly well put, perhaps, but apt enough to show the basic folly of arguing with umpires. Win, lose, or draw in the argument, no good can come of it since the decision on a judgment play, once made, must stand.

Harassment of umpires by a coach is not only fruitless, it is ruinous in its effect on squad morale. The coach is looked to not only as an instructor by his players, but as an example of correct behavior. If he constantly "jaws" at umpires, his players, and often the spectators, tend to follow suit. Only chaos can ensue.

A coach should make it an ironclad rule that no player is to abuse or even argue with an umpire. If a legitimate complaint on a matter of interpretation (not judgment) seems warranted, the captain, and possibly the coach, are the only members of a squad legally authorized to discuss the matter with an umpire. In the absence of strong league control and proper punitive measures for flagrant offenders, it is the duty of the coach to enforce conformity with this rule.

The exception to the rule of questioning an umpire's decisions is in the matter of balls and strikes. The vast number of these calls in the course of a game combined with the fact that ballplayers are human and become keyed up is reason enough to allow an occasional lapse. Disputing an umpire's decisions, however, must not be encouraged; in fact, it should definitely be discouraged. Baseball's outstanding stars never question an umpire's judgment. They realize that he is human and, furthermore, accept the bad with the good and go about their business like true professionals.

There is a correct way in which to talk to an umpire, based on a conscious effort to avoid making him look bad in the eyes of the crowd. When an occasion arises in which the umpire's judgment may justifiably be questioned, the catcher or batter should address him without turning in his direction. A pitcher who feels the need to speak up to an umpire should meet his catcher in front of the plate, turn his back on the man in blue and address him in a dispassionate manner.

An umpire is never "at home" and, to repeat, every effort should be exerted to keep from making him look bad in the eyes of the spectators.

Abuse of an umpire should not be tolerated by a coach. He and his players should aspire to the best. In order to earn it, they should deserve it.

THE CAPTAIN

The captain of a baseball team can be of tremendous value to coach and squad alike—if he is the right man for the job. He is the coach's alter ego (on the field) and can be the proverbial "second right arm" to the mentor (both on and off the field). Thus, his selection is not to be taken lightly nor should it devolve into a popularity contest.

The qualities to be expected of a man worthy of being team captain are several in number, but revolve around one common denominator—character. The man chosen to lead his teammates should be a player of ability who knows the rules of baseball and of proper conduct. He should be a man of good moral fibre, even temperament, courage, and clarity of mind. He should be the type of man whose deportment will serve as an example to his teammates, win or lose.

His game duties start with the pre-game ceremonies at which he hands the line-up to the umpires and clarifies the ground rules—for the visitors when his is the host club, for his own team when they are on the road. He then edifies his teammates on the ground rules and leads them into battle. Thereafter, during the contest, he keeps the umpires informed of line-up changes and handles any discussion with the umpires which may be warranted. The latter's judgment should never be questioned, interpretation being the only justifiable topic of argument to be broached —and then in a gentlemanly manner by the captain, alone.

The captain's duties as an intermediary between coach and players embrace both on- and off-the-field activity. He represents his coach on the field in so far as personal example and oral direction relating to the coach's orders to the team are concerned. He should report to the coach any pertinent information which might otherwise go unnoticed by the bench.

During practice sessions his value can increase vastly if he helps oversee and keep in operation the wide area and many men involved. He should be given formal authority to assist in the conduct of practice sessions.

Off the field he should not only set a good example for his teammates, he should serve as advisor and counsellor to them when the need arises. In this role he should, needless to say, act only on the authority of the coach and in a manner that will reflect only the coach's philosophy and system of play. This phase of his responsibilities further includes the pacifying of gripers. Legitimate complaints and any moot point put forth by a squad member should be brought directly to the coach by the captain. Covert criticism of coach, teammates, or school must not be tolerated.

Obviously, an exceptional man is needed to fill the captain's role properly. Furthermore, since he will be delegating authority to this emissary of his, a coach should have the type of man he wants, for his captain. For that reason, and to avoid the popularity contest and petty politics approach, the captain should be chosen by the coach. It is sufficient to allow the team to elect its own honorary captain at the close of the season.

39

Some coaches prefer game-captains. With the possibility of finding more than one real leader on a squad quite rare, a season-captain seems more logical. Should more than one man have outstanding qualities of the sort desired, co-captains may be a better solution than alternate ones since authority is involved and should not be transferred continually if it is to have real significance.

Another possible solution, if one outstanding leader has not made himself manifest, is to have co-captains for, say, the first two games, then select either the man or men deemed outstanding as team leader for the balance of the season.

Whatever course is followed, the coach should pick his own captain —with care.

ARRANGING THE SCHEDULE

The construction of an intelligent schedule is a difficult feat, for carefully laid plans often must be modified by practical considerations. In practice, the ideal can rarely materialize, yet it can be approached—but only if common-sense principles are applied in diligent fashion.

Financial and academic matters are primary considerations in scheduling. The amount of money allocated to baseball, and the scholastic standards which the players must meet should be determining factors in both the number of games arranged and the travel involved in playing them.

The most important consideration from the standpoint of the boy on the squad is his academic well-being. Baseball (or any sport) is not an end in itself. Rather, it should be made an integral part of his education. Baseball can serve as a wholesome outlet for the vigorous youngster. Its demands on a boy should promote health, purpose, and a budgeting of his time which can serve as a stimulus to his education. For this reason it should be carefully integrated with the academic program. Where scholastic demands are exceptionally high, the number of games and the travel involved should be held down so that no player's academic standing may be adversely affected by his obligation to the team. A boy in academic difficulty should be made to concentrate on his books —at the expense of the ball club. The only philosophy that can be justified is that, although we should strive for a strong mind in a strong body, the development of the mind must come first.

Merely because of his familiarity with his personnel, a coach should have the final say in schedule-making. Where possible he should arrange for relatively easy games early in the season, especially if his squad is an inexperienced one. It is experience in actual competition that breeds confidence, and nothing can boost a squad's morale better than some easy victories.

Needless to say, compromise with and accommodation of other teams is inevitable. Over and above this stand conference commitments. Within this framework a balanced schedule must be worked out, one in which natural rivals should be met near the end of the season (preceded, if possible, by an easy game and sufficient rest).

The first rule of thumb to be applied is that good equipment for the players should not be sacrificed for an over-ambitious schedule. It is far better to travel first class on a short trip than to ride the rods on a long one.

Squad strength is a factor to be respected. Baseball loses its educational value where victories are unduly easy or hopelessly difficult. Granted that this is often unpredictable at the time schedules are being fixed, it should, nevertheless, be the endeavor of a coach to send his squad against an opponent with whom they have an even chance in at least eighty per cent of their games.

A sensible schedule at the secondary school level is two games per week, properly spaced. College men, because of their greater maturity and need to experience the full development of the game, can and should be given more competition. Distribution of playing dates, however, is also a matter for consideration here. Size and strength of the pitching staff and, to a slightly lesser extent, the squad constitute the chief temporizing element.

Rain will, of course, curtail the number of games played. Because it is completely unpredictable it should not bear direct influence on schedule-making. Rather it should promote balance—sufficient games to insure that a rainy spring will not cause too little competition, few enough games to insure that a dry spring will not find a team's manpower overburdened.

Secondary schools normally will confine their activity to a localized area. Colleges must usually go further afield for suitable opponents; but budgetary limitations may preclude long trips. Where they can be arranged, however, they can provide a worthwhile experience. Logically, a long jaunt should include more than one game and should be followed by a day of rest. It follows that the ideal arrangement for an extended road trip would wind up with a Saturday game.

The most satisfactory mode of transportation is by bus. Here again, finances may enter the picture and force travel by automobile. Whichever method is used, long journeys should be arranged so that arrival at the team's destination will allow a good night's rest before a game is played. If necessary, automobile transportation is acceptable when its use will enable a squad to have the financial means for an extra night's lodging. If this basic requirement cannot be met, long road trips should not be taken.

41

For the team that is badly strapped financially, a preponderance of away-games in a localized area is justifiable, since they often cost less than home games, in which the expenses of umpires, balls, and visitor's guarantee are involved.

The ideal schedule at various levels of scholastic competition would be something like this:

High School   —Tuesday and Friday
Prep School   —Wednesday and Saturday
College   —(Two games) Wednesday and Saturday
(Three games) Tuesday, Thursday, and Saturday
(Long Trip) Friday and Saturday.

FALL BASEBALL

A recent development in college baseball circles in the New York area is the playing of an abbreviated schedule in the early fall. The practice has met with success amongst the handful of schools trying it, and for good reason—physical conditioning of the squad and inclement weather are relatively minor problems.

With a summer of activity behind them, the players will need no pre-season conditioning. Two weeks should be sufficient for the achievement of playing readiness. Then, with at least four weeks of better-than-April weather at his disposal, a coach can play an eight-to-ten-game schedule.

Booking two games a week will enable a team to make up rain-outs with no great strain on manpower. Tuesday and Friday are the logical game days, the latter to avoid a conflict with football, the former merely to make for proper spacing of the contests.

In many cases, particularly in smaller schools, a number of baseball players will be engaged in football and, thus, will be lost to the baseball squad. Yet, fall baseball is a worthwhile undertaking, valuable not only in itself, but of great merit for the carry-over effect that will be gained for the regular season.

An autumn schedule will be of particular advantage to teams in the northern section of the country. The month of October almost invariably affords more favorable baseball weather than does April and it seems only right to profit by the opportunity thus presented.

MULTI-SPORT MEN

With many baseball players being all-around athletes, occasional conflicts with other sports are inevitable. This problem revolves primarily around winter sport participants and concerns the inroads that this activity makes on their baseball conditioning program.

Since there is no seasonal conflict involved, football players need concern us here only in so far as possible injury is involved. The school and its football coach should not be deprived of the services of a good performer merely because he happens to be a baseball player. It is only in the case of a boy who is a truly outstanding ballplayer but only mediocre in football that a choice is called for. In this case his value to his school and his potential in higher levels of baseball should determine how advisable it is for him to partake of the gridiron game; this determination should be weighted also by the possible effects of *two-sport participation on his health and his school-work*. Generally speaking, football should be discouraged if a boy's contribution to that sport will be a minor one, especially if he needs the extra time for study, is not overly robust, and/or is a baseball player of really exceptional ability.

The same standards are the basis for deliberation where winter sports are concerned, but to a lesser degree. Basketball players, for example, pose a problem to the baseball coach primarily because of the loss of valuable pre-season baseball work that can be involved. This stems not only from an overlapping of seasons but from the need for a period of recuperation from the basketball grind.

A boy's health and his academic status far outweigh the need to report early for baseball. The winter sport participant should be required to take a definite period of rest between seasons. A reasonable lay-off at the high school level would be one week (no less)—for essentially physical reasons. College men should have a mandatory two-week respite—for physical and scholastic reasons. The baseball routine for them may then have to be condensed. This is the proper approach—closely observing the master plan, and not eliminating any of it.

Obviously, the only rational guide to be followed is a careful consideration of the possible consequences of dual participation on the health and scholastic standing of the boy involved, with contribution to school and baseball potentiality as contingent factors.

EQUIPMENT

In order to fulfill its educational function baseball should contribute a truly worthwhile experience to the maturing youngster. As is the case with the schedule, equipment for the squad should be first-rate if the sport is to serve its desired purpose. Here, once again, it enters the realm of fiscal affairs and demands careful calculation and weighing of objectives in the case of all but the most affluent of budgets.

Regardless of the size of the budget, the key to its proper management is the economical use of available funds. This means good quality at a good price. The purchase of certain equipment is long-range in character (uniforms, jackets, etc.), thus a little extra expenditure for quality merchandise will pay dividends over the years—good equipment lasts longer and looks better, *ergo* it is more economical.

Rather than completely outfit a squad with inferior equipment, it is much better to omit nonessentials and buy quality in the essential items.

Since price, quality, and service are the major considerations in outfitting a ball club, a reputable firm should be sought. Local merchants often handle the best line, cooperate financially, and are available for service. If none is readily at hand, the major manufacturers have agencies centrally located, and their representatives can be called on for a visit to a school with no great difficulty.

Equipment has priority in the budget and should be the last item to suffer if financial difficulty is encountered. Wise buying, in itself, can help greatly in avoiding fiscal distress. Its practice implies the observance of several basic rules.

1. Buy with the future in mind.
2. Purchase the best quality within your means.
3. Plan carefully and buy early.
4. Don't overstock.
5. The coach, not the player, should select all equipment. In the case of bats, gloves, and shoes his recommendations should be followed; the player should try these items for size.

The stockroom is of utmost importance. One that is properly maintained can be a great aid as a guide to purchases and in the preservation of equipment.

The stockroom should be neatly shelved, with all equipment immediately accessible. Good ventilation is imperative, as is temperature control. A stockroom that is overly hot tends to destroy the life of leather products and one that is too damp promotes mold, which injures all other materials.

Before discussing the several items of equipment needed for a well-run baseball club, a word is necessary on two topics of a more general nature.

Textiles: Cleanliness is imperative; uniforms should not be worn in practice, they are for games only; woolen goods (jackets, uniforms, and stockings) should be stored in the off-season with one of the firms that specialize in equipment storage and also take care of necessary repairs. If this cannot be afforded, woolen goods should be cleaned, packed in moth balls, and stored in a dry place.

Personal equipment: If budgetary limitations preclude the possibility of equipping the squad with gloves, shoes, and any desirable yet not essential item, two methods of approaching the problem bear investigation.

(a) Share-the-cost: The school and the player split the cost of any piece of equipment he wants.

(b) Player-bear-the-cost: The most sensible way to do this is for the school to purchase the equipment (at discount prices, to which it is entitled) and sell it to the player at cost.

Items of equipment range from essential to luxury in classification. All will be listed, with method of supply given for each of three categories—ideal, fair, and good.

ITEM	IDEAL SITUATION	FAIR	POOR
1. Uniforms (and stockings)	A	A_1	B
2. Jackets	A	A_1	B
3. Caps	D	E	B
4. Sweatshirts	D	E	B
5. Supporters	D	E	E
(a) Cups (for pitchers, catchers, infielders)	E	F	F
6. Inner hose	D (three pair)	D (1 pair)	F
7. Sliding Pads	E	B (regulars only)	G
8. Rubber Shirts	E	B (regulars only)	B (pitchers only)
9. Gloves	E–B	G	F
10. Shoes	D	E	G
11. Traveling bags	B	F	F
12. Bats	C (new)	B–C	B
13. Balls	C (new)	B–C	B–C
14. Catcher's Equipment	B (two sets)	B (one set)	B (one set)
15. Sun-glasses	B (7 pair)	B (three pair)	B (one pair)

CODE

A = Four new ones per year A_1 = Two new ones per year   B = Replace as needed   C = Order according to number of games   D = Order yearly   E = Provide for new men   F = Not supplied by school   G = Share the cost

Hints on equipment

1. Uniforms and jackets: Buy quality. Keep clean and in good repair. Wear only during games. (Jackets may be used for practice.) Wear

correctly (see *Discipline*). Mend rips and tears immediately (a stitch in time does save nine here).

2. Caps: Buy the best. Caps alone, can make a team look good (or bad). Supply new ones yearly, if possible. Avoid crushing. Should fit tight to avoid blowing off.

3. Sweatshirts: Ideally a player should have three—heavy wool for cold weather; medium weight, long sleeves for normal wear; short sleeves for hot weather. Keep clean and wear one at all times. The same color should be worn by all players.

4. Inner hose: Must be worn (no sweat sox allowed). Keep clean.

5. Sliding pads: Advised for regulars.

6. Rubber shirts: Recommended for early-season wear for all players. An essential item for pitchers.

7. Gloves: Today's gloves are made so that little breaking-in is necessary. Keep clean. Do not oil. If too dry, a little vaseline or petroleum jelly may be applied. If too floppy, apply water to the pocket. A player's glove should be worn by that man exclusively.

8. Shoes: Ideally a player should have a practice pair (last year's) and a game pair; shoes should be two sizes smaller than street shoes and worn only with cotton inner hose; can be kept clean with saddle soap, soft and pliable with waterproof oil. Should be cleaned immediately after use on a wet day. Leather toe plates are mandatory for pitchers. Black shoe laces, only, are to be worn.

9. Bats: Buy quality. Each regular should have his own bat(s). Rub with bone or bottle to harden surface. Don't overstock, because bats dry out with age. Use last year's left-overs for early season workouts, when many are split. Bats should be light enough to be easily handled, but not so light that they cannot be well-controlled. Thin, whip-like bats are for experts. Inexperienced players should have thick-handled bats which make for better bat control, fewer broken bats, and more safe hits when the ball is hit off the handle or other non-hitting surface.

10. Balls: Good ones must be used in games. Allow for use of one per inning. "Seconds" may be used in practice as an economy measure. Pitchers should not be permitted to throw a ball which becomes heavier than normal.

11. Catcher's equipment: When not in use handle as though it were a valuable item—which it is. Keep clean, dry, and in good repair. This equipment should be light in weight. Glove should be easily handled but not small since it is used as a target and to block wild pitches.

Good equipment is essential to a really well-run ball club. Since it represents a large investment, careful planning and close observance of preservative measures are essential. The correct handling of the equipment problem involves detailed attention to procurement, care, and storage.

2

DEFENSE

PITCHING

TECHNIQUES—THE FUNDAMENTALS OF
GOOD PITCHING

If a pitcher were physically capable of overpowering every hitter his battle would be won just as soon as he stepped on the mound. Needless to say, such is not the case and, whereas exceptional speed and/or a baffling curve will enable him to get by at some levels of competition as he progresses up the baseball ladder, somewhere along the way to the Big Leagues he will encounter hitters whose physical prowess is the equal of, or superior to his own. He will then have arrived at the point where he must become a pitcher rather than a thrower.

Many qualities, both physical and mental, contribute toward the making of a polished performer on the mound. Sheer physical ability and the development thereof; knowledge of the hitters; poise, confidence, and the desire to win; and courage are the most important of those qualities.

The first fundamental

Probably the most important rule which should be followed by all pitchers, both young and old, is that every pitch should have a purpose. There should be no such thing as a waste pitch, if the term is taken literally. Regardless of what delivery is used, it should have a definite meaning and aim behind it. It might be a quick strike to get ahead of the hitter; it might be a change-of-pace to keep him off balance or set him up for the fast ball; it might be a calculated bad ball, a pitch which is not too good but will induce the batter to swing at it for an out. But, whatever the pitch, it should never be merely a random throw. Instead, it should always be one with a definite purpose behind it.

To go one step further, every single occasion on which a pitcher throws the ball should be one in which he has a definite purpose in mind. This pertains to warming up, pitching batting practice, or even a harmless game of catch—as well as to actual game competition.

MECHANICS

The basic objective of every aspiring pitcher should be to capitalize to the utmost on his physical equipment—to take full advantage of his

God-given attributes. This involves not only the acquisition of a sound tactical background and the development of a good operational method, but learning to put all of his mechanical ability to effective use in the actual throwing of the ball. In short, learning to pitch includes the development of maximum stuff within the limits of a man's physical capabilities.

Method

First, we should consider, from a strictly physical standpoint, some of the theory which lies behind the act of delivering the ball to the batter with the most telling effect. Strategy, tactics, and the development of operational proficiency will be covered in subsequent chapters. At this juncture we should delve into the mechanical means which have contributed greatly to the success of baseball's finest pitchers.

At the outset, it should be realized that overpowering stuff entails muscular adaptation to a greater degree than it does sheer muscular strength. Size and power, although a great asset to any pitcher—particularly in regard to endurance and sustained stuff—are not the predominant factors in enabling a man to throw hard and to break off a good curve ball. Men of short stature, slight build, and moderate strength have possessed exceptional stuff. To a great extent this is so because muscular control as it relates to pitching involves every part of the body—fingers, wrist, arm, and legs as well as the entire physical being. What these men have developed is the knack of putting something on the ball without exerting maximum effort. The key to this mastery of ideal pitching coordination is relaxation. It not only enables a man to get maximum stuff on the ball, it allows him to conserve his strength and to call upon that little bit extra which is needed in any clutch situation which might arise.

One of the main ingredients which goes into the making of a good pitcher is balance. It is, in fact, an absolute essential at all stages in the delivery of any pitch. A slight imbalance at any point in the pitching motion is magnified greatly in the full sequence of motion and in the resultant effect on the course and action of a pitched ball. Thus, it follows that all pitchers should strive for good balance and the maintenance thereof from the time that they take a stance on the rubber until the follow-through is completed and the squared-away fielding position is assumed. A simple means of testing one's balance is to wind up, rear back with the striding foot in the air, and then hold the position on one leg for several seconds. When this can be done consistently with good equilibrium a pitcher can be reasonably sure that his balance is proper at the start of his delivery and this will, in most cases, carry through to the end of his motion.

There are two distinct schools of thought on the physical effects created by the time element involved in delivering the ball. The first of these holds that a pitcher should work fast and waste little time on extraneous movements and undue deliberation, the belief being that taking excessive time means that the pitcher will remain on his feet just that much longer and add to his fatigue as the game progresses.

The other theory maintains that a pitcher should work slowly. The reasoning behind this is that working fast does not allow the arm muscles to contract sufficiently after the severe stretching they undergo in a hard throw. Consequently, the toll of working fast is too heavy on the arm.

The problem of which method to adopt is probably best left to the individual, since he is qualified to judge his own physical capabilities and limitations. A combination of the two methods could supply the most effective solution, provided that consideration were given to the game situation and—in particular—the hitter. It should be added that an unusually hot day calls for deliberate movements, which allow the pitcher to conserve his strength for the full nine-inning route as well as for any tough situations which may arise in the course of a ball game.

Preliminaries

Before he so much as toes the rubber a pitcher must concern himself with certain considerations that will leave him fully prepared to tackle the job at hand with the greatest possible effectiveness. First of all, there is the matter of equipment.

Shoes: The most important tools of the trade to any ball player are his shoes. They are, literally, the foundation from which he must work and are, possibly, of even greater moment to a pitcher than to any other man on the field. The extra few dollars required to equip himself with high-quality footwear will be well worthwhile in the long run. A light-weight kangaroo-skin shoe is predominant in use among professionals, who correctly assume that their base-of-operations is vital enough to on-the-field performance to demand both high quality and good condition. New shoes should be about two sizes smaller than ordinary footwear. They stretch considerably and a snug fit is necessary to assure a pitcher of good balance, a powerful push-off, and the ability to start quickly and cleanly when fielding duties so require. New shoes should be worn only a few minutes at a time until they are properly broken in, that is, until they feel comfortable and have become almost molded to the foot.

A toe-plate is essential since the shoe of the pivot foot is subject to great wear and tear. A piece of thick leather stitched over the inside of the toe of the shoe is recommended. This simple and economical device can be obtained from and applied by any shoemaker.

Baseball shoes should be given the loving care which their importance warrants by every ballplayer. This includes regular cleaning and polishing for the maintenance of good condition. Either shoe polish or saddle soap is an effective ingredient for this chore. As an extra precaution, wet shoes should be rubbed dry immediately after use and mud should not be allowed to remain on them overnight.

Every ball club should keep extra shoe laces in its medicine-kit. In the absence of them, a pitcher should carry an extra pair in the pocket of his jacket and should never allow himself to be handicapped by a broken shoe lace.

Another on-the-field precaution which should be observed is the removal of any excess mud or dirt from the spikes. Its presence can prevent a pitcher from getting effective purchase in both his push-off and stride. The spikes should be cleaned before the start of each inning and at any time that an accumulation of dirt appears.

Above all, a pitcher should see to it that his game-shoes are in good condition. They should fit snugly, be in good repair, and have spikes that are long and held tightly in place. The only place for old, worn baseball shoes is in practice sessions—if not the trash heap.

The Glove: Size is the main essential in selecting a glove. It should, needless to say, be of good quality and it should, by all means, be large—the larger, the better, within the rules of the game. The reasons for this are twofold and fairly obvious: (1) to permit the pitcher to hide the ball; (2) to aid him in fielding his position (a big glove enables him to stop or deflect many balls which might otherwise go through the box for hits).

As for glove care, one precaution should be observed by ballplayers in general and pitchers in particular. Oil or greasy solutions of any kind should never be applied to a glove. Oil which is rubbed into a glove is exuded by it and will get on any ball which is caught. Controlling a baseball is difficult at best and the slipperiness which is caused by oil imposes an extra handicap on the pitcher. The slight amount of extra life which the preservative qualities of the oil will add to a glove are far outweighed by the damage which it can do to a pitcher's control.

When a glove becomes dirty it can be cleaned with a damp cloth. When it becomes too loose and "floppy," application of water will help it regain the desired condition.

Protective Equipment: A pitcher should wear a long-sleeved undershirt at all times. On cold days this should be a woolen one, in warmer weather a lighter material—cotton, for example—can be used. When the temperature soars into the 90's a short sleeve can be worn on the gloved-hand arm but the sleeve of the pitching arm should always be long enough to cover the elbow. This is vital to proper protection of the pitching arm. Furthermore, a long sleeve will absorb much perspiration and prevent it from reaching the hand and causing the ball to become slippery.

It is strongly recommended that a pitcher keep an extra undershirt on the bench so that he can make a change whenever his original shirt becomes saturated with perspiration and uncomfortably heavy. This is particularly applicable to night games wherein the pitcher will invariably stop perspiring and be in danger of cooling off from about the fifth inning on. At this point it should be compulsory that he change shirts.

It is also advisable for pitchers to carry a washcloth or extra-large handkerchief in their pockets, to permit thorough drying of the hands and forehead when they become wet with perspiration. All teams should keep at least one towel on the bench, primarily for between-innings use of the pitcher; in cases where this is not done, the pitcher should attend to the detail himself.

A definite essential for every pitcher is a warm jacket; its use should be mandatory for him at all times when he is not on the mound or at bat. Even in hot weather or when running the bases the jacket should be worn. A pitcher's arm cools off too quickly to allow him to run any foolish risks and that arm is, after all, his bread and butter.

It is in the cool temperatures of early spring that the danger of contracting a sore arm is at its height. For that reason it is wise policy for a pitcher to wear a rubber or nylon shirt (in addition to the undershirt) during pre-season workouts. A rubber shirt not only promotes quick and relatively easy warming up, it also keeps the warmth inside the uniform once a sweat has been worked up, and affords good protection against the chill winds which are so prevalent in the early part of the season.

Of a more personal nature but, nevertheless, worthy of mention is the protective cup. Suffice it to say that this simple device can save a pitcher from serious injury and its use is highly advisable, from both a physical and psychological viewpoint.

Taking the mound

The impression will be given many times in this book that a pitcher's job starts long before he faces a batter. Even in an actual ball game he should not wait until he toes the rubber to concern himself with the task at hand.

As stated above, good balance is imperative to a pitcher, and this starts from the ground up. It follows that consideration should be given to the condition of the mound from which the hurler must work. Outside of professional ball there is wide divergence in the height and the material composition of pitchers' mounds. Because of the many varieties found in use we cannot concern ourselves with the mound per se—that is up to managers, coaches, and groundskeepers. The working condition of the mound is a different matter.

No two pitchers throw in identical fashion. All of them dig holes in the mound with their spikes. For these reasons it should be an absolute must for a pitcher to smooth the mound at the start of every inning. He should take care to fill in the hole dug at the rubber and the one made by the stride of the opposing moundsman. Furthermore, when his own stride marks become too deep they can throw him off stride, so these should be filled in when conditions so warrant. In other words, for proper working conditions, the mound should be smooth at all times.

To take the signal from the catcher, the pitcher should stand on the rubber. To speed up the game, the rules call for the pitcher to take the signal while in this position. To further accelerate action, he is now required to deliver the ball to the batter within twenty seconds after he receives it. For this reason alone, it is advisable to take the signal while in position to proceed into the wind-up. The same rule applies with men on base, with the exception that the pitcher is allowed to straddle the rubber while getting the sign. In addition to making for compliance with the rules of the game, this practice prevents the pitcher from walking around the center of the diamond and going through various purely extraneous actions which do nothing more than use up his energy.

Needless to say, consideration must be given to the condition of the baseball which is in use. When its surface becomes blemished in such a way as to impair the pitcher's ability to work effectively with it he should request a different ball from the umpire. If, on the other hand, a new ball is introduced which is too slick it should be rubbed until the sheen is removed. This duty is assigned to the umpire as a pre-game task and in those cases where it has been neglected can be done by the pitcher or one of his teammates as long as no foreign substance is applied to the ball. A little saliva, added to the dirt which is normally present on a ballplayer's hand should suffice to do the job satisfactorily.

A rosin bag should always be on hand for use of the pitcher. At any time that his hand becomes slippery or does not supply the desired resistance in releasing the ball the pitcher should dust his hands by gripping the rosin bag and squeezing it several times. Two words of precaution should be added—rosin may not be applied directly to the ball, since the rules consider it a foreign substance; and the application of rosin should be done judiciously, since an excess of it can cause the fingers to adhere to the ball sufficiently to impair one's control. In the absence of a rosin bag it is recommended that dirt or dust be used to dry the pitcher's hand.

The observance of these seemingly minor, but actually highly important preliminaries will assist any pitcher in making his task an easier one.

Grip

At this point we will not concern ourselves with the nuances of gripping the ball for various pitches or for the several styles of delivery. Instead, it is the grip on the ball, in general terms, which warants a few words here.

Regardless of how the individual moundsman holds the ball for his several pitches, he should strive for sameness of grip each time he throws a certain pitch. This similarity in grip helps a pitcher take advantage of the balance of the ball. By so doing he will be giving valuable assistance to his control, while at the same time lending uniformity to his stuff, thereby allowing him to gauge the probable action of the ball more accurately.

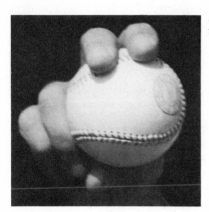

Pitching Grip (across the seams)

Pitching Grip (with the seams)

What this adds up to is that every pitcher should strive to get into a groove which will facilitate his over-all operations, and each facet of his pitching actions enters into the total picture.

Stance

The basic stance for a pitcher is one which finds him squarely facing the plate. In compliance with the previously mentioned rule which requires him to take his signal while on the rubber, and in order to enable him to go into his motion more effectively, he should place the front spike of his pivot foot over the edge of the rubber. This foot should be angled slightly toward the side from which the ball is thrown in order to facilitate the pivot and help get the body weight behind the throw. As a matter of fact, the foot must be in front of the rubber (not on top of it) if a pitcher is to reach peak effectiveness.

The striding foot should be kept a few inches back of the rubber and the weight should be forward. The body should be kept fairly erect and the shoulders should be level. While taking the signal, the pitcher should hide the ball from the batter. Holding it behind the thigh will accomplish this.

With men on base the same general principles apply. Main exception is that the stance is now a sideward one. The pivot foot can be angled along the inside of the rubber or placed as in the basic stance. The striding foot should be placed forward with the toe slightly to the left for a right-hander and pointed normally for a lefty. The body must remain motionless, although the head can be moved back and forth. The hands must come to a complete stop before the ball may be delivered to the plate (this does not apply to the pick-off throw to a base). The runner should be watched out of the corner of the eye. This phase of pitching is dealt with in detail in the section on "working with men on base."

The wind-up

The term "wind-up" is actually a misnomer. The windmill-like flailing of the arms is rarely employed by pitchers, probably because it accomplishes very little aside from tiring the arms. This phase of the motion can be more aptly termed the pump since that is the nature of the actions used by most successful pitchers.

The pump serves a two-fold purpose. It loosens and relaxes the arm and shoulder muscles and it helps the hurler to get his weight behind the pitch properly.

Complete relaxation is essential until just before the ball is delivered, if a pitcher is to achieve maximum results. Intentness of purpose is, of course, a vital factor in successful pitching, yet it should not interfere with physical relaxation. In order to help his cause in this respect it is recommended that a pitcher "break" his wrist in the forward and backward pump of his wind-up. This maneuver also makes for greater flexibility of the wrist and arm and should be practiced until it becomes automatic in those cases where it is not done naturally.

Another purpose which is accomplished by a pumping motion is the loosening of the shirt and undershirt around the arm and shoulder. Inconsequential though this may seem, it can bear heavily on a pitcher's effectiveness since a shirt can, at times, bind his shoulders and arms to a great enough extent to impair his normal delivery. For this reason, the arms should be fully stretched when the pitcher goes into his wind-up. By the same token, with men on base, a full stretch can be employed in order to loosen the shirt and undershirt thoroughly.

The pumping motions employed by different pitchers vary considerably. One thing which most good pitchers have in common, however, is the fact that their wind-up or pump is done above the throwing shoulder. There are exceptions but, in most cases, the hands and arms never actually cross the face, meaning, among other things, that the view of home plate will not be obscured at any time during the wind-up. As a matter of fact, some pitchers manage to get all the benefits of a full pump without ever raising their hands above their faces.

As the wind-up is started the weight should shift forward. Its primary purpose, however, is to move the body weight back and into the "rearing back" which puts power into the pitch. In order to facilitate this necessary transfer of body weight, many good pitchers take an initial step back on the striding foot. This process might be thought of as "gathering the weight" in preparation for the start of the wind-up. It is recommended as a means of getting increased power into the delivery. The entire pattern of action can be likened to a pendulum.

This pattern of action is highly important when consideration is given to that salient, but rarely emphasized, point: you can't add speed or stuff to a pitch after you let go of the ball. "Reaching way back" is one extreme of the pendulum-like motion which ends in the follow-through. It is, moreover, the more important of the two extremes. The follow-through is essential to a good delivery and is, as much as anything, a sign that all other phases of the delivery have been performed correctly. "Reaching way back" provides the explosive charge which actually propels the ball and, thus, is a definite must for all pitchers.

The pivot

The wind-up or pump leads quite naturally into the pivot. Momentum for the proper shifting of body weight has been started by the pump, and it reaches its "point of recoil" or of forward "detonation" at the rear extreme of the pivot. It is this phase of the motion which is the real source of power and wherein the very important "reaching way back" takes place. It is here that complete bodily relaxation is transformed into intense physical action—not by strained effort which will impair a smooth-flowing delivery, but by the controlled and natural actions which will impart maximum power.

As the pitcher's arms come up in his pump, the weight should shift back. It is then that the pivot actually begins. The pivot foot slides diagonally forward and the body turns toward the throwing side. As the pivot to the rear takes place, the striding leg should be swung up and around toward the pitching arm. At this stage of his motion the pitcher should be eyeing home plate and his target over the shoulder of his gloved hand. The kick itself should be moderate since an exaggerated one can throw the pitcher off balance, hindering his stuff and ruining his control.

During the wind-up and at the start of the pivot the legs should be relatively straight, not rigidly so, but straight enough to eliminate what would be purely extraneous movements which do not contribute to the desired pendulum effect but are primarily of a vertical nature. Needless to say, this is another factor designed to insure maximum stuff.

At the start of the pivot the pitcher's stance should be slightly open, that is, the toe of his pivot foot should be pointed out (slightly toward third base for a right-hander, toward first for a lefty). This will cut down excessive body action on the pivot while still allowing it to be a good, pendulum-like, one, thereby making for better control without impairing the power which can be imparted to the throw.

As indicated, the pivot should be a relatively short one which can be fully controlled. The upper body should remain straight during this phase of the delivery. Also, a very important consideration is that the pitcher should concentrate intently on his target at this point as well as at all times during his entire motion.

The stride

Quite obviously, the purpose of the stride is to shift the weight forward and into the delivery. It is the central link in the chain of physical movements which makes up the over-all pitching motion. It is a key factor in giving impetus to the ball. Yet, moderation is advocated.

The stride should not be exaggerated. It should be long and strong enough to provide full power but not to the extent that it interferes with good coordination, damaging both stuff and control.

As the pitching arm swings back, the striding foot comes straight forward and hits the ground with the toe pointed directly at the plate. The arm comes through as the body drives hard off the pivot foot.

There are three points in the last paragraph which bear elucidation: (1) The striding foot should hit the ground almost flat, or even slightly on the ball of the foot. When a pitcher lands on his heel he jars himself, hindering his balance and, consequently, his control; he also offers too much resistance to the forward shift of his body weight, thereby cutting down on his power—he should actually slide smoothly into his stride. (2) The toe should be pointed directly at his target. This simple device is a great boon to good control. (3) The body must drive hard off the pivot foot. A powerful push-off is an essential to getting the full weight behind the pitch and adding greatly to the power of it by so doing.

As the stride is taken, the arm should remain back of the rear shoulder which, in turn, lags behind the stride. The arm should start forward as the foot hits the ground and the stride should be definitely completed before the top point of the delivery is reached. It is not until this point in the delivery has been reached that the wrist-snap should take place. Needless to say, perfect balance is demanded during this entire series of actions, if good stuff and adequate control are to be achieved.

The pitch should be made against the front leg, which serves as a form of anchor in this case. This leg must be bent at least slightly to prevent the jarring effect which can hinder a pitcher's control and so that it will not serve as a brake which checks the smooth flow of motion that leads into the follow-through and which inhibits the power behind the pitch.

Consider the correct stride from the viewpoint of a right-hander: The stride, in order to assure a pitcher of his most effective possible delivery, should be not only forward, but slightly to the left. By the same token, a left-hander's stepping foot should move forward and slightly to the right. In order to ascertain the correctness of this move, a straight line should be drawn in the dirt pointing from the pivot foot toward home plate. The striding foot should land at a point three to six inches to the left of this line for a right-hander and three to six inches to the right of it for a left-hander, the only exceptions being those occasions when a cross-fire delivery is employed. The value of this lies in the fact that it prevents a pitcher from throwing across his body and thus creating unnecessary resistance, which decreases the power behind the pitch, hinders control, and can damage the arm by placing an unnatural strain on it.

"Throwing his glove" at the batter while taking his stride can prove a helpful maneuver to a pitcher. It not only aids in bringing his body weight into the pitch, but can add deception to his delivery since the motion of his glove can prove distracting to the batter in his efforts to locate and follow the ball.

The delivery

There are four basic types of pitching delivery common to baseball. They can be categorized generally as overhand, three-quarters, sidearm and underhand. All pitchers use one of these methods of throwing the ball and some employ a combination, usually adding an occasional side-arm pitch to a normally overhand or three-quarters style.

Overhand pitchers generally throw a fast ball which rises and a curve which breaks down. They release a fast ball off the ends of the fingers and employ a full downward sweep of the arm, which passes close to the head. By raising up on his toes during the delivery an overhand pitcher will gain added leverage that puts more hop on his fast ball.

The three-quarters delivery is, as the term implies, half-way between overhand and sidearm, and is most prevalent in use. Pitchers who employ this style throw a curve ball which breaks down and to the side. Their fast balls vary according to the method of release, rising when the ball is released off the ends of the fingers, but moving in and down (the sinker)

Sidearm Delivery (Allie Reynolds)

when the ball leaves the hand off the middle finger while the wrist is rotated to the outside.

Sidearm pitchers almost invariably throw a sinking fast ball and can add to this effect by rotating the wrist to the outside ("turning it over" as the arm comes through) and releasing the ball off the side and tip of the middle finger. The curve ball thrown by a sidearmer is usually a "flat" one. For this reason plus the fact that the ball can be so well hidden from the batter, the sidearm pitcher is more effective against a batter who swings from the same side, that is, righty vs. righty and lefty vs. lefty.

Underhand pitchers are few and far between, possibly because it seems to be more difficult to get good stuff on the ball in this way than by means of the other styles of delivery. An underhand fast ball will sink and an underhand curve ball will rise as well as move to the side when thrown with sufficient power.

The cross-fire is a variation which is occasionally used by pitchers who employ a sidearm delivery. It is the one method in which the striding foot crosses the line between the pivot foot and home plate. Consequently, it can cause considerable strain on the arm and for that reason must be used judiciously. Since the stride is made toward a point behind the batter and the sweep of the arm makes the ball appear to be coming from somewhere near third base for a right-hander and first base for a lefty, intimidation, as well as deception, are the principal reasons for its use. In this case, the angle of delivery rather than the action of the ball is the key factor.

It is the angle of delivery which marks the difference in these several styles of pitching. Each has its definite strong points. Perhaps the prime consideration in employing a particular style should be consistency of delivery. This refers to the motion used in throwing different pitches and pertains to the important element of deception which adds to their effectiveness. To cite a specific example, a pitcher who uses a three-quarters delivery should throw his fast ball and curve from the same angle so as not to tip off the batter as to what is coming. If every fast ball is thrown three-quarters and every curve sidearm, an opposing batsman will know exactly what is being thrown on each pitch. A smart hitter will be able to pick up even slight variations where they exist. Furthermore, in those cases where a combination of deliveries is used, a pitcher should throw his entire repertoire from each angle used—that is, every type of pitch he throws overhand, he should throw sidearm, and he should let the opposition know that he can do so.

One of the important requisites for sustained pitching success is smoothness of delivery. Though ungainly moves and jerky actions are no serious deterrent, the actual throwing motion should be smooth enough to allow a pitcher to fall into an easy, natural groove. All aspects of his pitching will be improved and, most important, his arm will be subject to much less wear and tear.

Good Pitching Form, left-hander (Fred Green)

Regardless of the style used, certain basic qualities are absolutely imperative. In any type of delivery there must be balance, the proper pivot, correct stride, and a good follow-through—plus the rapid coordination that comes with practice.

The release and follow-through

In breaking down the pitching motion into its various distinct segments and giving consideration to them individually and in the over-all aspect, we have reached the point where the body drives hard off the pivot foot and the arm comes through with good wrist snap. In the continuity of action the arm should then proceed through its arc of motion naturally, the hand reaching a point below the knee opposite the pitching shoulder. The body should be bent sharply at the waist. The finish of this sequence of action should find the pivot foot slightly ahead of the striding foot and the body in a crouch.

An important factor in achieving maximum stuff with a minimum of effort is getting the shoulder behind the pitch and leaning the weight into the delivery. A perfect example of the ideal execution of this technique is provided by Robin Roberts. This trait has contributed strongly to Roberts' endurance and his ability to call on the needed something-extra in clutch situations.

It is wrist action and the release of the ball which are primarily respon-

Good Pitching Form, right-hander (Paul Giel)

sible for imparting stuff to the pitch. For best results the ball should be released in front of the pitching shoulder. This not only provides necessary power but has a strong effect on control. Both will be at peak efficiency only when the ball is released in front of the pitching shoulder.

It has already been stated that a pitcher can not add stuff after he has let go of the ball. This lends emphasis to the importance of "reaching back" and then observing all of the fundamentals which have been discussed thus far. Nevertheless, the follow-through is extremely vital to good pitching. If nothing else, it is a sign that all of the other basic essentials have been performed correctly.

One of the first pieces of advice given to youngsters in any form of athletic endeavor is to follow through. Its importance in throwing a baseball can be observed in practice. A pitching motion which stops abruptly upon release of the ball hinders rather than contributes to the speed and control of the pitch. One which is only partial in its follow-through achieves only mediocre results within the framework of a man's physical capabilities. On the other hand, a full sweep of the arm and a complete follow-through will produce markedly better results in all respects. Merely by experimenting with these three methods in practice, a pitcher will readily come to appreciate the value of a good follow-through.

A simple method of checking on the completeness of the follow-through is to observe whether or not the pitching hand is below and to the outside of the knee of the striding foot upon completion of the throw. To go a step further, if the heel of that foot can be touched with no conscious effort, the follow-through is a good one.

At this final point in the delivery the pivot foot will be slightly in advance of the striding one. In order to be squared-away properly to be in good position for his fielding duties, the pitcher should employ a short shuffle-step with his striding foot to bring it in line with the other one. He will then be fully prepared to move in any direction to field the ball.

CONTROL

It is generally agreed that control is the main essential in successful pitching. Without it, the most overpowering of pitchers cannot rise above mediocrity. Ability to throw hard and to make the ball do tricks will go for naught if the ball cannot be controlled.

Its importance being widely accepted, let us try, first of all, to determine exactly what control is.

The prime requisite of good pitching is to throw strikes consistently. Although it is imperative for the pitcher to get the ball into the strike zone in order to be effective, perhaps this is too broad a definition in view of the ability of some batters to hit with authority balls in most parts of the strike zone.

The best definition of a successful pitcher's "control," is "the ability to put the ball *close to* the target with good stuff on it." The italicized words emphasize that merely getting the ball into the strike zone is not sufficient in the long run, although it must, of necessity, be the pitcher's initial objective.

Acquiring control

Since control is the most essential factor in good pitching, it is very fortunate that it is one quality which can be acquired. The observance of certain basic principles, the avoidance of several all too prevalent faults, the adoption of a sound mental attitude combined with the application of good common sense, and, above all, practice, practice, and more practice will help any pitcher to gain improved, if not really good, control. And, needless to say, the pitcher has never lived who could not afford to better his control.

Rule number one, for the observance of all pitchers, is: have a definite target. Although pinpoint control and the ability to thread the needle is not, in itself, essential, the attempt to achieve it is a must. Every pitcher should pick out a specific target (not merely a general area in the strike zone), should concentrate on it intently, and should make a determined effort to hit that target on every pitch. Its results, in terms of control, will come as a pleasant surprise to those who have not followed this practice.

Obviously, the catcher's glove is an ideal target. But, in the higher ranks of baseball, observant hitters will take advantage of this type of advance information. If the catcher's glove is used as a target and moved around from pitch to pitch they will be able to tell where a pitch is being aimed. Fixed targets should therefore be employed. There are four of these which can be used to good advantage by every pitcher—

Pitching Targets (the four corners)

the catcher's knees and his shoulders. For a low, outside pitch to a right-handed batter, for example, the target will be the catcher's right knee; for a high, inside pitch to a right-hander, his left shoulder; and so forth.

Other targets can be used, depending upon what suits the pitcher's purpose most effectively. Two things, however, must definitely be borne in mind: His target must be within the confines of the strike zone unless a pitch-out or waste ball is being used; and he must remember to keep his eye on one, fixed target during his entire motion.

One final word on this phase of the problem should be added. A pitcher, while he should strive for pinpoint accuracy, must definitely avoid aiming the ball if good control is to become an asset. Aiming the ball actually means that it is being held too long in an effort to point it at a certain spot. This causes full energy to be lost and a natural motion to be ruined. Needless to say, this results in both an impairment of a pitcher's stuff and an even greater loss of control than that which has caused him to aim the ball in the first place.

The first step in acquiring control is a simple, but effective practice technique. In throwing to a catcher, a pitcher should start by trying to throw every ball "through the middle." This should be repeated, using nothing but a three-quarters speed fast ball, until control to this partic-ular spot is well-nigh perfect. Once this has been accomplished, the target should be shifted to low and "through the middle," with repetition until perfection is reached. The same method can then be used at the letter-high level and, finally, when satisfied with his ability to hit these targets, the pitcher should follow the same procedure in throwing the ball over the inside and outside corners of the plate. This routine should be followed at frequent intervals, particularly during the pre-season training period, with the catcher offering a steady glove-target for each pitch. This simple drill will provide great benefits to the control of any hurler and can be employed with each of his various deliveries—but only after near-perfect control of his fast ball has been mastered.

The stride is very important in achieving control and it should be given careful consideration by a man who is attempting to perfect this essential phase of pitching technique. There are three facets of the stride which bear heavily on control of the ball—its direction, the part of the foot on which it lands, and its length.

As previously stated, the striding foot should land at a point three to six inches to the side of an imaginary line which runs from the pivot foot to home plate. This assures the pitcher of greater freedom of movement by preventing his throwing across his body, a practice which locks his arm and chest in such a way that both power and control are deterred. At the same time, the striding foot should be pointed directly at the pitcher's target. This last point is extremely important. Simple though this suggestion may appear, an analysis of pitching styles shows that it is too often overlooked, and regrettably so. The improvement in one's control will be quite noticeable if this idea is carried out faithfully.

In taking his stride, the pitcher should land on the ball of his foot. The man who lands on his heel when throwing jars his entire body sufficiently to upset his balance and temporarily blur his vision. These handicaps need not be imposed on a pitcher. They can be eliminated if he lands on the ball of his foot, a practice which makes for better stuff as well as improved control since it leads directly to a good follow-through.

The length of the stride should be moderate—of sufficient length to get good power behind the throw, but not so long that it upsets the delicate balance which is essential to a good pitching movement. Overstriding is a serious deterrent to good control in that it is usually accompanied by the above-mentioned landing on the heel which jars one's vision. Furthermore, it prevents the proper bending of the back which is required for a good follow-through.

The follow-through, itself, is vital because it maintains control right up to the last body movement of the pitching motion.

It should be fairly obvious that good control is dependent upon a repetition of actions for each type of pitch. This means that the fingers will be the same distance apart, the ball will be held the same distance out from the crotch formed by the thumb and forefinger, the angle of delivery will be similar for each throw, the finger pressure applied to the ball will be alike from pitch to pitch, and the feet will go in the same respective spots on each follow-through. A fraction of an inch difference at the rubber can mean inches at the strike zone.

In short, control can be acquired by constant, systematic practice, applying the principles of the fixed target, the well-controlled stride, and similarity of actions.

The causes of wildness

Granted that some pitchers are inordinately wild and that all of them can well afford to improve on their control, what are the basic, underlying reasons for wildness in any degree? Under analysis, the fundamental causes of this damaging affliction seem to resolve themselves into nine distinct categories, each of which will now be listed and touched upon briefly.

1. Changing finger pressures on the ball: The finger pressure for each kind of pitch—fast ball, curve, change, and so forth—must be kept the same each time it is delivered. This rule goes right back to the principle of similarity of actions. Inconsistent action in this case means that more pressure is applied on one side of the ball. This causes a general im-

balance in grip and results in a different release of the ball from pitch to pitch. The result is a complete absence of consistent release, which will hurt control and compound any wildness which already exists. Thus, it is imperative that every fast ball, every curve, every change-up, and so forth, be gripped in identical fashion.

2. Failure to concentrate on a fixed target: The need for a pitcher to keep his eyes focused on a definite target is so important that it can bear frequent repetition. Even when a fixed target is selected it is often lost from view during the pitching motion. When present, this fault is almost invariably caused by the turning of the head and eyes during the pivot. This means that the eyes must refocus on the target as the pivot is completed and, needless to say, can do little but harm a pitcher's control.

3. Excess rocking: This is closely allied to the second category. Most effective is a motion of the pendulum type. When the body is rocked excessively during the pivot the head and eyes will move and lose sight of the target. The suggested remedy is a shortened pump and concentration on restricting the shifting of the weight to backward and forward movements, thereby eliminating extraneous and harmful body actions.

4. Throwing across the body: This habit locks the hips and shoulders to such an extent that a good follow-through is impossible, meaning, also, that a smooth continuity of motion will be absent from the delivery. To revert to a device which has been previously explained, it can be corrected by drawing a line from the pivot foot to home plate and planting the striding foot about four inches to the side of this line—first base side for a right-handed pitcher, third base side for a left-hander.

5. Lack of proper follow-through: A partial follow-through interrupts the continuous control which should be maintained from start to finish of the pitching motion. In addition, it means that the body is not completely behind the throw and can give rise to the sore arm to which "arm-throwers" are prone. It is characterized by a relatively straight back and can be remedied by a full bending of the back and the effort to complete the delivery with the pitching hand below and to the outside of the knee of the striding leg.

This is closely related to poor balance on release of the ball, a habit which is equally injurious to control. This is caused by an uneven follow-through, which, in turn, arises from the fact that the pitcher does not "follow the ball" with his motion. It can be corrected by striving for a squared-away follow-through which can, in most cases, be achieved by a short shuffle-step with the pivot foot upon completion of the delivery.

6. Overstriding: This has already been discussed. It prevents the proper bending of the back in the follow-through and leads to the landing of the weight on the heel that causes the ruinous jarring of the vision. It can be corrected only by the use of moderation in striding.

7. Improper footing: This is harmful to all aspects of pitching form. It can be caused by poor shoes or an accumulation of mud on the spikes. More often, however, the improper planting of the pivot foot is the contributing factor. The spikes should not be placed on the rubber and the push-off made from that spot. Rather, the front spike should extend over the rubber at the start of the motion, the foot should pivot toward the pitching side, and the shoe should slide from the rubber and be braced against and parallel to it for the push-off.

8. Poor physical condition: This is definitely harmful to a pitcher's control, particularly in the late innings when fatigue begins to set in and take its toll. It should be emphasized that a pitcher's control is no better than his wind and legs—and, of course, a pitcher without control has nothing. Plenty of good hard running is the logical solution.

9. Mental factors: Lack of self-control is displayed most conclusively when a pitcher becomes upset by poor support from his teammates or infuriated at his own failings. Lack of courage, more accurately lack of confidence in the vast majority of such cases, can be caused by an unfamiliarity with game conditions or a lack of faith in one's ability to get the ball over the plate with something on it. Aiming the ball is another fault which is essentially mental in nature, since it stems primarily from lack of confidence.

Experience under game conditions, a full realization of the percentages which lie in his favor, and the resultant faith in his own ability comprise the proper mental outlook that will help a pitcher overcome these difficulties.

The faults listed in this section are the most common causes of wildness. Where one of them exists it is usually inadvertent and unconscious on the part of the pitcher. Careful self-analysis may uncover such a root of evil. Cooperation from coach, manager, catcher, or a fellow pitcher is a more certain method of detecting a flaw. Suffice it to say that if none of these basic faults is present in one's pitching style, the control problem will be greatly minimized—if not eliminated entirely.

Correcting wildness

When a pitcher's control is faulty he must adopt an attitude which is simultaneously realistic and optimistic. Mere hope and dogged persistence with his present style is not enough; it amounts to expecting a divine miracle to rectify the situation. Informed, outside help should be sought and the proper therapy should be diligently applied, once the cause of the trouble is discovered. The pitcher, in setting out to improve his control, should realize that: (1) his wildness is almost invariably caused by a flaw in his delivery; (2) he must discover the source of his trouble and work hard to remedy it; and (3) the situation is far from hopeless—control can most definitely be improved by a sensible approach and a determined effort.

Experienced baseball men, in appraising the control problems of many pitchers over a great number of years, have arrived at the conclusion that when wildness is consistent, it can be corrected, usually by an alteration in bodily movements that has the effect of adjusting the sights. This means that if a pitcher's wildness results in his throwing the ball consistently to one general area outside the strike zone, his trouble can be rectified. If, on the other hand, his throws go "all over the place" with no regularity, he is releasing the ball differently on all of his deliveries, due to changing finger pressures. Unfortunately, this is a bad situation, one which demands a complete change of style, a fresh start, as it were, if the situation is not to progress to a point which is beyond all hope.

Wildness is either horizontal or vertical in nature. In other words, a bad pitch is primarily inside, outside, too high, or too low. Of course, combinations of two of these qualities do occur frequently but wildness on pitch after pitch will be predominantly in only one of these general areas.

The pitching rubber is six inches wide by twenty-four inches long. This twenty-four-inch length provides a pitcher with sufficient space in which to make the adjustments needed to correct horizontal wildness. By moving to either side of the rubber he can correct this horizontal wildness, the exact amount of the shift being determined through experimentation. Both over-all wildness and temporary loss of control on a horizontal plane should be treated in this fashion. To cite a specific example, if a right-handed pitcher finds that he is consistently wild-inside in relation to a right-hand batter, he can eliminate this trouble by moving to his left on the rubber. A comparable application of this basic principle can be used to correct other instances of horizontal wildness in its varied forms.

Vertical wildness revolves primarily around the follow-through and is greatly affected by the length of the stride. A good follow-through, with the back bent and the pitching hand below and outside of the knee of the striding leg, is vitally important to good control and should be practiced continuously. Specific adjustments which may be needed can be effected by alterations in the length of the stride. If a pitcher is wild-high he is releasing the ball too soon and can remedy the fault by shortening his stride, a move which brings his body weight forward more quickly in relation to his arm motion, making for a lower point of release and promoting a better follow-through, both of which will help him to bring the ball down. Conversely, when he is plagued by being wild-low, a lengthening of his stride should offset the faulty equilibrium which is causing him to release the ball too late and making his pitches consistently low.

Similarity of actions has already been noted as imperative to good control. In so far as the stride is concerned, wildness is often caused by a lack of this desired sameness. The striding foot should come down in the same place and in the same manner each time one of various pitches— fast ball, curve, change, and so forth—is thrown. A check of footprints can reveal when this is not being done and an effort to stride in the same place for each pitch should bring about the necessary cure.

Keeping the eyes on a fixed target is so important that it merits repetition. A pitcher should have a specific mark at which to throw and his eyes should remain on that spot throughout his entire motion. Above all, his eyes should be focused on his target prior to any forward movement of his body, otherwise his pitching will be tantamount to throwing at a moving target. One method to insure the performance of this vital act is to hesitate momentarily at the top of the wind-up. This allows for applied concentration on the target, free from any distracting movements, and is a definite boon to control in the case of a pitcher whose wildness is due to his eyes wandering from the target.

Control sometimes is affected by the presence of runners on the bases. Chief cause of this is the failure of the pitcher to sight his target properly. The sideward stance provides a less full view of home plate than does the normal delivery in which the pitcher faces the batter squarely. Two things should be indelibly impressed on a hurler's mind when he works with men on base—(1) he should look at his target with both eyes (the tendency in working from a stop-position runs counter to this); (2) he must never pitch from memory—in other words, he should take a good look at his target before delivering the ball plateward, even at the cost of allowing the runner an extra step or two of lead. If these two precautions are observed, a man's control should be no worse with men on base than it is with the bases empty.

A further word of advice on correcting wildness revolves around the desirability of acquiring a pendulum-like motion in which movements are primarily backward and forward in relation to home plate. Excessive rocking moves the head and eyes and causes temporary loss of the target. An effective method of steering the ball toward the target and, at the same time, not disrupting the smooth, pendulum movement which helps control, is to turn the body further in the direction in which the pitcher intends the ball to go. The ball should, moreover, be released in the same way, the striding foot should point directly at the target, and the ball should not be aimed, all of which are merely reversions to the basic principles of good control.

The acquisition of proper techniques for good control and the application of corrective therapy where wildness exists can best be accomplished on the sidelines during practice sessions. When throwing for control, it is best to work from a mound. Having a batter standing in hitting position is also desirable and is, incidentally, beneficial to him in his efforts to learn and familiarize himself with the strike zone. The use of strings which can be erected to outline the strike zone is also of great value. Any of these devices can be fruitfully employed; a combination of all is ideal. Attempts at correcting wildness should give further emphasis to the need for giving every pitch a definite purpose—even in simple warm-up sessions.

The performance of any of the above measures which may apply to a particular case, the repetition of similar actions for each pitch, and the development of the proper mental attitude should do the trick for any pitcher desirous of achieving good control.

The mental side of control

Some pitchers seem to have good control naturally. Others succeed in developing it. Still others never acquire it. Yet, it is one of baseball's truisms that *anyone* can improve his control unless he is convinced that he cannot.

A pitcher's frame of mind is of tremendous importance to his over-all performance in general and his control in particular. Confidence, poise, and, to a certain extent, competitive spirit are increased by the assurance which comes from familiarity with the job. All of them influence a pitcher's control and, paradoxically enough, at the same time are in-fluenced by his control. There is a very close interrelationship between them.

The successful pitcher takes keen delight in outsmarting the hitter. He also realizes how strongly percentages will work in his favor if he throws strikes. Even when he cannot overpower a batter, he is fully aware that the best of them do not hit safely more than once in three times at bat. Thus, if he gets the ball over the plate with good stuff on it, the law of averages is definitely on his side. When he can stay ahead of the hitter and then put the ball in the general area of that man's weakness he will be well on his way to real success.

Yet, there are pitchers who are actually afraid to put the ball over the plate. This is, of course, a sign that they lack confidence in their stuff. It also indicates that they are not fully aware of the way in which percentages favor them. Even in batting practice, when the ball is "laid in there" for the hitter, more balls are hit which would be outs than which would go for base hits. Obviously, this phobia can lead to noth-ing but trouble.

A pathetic and too often heard description of pitching ineptitude is, "He got behind the hitter and had to come in with a 'fat' pitch." A survey has shown that in the Major Leagues, a .250 hitter becomes a .350 hitter

71

with the pitcher in the hole and, just as conclusively, a .350 hitter becomes a .250 hitter when the pitcher has him in the hole. These are not exact figures but they are close enough approximations to demonstrate that the pitcher who consistently falls behind the batter in the count is committing baseball suicide.

Occasional and usually inexplicable wild streaks will arise to plague every pitcher. These are all but inevitable occurrences and the surest way to prolong one when it comes along is to fall prey to excessive worry over it. A pitcher must never allow himself to ease up and aim the ball in order to get it over the plate. Instead, he should combat a spell of wildness by firing away naturally until he once again finds the proper groove.

Pressure can also take its toll on a pitcher's control. There is actually no need for him to allow the situation to become too big for him. He must bear in mind that the hitter is in an equally tough spot. Furthermore, it is the pitcher who has the odds in his favor. He has eight other men waiting to help him and the law of averages dictates that, even when the batter does hit the ball, it will fall in safely only a small percentage of the time.

The conclusions should be obvious. The pitcher who realizes that the advantage lies with him, who exhibits poise and assurance at all times, and who has confidence in his ability to get the ball over the plate with something on it will have little difficulty with his control and can quite reasonably expect to be a winner.

THE BASIC PITCHES

Baseball's basic pitches are three in number. They are the fast ball, curve, and change-of-pace. More accurately, it might be said that there are four of them, since the change-of-pace includes a change-up on both the fast ball and curve.

The basic pitches, plus control of each of them are all that any pitcher needs in order to be successful. At the same time, all four pitches must be perfected if a pitcher hopes to reach real stardom.

The slider has become prevalent in use of recent years and is a valuable addition to a pitcher's arsenal. The knuckler, screw ball, palm ball, fork ball, and so forth are the so-called off-pitches and all have their staunch advocates. For the time being, however, we should concern ourselves with the basic three, the ones which are really essential in making a pitcher. They should be mastered one at a time and, when each is perfected, will combine to give a pitcher an effective repertoire. Only after mastery of the basic pitches has been achieved should any thought be given to the other deliveries and, even at that time, their acquisition is not really vital to success on the mound.

When thrown at different speeds and, if possible, when delivered both overhand and sidearm, the basic pitches will furnish a pitcher with the material needed to inject an almost unlimited amount of variety into his method of operation.

The fast ball

A good fast ball is, of course, a gift of nature. The ability to throw exceptionally hard cannot be learned. Any natural attributes, however, can and should be exploited fully. There are certain techniques which, if perfected, will enable a pitcher to get the maximum benefits from his physical ability and will actually increase the speed of his delivery. Those we will consider at this point. Later, in the section on tactics, we will explore the strategy which makes possible the judicious use of various pitches in such a way that a fast ball can be made to seem considerably swifter than it actually is.

DEFINING THE FAST BALL. A fast ball is, by literal definition, the swiftest pitch that a hurler is capable of delivering. More precisely, it is a normal, hard throw delivered with a full sweep of the arm and a completely natural motion.

The laws of physics have demonstrated that force cannot exist without resistance and that resistance will be nonexistent in the absence of force. In other words, one must be present in order for the other to develop. In relation to velocity, it has been conclusively proven that the speed of any object will be greater when resistance is built up against the propelling force.

These statements sound highly technical in the light of a discussion on pitching but they most certainly apply to this phase of baseball. Furthermore, an understanding of them may furnish the means for the development of a really good fast ball.

Force, in pitching, is provided by the long, whip-like action of the arm combined with a snap of wrist and elbow. Resistance, in this case, is furnished by finger pressure against the ball and the shifting of body weight brought about by the stride and push-off. The application of our physical laws to the act of throwing a baseball leads to the conclusion that the greater the resistance provided by the fingers and the momentum (not the sheer bulk) of the shift of body weight, and the longer the arc of the arm and the stronger the wrist-elbow snap, the greater will be the velocity of the pitched ball.

The term "good fast ball" applies not only to the actual speed of the pitch but, even more so, to the movement of the ball in flight. Mere

73

velocity is generally not sufficient to nullify the ability of really good hitters. The most effective fast ball is one which is not only swift, but "live." That is, it deviates slightly in course, or "moves."

The movement of the ball in flight varies according to the spin imparted to the ball as it leaves a pitcher's hand. A fast ball which "moves" can deviate on either a horizontal or vertical plane, and often does so in a combination of the two. Generally speaking, a "live" fast ball delivered overhand has a tendency to rise; if thrown sidearm it usually sinks; and hurled with a three-quarters delivery it may do either. In addition, sideward deflections in course will be present in a great many cases. Through experience the individual pitcher can tell what tendency his fast ball has and can gauge himself accordingly in his use of it.

Pitchers who compile impressive strike-out records invariably possess an exceptionally good fast ball. It is their "strike-out pitch." Even in the case of pitchers who are not overpoweringly swift, a good, well-controlled, and judiciously used fast ball is most likely to be their "out pitch." This leads to the idea that the individual pitcher should have two broadly defined types of fast ball—a good one which is thrown naturally and with no extra effort, for use in getting ahead of the hitter and in what might be called normal situations; and an extra fast one which is held in reserve for those instances when the pitcher finds himself in a tight situation or in which he has two strikes on the batter.

A further breakdown of fast ball types can be made and would include a sinker, a slider, and a power-pitch. Some pitchers are fortunate enough to have developed all three. They can be employed for different purposes, exemplified by the sinker, which breaks down and can be used when it is most desirable to induce the batter to hit the ball on the ground; the slider, which moves to the side and can prevent the batter from getting good wood on the ball when he is set for a normal fast ball; and the extra-fast pitch which can be used to "drive it" in on the batter and overpower him when he has been properly set up for it. Needless to say, the pitcher who possesses all three has a most valuable weapon with which to combat the hitters—variety in his most basic pitch sufficient enough so that the one pitch can be used in several widely differing situations.

THROWING THE FAST BALL. The ultimate objective of a pitcher who is working to perfect his fast ball should be the development of maximum speed with minimum effort. Relaxation is the psychological basis for this. The bodily actions which produce maximum speed are a firm grip; a good push-off with the pivot-foot; full utilization of the body weight; getting the shoulder behind the throw; a strong wrist and elbow snap; and a good follow-through. All these are absolute essentials.

All deflections from a horizontal or vertical line and all changes in speed are caused by varying spin and pressure. It is the grip on the ball and the snap of the wrist which are responsible for this.

For best results, the first two fingers should be close together in gripping the ball. This makes for a firmer grip and more fluid wrist action which, in turn, gives greater rotation to a pitch. (A wide grip, on the other hand, can help one's control.) The ball should be placed as far out from the crotch formed by the thumb and fingers as is possible while still permitting control over the ball. Furthermore, the ball should be gripped firmly in order to provide resistance for the propelling force of the arm-sweep, but not so tightly as to create a tense wrist. A grip that is too tight has a tendency to lock the muscles and, conversely, a loose wrist supplies the rapidity of rotation that gives the ball its "life."

Adopting the proper grip is sometimes an involved matter and often calls for experimentation. This is occasioned, to a great extent, by the need to employ a grip which is just right—not too loose, not too tight—in other words, firm, yet fluid. Obviously, "feel" is an important factor. It cannot be taught in lectures or books but must be arrived at by the pitcher himself. The thumb should not be overlooked during the period of trial and error. Its role is vital in contributing the delicate balance which provides maximum results.

Getting the weight and pumping power behind the pitch in correct fashion is accomplished by three elements of the pitching motion—the pivot, the push-off, and the stride. It is desirable to use a full body pivot. This will transfer the weight, in balance, to the rear leg, which should be rigid though bent, like a coiled spring. Then follows the push-off, which is extremely important in imparting power to the throw. A pronounced push—slightly up as well as forward—should be employed off of the rear foot. This not only provides power but serves to prevent the arm from coming through too late in the motion. This leads naturally into the stride, which should not be so exaggerated as to dissipate all of the force and not leave any for the throw itself. Landing on the ball of the foot (not the heel) lessens resistance to the body's momentum and facilitates the continuous flow of motion which ends in the follow-through.

The direction in which the body weight should move warrants at least passing mention. The push-off and stride help to get the shoulder and body weight properly behind the throw. Only when the momentum imparted is directed in a straight line toward home plate will the full propelling power be brought into play. It is imperative that the throw not be made across the body. For this reason, previous reference has been made to the advisability of pushing off and striding directly toward home and planting the lead foot slightly toward the side opposite the throwing arm. In order to insure the channeling of the body weight in the right path this principle should be extended to the pumping motion which is the inception of a pitch. Preliminary moves of this nature will lead to a more effective utilization of a man's bodily capacities, i.e., it will help him to throw a better fast ball.

A good follow-through is an absolute essential and this is the natural culmination which stems from reaching way back. It is actually a result rather than a cause and furnishes proof that the other fundamentals have been properly observed.

Reaching-way-back and the follow-through are closely allied and comprise the start and finish of the prescribed pendulum-like motion. The delivery should be in the form of an arch which has as its initial low-point the end of the backswing, its high-point the release of the ball, and its concluding low-point the follow-through.

Each pitcher can tell what tendency his fast ball has and can take steps to improve its action. The guiding principle is to hold the ball in the way that will bring it into the position in which it will be subject to the fullest degree of air resistance. For instance, in order to impart maximum backspin to a rising fast ball, an across-the-seams grip should be used. A sinking fast ball, on the other hand, should be gripped with the seams. The former applies primarily to overhand pitchers, the latter to sidearmers.

By releasing the ball off the ends of the fingers with a strong wrist-snap an overhand pitcher can impart the backspin needed to make his

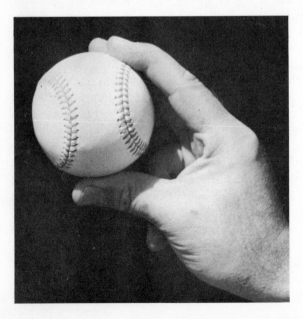

Release of the Ball (fast ball)

fast ball "hop." The heavy backspin exerts an opposite rising force that at a certain point succeeds in overcoming gravity for a split second, enabling the ball to rise slightly in its course of flight.

Much publicity has been given the "sinker." In the majority of cases this is not a separate pitch, but merely a fast ball which has a natural tendency to sink, rather than rise. This is a regular characteristic of a sidearmer's fast ball and is shared by a good number of hurlers who deliver the ball in three-quarters fashion. A downward follow-through is one of the chief factors in making the ball sink and this should be emphasized in the case of a pitcher who throws this type of fast ball. When combined with an outward roll of the wrist and the release of the ball off the side of the middle finger the effect will be more pronounced.

Because the middle finger is longest and since it is the last one in contact with the ball at the point of release, the fast ball also has a tendency to move toward the side from which it is thrown, particularly in the case of a pitcher who rolls his wrist to the outside. Different spin can be imparted merely by moving the tip of the middle finger back or by gripping the ball off-center. Thus the fast ball can be made to move to either side. This is the underlying principle of the slider which is, in reality, a variation on the fast ball, and will be discussed later.

In brief, the ingredients which make for a good fast ball are—a firm grip, a good push-off on the pivot foot, getting the shoulder and body behind the throw, a strong wrist-elbow snap, and a complete follow-through.

IMPROVING THE FAST BALL. The most effective method of throwing the fast ball has been rather thoroughly covered in the last section as well as the various ones which came under the general heading of *Mechanics.* Yet, one problem remains. What should be done in the case of a pitcher who is not blessed by nature with a good fast ball or in the case of one who feels that he is properly observing all of the basic fundamentals but whose fast ball still leaves much to be desired in the way of effectiveness?

One phase of this question revolves around pitching strategy and is the subject of a later chapter that shows how to put all these principles to correct use. The other concerns itself with ironing out flaws that may be present in the delivery, and with learning some of the tricks of the trade that accomplished moundsmen have discovered through hard work and experimentation.

The first step to an improved fast ball is, needless to say, the uncovering of any basic flaw that may be hindering its delivery or the lack of that little something which will make a big difference in quality. Self-appraisal, while always helpful, is not the complete answer. Close observation, analysis, and instruction by an interested party are needed.

A coach, manager, or experienced teammate can often provide the solution to the problem and should be consulted.

Several simple measures which can be of help in developing a good fast ball will be discussed briefly in the following paragraphs. Some of them have been mentioned in the preceding material; any or all of them may possibly provide the means by which a pitcher can acquire a more effective fast ball.

1. The fast ball is improved by practice while a pitcher is at a youthful age. The muscles which are most important to throwing well will develop along with a youngster's physical growth. Plenty of free and natural throwing is a boon to the materialization of a pitcher and should be indulged in to the fullest possible extent—but should not exceed that point where any undue strain on the arm is felt.

2. The grip is basic in importance. The pressure of the two fingers increases the rotation of the ball; the seams aid the grip and should be utilized to the fullest extent. In his eagerness to throw hard a pitcher may allow himself to grip the ball too tightly or to "choke the ball" (insufficient space between the ball and the crotch of the hand). The former causes tension which locks the muscles and wrist; the latter cuts the speed of a pitch by decreasing the leverage provided by the wrist and arm motion. Both must be avoided if best results are to be achieved.

3. The body movement should not be expended in any direction other than toward home plate. One of the chief causes of a lack of speed (and of sore arms) is throwing across the body. The motion should be directly toward home plate and given impetus by a powerful push-off. The push-off should be slightly up as well as forward, particularly in the case of overhand pitchers who will find that this gives a better angle of delivery and increased leverage, both of which help impart the "hop" which makes this pitch most effective.

4. The gloved hand and arm help bring the weight into the pitch correctly. They should be thrust toward the plate (thrown at the batter) in such a way that the action will start a good body movement.

5. One practice may help relaxation and contribute to the value of the pump: when bending forward the pitcher should exhale; when going up and back he should inhale; the lungs should be full on the "reach-back."

6. Rosin can be helpful when properly used. In hot weather it dries the hand; on a cold day it offsets the dry, smooth condition which is present. It definitely helps give rise to the needed friction. An added note: for most telling results, it should be applied only to the first two fingers.

7. The condition of the ball can contribute to the effect achieved by a fast ball. A slick, new ball has a tendency to sail. A cut ball will break in the direction away from the cut as it is prior to release (with a

blemished surface facing to the right, the ball breaks down and to the left). A rough spot will add to friction, thereby increasing the ball's rotation. When present, these conditions should be capitalized on fully.

The curve ball

It is not only a consensus of informed baseball opinion, but a well-proven fact that a curve ball can be learned, improved upon, and perfected by almost any pitcher with average physical equipment. Its mastery depends on aptitude, flexibility of wrist, suppleness of arm, and the determination evidenced by the man who is endeavoring to acquire an effective curve ball.

The only individual likely to prove incapable of developing a good curve is one who is affected by a stiff wrist which has resulted from an injury. In any case, a first-rate curve rarely comes easily. It must be practiced assiduously until it can be thrown with a consistently sharp break and with the degree of control that will enable the pitcher to "move it around" as well as he can his fast ball.

Accepting the validity of the above statements, an attempt will be made here to set forth principles and methods which can be of great assistance to any pitcher attempting to master the curve.

THEORY. Theoretically, two basic methods exist by which a pitcher can retire a batter: on a vertical plane and on a horizontal plane. A fast ball which overpowers the hitter or changes of speed which upset his timing are examples of the latter, which is essentially a method that does not necessitate changes in the course of a pitched ball. The curve ball is the principal means of retiring the batter on a vertical plane since it is the one pitch which deviates most radically on this plane.

By way of further contrast, the basis for the curve ball is forward spin, whereas the fast ball derives its "life" and effectiveness from the backspin which is imparted to it.

That the ability to throw a curve ball is an absolutely integral part of a pitcher's operating equipment is a superfluous statement. Discussion of its importance is unnecessary. Some theoretical background can prove invaluable to a pitcher in mastering the curve, however, and for that reason a few introductory remarks on the scientific aspects of curve ball pitching are in order at this point.

It is air resistance which makes a curve ball break. This is the reaction of air to any object moving through it at high speed. Resistance will cause a deviation in the course of a ball which is rotating at an exceedingly rapid rate. It follows that the faster the rotation, the bigger the curve will be. Quite logically, the ball will break in the direction in which it is spinning.

To illustrate the importance of air resistance, first of all, consider the fact that a curve ball breaks more pronouncedly on a damp day when the air is heavy and, to pursue the point further, that at high altitudes (Denver or Mexico City, for example) a curve is little more than a "wrinkle" due to the rarefied atmosphere prevalent there. To lend additional emphasis to this premise, consider the fact that, paradoxically enough, a curve ball pitcher operates more effectively when throwing into the wind. Once again increased air resistance is responsible, here in the form of the better "bite" which a ball gets when going into the wind.

There are, needless to say, several types of curves. The two broadest categories thereof are the sharp and the sweeping variety. The sweeping one may have a much larger arc but is, in most cases, less deceptive than the sharp-breaking one, which is more difficult for the batter to pick up. The sharp curve is given a more elaborate twist in its delivery than is the sweeping one.

The specific uses which experienced pitchers make of the curve ball also call for further classification, namely swinging, taking, and wasting types: when the pitcher wants the batter to hit the ball (or, at least, swing at it) he deals him his best curve and tries to hit a corner with it; when the batter is least expecting a curve and most likely to take it for a strike the pitcher can afford to cut the middle of the plate with it knowing that the element of surprise will often give him a called strike; finally, when ahead in the count the pitcher can afford to waste a pitch and can throw his curve for the plate in such a way that it will break outside of the strike zone, yet have a good possibility of enticing the batter to swing at a bad ball.

Before delving into curve ball techniques, one fallacy should be dispelled. The deliveries to which uninitiated fans and players refer as curve, drop, and out-drop are actually one and the same. They are all lumped together under one heading and known merely as a curve ball to experienced ballplayers, the drop and the out-drop being curve balls thrown from different angles, ones which will cause them to break down and/or to the side. For practical purposes, they are all called curves, with the possible further qualification of delivery angle—sidearm, overhand, or three-quarters.

DEVELOPING A CURVE. In learning to throw a curve ball a pitcher should attack the problem in stages, working from gradually increasing distances until he reaches the full sixty feet, six inches. To set an arbitrary figure, he should start at thirty feet, spinning the ball with a full curve ball action. The next step should be to repeat the process at forty-five feet; then the regulation pitching distance can be used. The idea behind this method is to develop that curve ball motion which will impart maximum spin to the ball. The pitcher should strive for a delivery in which his elbow straightens with a definite snap movement and an inward rotation of the wrist which will find the back of his hand facing the catcher as the ball is released. He should go through this procedure with the idea in mind of trying to see how fast he can spin the ball. This, of course, is the key to a really good curve ball.

Several essentials of the curve are similar to those required for the fast ball. A strong push-off on the pivot foot is a primary requisite. The shoulder should be behind the throw as much as possible. The follow-through is especially important in bringing the ball down to a point where it will be most effective—there is no such thing as a *good*, high curve (the ball "hangs"). A right-hander's arm should be alongside or below his left knee upon completion of his motion and, quite naturally, the left arm and right knee apply in the case of a left-hander. The achievement of this finish-of-the-motion is even more important in the case of the curve ball than it is when the other pitches are thrown.

Any grip which produces maximum spin can be used, but it is preferable to employ the same one with which the fast ball is held. In order to make for more fluid wrist action the ball should not be gripped as tightly as it is for the fast ball. The seams should be made to work for the pitcher since their action can give the ball greater rotation and can induce a sharper break to the curve. Thus, the grip should be such that as much of the seamed surface of the baseball as possible is rotating in the direction in which the ball should curve. Good curve ballers make four seams, the maximum number which can be brought into play, work for them when throwing this pitch.

Most of the pressure of the grip should be applied with the middle finger as this is the one which does the major part of the work. The ball rolls off the index finger as it is released and the part played by this particular digit is to serve as a guide for the pitch.

The wrist should be bent for the curve ball, but not until the pitcher is well into his motion. Bending the wrist as the ball is gripped is too good a tip-off to the hitter and, no matter how good the curve, deception is still a highly important element in its effectiveness. It should be added, here, that the more the wrist is bent, the bigger and slower the curve will be.

By way of confirmation of some of these ideas, the words of Sal Maglie can be cited. Probably the finest of modern-day curve ball artists, Maglie states that he used the same grip for all of his deliveries, adjusting the finger pressure for the change from one to the other. His grip for the fast ball was similar in finger position but tighter than the one he used for his curve.

The proper stride for the curve is several inches shorter than that used in throwing a fast ball. This is very important. Employment of the shorter stride produces a lower point of release for the ball and a better follow-through, both of which help to impart greater spin. To take full advantage of the effect of his wrist-snap the pitcher should try to release the ball in front of his forehead. And—repeating this for emphasis—his arm should be alongside of his knee on the follow-through.

In practice, the curve ball, as a separate delivery, should not begin to materialize at the very start of the motion. The pitch actually begins to take shape when the arm reaches a position behind the ear. At this point, where the arm starts its forward motion, the forearm and wrist should be turned in toward the shoulder and head until muscular tension is felt. This brings the wrist and hand into position to release the ball, with a rolling motion, off the first and second fingers. The hand is given an outside-in twist as the wrist-snap takes place.

The act of snapping the wrist should occur when the hand comes into a position where it is even with the body in its full sweep. The curve ball will be completely ineffective if the snap takes place any sooner, since the ball must be released in front of the head if it is to achieve a good break. Conversely, too late a snap will cause a delayed release, resulting in a low pitch and insufficient spin. Consequently, the curve ball motion must be practiced diligently until the wrist-snap and release of the ball are performed at a point which will produce a sharp break and allow for good control of the pitch.

There are two methods of releasing the curve ball—off the ends of the fingers or off the inside of the index finger (the side toward the thumb). Either manner of release can be used, although the latter is favored by most pitchers, probably because it entails a more natural motion and permits the ball to be controlled with less concentrated effort. If, however, the more natural side-of-the-fingers release produces insufficient spin, the other method should be tried. The end-of-the-fingers release requires a fuller wrist-roll, since the palm must be brought into a position which will find it directly facing the pitcher. This technique will impart better spin to the ball because the wrist has a greater latitude of movement up and down than it has from side to side. Needless to say, some experimentation may be required until the method is found which effects good results and is easily mastered. If, however, a pitcher can throw a good curve ball using one of these styles he should be satisfied with it and not try a change to the other method on the possible chance that it will help his curve—it might well do just the opposite, and cause impairment of his original method in the process.

To recapitulate—throwing the curve ball entails the extension (straightening) of the elbow, a slightly inward rotation of the wrist so that on release of the ball the palm is facing the pitcher and the back of the hand is toward the catcher, a good snap which takes place as the arm comes even with the body, and a relatively short stride which makes for a full follow-through and helps impart maximum spin to the ball.

PERFECTING THE CURVE. Let us assume that the principles of the curve ball are understood and that the basic techniques of throwing it have been properly observed. This should result in at least a better-than-average curve for most pitchers, but such is not always the case. The action of the pitched ball is the consideration here, not its tactical use, an aspect designed to increase the effectiveness of the curve, which will be discussed in a later chapter.

When a curve ball is delivered correctly but still fails to respond with a sharp break, additional means may be needed. That is the concern of this particular section and it is hoped that an idea may be gleaned therefrom which will enable a mediocre curve ball pitcher to break off a really good curve.

Since the secret of a good curve is the imparting of a maximum amount of spin to the ball, an exceptionally good wrist-snap is required. An exercise which may prove invaluable in abetting wrist-action is to snap the wrist with a curve ball rotation while holding the elbow stationary. A few minutes a day spent in this fashion should contribute greatly to the development of a really strong wrist-snap. This exercise is performed without a ball and is highly recommended to any pitcher who is desirous of improving his curve ball.

In many cases, the pitcher whose curve ball is a poor one contributes to his shortcoming by waiting too long in snapping his wrist. This delay makes for weak wrist-action and means that insufficient spin will be imparted to the ball.

Another fault which hinders the wrist-snap and which, consequently, must be guarded against is attempting to throw the curve ball too hard. This causes a stiff wrist and, in order to break off a good curve, the wrist must be relaxed and its motion fluid. The curve simply cannot be thrown as swiftly as the fast ball and no attempt should be made to do so if the curve is to be a good one.

The curve ball should not be "pushed." The correct wrist-action is similar to that used in "pounding a nail into the wall"—the ball should be behind the elbow as the elbow passes the shoulder. A pitcher should feel that he is bringing his hand over the ball and almost pulling it along. This fluid-type motion furnishes the fast rotation which is so essential.

Another "must" for a curve ball pitcher is to strive for a full sweep of the arm. In this respect, the elbow should be kept away from the body so that the entire arm will enter into the delivery.

The thumb can be brought into play to give valuable assistance in producing spin. If not done so noticeably that it will tip off the opposition as to the pitch, the thumb can be tucked slightly under the ball. A quick flip of it as the ball is released will then help to impart just that much more rotation to the ball, adding to the sharpness of the break.

The curve should, of course, be hidden from the batter to the fullest possible extent. For that reason the wrist and elbow should not bend in toward the head until the arm is moving forward. The temptation to "crook" the arm prematurely is often present due to a pitcher's anxiety to get something extra on his curve. The desire to do so must be controlled. Too much snap or elbow bend is not necessary—a good sharp twist should suffice. The object of all this is to make the curve ball motion appear the same to the hitter as that used for the fast ball. A key to spotting the fast ball—as opposed to the curve—is the appearance of more white (the ball) as the arm comes forward. An exaggerated wrist and elbow bend contributes to this contrast between the two by its greater concealment of the ball from the batter. Masking one's intentions is, of course, desirable. Concealing the ball until the last possible moment is highly important. The idea here, however, is to achieve the effect of making the fast ball and the curve appear similar to the batter when he picks them up visually. Thus, it is good practice to show "a little white" on both pitches.

The wisdom of adopting the same grip for both fast ball and curve has been mentioned previously. It is an invaluable device in keeping the enemy from "reading" one's pitches and, where feasible, should definitely be put into practice. Yet, its need is not so compelling that it should be allowed to detract from the quality of a man's curve merely for the sake of similarity of grip. In other words, a pitcher should not sacrifice his best stuff for a particular grip on the ball. The primary consideration should be to impart the greatest possible spin to the ball and to acquire a sharp curve thereby, regardless of what grip must be used in order to do so. Whereas the pitch should not be telegraphed, it is, nevertheless, entirely unlikely that a batter will be able to put advance knowledge of the pitch into physical action if his discovery of a curve ball grip does not take place until the pitcher's arm is well into its forward motion. The time interval in this case is too minute for the difference in finger position to bear heavily on the situation. Thus, the best policy is to use the grip which produces the best curve, keeping it concealed from the batter long enough to nullify the effect of possible discovery on his part, and hiding it from the baseline coaches until the actual throwing motion has begun.

Where a sidearm fast ball is thrown, even if only on occasion, a curve should be delivered from the same angle. Unfortunately, a sidearm curve is not only flat in its action, but cannot be made to break as sharply as one thrown overhand. Its value against a batter who swings from the opposite side of the plate is doubtful since it breaks straight-in to him. Yet it is a potent weapon if for no other reason than that it gives needed variety to a pitcher's repertoire. Moreover, a sidearm curve will not be so flat when the pitcher delivers it with a slightly open stride.

Obviously, experimentation is called for on the part of the pitcher until he succeeds in arriving at the right combination of techniques to give him the best curve ball of which he is capable. Any or all of the suggestions which have been enumerated above might help and can be applied according to the needs of the individual. The principle of building up to the task by throwing for maximum spin at short distances will prove a great boon in learning and perfecting the curve, particularly when stress is placed upon the observance of the basic fundamentals at each stage in its development.

In brief, these essential ingredients are a comfortable grip, similar to the fast ball where practicable; heavier pressure on the middle finger; an adjustment of the stride as may be necessary; release of the ball off the ends or sides of the fingers with good elbow and wrist-snap; and keeping the ball low and away, with an emphasis on the word "low."

The change-of-pace

The change-of-pace, employed judiciously, can be the most valuable weapon at a pitcher's command. This is due to its dual purpose in serving as a good pitch in its own right while at the same time making his other deliveries more effective by preventing the batter from getting set for them.

Changing speeds in such a way that it keeps the hitter off balance and upsets his timing is an example of retiring him on a horizontal plane. In other words, the batter can be fooled by differing velocities in the pitches that are delivered to him even though they involve no deviation in line of flight, the idea being to nullify his power by making him swing too soon or too late to hit the ball with authority. Added to breaking stuff and a live fast ball, the change-of-pace will give a pitcher sufficient equipment to cope with any hitter.

THE VALUE OF THE CHANGE-UP. Every pitcher will sooner or later encounter batters whose physical ability equals his own and whom he cannot overpower. It is here that he must become a pitcher rather than a mere thrower. At this point, the change-of-pace proves most valuable and really becomes a necessity. Taking something off a normal delivery can completely upset a batter's timing and make him relatively easy prey for a smart moundsman.

A pitcher should use no less than three different speeds. First comes his normal fast pitches; second, the extra something which he should hold in reserve for use in tight spots; and third, the slow pitch, or change-of-pace, with which he keeps the hitter off balance. The thing to be avoided is firing away with everything he has on every pitch, thereby getting in an operating rut that will enable the batter to adjust his timing to every delivery of the ball. The objective to be sought, in this respect, is the ability to retire the batter on a horizontal plane.

Every pitcher should strive to develop a change-of-pace just as soon as he possibly can. It has strategic value in giving a man a wider variety of pitches with which to operate, psychological value in making the batter realize that he must be on the alert and not allow himself to be set for only one speed, and physical value in that it imposes little strain on a pitcher's arm and is less tiring than his fast pitches.

MASTERING THE CHANGE-OF-PACE. The most effective change-ups are those that most closely resemble the fast pitches in everything save velocity of the ball in flight. Exaggerated movements or differences in method of delivery should be avoided. Not only should the same motion be used, but the same amount of effort should go into that motion if the pitch is to have maximum deception. The objective is to make the batter swing at the pitcher's motion rather than at the ball itself.

The means by which professionals lend similarity to the appearance of their fast and slow pitches are several in number and involve either the grip or the stride. They are as follows:

1. Probably the most commonly employed method is one in which the ball is held well back against the crotch of the hand, gripped loosely, and thrown with a tight wrist. The fingers remain crooked to serve as a brake.

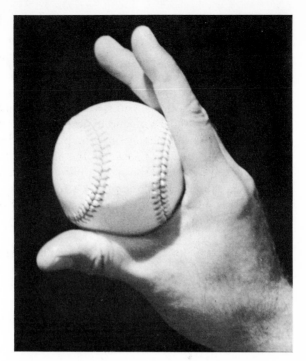

2. The finger tips are raised and the ball is gripped as though the fingers were cut off at the second joint. Pressure is applied at that point (the middle joint) and the ball is thrown with a stiff wrist and no snap, the motion being closely akin to that used in pulling down a window shade. The raised fingers mean that the ball is shoved in shot-put fashion.

3. A more effective method is a combination of these two and should be tried when the pitcher feels that he is up to it. Here, a fast ball grip is used but the ball is held back in the crotch of the hand. As the release is made the finger tips are raised. This manner of throwing the change is more deceptive because it imparts a backward rotation which makes the pitch more closely resemble a fast ball.

4. Another way in which something can be taken off the fast ball is by lengthening the stride and dragging the rear foot, thereby slowing the weight shift and lessening the force which is put into the pitch. This is particularly helpful in throwing a change-of-pace curve ball wherein a good wrist-snap is needed to get any real break on the ball and, consequently, the arm motion and grip should be practically the same as that used for the fast curve.

5. Some pitchers use a screw ball for a change-of-pace, not so much for the action of the ball (although this does add to its effectiveness), but because the screw ball will not be a really fast pitch, even when thrown hard. The reverse twist of the wrist and the dragging action of the hand

in releasing the ball serve to take away much of the speed which is normally provided by natural arm and body action.

6. If these tricks prove too difficult to master, merely taking something off one's fast pitches can be effective, the main idea still being to lend variety to the repertoire and to upset the hitter's timing.

One thing about the change-up which should always be borne in mind is that the looser the grip, the slower the pitch will be.

The change-of-pace is the most difficult to control of the three basic pitches and requires constant practice for mastery. Really accomplished mound artists develop it to the point where they can move it around at will, not merely get it over the plate. This is a goal well worth aspiring to.

The change should not be thrown too slow lest the batter succeed in double-timing it. Neither should it be so fast as to offer too little variation in speed from the regular pitches. Above all, the ball should be kept low if the pitch is to be most effective.

No man will ever become a real pitcher, in the truest sense of the word, until he has learned to throw a deceptive, well-controlled change-of-pace with complete confidence.

THE SLOW CURVE

Baseball's better pitchers throw a change-up off the curve as well as off the fast ball. This immediately gives them one more pitch with which to work on the batter. A thoughtful approach will show that the slow curve can be, in itself, the most effective pitch in a hurler's repertoire, because it will provide him with a single delivery that can fool the batter on both a horizontal and a vertical plane.

Several of the principles used in throwing a straight change-up apply to the slow curve. Use of a longer stride and the dragging of the rear foot is a method which has already been mentioned in connection with this pitch. Its great value lies in the fact that it allows a normal curveball arm motion and wrist-snap to be used while deterring the speed of the pitch, thus promoting a slow curve with a good break.

The slow curve can also be thrown by employing a loose grip, the rule of thumb being the looser the grip, the slower the pitch; by keeping the elbow relatively close to the body for an overhand delivery, preventing the full arm sweep which imparts speed to a pitch; by using more body motion, thereby dissipating most of the force in this action rather than in the sweep of the arm; and by raising the fingers and tightening the wrist-action, just as in the straight change.

Any of the above ideas might prove adaptable and helpful to a pitcher in acquiring the knack of throwing a change curve. Regardless of the technique used, this pitch should be practiced diligently in the same manner advocated for developing a good curve ball. That is, the process should be gradual, with the pitcher spinning the ball from a short distance and working back to the full sixty feet, six inches, striving for a deceptive motion and maximum rotation while so doing.

An aspiring pitcher should, quite naturally, use the method which he finds will give him the best results, keeping in mind that the slow curve should be gripped well back in the hand since this technique prevents a man from throwing the ball fast while still enabling him to impart good spin to it.

The slider

Emphasis has been placed on the three basic pitches with the firm conviction that mastery and control of them are difficult in themselves and should provide any pitcher with the necessary equipment to cope with the best of hitters.

As he advances through the various stages of baseball, a pitcher may find it advisable to add an extra pitch—but only after the basic three have been perfected.

Most favored of the off-pitches which hurlers strive to develop as added equipment is the slider. This is due to the fact that it is relatively simple to throw and control, and has great deception in that it resembles a fast ball, yet behaves like a quick, sharp curve as it nears the plate.

WHAT IT IS. The slider is often referred to as a "nickle curve." Nevertheless, it can be more accurately classified as a variation on the fast ball. It is thrown with a normal fast ball motion, refined by a minor alteration in grip or by a slight twist of the wrist as the ball is released.

Mention was made in the section dealing with the fast ball that the ball can be made to move to right or left by altering the grip or by moving one of the finger tips back, the theory being that by applying pressure at a different point, a different spin will be imparted to the ball.

This principle most assuredly applies to the slider. The basic idea in its development is to provide sufficient spin to make the ball move to the side (slide), rather than change courses in pronounced fashion (curve). The great advantage in using this pitch is that it approaches the batter almost as swiftly as, and looking like, a fast ball, while moving in the same direction as the curve ball—but with a quicker, smaller break.

HOW IT IS THROWN. As opposed to the curve ball, the slider is thrown with the index finger controlling its release and being the last digit to be in contact with the ball. In this respect it can be likened to passing a football or, to draw another parallel, the pitcher should experience the feeling of pointing his index finger at home plate as he throws the slider.

As intimated in the last paragraph, the first finger is the one with which pressure is applied. In further contrast to the curve ball delivery, the slider is thrown with a very late wrist-snap (immediately prior to the release) which is just enough to impart the rotation which will make the ball veer to the side opposite that from which it is thrown.

With these ideas to help him in developing a good slider, a pitcher should give consideration to the two principal methods which can be used for this delivery and should then adapt one of them to his own use with any refinements that may be needed to achieve good results.

One of the techniques which can be used involves a fast ball grip and motion, modified by a slight inward rotation of the wrist as the ball is released. It is analogous to shaking hands with the ball—the hand is brought down, more or less to the side of the ball, which slides off the fingers as it is let go. Sufficient spin is imparted to make the ball move to the side but not enough is given to it to slow it up and make it break in a big arc, like the curve.

The other principal method is one which enables the pitcher to achieve the same effect by gripping the ball off-center, with the greater part of it being toward the side to which it will move. It is thrown with a fast ball motion, the off-center grip giving it the desired rotation.

One word of caution should be interjected at this point. The slider can impose an extra strain on the elbow and for this reason should not be attempted unless the arm is in good condition and until it is thoroughly warmed up.

The other off-pitches

The above-mentioned deliveries generally suffice to provide a pitcher with all the equipment he needs to deal with any hitter he may be called upon to face. If, however, deficiencies exist in his command of the more conventional pitches and their effectiveness, he may find it advisable to develop one of the so-called off-pitches. It must be understood that they should be used only as a last resort in the cases of pitchers of limited experience. More accomplished hurlers who employ them often do so because their fast ball or curve is of inferior quality and usually rely very heavily on whichever of these off-pitches they include in their repertoires.

THE KNUCKLE BALL

The knuckler has enjoyed much popularity due, no doubt, to its sometimes baffling actions. It can be so unpredictable that at times it will fool batter, catcher, and pitcher alike. Furthermore, it is not only difficult to control, but easy to run on, consequently allowing base runners to take liberties at the pitcher's expense.

The knuckler is held with the ball cradled against the first joints or fingernails of either the first two or first three fingers, which are bent for this pitch. The thumb and remaining finger(s) encircle the ball in a tight grip and serve primarily to control it.

A spinning ball is held on course by its rotation. It can be likened to a bullet fired from a gun. The knuckle ball, on the other hand, since it revolves slightly, if at all, does not hold its course and derives its erratic actions from the resistance of the air or wind against the seams of the ball. For this reason the knuckler will have a better break when thrown into a wind which blows toward or across the path of the ball. A good one floats toward the plate, breaking suddenly, just before it reaches the batter. Variations in the cleanliness of the seams cause the inconsistency in the actions of this pitch.

There are two principal types of knuckle ball: (1) The floater or butterfly type which is thrown at half-speed, with a stiff wrist, and seems to dance as it approaches the plate, reacting to each shift in air-currents; (2) The fast knuckler or "dry spitter" which is thrown at full speed. As the ball is released the fingers are extended and the wrist snapped, giving the ball extra velocity and sufficient downspin to make it dip sharply as it nears the batter, "rolling off the table," as it were.

A pitcher will find it next to impossible to hide this pitch from the batter and coaches. Its success is due to its actions, not to any element of surprise.

THE SCREW BALL

The screw ball is, to all intents and purposes, a reverse curve. It is gripped similarly to the fast ball and thrown with an inside-out twist of the hand and wrist. It is spun out of the hand between the middle and ring fingers and is given its rotation by the reverse quarter-turn of the wrist, the middle finger release, and the thumb, which is used to increase the reverse spin by being given a last-second flip as the ball is released.

The screw ball is usually thrown overhand and breaks down and toward the side from which it is thrown. It is a relatively slow pitch and its break is far less pronounced than that of the curve ball.

Because of the manner of delivery, the fingers go through first, then the ball, creating the effect of a change-up. As a matter of fact, the screw ball can be used to good advantage as a change-of-pace.

This pitch often proves a great strain on the arm because of the unnatural motion used in throwing it. If for no other reason, its use is not encouraged on the part of inexperienced pitchers.

The Fork Ball

The fork ball is so named because of the manner in which it is gripped. The index and middle fingers form a fork which encircles the ball. This pitch is thrown with a forward wrist-snap and the ball slides from the hand between the spread fingers.

The fork ball, like the knuckler, has little rotation and, consequently, floats toward the plate. Its break is almost invariably downward and is more predictable than the knuckler. Furthermore, it can be much more easily concealed than the knuckle ball and, for most pitchers, is less troublesome control-wise. Achieving really effective action of the fork ball is, however, far more difficult.

The fork ball cannot be thrown with great speed, no matter how intense the effort, and for that reason can be used as a change-of-pace.

The Palm Ball

This pitch is gripped with all the fingers on and around the ball and spread slightly. The ball is held back against the palm of the hand and slides from the thumb and palm with little wrist-action, the fingers resting very lightly on the ball and acting primarily as a guide.

The palm ball revolves very little and floats in with a slight downward break, much like the knuckler and fork ball. It is an even slower pitch than those two.

This pitch can also be thrown with the two-finger, second-joint grip delineated under the heading, *Change-of-Pace*. In this case, the ball is slid from the hand with the palm to the side (curve ball fashion) or down (like a fast ball).

As a final word on the various pitches—let it be emphatically stated to all young pitchers that they should give no consideration whatsoever to the off-pitches until the basic three can be delivered with control, consistency, and effectiveness.

FIELDING FOR THE PITCHER

According to an old baseball maxim, a successful pitcher is one who rarely, if ever, hurts himself. One facet of his job wherein a pitcher can definitely help himself is fielding his position. Too often the pitcher's job is thought of as merely throwing the ball, and his defensive play is left to instinct and natural athletic ability. The study and practice of correct techniques and tactics relating to this phase of the game can contribute immeasurably toward making a pitcher's main task much easier and, at the same time, make him a well-rounded ballplayer who contributes in all respects to the success of his team.

On being prepared

A pitcher should literally be a fifth infielder. Through fielding dexterity and knowledge of the correct move to make he will prevent many base hits and possible runs should he be involved in a play.

In order to be that fifth infielder, certain preparations are essential. First is the matter of equipment, A big glove is a requisite for a pitcher not only in covering his pitches, but in enabling him to stop many batted balls that would otherwise go for hits. In addition to being able to field batted balls himself with a large glove, he will succeed in deflecting many otherwise unstoppable balls, making them playable for the other infielders.

Next, the pitcher must have the correct play in mind any time the ball is hit. This includes knowing what to do with the ball when he fields it, carrying out his duties as a back-up man when the batter drives one to the outfield, being fully aware of the responsibilities involved in any situation which demands that he cover a base, and filling his role in lending vocal and occasional physical support on foul flies. He should be prepared to make the right play before the occasion actually arises, taking into consideration the game situation and all possible plays and ramifications thereof. He should also include in his mental preparations a definite plan of action in case of an error.

Finally comes the physical preparation entailed in the completion of the act of throwing the ball. The pitcher should be in a squared-away position in his follow-through, with his feet relatively parallel and his weight evenly distributed. Needless to say, this will give him better balance and enable him to move quickly in any direction. In cases where the natural motion finds the pivot foot either in advance of or dragging behind the striding foot, an extra shuffle-step or hop, a short one in either case, is a good method of achieving a balanced, squared-away position. Bringing his glove into position in front of his body can also prove very helpful when quick reactions are demanded.

Although not particularly germane to the subject of preparation, mention should be made of the act of receiving the return throw from the catcher. It is advisable, in this instance, to catch the ball with one hand (one of the few times when this is advocated) in order to offer proper protection to the fingers of the pitching hand.

Playing the ball

The outstanding fielders among pitchers are men possessed of great agility and quick reflexes. These traits are, of course, inherent to a great degree. They can, however, be improved in the case of anyone who is willing to work at becoming a better fielder.

The seemingly harmless and time-killing pepper games in which Major League pitchers engage during pre-game practice actually have a definite, two-fold purpose. They not only serve as a fine conditioner, but help greatly with regard to fielding, since they promote good balance, agility, and sharp reflexes. A pitcher cannot play too much pepper.

Another drill which can be engaged in during practice sessions and which is very helpful to a pitcher in becoming accustomed to handling ground balls under game conditions goes as follows: with a batter at home plate, the pitcher throws to the catcher; simultaneously with each pitch, the batter fungoes grounders through the box. This drill gives the pitcher experience in fielding batted balls after going through his complete motion, while helping him develop a balanced follow-through and agility.

The pitcher should keep his eye on the ball while fielding it; in fact, he should follow it visually right into his glove. This statement seems almost superfluous but is necessary in that, because of his proximity to the batter, the pitcher is often prone to a tendency to go for a batted ball without full concentration; or, on a bunt or slow roller, he may pay too much heed to the runner(s). Obviously, he cannot make a play until he is in complete possession of the ball and that should be his primary consideration.

The pitcher should try to block any ball hit through the middle. Every precaution should be exercised to make sure of the stop since the ball comes to him so quickly that he will have time to make a play even if he does not field the ball cleanly.

A good moundsman does not wait for the ball to be on the ground before he breaks for the plate; he does so just as soon as the batter shows his intentions, since the least delay will allow the bunter to beat it out for a hit.

Occasionally a bunt or slow roller must be played to first base very quickly; the pitcher must field the ball as best he can, throwing underhand or sidearm from a bent position, as an infielder does on a close play. Gen-

Fielding a Bunt

erally speaking, however, bunts and slowly hit balls should be played with two hands, the safest way usually proving the surest. When the play is not hurried he should use his normal throwing motion.

After fielding a ground ball, the pitcher should make the shortest possible pivot to throw to first or second base. For example, a left-hander fielding a grounder to his left should turn to his left to throw to first; when he fields the ball in the home-plate area he should turn to his right after having handled the ball in front of his left foot. If the play is at second base he should turn to his right on any ball fielded in front of him. A right-handed pitcher should make his turn to the left when throwing to either first or second.

A left-hander turns to his right on any throw to third base. When a right-hander fields a ball close to the third base line and his back is toward third, he should pivot to his left for the throw. If, on the other hand, he is partially facing third as he fields the ball, he should turn to his right.

The throw itself depends, to a great extent, on the distance involved. Long throws should be hard for the sake of both carry and accuracy, while shorter ones can be slower so as to make matters easier for the receiver. The lob throw should be avoided if at all possible, since it is generally lacking in accuracy and often confusing, because of the change in speed, for the player who has to catch it.

The ability of the pitcher to handle batted balls and diagnose play situations can be as important to his success as the stuff and control with which he delivers the ball. Conceivably, in the course of a single play, he can be required to pitch to the batter, handle a batted ball, throw to the appropriate base, cover another base, and finally back-up the play. His failure to do any of these things properly might completely destroy the effect of throwing the right pitch in the first place. He must literally be a fifth infielder.

What to do and when to do it

Fielding, as all phases of pitching, demands far more than mere mechanical ability. Common sense, an awareness of all possible play situations and the duties which they entail, and quick thinking are requisites to a good fielding pitcher. Not only must he know where to throw the ball when he makes a play himself, he must recognize the need for performing other fielding duties, and should have a knowledge of the correct techniques involved in carrying out these maneuvers with efficiency and dispatch.

INDECISION—A PITFALL TO BE AVOIDED. Baseball is literally a game of inches. Defensive plays must be carried out with split-second rapidity if they are to succeed. Like all of his teammates, a pitcher must think ahead and take quick, decisive action when the occasion for it arises.

Among the general points which will help the pitcher to avoid indecision are three which warrant mention. (1) A slowly hit ball or fumble should be played to first base. The delay caused by a fumble or a slow roller will make it all but impossible to retire a base runner who has taken a lead and, in many cases, enjoyed a running start. The batter, on the other hand, must complete his swing before setting out for first base and must run a full ninety feet to reach his objective. (2) The catcher is the field general and has a much better view of the play. His advice should be heeded and, when contrary to the first point, is the only time that that rule should be ignored. (3) Any time that a runner is hung up between bases while the pitcher is in possession of the ball, the latter should run directly at the runner, waiting until he commits himself before making a throw.

WORKING WITH THE FIRST BASEMAN. A pitcher must coordinate his efforts with those of the first baseman on any play which involves both of them. This includes not only ground balls to the right side of the infield on which the pitcher must cover first base, but ones which he fields himself.

When a pitcher fields a hard-hit ground ball he should take two or three steps toward first before making his throw to that base. This will give the first baseman time to reach the base and set himself for the throw. It will also serve to ease some of the tension which can build up during this period of waiting, and impair the accuracy of the throw. The throw should be made to the inside of the base to facilitate handling of the ball by the first baseman and to eliminate the possibility of a collision with the oncoming base runner.

The pitcher's role in covering first base is highly important and, because it is an intricate maneuver, is the subject of many hours of practice on the part of Major League teams. The pitcher should break toward first base on all balls hit to the right side of the infield. Covering first is necessary on every play and there are times when this duty falls to the pitcher.

There are two methods of performing this play. On a ball hit to the first baseman's left, or straight to him, the pitcher should go to the foul line about twenty feet in front of the base and cross the bag running parallel to the line. As the bag is neared he should slow down slightly and bring his speed under control. This manner of making the play reduces the danger of collision with the runner and its attendant fumble and, at the same time, permits the first baseman to time his throw more accurately.

96

On a ball hit to the first baseman's right or on a slow roller, the pitcher should go directly to the bag and anchor there. This also applies to the first-second-first double play with the shortstop. In these instances the throw to first will be delayed and there will be no time for a carefully-timed play.

In those cases where doubt arises as to who should field the ball or cover the base the play should be called. "I've got it" and "You take it" are the initiating and answering calls to be used. When the first baseman makes the play himself, the pitcher should get out of the way.

With a runner or runners on any other base, the pitcher, after taking the throw at first, should take care not to continue running down the base line toward right field. Instead, he should stop quickly and turn, and run the ball back toward the plate in order to check the advance of any other runner or possibly to catch him rounding the base too far.

(a) *Ball hit straight at 1B or to his left*

(b) *Ball hit to 1B's right, or slow roller*

COVERING AN UNGUARDED BASE. On many plays one of the bases is left unprotected and some player must leave his normal position to cover it. Quite often this is the pitcher's responsibility.

In addition to covering first base on some ground balls, the pitcher should go to that base in readiness to handle a throw whenever the first baseman tries for a fly ball. This is particularly important when there is more than one runner on base and the first baseman makes the play on a foul fly. Here, the pitcher not only covers first base, but serves as a relay man should more than one runner try for the next base or bluff an attempt to do so in an effort to draw a throw.

Second base should be covered by the pitcher when both the second baseman and shortstop go for a fly ball in short center field—unless either the first or third baseman can leave his position to do so, in which case the pitcher should go to whichever base has been vacated.

There are two occasions on which the pitcher should cover third base. One of these is when both the third baseman and shortstop go after a fly ball with a runner on base. The other occurs when, with a runner on base, the third baseman fields a bunt or slow roller for which both he and the pitcher have tried and the catcher or shortstop is unable to get to third base in time to cover it.

Home plate is the runner's ultimate objective. It should be covered at all times. Whenever home plate is left open with men on base, the pitcher should cover it. This duty should be performed any time a pitched ball gets away from the catcher and whenever he leaves his position to catch a pop-fly. In taking a throw from the catcher, for a play on a runner attempting to score, the pitcher should take a position in fair territory just in front of the plate, facing the catcher. After receiving a good throw he should turn to his right for the tag, clutching the ball in his bare hand and holding his gloved hand between the ball and the runner for protective purposes. If the throw is a wide one and there is still a chance to retire the runner, the pitcher should dive for the third base side of home plate after catching the ball.

THE PITCHER'S ROLE ON POP-FLIES. Mention has been made of the need for the pitcher to cover a base which has been left unguarded when the man who usually protects it must leave it to field a pop-fly. There are other considerations to be observed when a pop-fly goes up over or near the infield.

The pitcher should let the infielders handle any fly ball in the vicinity of the mound. They are in better position and better equipped to play such balls. Consequently, the only fly balls which the hurler should field are popped-up bunts and weak taps which are too low for the infielders to reach.

On a foul fly the pitcher should go toward the ball and call the play, lending both aid and encouragement to the player(s) involved. In this case he has a better view of the play then has a player who is concentrating on the ball. Exceptions to this are the above-mentioned instances in which he must cover a base which has been vacated.

A foul fly, because of its drift and the fact that it is easily lost in a bright sun, is one of the most difficult plays for a catcher to make. For this reason, the pitcher's help is needed. Not only can he lend valuable assistance in calling the play and giving encouragement, he will be in position to catch the ball should the catcher lose it in the sun or wind.

Still another advantage to the pitcher's going toward a foul fly is that he will be in position to serve as a relay man when base runners make a move toward the next base after the catch.

THE DOUBLE-PLAY THROW. The double play is the pitcher's greatest aid in breaking up scoring threats when the opposition has runners on base. The throw to start a double play is of paramount importance, for the cardinal principle behind a double play is to make sure of the first out, for without it the play will go for nought and the pitcher will be in real trouble.

On a ball hit back to the pitcher, the double-play throw should always go to the shortstop unless a decided right-hand pull hitter is at bat and the shortstop is stationed in the hole, far out of his normal position. On any ball hit through the middle he will be going toward the bag and should be in good position to take the throw and complete the double play.

In making this play, the pitcher should pivot quickly and throw after deliberating long enough to allow the shortstop to get in proper position to make the play with little trouble. He should take a look at the base before getting rid of the ball, taking care, above all, to make sure of the first out.

The throw should be chest-high and about one-half step to the left of the bag in order to facilitate handling of the ball and to allow continuity of motion on the part of the shortstop. The only exception to this is when the shortstop is out of position and the play must be handled by the second baseman. In this case the throw should be chest-high and about one-half step to the right (first base) side of the bag.

This maneuver should be worked on during batting practice on balls hit back to the pitcher. Then, he should practice his pivot and throw— even when no one is covering second base. Simulated game conditions are always best for developing successful mound techniques.

With the bases loaded, a pitcher's double-play throw should go home, then to first (this is a relatively easy double play on a ball hit directly to the pitcher). With men on first and second, the double-play throw goes to second base, unless the batted ball is a slow roller between the mound and third base, in which case the throw goes to third since a double play is very unlikely and, consequently, the closest play is the logical one and will, moreover, cut down the lead runner.

LOOKING THE RUNNER BACK. Lest this term prove confusing, consideration should be given to the following situation: With a runner on third base, or runners on second and third, a ground ball is hit to the pitcher. Unless the runner on third makes a foolhardy break for home, the play is obviously to first base. In order to prevent the runner from scoring while the play is being made on the batter, the pitcher should "look him back" to third before throwing to first. A mere glance at the runner will usually succeed in driving him back, and the pitcher who neglects this very sensible move deserves no better than the occasional run with which the opposition will be gifted.

The same thing applies with a runner on second base. He should be driven back to his base before the play is made on the batter. As an added benefit, this slight delay will allow the first baseman sufficient time in which to reach the bag and position himself to receive the throw.

When the glance at the runner reveals that he is foolishly trying to advance to the next base, the play should be made on him.

DEFENSING THE SACRIFICE. The sacrifice bunt presents two problems—the mechanical and the tactical aspects of the situation. Because the sacrifice can, to a great extent, be anticipated, the mechanical phase of defending against it is simplified. The pitcher should not wait for the ball to be on the ground to break toward home but should do so just as soon as the batter shows his intentions.

For safety's sake, the ball should be fielded with two hands—even if it is rolling very slowly. The throw should be made to the base to which the catcher directs the play, since he has a better view of the situation. If, however, the bunt is a hard one, directly back to the mound, there is little cause to wait for the catcher's call—a force-out will be relatively easy to achieve and the throw should be made for it.

With a right-hander at bat, most sacrifice attempts will go toward first base. This is the easiest bunt for a right-hand batter and is, strategically, a wise move against a right-handed first baseman since he must turn to make a throw to second.

The sacrifice bunt with a runner on second will usually go toward third in an attempt to draw the third baseman in to field it, leaving the base unprotected against the advancing runner.

The accepted technique for fielding a bunt has been worked out quite logically from a physical standpoint. A left-hand pitcher should overrun the ball slightly so as to field it to the inside of his left foot and in front of him. A right-hander should overrun the ball slightly so as to field it to the inside of his right foot and in front of him. This will lead to an easier pivot, which results in a quicker, more accurate throw. Regardless of the base to which the throw should be made, a left-hander's pivot should be to his right, while a right-hander should turn to his left. In effect, this means that the pivot will always be made toward the infield.

On a sacrifice with runners on first and second, the pitcher should charge toward the third base line as soon as he releases the ball, in order to give proper coverage to that area and allow the third baseman to remain at the bag to receive the throw for a force-out. To repeat for clarification—for a throw to third, a right-hander pivots to his left, a left-hander to his right; for a throw to first, a right-hander once again pivots to his left and a left-hander to his right. If it is apparent that the runner is "in" at third base the throw should go to first, not second, since the other runner will have enjoyed an even bigger lead than the one who is already safe.

The setup is the same for the sacrifice with a runner on second base only.

THE SQUEEZE. The "suicide squeeze" is a play in which the runner at third breaks for home with the pitch and the batter merely has to bunt the ball on the ground in fair territory in order to score the run. If properly executed it is almost impossible to stop. The only defense against it is early detection and an unbuntable pitch. For that reason, when a squeeze situation exists, the runner should be watched closely for an indication to the play since, in many cases, he will tip his hand by a premature start. It might even be wise to work from a stretch at a time like this. (The most logical time for the squeeze is with one out in a close ball game and with someone other than a power hitter at bat.)

When the squeeze is detected, the pitch should be made unbuntable. Regardless of what the catcher's signal has been, a fast ball should be delivered—high and well outside the plate to a left-hander; at the head of a right-hand batter. The latter act does not constitute a bean-ball since this is one occasion on which the batter can expect to be "knocked down." Pitches delivered to these spots will be both unbuntable and easy for the catcher to handle in making a play on the runner.

When a squeeze play is worked successfully with runners on second and third, the throw to first should be made quickly, and care should be exercised that the runner who has been on second is not allowed to score when the play is made at first.

With runners on first and third, the opposition will occasionally attempt a safe squeeze in which the runner holds third until it is apparent that he can score. This should be played like an ordinary sacrifice, with two exceptions: the catcher must cover home, putting the greater responsibility of fielding the ball onto the pitcher; when a defensive player has fielded the ball, he should glance at the runner on third before making his throw to first. If the runner is far off his base at third, the play should be made on him.

Any time that a bunt is played to first base the throw should be to the inside of the base, so that the runner will not obstruct the first baseman's view of the ball and, quite possibly, interfere with the throw. A throw to either second or third should be directly over the base.

BACKING UP THE PLAY. One of a pitcher's primary duties is backing up the right base on any ball hit to the outfield. He should know which base to back up under any circumstance which might arise, and should never hesitate to get into position to do so.

An alert moundsman will be one base ahead of the lead runner so that he can prevent him from taking an extra base on any ball that might have to be retrieved. Generally speaking, the pitcher's position is in foul territory when he is the back-up man and he should station himself about forty feet behind the base which he is backing up. Being too close to the play is ineffective, since it will not allow him to cover sufficient ground to retrieve most overthrows.

Deciding which base to back up is dependent of where and how the ball has been hit, the strength of the outfielder's arm, the speed of the runners, the inning, and the score. Nevertheless, staying one base ahead of the lead runner is a safe rule of thumb to follow and, in the vast majority of cases, will provide the correct solution to the problem.

Another principle which the pitcher should follow in backing up a play is to get off the mound and into position quickly so that there will be no possibility of interfering with the cut-off man, who also has a definite station to take.

An overthrow which must be fielded by the back-up man should be blocked. To eliminate any danger of the ball's getting through him the pitcher should drop to one knee to stop it.

The pitcher's duties in his backing-up role also include run-down plays. On a run-down between first and second he should cover first base unless there is a runner on third, in which case he should back up home plate. On a run-down between second and third, the pitcher should cover third—with the same exception. On a third-home run-down, he should cover the plate—with no exceptions.

Many of these situations involve the cut-off play; consequently this important maneuver should be understood by all pitchers. Briefly, the cut-off play, by means of an intercepted throw, enables a team to prevent another runner from advancing when the lead runner is obviously safe at his destination. At times, it makes possible the *sure* out.

The shortstop is the cut-off man on plays at third base. When the throw should go home, the third baseman acts as cut-off man on a hit to left field, while the first baseman assumes that role on hits to center and right field. The cut-off man stations himself about forty feet from the base at which the play is made, in a direct line between the throwing player and that base. On a good throw he listens to the baseman for instructions. On a bad throw he intercepts the ball on his own and without hesitation.

In all such situations the pitcher backs up the play, with two possible exceptions. The first arises when the game is being played on a field where the backstop is very close to home plate. Here, since there is little need for the pitcher to back up the play, he can serve as cut-off man, allowing the first and third baseman to cover their respective bases.

The other exception is more in the nature of a tactical variation, and its use can be left to the discretion of the team involved. When a single is hit to either center or right field, with a runner on second base, the cut-off position is assumed by the first baseman. In such instances, the pitcher can cover first base. This is a relatively unexpected move and can result in a put-out on the batter, who almost invariably takes a wide turn at first base when the throw goes home. It can be used to good effect by any ball club and is definitely advisable for teen-age teams, with whom there is little danger of a powerful throw which will sail well over the catcher's head.

To return to the pitcher's role in backing up a play: the following situation should be visualized as a good example of how important his role is. With a runner on first base a single is hit to the outfield. The runner will probably try to reach third, with a consequent play at that base. Should the ball go through the third baseman, the runner will score and the batter will reach second base, meaning one run home and another in scoring position—unless the pitcher is in position to back up the play at third.

WORKING WITH MEN ON BASE

If a pitcher could achieve a perfect game every time he went to the mound he would have no worries as far as base runners are concerned. Needness to say, such is not the case. To be realistic about his situation, in order to be successful, a pitcher must learn how to work effectively with men on base. This means that he should not only be able to hold the runners close to their bases and foil such offensive plays as the sacrifice, squeeze, hit-and-run, and steal, but that he should be able to get good stuff on the ball and control it despite the presence of base runners.

The approach to the problem

While it is true that no pitcher can get his very best stuff on the ball while working with men on base, and that few hurlers can keep every runner from getting a good jump on the ball, the fact remains that this obstacle is not insurmountable.

A realistic approach acknowledges the fact that the problem is going to exist at all too frequent intervals and that the situation is not conducive to peak efficiency. Yet, the smart pitcher accepts this set of circumstances as a necessary evil, works hard to learn the most efficient method of operating under these conditions, and, in the case of the real mound artist, looks on the situation as a definite challenge. The true competitor is often a better pitcher with men on base because he does not allow himself to become upset and bears down even harder when the opposition confronts him with a scoring threat.

The problem of working with men on base resolves itself around a two-fold task—preventing the runner(s) from taking undue liberties on the base paths, and maintaining a high degree of effectiveness in dealing with the batter.

In delving into the methods of coping with the problem, two basic principles should be advanced in order to give reassurance and the proper attitude to all pitchers. (1) Relax. The runner is probably more keyed-up over the bigness of the situation than you are. (2) Don't forget the batter. He's still the man you want.

The right move(s)

The first fundamental is, of course, assuming a proper stop-position. Although minor differences exist in this phase of various pitching motions, basically a strong similarity must, according to the rules, and does, in practice, exist.

The rear foot must be in contact with the rubber and the only movement of the feet which is permitted, other than in delivering the ball, is a lateral movement of the front foot preparatory to coming to an actual stop. After the stretch is taken, and before the delivery, the pitcher must come to a complete stop and must not take his hand from the ball or make a perceptible movement of any part of his anatomy except his head. After the stop he can deliver the ball to the plate, throw to an occupied base, fake a throw to second or third if it is occupied by a runner, or step from the rubber and call "time." He can, however, throw to a base *before* coming to a stop. As long as his foot is in contact with the rubber he cannot make a move toward first base without throwing the ball to that base. If, on the other hand, he steps back off the rubber before making any move, it is almost impossible for him to balk. Thus, though not practicable in throwing to first, this is a good policy to follow in coping with base runners.

A good pick-off move is a great asset to a pitcher and should be practiced diligently until perfected. Just the reputation of having a good one is often enough to keep runners close to their bases.

In developing a good pick-off motion, it must be emphasized that a pitcher should assume a position that will enable him, with a quick glance, to keep an eye on the runner, yet not cause him to "lose" home plate. In fact, he should never "pitch from memory." Rather, he should always take a good look at home plate before delivering the ball to the batter.

ASSUMING THE STOP-POSITION. The basic stop-position, quite naturally, should be developed in relation to a runner at first base. Its primary purpose is to hold the runner close to his base, making it as difficult as possible for him to advance to scoring position. Also, with less than two outs it facilitates a double play. A left-hander, of course, enjoys a big advantage in holding the runner close, because he faces in that direction. A right-hander, to offset some of the natural disadvantage under which he must work, should assume a slightly open stance—one which will enable him to see the runner out of the corner of his eye without turning his head completely toward first.

With men on base, all moves on the part of the pitcher must be faster and, because of the natural loss in power which results from working out of a stretch, the push-off from the rubber is even more important in contributing to speed and stuff. A long, slow stretch is not necessary but enough of one should be used to relieve tension and loosen the uniform around the shoulders and armpits.

When the hands are held in a relatively high position (at the letters) upon completion of the stretch, excess body motion will be cut down and movements will be quicker and more deceptive. In order to hold the runner(s) in check, the striding foot should pass closer to the ground in delivering the ball to the plate from a stop-position. As for the centering of the weight, a well-balanced stance is advisable because the placing of too much weight on the rear foot will slow the move to a base, while too much weight on the front foot takes stuff off a pitched ball. All of these ideas are designed to help speed up a pitcher's moves and enable him to hold the runner close to his base.

The pick-off at first

A RIGHT-HANDER'S MOVE. A right-hander's main hope is a quick motion and a low, hard throw that should be aimed at the first baseman's right knee to allow him to catch the ball and apply the tag quickly, with little lost motion.

Right-hander's Pick-off at First (Hal Schumacher)

Although the runner should be watched, if a right-hander faces third base less body movement will be needed for the pitch. However, when he finds that he is slow in delivering the ball to the plate (allowing the runner to get a big jump) he should move his front foot further to the side (first base) and place a little more weight on it. This will also lead to a quicker move to first.

The initial move in throwing to first should be the lifting of the rear heel since this properly launches the pivot which is made on the ball of the rear foot. A right-hander's most effective throw to first is based on what might be called a "deception move," one that involves a feint of the head or movement of the knee which closely resembles that used in delivering the ball to the batter.

A LEFT-HANDER'S MOVE. A left-hander can be more deceptive in his move to first base since he faces in that direction when working from a stop-position and can keep an eye on the runner with no trouble.

According to the rules, he must step toward a point at least half-way between home and first when throwing to that base. If he steps more toward home than toward first he can be charged with a balk. Nevertheless, some left-handers succeed in getting away with half-balks by the simple expedient of stepping quickly toward first after having made a pick-off throw with a step that is almost directly toward home. These steps follow one another so rapidly that detecting a balk is very difficult and, needless to say, when performed in this fashion the move to first is very deceptive.

There are two basic ways for a left-hander to pick off a runner at first. (1) The "head move." Here he looks alternately at home and first, turning his head ninety degrees to do so. Then, after looking at first, instead of completing a full ninety degree turn to "go home," he stops half-way, turns back, and makes a quick throw to first. Warren Spahn of Milwaukee

Left-hander's Pick-off at First (Fred Green)

is a master of this type of move. (2) The "swing move." This is used primarily to hold the runner close to his base. Here, the body and leg are swung toward (but not further than) first before delivering the ball to the plate. When the "swing move" is made, the hurler can throw the ball to first if he sees that the runner has strayed too far off his base. Whitey Ford of the Yankees does this perfectly.

MAKING THE MOVE EFFECTIVE. The secret of picking a runner off first is to catch him off-balance and throw when he is leaning toward second and must take that little extra time to get back to the base. To catch the runner leaning, the pitcher should give his move variety. Occasionally he should throw to first without taking a full stretch. He can inject further deception into the maneuver by varying the interval between pitches and/or throws to the base, as well as in the time consumed in the stretch itself.

A device which is used with occasional success by experienced moundsmen makes good use of changes of speed in the throw to first. By means of half-speed throws, the runner can be lured into taking an extra-long lead. Then, a quick, hard throw may catch him off base. The pitcher should make sure to allow the runner to get back to first easily several times in order to "bait the trap."

The habits of base runners should also be taken into consideration. A man who moves off the base with a jump can occasionally be caught while taking the jump. A player who crosses his legs while taking a lead is easy prey for a pick-off throw when caught with his legs crossed. For the nervous type of runner who dances around in an effort to rattle the pitcher, the latter should stand and wait, causing the runner to tire of his own exertions and making him less likely to attempt daring tactics. A jumpy runner is rarely able to get off to a fast start and can be combatted by merely pitching to the hitter.

Just as long as the runner must slide to get back safely, the pitcher should keep throwing to first. This is an indication that his lead is too big and that he might be planning to steal.

These methods of picking the runner off base notwithstanding, it must never be forgotten that the batter is the man on whom to concentrate. The pitcher should never deliver the ball to the plate until after he has looked at his target with *both* eyes.

The most effective move to first is the one in which the pitcher looks like he is making his usual pitch to the batter—right up to the point where the pick-off throw is made.

The pick-off at second

There are two basic methods of working the pick-off at second base— by a signal from either the shortstop or the catcher, and by the "daylight play," in which the pitcher uses his own judgment. Random throws to second base are risky business—and rarely effective.

It should be explained at the outset that the shortstop is the proper man to use for the pick-off at second. The second baseman is actually only of nuisance value since he can be so easily watched by the runner.

Generally speaking, the time to throw is when the pitcher sees daylight between the shortstop and the runner—with the shortstop closer to the bag—otherwise there is little chance to get him. This is the "daylight play."

A count-play, worked out and practiced with the shortstop beforehand, is the preferred method. A signal from the shortstop starts the proceedings and the play can be executed like this: When the runner takes an extra-large lead he is fair game for this maneuver. While the pitcher is looking at the runner, the shortstop flashes the signal. He breaks for the bag as the pitcher turns back to face the batter. As the pitcher turns toward the plate he counts "one-two"—and turns and throws on "three." The throw should be knee-high and directly over the bag in order to facilitate a sure catch and a quick tag for the shortstop.

Right-hander's Pick-off at Second (Hal Schumacher)

Left-hander's Pick-off at Second (Fred Green)

A turn to the left is more deceptive and effective for a right-hander since it creates the illusion that he is delivering the ball to the plate before the pivot is completed and the pick-off throw made. A left-hander, by the same token, should turn to his right. In either case, the correct technique is a quick pivot and deliberate, but hard, throw. The pitcher should always look before he throws.

The pick-off at second can also be made on a signal from the catcher, who directs a throw to the base when he sees the shortstop break for it. Since this involves one more player and the additional room for error which follows, it is not highly recommended.

The "block play" may succeed where the shortstop pick-off fails. In it, the shortstop, after leaving the base to return to his position, passes in front of the runner, gaining the latter's attention by so doing. The second baseman, meanwhile, has edged over to the bag to take a quick throw from the pitcher that can catch an unwary runner napping.

A jump-turn is conducive to the necessary pause after the pivot and before the throw. Furthermore, the throw will be more natural (and accurate) when the striding foot is brought past a direct line to second base, that is, the pivot is one of slightly more than 180 degrees.

The first move, for both left- and right-handers, should be the lifting of the rear heel. This move properly starts the pivot, which is made on the ball of the rear foot.

One exception to this move can be in the case of the sidearmer. He will often find it easier to pivot toward his throwing side.

Regardless of the technique employed, there are several tactical points which should be borne in mind:

(1) A pitcher should not get into the habit of turning to look at the runner only once, then pitching. All moves should be varied to prevent a smart runner from gaining an unwarranted advantage.

(2) Runners can be categorized as "head-turners" (shifting the glance from pitcher to shortstop) and "leaners" (placing the weight on the right foot to get a good start toward third). They should be studied for these habits, which will aid in picking them off base.

(3) A pick-off throw to second is most likely to succeed on a 2-1 or 3-2 count, in which case the runner is more apt to take liberties. This is especially so with a left-hander at bat since the shortstop will be playing closer to the base.

(4) The pitcher should step off the rubber before throwing to second, so as to eliminate any danger of a balk.

(5) If it is apparent that the play will not succeed, the throw will be an unnecessary one and should not be risked. The rules do not require that a move to second be completed by a throw.

(6) The ball should never be delivered to the plate after an infielder has

made a move toward the base. He should be allowed to return to his position before a pitch is made.

(7) Once again, this reminder to pitchers—don't pitch from memory; take a look at the plate before delivering the ball, even if it permits the runner to get a big jump.

(8) The pick-off play must be practiced diligently until timing, including the meter of the count, is synchronized and the throw can be made quickly and with accuracy.

The pick-off at third

A pick-off throw to third base is very risky business and should be attempted only by experienced players who have practiced it many times. It is a prearranged play, signalled by either the pitcher or third baseman, and demands an accurate throw which arrives at the base simultaneously with the third baseman, if not slightly after he has reached the bag. Here again, the rules do not require completion of a throw to the base and a needless one should not be made. Since the main object is to drive the runner back to his base, a fake throw or stepping off the rubber is recommended as equally effective and far less hazardous than a throw to third base.

A pick-off with men on first and third or, especially, on second and third, is more feasible than one with only a runner at third base. In operation, it works like this—the pitcher, *after stepping off the rubber,* pivots toward second (or first, as the case may be), continues around to third, and throws. This move can be worked effectively only by a right-hander and should not be attempted until it has been practiced to the point of perfection.

The situation with runners on first and third presents another possibility for the offense which must be guarded against by the pitcher. The man on first base will occasionally break for second while the pitcher is holding the ball, hoping to draw a hurried throw which will allow the runner on third to score. The way to combat this is to step off the rubber, survey the situation quickly, and either make a play on the runner at third if he attempts to score, or fake him back to his base before throwing to cutdown the other runner. If a runner stops between bases, the pitcher should hold the ball and run directly at him, keeping an eye on the other runner while doing so.

Holding the runner

The idea of developing an effective method of operation with men on base revolves around holding the runner close to his base. Since a pick-off play is rarely successful, extra consideration should be given to the matter of preventing the runner(s) from gaining a big lead, which will allow him to advance to the next base with comparative ease.

The first time a man gets on base the pitcher should "look him back" and it is a good policy to do so more than once. This will let the runner know that he is being watched and cannot afford to take too big a lead. A left-hander can add to this effect by using the "swing move," which was previously described and which may enable him to drive the runner back to the base while in the process of delivering the ball to the plate. A right-hander must rely more heavily on a "head move" ("looking him back") and, at times, a throw to the base. A dangerous runner, in particular, will demand an occasional throw.

One thing that should definitely be avoided is allowing the runner to get a walking lead. He should be made to stop before the ball is delivered to the batter. The first step in preventing a walking start is to wait on the runner. If this fails, the pitcher should step off the rubber to insure that the man returns to his base. This involves correct technique. The pitcher should step back off the rubber with his rear foot. Any other movement prior to the lifting of the rear foot and the placing of it behind the rubber can be construed as a move intended to deceive the runner and may result in the pitcher's being charged with a balk. Furthermore, he is not permitted to step off once he has started his pitching motion.

Still another method of holding the runner close is to take a deep breath while at the stop-position. In this case, the runner will have difficulty in deciding whether the pitcher is breathing or moving to pitch.

Two additional precautionary notes which deserve consideration deal with the same phase of the problem and apply, one to a right-hander, one to a left-hander. When a right-hander reaches his stop-position with a runner on first and finds that the runner has disappeared from his field of vision when he has made a half-turn of his head toward the base, a throw is called for. The same principle pertains to a left-hander working with a man on second. When the runner can't be sighted by means of peripheral vision, his lead is too big and he should be forced back to the base.

Tactical points to be remembered in holding the runner close to his base can be listed as follows:

(1) If the pitcher is working with more than a two-run lead, he need pay little heed to the base runner—he's not going anywhere. At least, he certainly should not be going anywhere, since it is bad baseball to take chances when you are more than one run behind.

(2) If the pitcher so much as suspects a hit-and-run or steal, he should throw to first base. When the automatic run-and-hit is in order (a 3-2 count with a force play possible), the runner should not be allowed to get too big a jump on the ball. A well timed pick-off throw might catch him off base in this situation.

(3) If the bunt is in order but not certain, the pitcher should take his stretch, then step off the rubber. When this is done, the batter may give a tip-off as to his intentions.

(4) With the hit-and-run in order, a right-hand batter should be pitched tight and a left-hander should be pitched outside. This will make it difficult for either to hit behind the runner.

(5) With a fast man on third in a tight game, it might be advisable for a pitcher to work from a stop-position. This is particularly applicable to a slow worker and is especially pertinent to a left-hander, whose back is toward the runner.

(6) Under any circumstance, with a man on third base, a short pump and a quick delivery should be used. A right-hander can actually take a glance at the runner while in his pitching motion.

(7) If a teammate shouts a warning while the pitcher is taking his stretch or has reached the stop-position, his first move should be to step off the rubber and quickly size up the situation. Only then should positive action be taken.

In order to condition himself to working with men on base, experience is needed. The simplest means of achieving this is to put a man on first base during batting practice and have him jump around in an effort to disconcert the pitcher. This will serve to inure the hurler to operating under these game conditions.

The pitch-out

A pitch-out is a device which is resorted to with two purposes in mind —to pick off a runner who has taken too big a lead and/or to foil an attempted hit-and-run, steal, or squeeze. It generally calls for a fast ball, letter-high and wide of the plate (as the term implies), which will permit the catcher to make an unobstructed throw. It should never be too wide to permit easy handling and to afford the catcher a good chance to get the runner. While very useful in checking enemy runners, it should not be indulged in by a pitcher who is wild, or one who is momentarily having control trouble, since he can ill afford to waste a pitch.

With a runner on first base, in order to make a pick-off throw to that base, some catchers prefer an inside pitch with a left-hand batter at the plate. Their throw is then made sidearm, around the batter. This is a matter of personal preference and the pitcher should deliver the ball in accordance with his catcher's wishes.

When a waste-pitch is thrown with men on base, it should be a pitch-out. A curve ball pitch-out is a good maneuver with a bunt in order, since the batter will lean with the pitch and may lure the runner(s) into straying far enough off base to fall victim to a pick-off throw. This is especially so with a runner on second base—even if a bunt is not suspected.

Combatting the squeeze play and the steal of home have already been discussed, but further words are called for here since the pitch-out is the basis of dealing with them.

The best method of breaking up the squeeze is an unbuntable pitch that will catch the runner trying to score. A right-hand batter should be knocked down. The ball should be kept high and outside to a left-hander. Both can be considered pitch-outs. They should be unbuntable and in such a location that the catcher will have little trouble in handling the ball and tagging the runner.

When the squeeze is under way, a fast ball should be automatic regardless of the signal that has been given. It not only gets to the plate more quickly, but is easier for the pitcher to control and the catcher to handle.

The beginning of a steal of home looks so much like the squeeze play that the same tactics should be used in coping with it. When it can be distinguished from the squeeze, a low fast ball in the strike zone can be thrown, allowing the catcher to be in good position for the play; at the same time, this gives the pitcher a strike, since the batter is unlikely to be swinging.

A special situation for which the pitcher should be prepared is an attempted steal of home with two strikes on the batter. Here, the fast ball should once more be automatic; the pitcher should make it a strike, since the oncoming runner might interfere with the batter's swing.

To return to the pitch-out per se—it should be employed only in a close game in which the out at stake is a big one; it can occasionally be used in an attempt to discover the intentions of the offensive team; and once it has been signalled by the catcher, it should actually be thrown, since at least one infielder will have left his position to handle the pick-off throw and the infield will be inadequately defended should the pitch be hit by the batter. Consequently, it should be unhittable.

CONDITIONING

Warming up is an extremely vital phase of pitching which is too often taken for granted. It is a positive measure, not merely something which has to be done, and a pitcher should take full advantage of it to prepare himself properly to obtain the maximum results from his natural equipment, whether it be with a single inning, a specific game, or an entire season in mind.

Proper warming-up procedure varies for different pitchers just as do individual physiques. A man's muscular structure, his pitching style, his temperament, and other less personal factors, such as the weather, must

113

be considered and dealt with according to what past experience has shown to be necessary. For example, a thick-muscled pitcher needs a longer warm-up than one who is loose and smooth-muscled; a "junk ball" artist needs less time to be ready than does a fast-baller; and a cold day necessitates a slow, careful warm-up, whereas on a very hot day a pitcher can be ready with only a few loosening-up throws.

Bearing in mind that it is better to be over-warmed-up or conditioned, than insufficiently so, this section will consider various aspects of this important fundamental of good pitching.

Pre-season

This phase of conditioning should be done slowly and with care. The first consideration should be a pitcher's legs and wind—they are closely allied and must be in shape before his arm will be ready.

Legs, as well as the arm, should be strengthened gradually. Over-exertion at too early a date can result in a pulled muscle, and consequently can disrupt the entire training schedule. Long walks during the off-season will serve as a good build-up for the hard work which follows. Squeezing a hand-grip or rubber ball, snapping the wrist in a curve ball motion, and swinging an Indian club in an easy throwing motion will help in developing a strong, supple wrist.

Jogging, to condition the muscles, is the second phase of pre-season work. Calisthenics in general and leg-builders in particular are also very beneficial. The routine should include running; squatting, for the calves and thighs; twists and bends, to loosen and develop the trunk; and bicycling, to strengthen the back. Ten minutes of calisthenics is not enough to harden the muscles and it will promote stamina and looseness.

When his legs have begun to grow strong, the pitcher can engage in harder work. Wind sprints—short dashes at full speed—are the most effective of all conditioners. These should be continued all season and combined with shagging flies in batting practice and chasing fungoes hit by a coach.

Another great boon to good condition is an exercise which might be called "pick-ups." It is done with the aid of a partner who takes a position about eight feet away. He rolls a ball, first to one side, then the other. The subject of the drill picks up the ball, bending fully to do so, and tosses it back to his partner while straightening up. This is continued at a rapid pace while moving from side to side. About fifty of these pick-ups daily will prove highly beneficial.

Wind sprints are still the cornerstone of a good conditioning program. No less than ten good, hard ones per day should be the rule for every pitcher, the only exception being on the day of a game that he is scheduled to pitch.

Leg conditioning should be accompanied by daily throwing, with a gradual increase in the speed of the pitches. Getting the arm attuned to the curve ball motion should begin almost at the outset of the training period. This should start with merely spinning the ball—with a full arm motion. No hard curve balls should be attempted until the arm is fully prepared for it.

The arm will round into shape along with the legs, and should be ready to respond to hard work when the ball begins to feel light. Once a pitcher is ready to throw at top speed he should begin working up to a full-game routine, starting with two- or three-inning chores and gradually building up to a full nine innings. He should be ready for a complete game in about four weeks time (see section on coaching). After this period of preliminary work has been completed, emphasis should be placed on the improvement of skills, as well as the maintenance of good physical condition. When the arm is sound, the more throwing for accuracy, the better.

When he does commence hard throwing and working up to his game routine, the pitcher should begin to take a day of rest (running, but no throwing) between his pitching stints, taking care to forego all throwing whenever his arm feels tired or heavy. Some experienced pitchers believe in throwing every day until the arm feels a strain—then abstaining for a day.

At the same time that he is gradually conditioning himself for his full-game routine, he should also be working up to his full between-games rest period, usually consisting of three or four days interspersed with only running and light throwing.

Three important precautionary moves to be observed by all pitchers are:

(1) A damp sweat-shirt should be changed immediately after throwing.
(2) In early pre-season conditioning, a pitcher should throw hard enough to loosen the kinks, but not so hard that his arm will be strained.
(3) Soreness should not be pitched out; rest and heat are the best cures.

The over-all pre-season conditioning period should be conducted with the basic idea in mind that poor physical shape results in fatigue, which in turn ruins coordination and can cause injury to the arm. Each part of the pitching machine should be ready to go at full speed for nine innings by the time the training period has been completed.

Pre-game

A pitcher's pre-game warm-up should be taken slowly and should include plenty of bending and stretching. Calisthenics should not be indulged in, but exercises of the stretching variety are very helpful when performed just prior to the actual warm-up. It should be a scrupulously observed rule that no ballplayer attempt to throw unless he has taken the time to bend and stretch until his muscles are loose. For a pitcher, this should include revolving his arm above his head (to loosen his shoulder muscles) and massaging his elbow (to stimulate circulation).

The individual pitcher will come to know just how much and what kind of warm-up he needs in order to be ready. The weather is a factor to be considered, a cold day necessitating a long, slow warm-up and a hot day demanding only a few minutes of throwing. Moreover, in hot weather the pitcher should time his warm-up so as to be assured of a few minutes rest before the game starts.

When ready to throw hard, a hurler should try each of his pitches until satisfied that all are working properly. The curve ball should be merely spun at first, yet at all times should include concentration on a full arm-sweep and follow-through, and a good wrist-snap.

A certain portion of the warm-up should be devoted to throwing from a stop-position, with each of the deliveries being tried this way as well as with a full wind-up.

Every pitch should be in the strike zone. By striving for this during his warm-up, a hurler will be practicing the correct pitching habits that will get him in the proper groove for the game.

Each time he draws a starting assignment, a moundsman should be sufficiently warmed up to begin the first inning at peak efficiency but, at the same time, he should take care not to leave his game on the side-lines. Careful study has shown that the first inning and the last three are the most difficult for a pitcher, hence the need to draw a fine line between too little and too much warm-up. Eight to ten really hard throws at the close of the full warm-up should prove sufficient for readiness and, under normal conditions, about fifteen minutes of throwing should prepare a pitcher adequately for the game.

The warm-up throws should be made in the same direction as will those in the game. Wind can be a very important factor in affecting the action of a thrown ball, and a pitcher should become accustomed and adjusted to the wind before he starts the game.

Between innings

There should be a definite purpose to the between-innings warm-up. Every pitch should be thrown for a strike and with a full motion, and the last two should be thrown hard so that the pitcher will be fully prepared to start the inning.

Eight throws are permitted by the rules, and are the standard used by most pitchers. If the preceding half-inning has been a long one, the

116

maximum number allowed should be used—and in unhurried fashion. Under normal circumstances, however, five throws should prove sufficient. The extra three per inning will add up to twenty-seven per nine innings and that constitutes an extra inning or more of pitching to which the arm will be subjected. This can take its toll over the course of a complete game.

An important protective measure that should always be observed is the wearing of a jacket between innings. On an oppressively hot day it need not be donned fully but, even under these conditions, the pitching arm and shoulder should be covered. In line with this is the idea that during a night game a pitcher should change his sweat-shirt *before* he stops perspiring, something that generally occurs in about the fifth inning.

Bullpen routine

In the Major Leagues each club carries on its roster pitchers who are relief specialists. As we go down the ladder to the various levels of baseball, the trend is to a combination of starting and relieving for all pitchers. Every pitcher will be called upon for bullpen duty at some time during his career and, since it calls for a different warm-up technique, he should have some knowledge of this deviation from standard procedure so as to be prepared to provide his club with effective relief pitching whenever the duty falls to him.

The pitcher who excels in relief is distinguished by two major attributes —his ability to get the ball over the plate with something on it, under pressure; and his knack of warming up quickly at a moment's notice.

A reliever may find it advisable to loosen up in advance, at the start of the game. So as to save valuable time when the call comes, either he or his catcher should be equipped with a baseball from the time the game first gets under way.

A pitcher who gets the sign to warm up in the bullpen must be ready in a hurry. He should take about ten tosses and then throw hard. Once he is warmed up thoroughly, he should just lob the ball to stay ready for the call to action which may come at any time.

Between games

One of the problems confronting every pitcher is the adoption of a between-games routine by which he will be able to maintain good general physical condition and, at the same time, arrive at his pitching assignments with the desired degree of sharpness. There is no set schedule which is correct for every pitcher. Rather, each one will respond best to a pattern tailored to his own physical make-up and peculiarities. Experience and observation will enable him to determine just what his own conditioning program should be.

A three-day rest between starts is standard, although some hurlers work more effectively with an extra day's rest, while others are sharper, at times, with only two days' lay-off. Using three days as a norm, a sensible routine might go somewhat like this:

Game
First day —light exercise, such as backing up the batting-practice pitcher, which involves much bending and stretching; running; *no* throwing.
Second day—throwing for control, possibly one round of batting practice; pick-ups; running.
Third day —Running; a light warm-up.
Game

The day before a game is highly important and warrants further mention. Calisthenics should be eliminated so as to avoid a source of possible game-day stiffness. Plenty of good, hard running should be done. Five minutes of throwing should suffice to tune up the arm. Hard or prolonged throwing will rob the pitcher of the edge which he should have for the game itself. This easy warm-up will loosen the muscles properly and should be followed immediately by a shower.

The above routine is not inflexible. It is presented merely to serve as a guide. As stated above, each pitcher should develop the routine which best serves his purposes.

In relation to conditioning in general, set-purpose routines, and, for that matter, the entire business of pitching, the watchword should be: "Know your own arm."

TACTICS—GENERAL STRATEGY

The mechanical phases of the pitching game having been covered quite thoroughly; the applied study of them should succeed in the making of an improved thrower. What remains is to transform the thrower into a pitcher.

The natural attributes of any pitcher, if fully developed and properly applied, should suffice to make him a winner. It is the application of the previously discussed principles which is the topic of this section on tactics.

Without delving into the art of working on batters in general or the various individual types which will be encountered (these facets of the game are included in subsequent chapters), several basic ideas on pitching tactics are herewith presented.

The science of pitching

The science of pitching revolves around upsetting the batter's timing. No pitcher can overpower every hitter; his primary objective should be to nullify the power of his adversary so that the ball will not be hit solidly when it is met by the bat. Needless to say, the best method of accomplishing this is to give him the pitch for which he is least prepared at a given time.

Later on, the means for keeping the hitter off-balance will be investigated thoroughly. Since we are dealing more with generalities here, suffice it to say that a pitcher should avoid getting into too rhythmical a groove, the cadence of which can be timed easily by the batter. Rather, he should vary his working speed. This does not refer merely to the velocity of a pitched ball. It also involves the time interval between deliveries. For example, on one pitch he can take fifteen to twenty seconds before delivering the ball; on the next one he can fire away just as soon as he gets the catcher's signal; and on the following pitch he can get the signal, take a deep breath, pump once, and throw. Such a routine will keep the hitter from getting too well set at the plate and help make the pitcher's task just that much easier.

Changing speeds is, of course, a very effective method of upsetting the batter's timing. In more general terms it serves an equally valuable purpose. A pitcher should not invariably fire away with everything he has on every pitch, particularly in the early innings. He should save his very best stuff for the tight spots when he must call on that extra something to get him out of trouble. This is what is known as "pacing one's self" and it is a knack that has been mastered by practically every successful hurler in the game. And, quite naturally, if a pitcher has not saved something extra for the tight spots, it will not be there when he most needs it.

Trying too hard to put everything he possibly can on a pitch and straining himself in the process is never good practice for a pitcher. This bad habit actually works negatively in that it does not allow him to deliver the ball with his best possible stuff and, furthermore, it can have a definitely harmful effect on his control. What should be strived for by every pitcher is a quality which might be called "controlled relaxation."

Much emphasis has been placed on the value of getting the ball over the plate with something on it. This will always stand as one of the keys to mound success. Getting a batter out on a minimum number of pitches lessens a hurler's problems in every conceivable respect. Staying ahead of the batter is the secret to this, particularly in view of the fact that study of the game has demonstrated conclusively that the percentage of batters who hit safely with two strikes is quite small.

Generally speaking, low-ball pitching is the most effective. The pitcher who can throw low strikes consistently is going to be successful. Yet, each hurler should learn to take advantage of his own natural stuff. Robin Roberts, a true mound artist, has operated on the theory that the basis of effective pitching is keeping the ball high-and-tight or low-and-away. The foundation for this belief is that his fast ball, like that of most pitchers, rises and moves to the inside, while his curve ball breaks down and away. This philosophy can be applied to any pitcher in accordance with the action of his particular deliveries. It pertains particularly to an individual pitch on which a definite attempt is made to retire the batter. Nevertheless, although Roberts follows this theory for his key pitches and finds success, he is still essentially a low-ball pitcher.

A curve ball should always be kept low, because it will have a better break when thrown below the waist and because it generally breaks down as well as to the side. A sinking fast ball should be aimed at a low spot for the same reason. A fast ball that rises and, especially, a change-of-pace on which the batter must supply his own power are also effective when kept low since, when thrown around the knees, they are more difficult to drive for distance.

The physical aspect of a ball park is another factor which enters into the tactical side of the pitching game. Short fences demand careful work and spot-pitching. A big ball park permits more freedom of operation, and in one, the batter can, at times, be allowed to hit the ball more freely since percentages alone will account for many "long outs." A short fence in one particular field will dictate pitching away from the power of a batter who hits in that direction, with occasional variations in tactics when he is detected crowding the plate to offset this strategy. A park with short fences down both foul lines demands that the pitcher make a determined effort to keep the batter from pulling the ball. This involves judicious use of slow pitches and keeping the ball away from most hitters. As a general rule, a pitcher can expect to be reached for more extra base hits in a small park and a greater number of singles in a big one.

Since a smart coach at first or third base can often "read" a pitch from some tell-tale movement on the part of the pitcher, the latter must constantly guard against tipping off the opposition as to what pitch is coming. He should not only try to use the same grip for his fast ball, curve, and change-of-pace and throw them all with the same motion; he should also take care to cover the ball from the view of the coaches as well as the batter. A right-hander should cover his pitches from the third-base side and a left-hander from the first-base side, and both should cover the wrist as well as the hand in order to prevent a coach from "reading" the pitch and relaying this vital information to the batter. Peculiar mannerisms should also be masked from the probing eyes of clever coaches.

Naturally, the ball should be hidden from the batter as much as possible. Some pitchers with an abundance of stuff are not successful because they are too "true" in their deliveries. An extra turn or twist of the body during the pitching motion can be very helpful in overcoming this difficulty. The wisdom of concealing the ball from the batter until the last possible moment is proven by the effectiveness of a sidearm pitch to a batter who hits from the same side that the pitcher throws (right-hand pitcher, right-hand batter, and so forth). It is the fact that the ball is hidden by the pitcher's body until just before it is released which makes for its effectiveness. The same principle can be applied in concealing any pitch and, well done, will add greatly to the success of the pitcher.

In probing into the intricacies of scientific pitching, one fact stands out above all others. In order to develop a good command of sound tactics and to make for maximum utilization of his natural equipment, a pitcher most definitely will profit greatly by observing, asking, and listening. No matter how polished a performer he may be, he will never "know it all," and there is always someone from whom he can learn something new and valuable.

Working with the team

Baseball is essentially a team game and the efforts of each player must be coordinated with those of his teammates. Obviously, no pitcher is going to strike out every enemy batsman; to be assured of the good fielding support which he needs in order to be a winner, his pitching should be designed to work in close harmony with the defensive alignment of his team. There is a psychological, as well as physical, aspect of the situation. When a ball club has confidence in the ability of a pitcher to work in close cooperation with them, the various players will perform exceptionally well. If the pitcher has faith in the support which his teammates will accord him, his performance will be improved. This close cooperation and mutual confidence can produce an almost unbeatable combination.

Team defense is closely coordinated with the operating methods of a pitcher, thus his strategy should be developed in reference to it. Fielders will station themselves according to the way in which the batter will be pitched. By the same token, a pitcher should work on the batsman in such a way as to make him most likely to hit the ball to that section of the field which has the best coverage. Thus, when an exaggerated defensive alignment is employed against an exceptionally strong pull-hitter, such as Roger Maris, he should be pitched tight so as to make hitting to the opposite field, all but uncovered in this case, very difficult for him.

To cite other specific examples: When the game situation demands the use of a tight infield to cut off a run at the plate, the ball should be kept low, where it is most likely to be hit on the ground. The same principle applies with a double play in prospect. When the first baseman is holding a runner close to the base, the pitcher should refrain from giving a left-hand batter slow or inside pitches which will be easy for him to pull through the hole left by the first baseman. These are a few of the instances in which a pitcher should operate according to his team's defensive alignment.

Conversely, a team's defensive positioning depends, to a great extent, on the pitcher himself. For example, a batter will be played to pull the slower pitches; or, with two strikes, the batter will be "guarding the plate" and less likely to pull the ball, so will be played accordingly.

Thus, if a team is to function at peak efficiency, the pitcher should pay close attention to the defensive setup behind him and should operate in such a way that his teammates will be aware of his methods and intentions and will, in many cases, be able to get that jump on a batted ball which will enable them to turn base hits into put-outs. This, incidentally, is the underlying motive behind the strategy worked out at pre-game clubhouse meetings.

There are certain pitchers who seem to enjoy exceptionally good defensive support. There is a definite reason for this—confidence in them on the part of their teammates. An old baseball saying states that a team can go "up on its toes" only so many times. In other words, when the pitcher stays ahead of the hitter, when he uses a minimum of pitches, when he cooperates fully with his team, they will play much better defensive baseball behind him.

Working with the catcher

A smart catcher, by properly utilizing a pitcher's stuff on a given day, can guide him through a game with telling effect. When a pitcher follows his partner's lead closely, adding knowledgeable embellishments of his own, a really smooth-working battery will be the result.

Basic strategy should be dictated by the manager or coach. He should not, however, go so far as to call each pitch. Rather, he should teach his pitchers and catchers to think along certain lines and to evolve and improvise on a plan of operations which is basically sound and, at the same time, allows room for the sudden changes of tactics often dictated by alert observation. Doing this adds to a hurler's effectiveness by taking advantage of every possible opening as it arises. This will insure best results, since feel and touch are far more important than sheer theory, in coping with the batter. By close observation, the batterymen can detect slight changes in grip, stance, and even the air of determination shown by the hitter, and this information can always be put to good use.

The only really defineable guide that the pitcher and catcher possess is the instinct and courage to gamble. The ancient adage, "two heads are better than one," being especially pertinent here and the fact that the reasoning of one man, alone, can often lead him into a rut, both the pitcher and the catcher should do some thinking in the calling of pitches. True, the catcher gives the signals and by reason of proximity can better observe the batter. Yet, the pitcher knows his own arm and has a different perspective on the general situation. Thus, he not only can, but definitely should, shake off the catcher when he feels that his own instincts and ideas have merit. Between the two of them, sound tactics can be developed.

It is of the utmost importance for the catcher to know what pitch is being thrown. This statement is so obvious as to seem ridiculous. But the fact remains that such is not always the case and, when the catcher is crossed up or caught unawares, a passed ball and possibly even a broken finger can ensue. For this reason, the pitcher should give extra consideration to his battery mate (and the welfare of his team). At times, the game situation may demand especially intense concentration, or visibility of the signs may be poor. Yet, the pitcher should never allow himself to be so preoccupied that he will either miss altogether or fail to read properly the catcher's signal.

Developing strategy

Evolving a plan of operation at any stage of the contest is dependent on several factors: knowledge of the batter, his habits, and peculiarities; the game situation, including the inning, score, count, outs, position of runners, weather conditions, and physical characteristics of the ball park; the tactical approach generally employed by the opposition; the alignment of the defensive players; the condition of the pitcher, including the stuff and control at his command at a given time; the intangibles which revolve around alertness to rapidly changing conditions; and gambling instinct, modified by a sound knowledge of baseball percentages.

First of all, the pitcher should be fully aware of who is at bat. Past experience will furnish at least the beginning of a book on each batter. In the absence of previous encounters, study of an opponent in batting practice, his general physical characteristics, and his stance and attitude at the plate can provide at least a sketchy guide. An additional factor which can shed light on the situation is the hitter's position in the batting order and what can reasonably be expected of a man who occupies that particular spot in the line-up.

One of the basic principles of good pitching is to give the batter the pitch that he is least expecting and/or to make him hit the one that the pitcher wants him to hit. This involves the establishment of a sequence of pitching (variable, when advisable) which will set up the batter. It also allows development of strategy that will permit the hurler to use his best pitch in the clutch.

The last sentence should be reminder enough of the importance of pitching to one's own strength. Regardless of how well a batter's weakness may be known, there are occasions when this knowledge can be ignored. One such case is general in nature: in a tight spot it is usually best to rely on one's most effective pitch. Another is the strength vs. weakness dilemma which has only one logical conclusion. To be more specific, consider a pitcher with a good overhand curve and a sinking fast ball. Obviously, he is most effective when he keeps the ball low. It follows that, even with a low-ball hitter at bat, he will probably be more successful by keeping the ball low, since the value of pitching to his own strength outweighs the fact that this will mean putting the ball in the batter's strong zone.

There are times when a moundsman will find that one of his basic pitches is not up to par. If one pitch is working well, and another is not, on any given day, he should merely *show* the batter the one that is not working, but should make him *hit* the one that is. For example, on a day when his curve ball is behaving poorly, he should use it as a waste pitch, letting the batter know that he has a curve—but without putting it in the strike zone. The fast ball is the one that should be thrown for strikes and which the batter should be made to hit. Actually, this is merely a variation of the idea that a hurler should rely on his best pitch or, in other words, pitch to his own strength.

Setting up the hitter and developing an effective sequence of pitches is an art in itself. Its mastery should be an aspiration of every pitcher. Yet, using a predetermined method of setting up a batter is not always good practice. The idea in occasionally avoiding it is to keep the batter from learning exactly how a pitcher operates and to prevent him from getting set for a certain pitch. What this amounts to is staying out of a rut. In a slightly different fashion than the planned routine, it also accomplishes the purpose of keeping the hitter off balance.

An oft-repeated maxim for success on the mound is "stay ahead of the hitter." No matter how often it appears on these pages its value makes it worthy of even further repetition. To achieve a first-pitch strike it is occasionally wise to try something a little unusual. The time to go to the "pattern" or one's best pitch is when the batter must swing. If a hurler finds that the opposition is consistently hitting the first pitch, he should resort to pitching to the batter's weakness on his initial delivery.

The game situation and strategy

As mentioned above, several factors influence the development of sound pitching strategy. Among these, and of great importance, is the game situation. Every ballplayer should, at all times, be fully aware of the score, the inning, the outs, the count, and the position of base runners. The pitcher should base much of his strategy on it.

Following is a brief listing of specific factors which come under the general heading of game situations and which should be taken into consideration when deciding on the proper pitch to be used at a certain time.

(1) When the pitcher is behind in the count he should concentrate primarily on getting the ball over the plate.

(2) The time to pitch to spots is when the pitcher is ahead of the batter.

(3) A pitcher should try to "thread the needle" only occasionally. Attempting to have ultra-fine control of every pitch can only lead to trouble for all but the very few who possess this control.

(4) When the pitcher is one or two runs behind with men on base, no "fat" pitches should be thrown. A base hit, in this case, could put the game beyond control.

(5) No "fat" pitches should be thrown with first base open and either or both of the other two occupied. Here, a pitcher can afford to be extra careful since a walk will do no great additional harm. Furthermore, with a man in scoring position, a batter is more likely to go for a bad ball because of his anxiety to bring home a run.

(6) Close consideration should be given the weather. On a hot day the pitcher should try to conserve his strength by throwing a minimum number of pitches. In damp weather he should rely heavily on his curve. When it is dark he should place special emphasis on the use of his fast ball.

(7) It is easier to pitch with a used baseball than with a new one. The catcher, first, and third basemen should retrieve foul balls in an effort to keep the same one in play.

(8) When a slick, new ball is introduced into the game a curve is more difficult to throw. For this reason, plus the fact that a new ball has a tendency to sail which adds to its effectiveness, the fast ball should be relied on heavily.

(9) A 3-2 curve ball is an effective pitch and will often catch the batter looking at a called third strike, because he rarely anticipates such tactics.

(10) The 3-2, two-out pitch with the bases loaded or men on second and third, should be from a set position since the base runners will be moving and should be held close to their bases, so that all of them will not be able to score on a base hit.

(11) With a runner on second base and no outs, extra effort should be applied to prevent the batter from hitting toward right field since this will probably move the runner to third base from where he will be able to score on a fly ball.

(12) If a first-strike bunt attempt is fouled off or missed, the next

delivery should be a pitch-out. A curve ball pitch-out is especially effective in this case since the batter leans with it and the runner is more likely to take a few extra steps.

This, by no means, covers every possible game situation. However, it can serve to channel a pitcher's thoughts in the right direction and aid him in the development of sound strategy and tactics.

The intentional pass

The intentional pass is a highly controversial part of the game, but a tactically important one to the pitcher. No matter how much scorn and ridicule it may arouse, there are certain situations in which its use is wise, others in which it is all but mandatory. Though generally called for by the manager, the principles and theory behind it should be thoroughly understood by the man who puts it into execution—the pitcher.

The catcher must remain within the confines of the catcher's box until the ball is on its way to the plate. Thus, care must be exercised in throwing the four wide ones which constitute an intentional pass. He stands at the extreme outside limit of his box and extends his bare hand to the side with a right-hander at bat, and his glove with a left-hander at the plate. Either of the two is the target for which the pitcher should aim, the catcher stepping to the side to receive the ball as it leaves the pitcher's hand.

No signals are necessary for individual pitches once the intentional pass has been decided upon. A medium-speed fast ball should be delivered from a stop-position to carry out this maneuver. When it is employed with less than two out and a runner on third, the catcher should squat behind the plate and give a conventional signal for the first of the four pitches in order to discourage an attempt at a squeeze play.

The intentional pass is generally dictated by sound strategy rather than fear of a particular batter. The primary object of it is to pitch to a more logical opponent, while, at the same time, setting up a force or possible double play. It is used only with first base open since there would be no sense in moving an important run nearer to home. With a runner on third it sets up a double play; with runners on second, or second and third, it makes possible a force at any base.

In setting up a double play, consideration should be given to the fact that the following batter will be much easier to double up if he swings right-handed, especially when he is a pull hitter who may drive the ball sharply to either the third baseman or the shortstop.

Occasionally a batter will be passed to get at the pitcher or to force the other team to pinch-hit for him if he is pitching a strong game. The advisability of this move can be tempered by other factors, one of which is

126

the strength of the batter who precedes the pitcher. If he is a weak bats-man it is wise to pitch to him, particularly when there are two out. In this event, the pitcher, usually an "out man," may lead off the next inning, always an advantageous occurrence to the defensive team.

Another time when the intentional pass may be put to good use is with the winning run on third and either none or only one of the other bases occupied. Here, a walk will not only set up a double play, with one out it will eliminate the necessity of playing the infield in close, an alignment that gives the batter a much greater chance of hitting safely.

One variation on this maneuver could be called the partial-intentional pass. Assume that first base is open, one or more runners are in scoring positions, and an exceptionally good hitter is at bat; if the count goes to 3-0 or 3-1 it may prove wisest to walk the man purposely rather than risk throwing him a "fat" pitch.

A more subtle variation, used by some experienced professionals, is the "hidden" intentional pass. It can be occasioned by the situation which finds runners on first and second or first and third, and the defensive team one or two runs behind in the late innings. Here, the pitcher should give the batter nothing good to hit. A walk, in this case, will not score a run, whereas a "fat" pitch can be driven out for a base hit which would put the game beyond recall. The word "hidden" enters the picture because the batter should be tempted with carefully aimed pitches on or around the corners of the plate, but given nothing down the middle.

One of the cardinal rules of baseball is "never walk the tying or winning run, intentionally." This should not be considered as an ironclad princi-ple, however, since there are situations when such a maneuver can be justified. Nevertheless, the percentages must be heavily in the pitcher's favor if he is to issue an intentional walk to a batter who represents the tying run, and they must be overwhelmingly in his favor if it is the win-ning run that is involved.

WORKING ON THE HITTER

The primary aim of every pitcher should be to get the ball over the plate with something on it. Percentages definitely favor the pitcher as he faces each batter individually, since even the finest of batsmen rarely hit safely more than once every three times they go to the plate. It follows that if the pitcher can avoid the base on balls and, because he paces him-self, has that little extra for the tight spots, the odds will be greatly in his favor.

The secret of good hitting is timing; consequently the pitcher should constantly endeavor to upset the batter's timing.

This, of course, brings us back to one of the fundamental rules: every pitch should have a purpose. The smart hurler will use a sequence of pitches, each of which will set up the batter for the next one and, in itself, may be a pitch that he is not expecting. If successful in his intentions, the pitcher will be able to keep the batter slightly off balance and will upset his timing sufficiently to keep him from getting really good wood on the ball.

There are so many ideas on the subject of working on the hitter, ones which seem only loosely connected but which fit into one over-all method of operation—that categorizing them is difficult. In studying them, the reader should be aware of the basic philosophy behind them and should make it part of his own approach to pitching tactics. That philosophy is: "A pitcher's greatest asset is the batter's imagination."

Establishing a pattern

Each pitch delivered during a ball game should form part of a definite sequence in so far as any one hitter is concerned. This pitching pattern is dependent on several variable factors—the score, outs, inning, position of runners, count, performance in previous times at bat, characteristics of the batter, and physical condition of the pitcher. As a consequence, the pattern can and should be varied from pitch to pitch. A real mound artist has a carefully planned method of operation, yet is, at the same time, an astute improviser. He employs psychology and guile in the over-all aspect of his sequence and remains alert to any momentary change which can be turned to his own advantage.

The time for concentration on the batter's weakness is when the pitcher is ahead of him in the count and he is forced to swing at a ball that is close to or in the strike zone. It might be added that if he gets nothing but pitches on which he is weak, they will give him enough practice to eventually overcome the weakness. Furthermore, he will be expecting the pitch that gives him trouble. For these reasons the batter's weakness should be exploited primarily when the pitcher wants him to hit the ball.

The sequence or pattern should be so arranged as to take full advantage of the batter's weakness. Of course, it is desirable to retire the hitter on the first pitch (or any one, for that matter) but this is a rare occurrence. Consequently, each pitch should have some element of surprise and the overall pattern should be designed so as to build-up to a climax or "out pitch," the one on which the batter is weakest. It need not be one, single delivery—a particular pitch can certainly be used more than once on each batter. The idea is to operate in such a way that, by setting him up for it, the hitter is made even more vulnerable to a ball geared to his weakness.

Specialty pitchers operate in this fashion. These are the hurlers who rely primarily on one of the "off" pitches for their effectiveness. They set up the batter for the delivery that is their chief stock in trade and use that one when they especially want the batter to hit the ball.

During the early innings of a ball game a pitcher should feel more free to throw what he wants. If for no other reason than the psychological one, it will do him good to use the pitch in which he, himself, has the greatest confidence. As the game progresses, however, the situation undergoes a perfectly natural alteration. The catcher is in a better position to judge the effectiveness of the action of each of the various deliveries and his proximity gives him a better "feel" of the batter. Thus, his judgment should be relied on more heavily in the late innings. This does not mean that the pitcher should relinquish whatever control he has over the selection of pitches. It is still a joint undertaking; the catcher's influence at this point should simply be the stronger of the two.

A simple example of an effective pitching sequence might go like this: With a good pull-hitter at bat, the pitcher tries to cut the outside corner of the plate with two or three pitches, then fires one in under the hands of the hitter, who will probably have geared his swing for another outside pitch. Or, after throwing a medium speed and a slow pitch, the hurler throws a good fast ball over the plate, finding that even the best of hitters is not fully prepared for it.

Observation, imagination, and an intelligent approach will enable any pitcher to work out effective patterns for dealing with each batter. Among the factors which should be borne in mind and which can materially affect the sequence of pitches are the following:

(1) With men on base the ball should be kept low. This needs little elucidation since, in this case, it is desirable and advisable to make the batter hit the ball on the ground.

(2) Giving the batter a "fat" pitch should be avoided with first base open and either or both of the other two bases occupied. This is one case in which a pitcher can take extra care in working on the hitter and not be too concerned should he walk the man.

(3) With runners in scoring position, an exceptionally good hitter should not be fed the same pitch that has retired him early in the game. He will be expecting it.

(4) When ahead of the pitcher, a smart hitter will set himself for "his pitch," one in his strong zone; he may pass up a good pitch if it is not just what he wants, since he can afford to take a strike.

(5) A first-ball hitter generally does not like the curve and is set to swing at the fast ball. Since he is over-anxious, he is the easiest type to make go for a bad ball (but it should not be so bad that he will pass it up).

129

(6) Most young and inexperienced batters fall into the "over-anxious" category and will have a tendency to swing at anything. Bad balls should be used on them.

(7) A waste-pitch should not be literally wasted—it should be off the plate, but close enough to the strike zone to tempt the batter. This is one more application of the principle that every pitch should have a purpose, and demonstrates cognizance of the fact that a bad ball is far more difficult to hit than is a good one. However, when the pitcher gets ahead of the batter and can afford to waste a pitch his main purpose should still be to get the man out. Thus, the pitch should be neither too good nor too bad.

(8) Regardless of the pitch selected or the sequence developed, a sudden change—often in mid-motion—is demanded whenever a bunt, squeeze, or steal of home is detected. An unhittable fast ball is in order.

Varying the pattern

The pitching sequence should never be rigidly set. Momentary changes in the pitcher-batter relationship make sudden alterations in plans advisable at times. In general, working speed, velocity of pitches, and *modus operandi* should be varied so as to keep the batter off balance.

When "the book" on a hitter is followed too closely, and without deviation, he will become adjusted to it. Furthermore, a pitcher's stuff varies in its behavior and he may find that, because of this, the "right pitch" may turn out to be the wrong one.

This is particularly so when dealing with good hitters. There are, however, certain batters (never really strong ones) who can be retired in the same way over and over again. Any pitch near their weakness will dispose of them with little trouble. This type of hitter hangs on in professional baseball primarily because he succeeds in getting an occasional base hit when a pitcher suffers a lapse in his control or the quality of his stuff.

One special situation in which the pattern can be ignored should be recognized by all pitchers. This is the occasion when the batter is taking a pitch. The pitcher should try to anticipate when the take is on—and should throw a strike. If the batter shows his intentions and squares-away or moves around in an attempt to rattle the pitcher, he is giving away a strike and the pitcher should be sure to get the ball over the plate. In this case, a fast ball should be used. An arrangement can be made with the catcher which will make this an automatic fast-ball situation.

One other qualification in establishing a pattern bears repetition. When he finds himself in a tight spot, a pitcher should employ his best pitch. In other words, he should attempt to get out of difficulty by "pitching to his own strength."

Varying the delivery

It is wise policy for a pitcher to perfect both an overhand (or three-quarters) and a sidearm delivery. Not only will this lend variety to his pitching; it will also enable him to cope more effectively with otherwise troublesome hitters.

A pitcher who uses both an overhand and a sidearm delivery should have both a fast ball and a curve with each motion and should mix up the two pitches. The batter should be made aware that the pitcher has both so that he will not be able to take a toe hold in anticipation of one particular pitch every time the hurler changes from overhand to sidearm and vice versa. Mixing up the fast ball and curve applies also to different times at bat for the same man: he'll remember the last time.

Ordinarily, it is bad practice for a right-hander to pitch sidearm to a left-hand batter since the latter can follow the ball so well when it is delivered that way, and because a sidearm curve ball breaks directly in to him. This applies, needless to say, to a left-hand pitcher and a right-hand batter.

On the other hand, because the pitch is so well hidden and difficult to pick up and follow, it is strongly recommended that a right-hand pitcher throw plenty of sidearm stuff to a right-hand batter and that a left-handed pitcher do the same to a lefty batter. Most hitters have trouble with a sidearm delivery when it is used by a pitcher who throws from the same side on which they bat. This is particularly so of left-handed hitters, possibly because facing a southpaw is a relatively strange experience for them. There are sound baseball men who maintain that a left-hand batter will never consistently hit a left-handed sidearm delivery.

By the same token, a right-hander's curve ball to a left-hand batter (and a lefty's curve to a right-hand batter) is most effective when thrown "over the top," that is, directly overhand. Thrown in this manner, the curve's break will be primarily downward, rather than into the batter, and will be more difficult for him to hit squarely.

An extreme example of the sidearm delivery is the cross-fire. The technique of throwing it has been explained in the section on mechanics. In tactical terms, the cross-fire should be kept away from the batter, who, in the vast majority of cases, will pull back from the plate.

PSYCHOLOGY AND PITCHING

"He pitches with his head as well as his arm," is a highly complimentary phrase when used to describe a pitcher. Anyone familiar with baseball has heard it used in reference to an exceptionally smart mound operative. It is a fitting commentary on the skill of a really polished performer because one who belongs in this category is both a strategist and a psychologist. By a well-conceived plan of operation, by disarming mechanical moves, and by taking advantage of the batter's emotions and thought processes, the pitcher succeeds in nullifying the batter's power by out-thinking him.

Guess-hitting is a bad habit for a batsman, but it is only natural that batters try to outguess the pitcher. Therein lies one of the big advantages enjoyed by a hurler. Baseball's outstanding hitters do not try to outguess the pitcher, yet even they can be maneuvered into a position where they will more or less anticipate a certain pitch in a certain situation. It is up to the pitcher to try to stay one jump ahead of the batter in his rea-soning and to exploit the perfectly normal reactions which any ball-player will evidence in response to a given situation, in this case one that can be conceived and, to some extent, controlled by the pitcher. The poorer hitters can be outsmarted with greater frequency because they are more prone to guessing. Thus, the pitcher who combines psychology with his physical skills is a tough man to beat.

Mound psychology is a very difficult thing to teach. Game situations are so great in number and have so many ramifications that set policies to cope with each of them could not possibly be delineated. The solution, then, is to make the pitcher think along certain lines by citing examples used by smart moundsmen. Through imitation modified by improvisation he can profit greatly by exploring only a few of the methods employed by masters of the trade. For example—

(1) Carl Hubbell was one of baseball's all-time greats. Although an artist at pacing himself, he always exerted extra effort to hold the opposi-tion scoreless until his team had gone ahead. He was a firm believer in the philosophy that having a lead gives the pitcher a definite psycho-logical advantage.

(2) If a pitcher's success over the early innings of a game has found him relying principally on one particular pitch, he will have the op-position looking for it. A switch to emphasis on another pitch will give him a valuable extra weapon in outsmarting enemy batsmen.

(3) Most batters set themselves for the fast ball when the pitcher is behind in the count. This is only natural, since most hurlers have better control with the fast ball than with any other pitch. Consequently, a curve or change-of-pace will often catch the hitter off balance in this situation. The fact that he tends to become overanxious is another good reason for changing up on him at this time.

(4) Pursuing the above theory, this pitch should be thrown for a strike because it is the element of surprise which makes it effective. The change-up, in particular, is difficult to control; so the pitcher should concentrate on getting it into the strike zone on the 2-0 or 3-1 pitch since a smart hitter, when fooled, will often pass it up.

(5) Many smart pitchers will go to the curve when behind the batter and the fast ball when ahead of him, knowing that most ballplayers do not expect such tactics.

(6) A special case—when the first pitch is a curve and misses the plate for a ball, the next pitch should be another curve ball, right over the middle of the plate. Nine times out of ten the batter will take it for a strike.

(7) With men in scoring position—if the batter takes a strike, the pitcher should come back with the identical pitch. In this case, the batter is up there to hit and if he lets a strike go by without offering at it, he is looking for "his pitch," the one which he wants to hit. The fact that he passed up a strike indicates that he does not want to hit that particular pitch.

(8) Nervous characteristics displayed by the batter can serve as a good guide to the right method of dealing with him. The pitcher should wait on a nervous hitter, taking the full time allotted to him by the rules. Conversely, he should work rapidly when facing an especially calm batter or one who waves his bat in pronounced fashion, the idea being to catch this type of hitter before he is set for the pitch.

(9) Occasionally the pitcher will encounter a batter who is a sign-stealer, that is, he sneaks frequent glances at the catcher in an attempt to see the signal. The logical way to handle this man is to quick-pitch him, both to catch him unawares and to discourage this habit in the future.

(10) Shaking off the catcher can prove an effective weapon to a pitcher because it can make a guess-hitter of almost any man he faces. This bit of psychology should not be limited only to those times when the pitcher gets a signal for a delivery that he does not want to throw. On occasion he should shake off the sign for the pitch that he wants to use and continue to shake off each subsequent signal until the catcher returns to the original one.

The brush-back pitch

Brushing the hitter back from the plate can be classed under the psychological phase of pitching. A hurler must occasionally throw close to the batter in order to be successful. If he does nothing but keep the ball out, over the plate, he is merely inviting his opponents to dig in and swing from the heels.

While intimidation is a motivating factor in using the brush-back pitch, its real purpose is to keep the hitter off balance and to prevent him from taking a toe hold and a full swing, safe in the knowledge that every pitch will be over the middle of the plate. Needless to say, a pitcher who tends to wildness has no need to resort to these tactics and should not do so.

When the batter digs in at the plate, setting himself to step in to the ball and hit it out of sight, it might be a good idea to brush him back. The best time to do this is with two strikes and no balls, when a waste-pitch is in order. It must be emphasized, and most emphatically, that a pitcher should NEVER throw at the batter with the intention of hitting him.

The term, "brush him back," means that at certain times when the hitter digs in, looking for a ball to hit, a waste-pitch can be thrown high and tight, or under his chin, since this is a very difficult one to hit solidly. It will also serve to "keep him loose" and make him less anxious to take a toe hold.

In professional baseball, umpires are empowered to eject from the game any pitcher who, in their judgment, throws at a batter intentionally. The umpires can recommend a fine and suspension for him. A baseball hurled at great speed can be a deadly weapon and, emphatically, no pitcher should, under any circumstances, throw at a batter with intent to hit him.

When the brush-back is used on a good hitter he may, quite possibly, become both angry and overanxious. In this case he will generally be vulnerable to a change-of-pace. Whatever pitch is used, the ball should be kept away from him since he will now stand back from the plate at least slightly.

PACE AND PITCHING

The importance of pacing oneself in order to conserve strength and save something extra for the tight spots has been stressed, and rightly so. Its value in coping with the batter also makes its mastery imperative.

Varying the speeds of his pitches is the most effective way for a pitcher to keep the batter off balance and upset his timing. Since the majority of pitches are fast balls, they will be considered as the normal speed and deviations will refer primarily to slower pitches, or the change-of-pace. The change-up, sometimes described by the term, "taking something off the ball," can be a pitcher's best weapon if properly used.

Much mention has already been made of the change-of-pace. However, a few additional ideas can give it the refinement needed to make it really effective:

(1) It is rarely good practice to change up on a late swinger, whether he is merely a man whose reflexes are slow or one with exceptionally good wrists who can wait longer on a pitch and still get around on the ball.

134

(2) Another type of hitter who is rarely bothered by a change-of-pace is the nonstrider who is usually well-planted, with a wide stance. This man is not a lunger and he generally maintains good balance at the plate; consequently a change is merely a slow pitch to him and he will be ready for it. This does not mean, however, that every pitch to him should be thrown as hard as possible—variety is still an effective tool—but it means that he is less likely to be caught off balance by a change-of-pace.

(3) It is seldom good practice to change up with two strikes on the hitter. This is a spot in which the pitcher has his opponent at a disadvantage and he should call on his best stuff to get the out. An exception to this is the case in which a batter has fouled off several fast balls and is geared to that speed.

(4) A weak hitter should not be thrown a change-of-pace. The fact that this man usually likes slow and high pitches and that his timing is inconsistent are closely related. He is a poor batsman because of his inability to hit the fast ball and curve, the pitches he most often sees in a game. A slow pitch will seem like batting practice to him.

This last point is important because it pertains directly to one of the cardinal rules of good pitching: a pitcher should never fool around or "get cute" with a weak hitter. A poor batsman is an out, and since achieving that is the main objective of the pitcher, he should waste no time on this man but should go to work on him and get the out just as quickly as possible.

OPERATING SPEED. The pace and changes therein used by a pitcher also refer to his operating speed. This, too, can be used to upset the batter's timing. Varying the interval between pitches, hesitating momentarily at some point in the motion, adding an extra body-twist, and speeding the delivery are all methods which can be employed to attain this purpose.

The "no wind-up" technique is closely related to this. This pitching style was brought into great prominence by Don Larsen's performance in the 1956 World Series. As originally conceived, its principal aim was to prevent enemy coaches from "reading" Larsen's pitches. It not only accomplished this, it furnished him with two extra benefits: it improved his control by eliminating purely extraneous movements that hindered his natural delivery; and it gave him an effective weapon in upsetting the batter's timing, because pitching without a wind-up means that the man at the plate can never relax but must keep himself in constant readiness for the pitch. Psychology is also involved because the need to remain constantly alert tends to keep the batter on edge and builds tension within him.

Setting up the hitter

In formulating his operating method and sequence of pitches a hurler should understand fully two general principles upon which the majority of outstanding mound artists base their approach to the art of setting up the hitter.

First, there is the effect which changes of speed have on a batter when they are properly applied and catch him off balance. If he is expecting a slow pitch or curve ball, a fast ball will either get by him completely or cause him to swing late and hit the ball without full power behind his swing. When he is set for a fast pitch, a change-of-pace will cause him to place his weight on his front foot too soon, making him hit the ball with an "arm swing" rather than with the weight of his entire body behind the blow. In either case, no great reliance is placed on his missing the ball completely; the basic principle is to nullify the power of his swing by upsetting his timing.

Secondly, there is the reasoning behind the definition of the strike zone, which includes all of that space over the 17-inch-wide plate between the batter's knees and his shoulders when he assumes his normal stance. It was drawn up to embrace that area in which the batter has the greatest likelihood of hitting the ball. Theoretically, the closer to the center of that area a pitch is, the greater will be the batter's chances of hitting it. It follows that if a pitcher can induce a man to swing at balls outside of the strike zone, his possibilities of getting an out are greatly enhanced.

Basing his approach to the job on these well-founded theories, a pitcher should endeavor to set up the hitter by combining pace and control in knowledgeable fashion.

Because the various segments of this section dealing with working on the batter have a strong tendency to overlap and because many of the salient points pertaining thereto are difficult to categorize, this presentation may lack rigid organization and categorization. Yet, in the over-all aspect, all of the really important points have been covered and many ideas on tactics have been advanced. In an effort to provide tactical examples designed to serve as a guide to setting up the hitter and to complete the coverage of the subject matter of this section, several additional tricks of the trade are included below.

(1) Close attention should be paid to where the batter stands, how he stands, how he holds his bat, how he strides, and his attitude at the plate. These things can help in developing effective strategy in both pitch-to-pitch and over-all aspects.

(2) The pitcher should move the ball around on the batter. When done from one pitch to the next this will keep the hitter from setting himself

for a ball in one location. When done after delivering several pitches to one section of the strike zone, it will find him set up for a pitch to another spot.

(3) If a batter likes a certain pitch he will more than likely bite at bad balls in his strong zone. For instance, a man who is a decided high-ball hitter is usually so anxious to get his favorite pitch that he will go for a bad ball in that general area. A shoulder-high fast ball will probably induce him to swing and will prove a very difficult pitch to hit solidly. The same thing applies to hitters who have other definite strong zones, whether they be low-ball hitters or hitters who like an inside or outside pitch.

(4) A bad ball in the strong zone of a batter has the added advantage of setting him up for a pitch to his weakness. If he takes the intentional bad one for a ball, the next one should be delivered to his weak spot.

(5) If the pitcher goes to a 3-2 count using only one pitch, he should resort to another delivery for the pay-off pitch. The element of surprise in the switch will often fool the batter.

(6) If he goes to a 2-2 count with one pitch he can also try this change in deliveries. Should that one be a ball, he should come right back with the same pitch as the last one. The batter will expect him to return to his original pitch if the sudden switch goes astray and thus often will be badly fooled.

(7) Many times, even a good curve ball hitter will miss the first curve he sees after being fed only pitches other than the curve. This pertains primarily to the late innings after this particular batter has received one type of treatment in several trips to the plate. It also applies, although not quite so strongly, to the good fast ball hitter and the first swift one he sees.

(8) The change-up is most effective when the batter is maneuvered into setting himself for a fast pitch. It can also be used with good results when over-anxiousness on his part is detected or anticipated. A logical time for this is when the pitcher is behind in the count. Another example of this is a first-pitch change-up to a good hitter when runners are in scoring position. In this situation a good hitter is at the plate with one primary purpose—to score the runners—and he may be over-anxious on the first ball pitched to him.

(9) An old pitching adage is, "When in doubt—curve him." In other words, if a hitter poses a particular problem and the pitcher has difficulty in deciding exactly how to operate on him on a particular pitch, relying on the curve ball is probably the safest procedure.

Because of the fact that most batters have more trouble with the curve than with the fast ball and since a breaking ball is generally more difficult to meet squarely, this seems like logical advice.

(10) A bad ball hitter presents a peculiar problem in that a waste-pitch or calculated bad ball has little effect on him. For that reason, the pitcher should try to get every ball into the strike zone—with good stuff on it. Changing speeds and moving the ball around should be done within the confines of the strike zone. His unpredictability is what makes this man troublesome. Fortunately, bad ball hitters are few and far between.

(11) Most ballplayers are fast ball hitters. It is ability to hit the curve ball that generally differentiates good batsmen from mediocre ones. Consequently, pitching sequence is of paramount importance in dealing with them. Fast ball, curve ball, slider, change—whatever the delivery, a good hitter must be properly set up for it if real effectiveness is to be achieved.

(12) An excellent example of how a smart pitcher avails himself of every opportunity to set up the hitter was provided by Clem Labine of Brooklyn in a game against the New York Giants early in the 1957 season. Labine was called in to the game as a relief pitcher with men on base and a 2-2 count on the batter, Andre Rodgers, the Giants' rookie short-stop. With Rodgers watching closely as he took his eight warm-up throws, Labine threw eight fast balls. Then, upon resumption of play, Labine came in with a curve ball—right over the middle of the plate. Rodgers was completely unprepared for the curve and took it for a called third strike.

Any or all of the above suggestions can be applied with necessary alterations and embellishments according to any pitcher's particular needs. They should help make him a much more successful operator on the mound. If he remembers and puts into practice only the more basic fundamentals outlined in this section—that every pitch should have a purpose, that his primary aim should be to get the ball over the plate (preferably low) with good stuff on it, and that he should save a little extra for the tight spots—a pitcher will be able to perform with far greater effectiveness and should win more than his share of games.

TYPES OF HITTERS

In the last section consideration was given to pitching strategy in a general sense and as it applied to all hitters as a group. The suggestions listed above are good practices to be followed under any circumstance, regardless of the hitter.

There are certain mannerisms and characteristics shown by some hitters which are fairly reliable indications as to their potentialities and possible weaknesses at the plate. A number of these peculiarities are discussed here but, needless to say, they are not guaranteed to be 100% accurate. They do, nevertheless, apply to the large majority of hitters who fall into these various classifications.

First of all, it must be recognized that a really good hitter cannot be categorized easily and that he is going to get his share of hits regularly, no matter how he is pitched. Applying the general rules already mentioned or, in other words, using good common sense from a pitching standpoint, is the best method to follow against a really good hitter. Fortunately, the really outstanding hitters constitute only a small minority of those who will be faced in the course of a game or, for that matter, a full season.

Following is a brief description of, and operational guide to, specific types of hitters:

(1) A man who carries his bat particularly high is usually a low ball hitter. His swing is started by a downward movement of the bat and it is usually easier for him to continue the motion which he has already begun and meet a low ball than it is for him to check the downward motion of the bat and begin his forward swing in a separate motion.

By the same token, a man who carries his bat particularly low is usually a high ball hitter.

(2) A batter who stands away from the plate is usually an opposite-field hitter. He strides toward the plate to meet the ball and, following the line of motion established by his stride, he should drive the ball toward the opposite field.

This type of hitter stands away from the plate because he likes to hit an outside pitch. Since he has an exaggerated stride into the ball it would seem that an inside pitch will give him trouble, although a wide curve ball or a fast ball on the outside corner might elude the sweep of his bat.

This category also covers any right-hand batter who attempts to hit behind the runner on a hit-and-run play. If the pitcher suspects the hit-and-run, he should pitch a right-hand batter in-on-the-fists, making it almost impossible for him to push the ball to right field.

(3) An open-stance hitter, as opposed to a man who steps toward the plate, almost invariably likes inside pitches. His very stance, stride, and swing indicate that only the very end of his bat will cover the outside corner of the plate and that he is a pull hitter whose power will be greatest on an inside pitch. The ball should be kept away from an open-stance hitter.

(4) A batter who takes a long stride is usually a low ball hitter and will have more trouble with a high pitch because his long stride lowers the center of his body weight and means that a high strike will be a bad ball for him to hit.

Conversely, a short strider generally hits high pitching well and should be pitched low.

The overstrider fits in here, too. He is a quick, as well as long, strider and will have difficulty timing the ball if the pitcher changes speeds on him.

(5) A batter who drops his rear shoulder is an uppercutter with a golf-type swing and is a good low ball hitter. He should be pitched high and tight. This will give him trouble since he is swinging up at a ball which is already high.

(6) A man who crouches usually does so for a good reason. He likes low pitching and wants the pitcher to bring the ball down to him. It follows that he should be pitched high.

(7) Some batters have a tendency to lunge at the ball. Thus, they commit themselves too soon and a change-of-pace will catch them off balance. A high, tight fast ball will also give this type of hitter trouble because his stride is a long one and the ball, when pitched high, will be above his strike zone after his stride has been completed.

(8) The batter who has a hitch in his swing must time the hitch as well as the swing. Changing speeds will cause him trouble. Pitching him tight and fast is, however, probably the most effective method (particularly when he is set up for it with a low change-of-pace) since he will have difficulty getting around on the ball.

(9) The nervous, jittery type of hitter is very eager to hit the ball and get his job over with. The pitcher should take his time and wait on this man—he will become overanxious and lose some of his hitting ability.

(10) The batter who turns his head when taking his cut is usually weak on curve ball pitching since he does not follow the ball well. The turn of the head also pulls his front shoulder away from the plate. Consequently this man will have trouble hitting an outside pitch.

(11) The "bucket-hitter" (one who steps away from the plate) will have trouble with outside pitches and curve balls breaking away from him unless he compensates for his foot-in-the-bucket stride by moving the upper part of his body into the pitch. If he does this he can occasionally be pitched tight.

(12) The sweep-hitter is one who brings his bat through on the swing with a sweeping motion of his arms and does not break his wrists properly, if at all. He is invariably weak on inside fast balls, especially high ones.

(13) A "guess-hitter" is one who continually tries to anticipate what pitch is coming. He usually looks for the fast ball. Quite obviously, the way to fool him is to give him a pitch which he is not expecting. It is to this man, in particular, that a pitcher can put into practice some of the strategy previously discussed—such as a curve or change-of-pace when

behind in the count, or a fast ball when the batter is "in the hole" and likely to be expecting a curve. Mixing up his deliveries in general is a good method for a pitcher to follow in dealing with a guess-hitter since this very characteristic all but eliminates the possibility of using a set pattern of pitching against him.

(14) *General Categories:* While all hitters do not fall into one of the above-mentioned groupings, they definitely can all be categorized under one of several more general headings—pull, straightaway, or opposite-field hitters.

The pull hitter is usually a free-swinger who takes a good cut at the ball. He is more apt than other hitters to strike out, but is also more likely to hit the long ball.

The straightaway hitter sprays his hits to all fields, hitting the ball where it is pitched. That is, he will hit an outside pitch to the opposite field, will pull an inside pitch, and will hit a pitch directly over the plate to center field. He usually has good control of the bat.

The opposite-field hitter waits on the ball a little longer than do the other types and is generally a "slice-hitter" who merely pokes at the ball rather than taking a full cut. He is the toughest man to strike out, but the least likely to hit for distance.

Close observation by both the pitcher and catcher, in batting practice as well as during the game, will help them to categorize the hitters and compile a guide for pitching to them as they come to the plate during the ball game.

For general purposes, low-ball pitching is still the most effective. The lively baseball in use today and the short fences which are found in most enclosed parks make this a particularly apt principle because a low ball is relatively difficult to hit for distance.

A PITCHING CHECK-LIST

In order to help a pitcher master the various mechanical moves which pertain to good pitching and to improve his over-all performance thereby, the following check-list is offered. In rating himself, he should consult with his catcher and coach, and should work hard to perfect each phase of the pitching game in which he is deficient. When he checks out with a passing grade on each of these items, he will be well on his way to becoming a finished performer on the mound.

1. Condition—Is he in shape to make the most of his natural ability? To bear down with something extra in the clutch? To go nine innings at full speed?
2. Grip—Is he choking the ball? Does he telegraph his pitches by the grip?

141

3. Stance—Is it correct in accordance with the rules? Is it conducive to maximum stuff and good control?

4. Hiding the Ball—Does he hide the ball from the batter and cover it properly to prevent detection by the coaches?

5. Eyes on Target—Does he sight his target properly and keep his eyes glued to it throughout his entire motion?

6. The Push-off—Is it powerful enough to get his full weight into the pitch?

7. Stride—Is it free from the serious defect of throwing across the body? Of landing on the heel? Of being too long?

8. Follow-through—Is it complete, with fully bent waist and squared-away finish?

9. Spin—Is proper backspin being imparted to the fast ball and maximum rotation to the curve?

10. Control—Can he throw seven out of ten pitches for strikes with each of his deliveries? Can he consistently get the ball close to where he wants it?

11. Curve—Is it effective when used and can it be thrown with control and confidence on any ball-and-strike count?

12. Change-of-Pace—Is it similar in appearance to the fast ball? Is it neither too fast nor too slow? Can it be controlled?

13. Holding the Runner—Has he developed a good head-move? Does he prevent runners from getting a big jump on the ball?

14. Pick-off—Has he developed a deceptive move to first? Can he make the pick-off play at second?

15. Fielding—Does he protect his position adequately against ground balls? Does he perform well his allied duties such as backing up bases, covering first, and starting the double play?

16. Bunts—Does he get off the mound quickly, handle the ball cleanly, and make the various plays properly?

GENERAL DEFENSE

Defensively a ballplayer must think of himself as part of a unit, and his moves must be considered in relation to what each of his eight teammates is doing. Thus, team defense is a matter of coordinating the individual skills of nine different players.

Good hands, a strong arm, and speed of foot are important assets in the fielding skill of any player. Yet, many men have overcome the lack of one of these attributes and have become sound defensive players.

Hustle, the ability to anticipate a play, knowing where to throw the ball and getting rid of it quickly, and the practice of consistently sound habits are qualities which, if developed, will turn a mediocre natural ballplayer into a valuable defensive performer.

GENERAL RULES

Each defensive player should give careful consideration, on every pitch, to the game situation and the ability of the batter. His positioning and subsequent actions will be dictated by these factors.

Defensive alignment of the team as a whole should be decided upon by the coach. The individual player can adapt certain principles which will enable him to be fully prepared for almost any play.

(1) Every player should figure that the next ball will be hit to him and should know what to do with the ball when he gets it.

(2) Baseball is a team game—players should help each other at all times. All should be aware of what the others will be doing on every play.

(3) There should be a good reason for every throw. The more throws, the more chance a base runner has to advance.

(4) Each player should have a mental plan of action in case of an error.

(5) Defensive players should shift position according to the game situation so that they will have the best possible chance to get to the ball and/or make the proper play. The pitch being thrown is another indicator—the slower the pitch, the greater the chance of its being pulled. These shifts should be done subtly so that the pitch is not tipped.

(6) Any time a fly ball goes into the air it should be called for—in loud, clear tones—by the man who intends to take it. Other nearby players should call the name of the man who is to make the play.

(7) On a high fly in the sun, the fielder should glance toward the ground once he has the ball located, then look back at the ball. He should shield his eyes with his glove, even when wearing sun glasses.

Playing a Fly-ball (eyes shaded by glove)

Catching the Ball

(8) Whenever possible, two hands should be used to catch the ball. A ball below the waist should be caught with the little fingers together; above the waist, with the thumbs together.

(9) To play a ball directly in front of him, a fielder can start on either foot. If the ball is to the right and in front of him he should use a cross-over step with his left foot; if it is to the left and in front of him, his start should be a cross-over step with the right foot.

(10) To play a ball behind him and to his right, the fielder should start with his right foot; on one behind him to the left, he should start with his left foot.

(11) A defensive player should always play the ball, not let it play him. Whenever feasible, he should make an attempt to move in on it.

Starting for the Ball (front, right)

Starting for the Ball (front, left)

INFIELD PLAY

A team is rarely stronger than its infield. Whereas individual skills should be perfected, it is coordinated effort and team play that are the real essentials to an infield as a whole. Nevertheless, the improvement of the mechanics of his game not only helps the player individually; when accomplished through sound practices, it also contributes to cohesive team play by making the work of every player predictably uniform and doubly effective.

The ready position

The objective of the initial stance is to assure a quick start in any direction. An infielder should assume a position with his feet comfortably spread; his shoulders, knees, and hips relaxed; and breathing deeply until the pitcher is ready. He then should become alert, his knees bent, weight forward on his toes in a modified crouch, his arms between his knees and slightly bent (the hands-on-knees stance can push the spikes into the ground). In order to get the best possible jump on the ball he should keep his eyes on the batter rather than the pitcher.

Defensive Set Position

Fielding a Ground Ball to the Right (Dick Groat)

The fielding position

As the ball nears him, an infielder should be bent at the waist and knees; his feet should be staggered and spread, with his right foot at a slight angle outward for balance; and his weight should be forward. The wrists should always be loose and flexible with the face of the glove and bare palm toward the ball. For a ground ball, the glove should be flat on the ground and in front of the left foot. An infielder should keep his head down on a grounder—when lifted it pulls the entire body up—and try to follow the ball right into his glove with his eyes.

When an infielder plays the ball in front of him it will be easier to handle and, even more important, easier to recover if fumbled—as well as less likely to roll through him.

If possible, an infielder should be in correct throwing position before the ball arrives. When going far to either side, needless to say, he cannot pay close attention to the position of his feet and concentrate fully on getting to the ball. Even then, he should try to set himself for the throw before the ball hits his glove—every split-second is important in infield play—by coming to a stop in throwing position. This is done through applying the brakes by sliding on the inside of the foot nearest

Fielding a Ground Ball to the Left (Dick Groat)

the ball. After "braking" to the right, he should perform a hop-step action for the throw.

Playing the ball

Catching the ball and throwing it should be combined in one continuous motion. In order to achieve this, one's glove should give with the impact and circle toward the throwing side. As the arms start upward the throwing hand should be removing the ball from the glove. At the same time (as ball hits glove), the right foot should move forward in a short step.

Timing is of the utmost importance in playing the ball, as opposed to charging it blindly. Timing consists of perfect balance while moving and can be defined as fielding the ball at the top of its hop, with one's weight forward. Use of a rubber ball in practice helps develop this knack.

A slow-hit ball should be fielded with two hands. The throw should be made as the ball is fielded and the infielder begins to straighten up; the body continues on in the direction of his approach to the ball. A slow roller inevitably involves a close play, thus any move that wastes time should be eliminated.

Getting the out

The throw should go to a spot which will best enable its receiver to handle it and make the play. In general, the throw for a force play should be above the belt; for a tag, below the belt.

In order to make the ball easy to follow, an infielder should pull his glove away from it when making a throw, especially a short one. On a long throw the fingers should be spread to reduce the curve of the ball.

An infielder should not hesitate in throwing a man out at first. He should "fire the ball"—in relaxed, unhurried fashion. This makes for an easy out and is important for two reasons—

(1) Whenever a defensive player takes a step to complete a play, a base runner is taking a step toward his objective.
(2) The more quickly the ball arrives, the greater will be the chances of recovering a fumble in time to retire the runner.

Fly balls

The man who will take a fly ball should call for it in unmistakable tones and should be guided by the other infielders. If two men can handle the ball, the one who can take it while coming in on it is the one who should make the catch. This is especially so on a fly that can be caught by either an infielder or outfielder. The outfielder should always call for it since he is coming in on the ball, has the play in front of him, and is in good position to make a throw. This rule also applies to any fly ball near the mound. The pitcher should never take a high fly in fair territory.

Fly balls or relays handled by an infielder in outfield territory should be run into the infield—not thrown, unless the ball is specifically called for by another player.

It is extremely important that all players, especially infielders, realize that a fly ball to the infield will always drift away from home plate.

Tagging the runner

In taking the throw, an infielder should straddle the bag. This insures the runner's sliding into the ball instead of into the defensive player's feet. When the ball is placed between the runner and the bag he will, in effect, tag himself. An experienced player can hold the ball cocked to one side and time his "sweep."

148

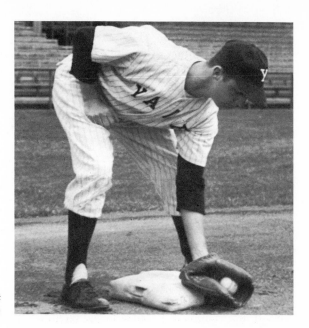

Position for the Tag (let the runner tag himself)

The ball should be held in the gloved hand, which affords greater protection, and it should be pulled away from the runner as the tag is made, thereby reducing the danger of losing the ball from the force of the base runner's slide. When the glove is folded a kick will drive the ball into the pocket. The sweep of the ball as the tag is made will also pull the body away from the runner.

When the throw is wild, the infielder should try to get the ball at the expense of losing the runner.

Backing up the play

One of the infielders should back up every throw to another, the second baseman moving toward first to do so on a throw to that base from the catcher, the shortstop or second baseman backing up the play at second depending on who covers the bag, and the shortstop backing up throws from the catcher to third base.

Defensive alignment

Correct infield depth depends entirely on the game situation. A tight infield should be played only when a run cannot be given—in other words, if the man on third is the tying or winning run, late in the game. Otherwise, it is best to play at normal depth and take a chance on the batter since a normal .200 hitter becomes a .600 hitter with the infield drawn in.

149

Several rules-of-thumb for infield positioning can be adhered to with little deviation—and to good effect.

(1) Play deep and give up a run early in the game or when more than two runs ahead.
(2) With men on first and third and less than two out, play for two—unless the man on third is the winning run.
(3) A tight infield is less risky with one out than with no outs since there is less chance of a big inning should the batter hit safely.
(4) Play at normal depth with men on second and third (unless the man at third is the winning run) since only one run will score when the ball is hit to the infield.
(5) Cut off the tying run at the plate unless a single will put the winning run in scoring position.

Tactics

An infielder should occasionally be a "groundskeeper," smoothing the ground and removing pebbles in his territory. This can prevent the bad bounce that may cost his team an out, or possibly even a run.

This "tending" also applies to the bases. First and third should be nudged toward the infield after every play, giving the batter slightly less fair territory at which to shoot. Second base should be as far toward left field as it will go. The extra inch or so that a runner must slide may be the one that saves an out.

The infielders should make sure that a runner touches every base. If he does not do so, a defensive player should call for the ball and touch the base. The omission must be called to the umpire's attention, since this is an appeal play.

In shifting with the pitch, infielders should avoid obvious moves that will tip off the pitch to the batter. An effective way of using advance knowledge of the pitch for getting a jump on the ball is merely to lean to the appropriate side. Placing one's weight on the right foot for a curve ball to a right-hand hitter, for example, will mean a difference of a step in getting to the spot where the ball is most likely to be hit, yet will in no way telegraph the pitch to the batter.

A return signal should be given by the infielder involved in a pick-off play, if the catcher has called for a pitch-out. This avoids confusion and assures the catcher that someone will be in position to receive his throw.

With rare exceptions, an infielder should not make a long throw for the out when a short one will do it. The safer and surer out is the one that should be played—especially with two outs.

When an infielder takes a ground ball with a man on third he should "look him back" (drive him back to the base with a quick glance before throwing). This also applies to a runner on second base when a ball is hit to the left side of the infield.

A good rule for all ballplayers to follow is "Keep the winning run as far from home as possible."

SPECIAL DEFENSIVE PLAYS

Every player should make himself a part of every play. Even if he does not actually handle the ball, he performs a vital function for his team, when he assumes a back-up, cut-off, or relay position, one of which might well be needed if execution is not perfect on the part of his teammates.

Several specific defensive plays have been perfected over the years and have proven to be the most effective methods of combatting the offensive moves of the opposing team. They are used with only occasional slight variations by professional teams and operate on the principle that a well-conceived team maneuver is far more effective than loosely coordinated individual efforts in keeping the other team from gaining any unwarranted advantage.

The cut-off

This series of alignments has two purposes—to provide a target for the throw from the outfield; and to allow the interception of a throw that will not get the lead runner but may cut down or check the advance of another runner.

The Cut-off at Third

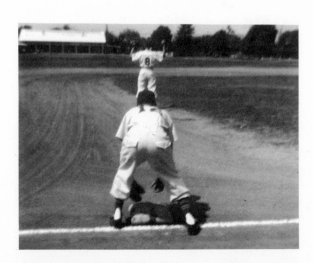

A long hit calls for an infielder to go to the outfield to serve as relay man. Since *the second throw should be the short one,* the relay man (almost always the second baseman or shortstop) should not go too far from the infield.

The use of the voice is very important in the cut-off play. All along the line, from the outfield to the final destination of the ball, instructions should be shouted to any player who throws or handles the ball. The man at the end of the line calls the play as far as the cut-off is concerned, shouting "cut" or "let it go" as the situation warrants. Both relay and cut-off men should wave their arms to give a better target.

Hints which will help the effectiveness of the cut-off man are—

(1) Catch the ball on your throwing side.

(2) Fake a catch when letting the ball go through.

(3) If no call has been made and the runner passes you before the ball arrives—the run should be conceded and the throw cut off.

(4) Rush forward to intercept a wide or late throw.

Cut-off situations

1. Single, no one on base; or fly on which throw goes to second: The shortstop covers, the second baseman backs him up on a ball to left field; positions are reversed on a ball to right field; when the ball goes to center field, the man nearest the base covers it. This gives the outfielders practice in throwing and, if the ball gets through, the man covering the base can get out there in time to serve as relay man.

2. Single with a man on second; or fly ball to the outfield with a man on third and at least one other base occupied (see diagram top of page 153).

3. Single with a man on first (cover second only on the batter); or fly ball with men on first and second:

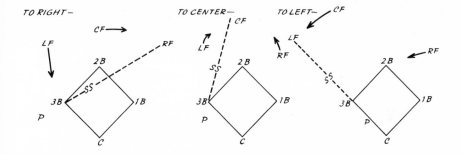

4. Extra base hits: The second baseman is the relay man when the ball goes to right, the shortstop when it goes to left; the man with the stronger arm when it goes to center; and the first baseman when it goes down the right field foul line.

On a sure double, both second baseman and shortstop should go out for the relay, one backing up the other, since the cut-off man does little good here and two relay men prevent an extra base on a fumble.

5. A variation: When the first baseman is the cut-off man, the pitcher might do well to cover first base. Then, when the ball is cut off by the first baseman someone will be in position to take a throw to retire a runner who has taken a wide turn at first. This play involves a calculated risk in so far as an overthrow of home is concerned. Yet, especially in amateur competition, there are very few outfielders with arms powerful enough to propel the ball far past the catcher.

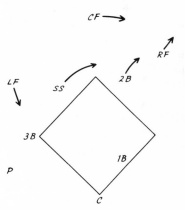

6. General rules:

(a) The *second* throw should be the short one.
(b) The cut-off man's head is the target.
(c) With bases loaded, the throw should go home.
(d) The pitcher's position is in foul territory, backing up the play. He should not serve as cut-off man.

153

The double play

Infield depths:

(a) Deep—normal position; 2B and SS move two steps in for DP setup

(b) Modified—1B and 3B in on grass; SS and 2B at Double Play depth.

DEEP—

SS 2B
3B 1B

MODIFIED—

SS 2B
3B 1B

1. *Man on First:* The first baseman ordinarily holds the runner close to first. The second baseman and shortstop play two steps in; the throw to second should be chest-high and directly over the bag.

The moves involved around second base are discussed at length in the section on the second base combination.

A notable exception to standard procedure comes when the ball is hit to the third baseman by a left-hand batter. In this case, at the amateur level of play, the throw should go to first base since no one will be in position to cover second properly.

2. *Men on First and Second:* The first baseman plays off the bag, the second baseman and shortstop play two steps in.

The double play with men on first and second should be made second-to-first, except in the following instances:

When the ball is hit in the hole, far to the shortstop's right—the throw goes to third.

When a ball is hit to the third baseman over the bag—he should step on third, then throw to first.

When a slow roller is hit to the pitcher's right—he should make the play at third base.

When a force play is made at second but the batter will definitely be safe—then a throw to third might catch the runner rounding that base.

3. *Men on First and Third:* The infield should be in normal double play positions with the first baseman holding the runner close to the base. The attempt to play for two should be made by way of second unless the runner on third represents the tying or winning run. If the play is made on the runner going home, the third baseman should follow him in to-

154

ward the plate for a quick put-out in case he attempts to get caught in a run-down and delay the out until the other two runners reach second and third.

4. *Bases Loaded:* If the run at third is an important one, a tight infield should be played and an attempt made to cut off the run at the plate. Otherwise, a modified infield is employed. The second baseman and shortstop then make the play by way of second. The double play goes home-then-first on a ball hit to the pitcher, first baseman, or third baseman. An exception to the latter is the case in which a ball is hit directly over either first base or third base. In these instances the bag should be touched and the throw then made to home plate; it must be remembered that the force is off after the bag is touched and the runner must be tagged at home.

The sacrifice

The most effective weapons in combatting the sacrifice are the alertness of the infielders and anticipation by the pitcher and catcher.

Only rarely will the signal for this play be picked up. However, with the bunt in order, when the runner fails to look alternately at the third base coach and the batter, it is probable that a signal has been given.

Pitcher-catcher strategy is covered in detail in other sections.

Man on First—The pitcher moves forward; the first and third basemen charge the plate, returning to their respective bases if they do not field the ball. The second baseman covers first and the shortstop covers second. The catcher pursues the ball and covers third base if the third baseman fields it.

Men on First and Second—(a) The batter should be allowed to bunt the ball. The pitcher charges the third base line; the third baseman covers the bag; the shortstop fakes the runner back to second and continues in to cover the mound. The second baseman covers first and the first baseman charges the plate. Worked properly, the play will be at third—then possibly to first.

(b) An alternate method, tried experimentally by some professional teams, brings in an outfielder to cover third, while the third baseman plays halfway to the plate. This method, risky at best, should be used only with a weak hitter at bat and the bunt almost certain.

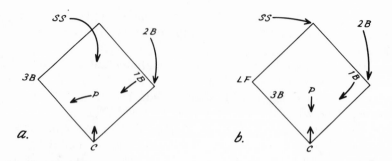

Man on Second—This is likely to be encountered only with a weak bats-man at the plate. Assignments are the same as for the sacrifice with men on first and second. Care must be exercised not to break with the pitch—alertness is the answer. A play at third requires the tagging of the runner.

The squeeze play

The only practical defense against the squeeze play is an unbuntable pitch that will catch the runner trying to score. The key to foiling it is spotting the runner's break for the plate. The pitcher should then throw high and outside to a left-hand batter, at the shoulder of a right hander. When the play becomes apparent the pitcher, first, and third basemen advance toward home plate and the second baseman covers first.

When the squeeze is worked with runners on second and third, and the play for the out must be at first base, the defensive team must be alert for the double squeeze (the man on second base continuing around third and in to score).

The hit-and-run

This play is most effectively thwarted by anticipation of it, followed by a pitch-out that cannot be hit and which should enable the catcher to throw out the runner at second base. Unfortunately, this can be accomplished only occasionally, thus the second baseman and shortstop must decide on their assignments as soon as they suspect a hit-and-run. Since the batter usually tries to hit behind the runner (to right field), the short-stop will cover second base most of the time. (A left-hand batter is the one most likely to try to hit toward left field.) The man who covers second should edge toward the base as the pitcher throws, playing the ball as best he can if it is hit to his position.

This is most likely to occur in a tight game with a good hitter at bat—especially with one out, even more so when the pitcher is behind the batter in the count and must throw a strike.

The steal

There are definite times when a steal should be anticipated: for instance, with no outs or two outs, a fast man on first and a good hitter at bat in a close game; or with one out and a weak hitter at the plate. The defense should be doubly alert for a steal of second in those situations when the count goes to 3-1 or, especially, 3-2. In addition to the role of the pitcher and catcher, the important factor in thwarting a steal of second is the base-covering assignments of the shortstop and second baseman. (See "The Second Base Combination," page 199.)

A steal of third base is relatively rare since the runner is already in scoring position. It should never be tried with two out. Nevertheless, the defense should be prepared for it. The third baseman should move toward his base after the ball passes the batter, the catcher should be in position to throw on every pitch, and, between them, the pitcher, shortstop, and second baseman should hold the runner close to his base since he is unlikely to attempt a steal of third unless he gets a good jump on the pitch.

Above all, the infielders should let the catcher know whenever a runner attempts to steal.

The double steal

The most common double steal comes with runners on first and third. The primary objective of the defense should be to prevent the runner on third from scoring. Its secondary aim is to prevent a steal of second base which will place two runners in scoring position.

The second baseman is the cut-off man, since he can see the runner on third while watching the ball. The shortstop covers second and must always be set for the throw, since the cut-off man may let it go through. An exception to this comes when the batter is a left-hand pull hitter, in which case the shortstop is the cut-off man.

The second baseman goes to the base (to lure the runner at third into starting for home) and continues in to a point about fifteen feet in front of the base. If the runner on third tries to score, the cut-off man intercepts the ball and throws home to catch him.

The pitcher can be used as cut-off man, in which case the throw should be head-high to him. This has a greater element of safety but is less effective in achieving an out.

The first baseman should follow the runner to second to make a quick put-out if a run-down develops since the runner, if he is played, will often pull up and try to delay proceedings in order to allow the man on third to score. By the same token, the third baseman should trail the runner home to make a quick tag if a run-down develops here.

The left fielder should move in to cover third in the event of a run-down, or if the play is at home and the other runner keeps going to third, which he can do with no one covering that base. The center fielder backs up second and the right fielder covers first base.

The double steal with runners on successive bases should be treated like an ordinary steal of the lead base.

The pick-off play

FROM THE CATCHER. This is most effective when a pitch-out is signalled and a play put on with an infielder. When this is done, the infielder involved should sneak behind the runner and go to the base as the pitcher delivers the ball to the batter. A missed swing or bunt should be construed as an automatic pick-off signal.

The throw to first or third should be on the inside of the diamond and, on a missed bunt, the second baseman handles a pick-off throw to first. Second base should be covered according to the batter, the shortstop taking it with a left-hander at the plate, the second baseman with a right-hander.

The outfielders should move into position to back up the throw just as soon as they see that a pick-off is being attempted.

FROM THE PITCHER. The technique of this pick-off play has been thoroughly discussed in previous sections. The throw to first can be made at the pitcher's discretion; a signal play should be used at second base; but an attempt to pick a runner off third base should rarely, if ever, be made.

To repeat: The outfielders should be moving into back-up positions on the throw.

The run-down

When a run-down develops, the baseman at the base from which the play started should return there after he throws the ball. The runner should always be forced back to the base from which he came and it should take not more than two throws to get him.

The man with the ball should hold it high, in plain view, and should use a modified overhand or sidearm throw to lessen the danger of hitting the runner with the ball. The man receiving the throw should move slightly to the side so that there will be no bodily contact with the runner as the tag is applied, with possible loss of the ball resulting therefrom. Furthermore, it should be kept in mind that the runner is entitled to the base line as long as the fielder does not have possession of the ball.

The ball should not be thrown until the runner commits himself and then only when he is slightly more than half-way to the man who will get the ball. This will keep him from ducking safely back past the thrower. On the other hand, the throw should not be delayed so long the runner will be past the infielder receiving the ball before it reaches him.

When a runner is hung up (caught between bases), the man with the ball should rush directly at him and force him to commit himself. Once the runner makes his move it is time to head him off with a throw.

The pitcher is strictly a back-up man on this play and should stay out of it unless he is needed to retrieve an overthrow, or to take the ball for a last-second tag in case the runner gets by one of the infielders and is close to the base.

Two aids to effective run-down procedure—

(1) A fake throw can make the runner commit himself.
(2) With two men on base, run the first one down fast and keep an eye on the lead runner if he is the other one.

THE CATCHER

His ability as a handler of pitchers, receiver, and field general far overshadow any other factors in measuring the value of a catcher to his ball club. A good man at this position will have an alert mind, keen powers of observation, and the ability to make split-second decisions, even as a play is in progress. The fact that he participates on every pitch and is the one player with the entire field in front of him means that he should be able to "take charge" and direct the play of his team.

Not only his pitchers, but every one of his teammates should be able to rely on the catcher as the really solid man on the ball club.

PREPARING FOR THE PITCH

Signals

The catcher's initial position is a squat, from which he surveys the situation and gives his signal to the pitcher.

Signals should be given *well back in the crotch* and should be *covered from the third base side with the glove*. The fingers should be spread and "squared" with the pitcher. Two basic ideas guide the philosophy behind these measures.

(1) It is of the utmost importance that the catcher know just what his pitcher is throwing. This is not as ridiculous as it sounds, since a missed signal can result in a passed ball and possibly even a broken finger for the catcher. Obviously then, the pitcher must know, see, and understand the set of signals being used.

(2) Signs must be hidden from the opposition. With the batter concentrating on the pitcher, it is the coaches who must be guarded against. As a precautionary move the first and third basemen should report the fact whenever either can see the signal.

Attention should also be paid to the arm and elbow, which can give away signals unless held in the same position every time a sign is flashed. Natural movements and a fair degree of precaution can protect even the simplest set of signals from detection.

Signals themselves can be very simple—such as one finger for the fast ball, two for the curve, three for the change, combinations for the off-pitches (more than three fingers may be misread)—just so they are not picked up by the opposition. When a runner is on second base they can, of course, easily be seen; here a more complicated set, or a switch-signal, should be used to confuse the runner and keep him from flashing the sign to the batter. To give a very simple illustration of a switch-signal—if the catcher touches his right knee with his right hand before giving his sign, the curve should be thrown when the fast ball is signalled for, and vice versa; if the knee is not touched, the signal is as given. There are, needless to say, many sets of signals and switches which can be used. It is when the catcher suspects that they are being stolen that a change is dictated.

Stance

The catcher should come up from his squat rapidly, be ready for the pitch, and give a stationary target. Remaining in a squat or resting on one knee is bad practice simply because a raised position presents a better target as well as making for easier shifting and quicker starts.

160

The stance should be balanced and comfortable with the weight forward, right foot back slightly, knees flexed, and rump high for mobility (the hips should be above the knees). The catcher's correct position is squarely behind the plate and close enough to the hitter so that his arm, if extended, will touch the batter's shoulder. (There is little cause for worry about the bat, since the hitter strides forward.) Thus, he will be closer to second base (inches count) and to a bunted ball; will find low pitches easier to handle; and *will catch more pitches in the strike zone.*

Catcher's Stance—Normal

Catcher's Stance—Man-on-Base (Bob Oldis)

The same stance should be used for both fast ball and curve so as not to telegraph the pitch to the opposition—the feet should not be shifted until the pitcher is delivering the ball. There is often a tendency to shift one foot to the side or to widen the stance when a curve ball is to be thrown; or to hold the glove flat for the fast ball and facing down for the curve. These tell-tale mannerisms must be eliminated.

With a bunt or steal in order, a more erect position—with rear foot further back—should be assumed. This is a modified sprinter's stance and makes for a quick start. The full-target stance, however, should be retained when the pitcher is wild.

Target

Giving a good target is one of the catcher's most important functions. His target should be prominent and stationary.

The pitcher should concentrate on a fixed object. Thus, the catcher should not move *noticeably* until the ball is being delivered, because the target will probably be some part of his anatomy. He should also make his target a large one, facing the widest part of his glove directly at the pitcher. Or he should stand so that his body will present a wide target, if he knows that the pitcher is sighting on it. Above all, he should make sure that the target being used is in the strike zone.

For a pitcher who is very wild, or exceptionally fast, the catcher should assume a wider stance. In this way he will have less difficulty in handling wild or very fast pitches, while at the same time making a slightly larger target. This in no way violates the idea of tipping off the pitch. It is merely a precautionary measure to cut down the number of wild pitches and passed balls.

RECEIVING THE BALL

Basics

The fingers of the catcher's right hand should be flexed, with thumb resting against index finger, preparatory to receiving the pitch. As ball hits glove, the right hand should be brought over it. Catching the ball with fingers extended or pointing toward the pitcher invites injury.

As for the act of receiving the ball—ideally, every pitch should be caught in the middle of the body. In fact, no ball should be caught by back-handing or reaching for it unless absolutely necessary. This marks one of the chief differences between a good and a bad receiver. The shifting-with-the-pitch that it implies must be practiced diligently until it becomes a well-ingrained habit.

The ball should be *met* with the mitt (not received), with the arms extended to a point where the catcher can see the ball hit his glove. In this way he can help himself in performing his main task.

The main task

The catcher's number-one duty is to *catch every strike in the strike zone*. Thus, in addition to standing close to the batter, he should bring every pitch *toward the belt buckle* as it is caught. Done smoothly, this prevents borderline pitches from being moved out of the strike zone—in effect, letting a strike speak for itself. A hinge-like wrist flick is sufficient without being too flagrant. Using this movement, it is quite natural that a low pitch should be caught from underneath, a high one from above; corner pitches should be brought in toward the center of the plate. The belt-high delivery may be handled from either above or below. Manipulating the knees (slightly bent for a high pitch, more erect on a low one) can also help keep the ball in the strike zone.

At the same time, the catcher should take care not to block the umpire's view of the ball by excessive jumping movements or body-raising. A strike should be called a strike, and the catcher can help his pitcher get his just due in this respect.

Receiving an Outside Pitch

Receiving a High Pitch

Receiving a Wide Pitch

Receiving a Low Pitch

Blocking a Low Pitch

163

Shifting with the pitch

In order to get his body in front of the pitch the catcher should shift his position by stepping in its direction with the foot nearest the ball. Naturally, this has reference only to a bad pitch.

On a wide pitch, the move should be forward as well as to the side, so that there is less chance of a mishandled ball rolling behind the catcher. This is especially so with a runner on base. The forward-lateral move is no problem on an outside pitch, since the batter will not be in the way.

A different move is called for on an inside pitch. With a right-hander at bat a quick step or hop should be used, replacing the left foot with the right, followed by a short, sideward step with the left foot. This will get the catcher in front of the pitch quickly, well-balanced, and in position to throw—if necessary. The reverse is used for a left-handed batter, the right foot being replaced by the left on the first step.

For low pitches a definite forward move should accompany the lateral shift (this shortens the hop) and is made by going down on both knees— left leg first on a pitch to the right side; right leg first on a pitch to the left side. In this way the catcher can move further to the side, making him a greater barrier against a wild pitch. The body should face the ball directly to prevent its being deflected to the side rather than in front of the plate. A high bounce should be blocked with the body, a low bounce with the glove. This helps to make the catcher impregnable when in front of the ball.

After the pitch

From a physical standpoint, the catcher's first move after receiving the pitch should be to take the ball in his bare hand and bring it into throwing position. This should be done on every pitch, then it will come automatically with men on base.

The return throw to the pitcher should be crisp and accurate, at chest level. A good throw will keep the pitcher on his toes. On the other hand, a poor throw, repeated often, may allow a runner to advance and definitely will use up too much of the pitcher's energy.

THROWING

With a man on base the catcher should make doubly sure that he is as close to the batter as possible without interfering with the swing. The few inches saved may mean an out rather than a stolen base.

Getting the ball away

The first move should be to "cock the arm" by bringing the ball up to a point behind the right ear. An across-the-seams grip and overhand throw will create backspin and impart greater "carry" to the ball.

As the pitch is received, the catcher's weight should shift quickly to his right foot, but with good balance maintained. He will then be in position to get off a good throw with only one step. The left foot merely serves to guide the throw, doing so with a stride directly toward the target.

On a pitch to his right, the catcher's right foot should step toward the ball, shifting his weight so that only a slight pivot on the right foot is necessary to make the throw with a single step. For a pitch to his left, he should go back on his right foot as he receives the ball (he has shifted toward it on his left foot) and then forward on the left for the throw.

Catcher's Throw to Second

In order to keep the runner from gaining an extra step and to facilitate easy ball-handling and a quick tag by the infielders, a catcher should keep in mind that—

(1) Where every pitch is caught in the middle of the body, throwing will come more easily.
(2) Only *one step* should be taken in throwing to a base.
(3) The throw should be directly over the bag at knee level.
(4) With a man on base, every pitch should be caught with the intention of throwing the runner out on a steal attempt.

Using the pitch-out

Any premeditated pick-off attempt should involve use of the pitch-out. It should be signalled by the catcher, with a return sign from the infielder who is to take the throw.

A pitch-out should be wide of the plate to prevent interference by the batter with the catcher's view of the play or his throw. In this way the ball can be thrown without obstruction to catch a runner stealing or wandering too far off base, or to break up the hit-and-run.

165

Receiving a Pitchout

For easy handling of the ball plus little wasted motion and lost time in making the throw, the pitch-out should be chest-high as well as away from the batter. With a right-hand batter the catcher should place his left foot behind his right as the ball is delivered. Next is a step to the outside of the plate with the right foot. This prepares him to throw by taking his normal stride forward with his left foot. An exception to this is possible with a man on third when a brushback pitch-out may be used since it may divert the runner's attention.

With a left-hander at bat the pitch-out will be to the catcher's left. As the ball is delivered he should replace left foot with right, step to the side on his left foot, pivot on the right one, and step forward on the left as he throws. To insure that the weight will be behind the throw and moving directly toward the target, the catch should be made with the head to the outside of the ball, i.e., on the right side for a pitch-out to the catcher's right; to the left side for one to his left.

To increase its effectiveness, the pitch-out should be employed intelligently in accordance with the following principles:

(1) The best time for the pitch-out is with two out and the count in the pitcher's favor.

(2) It should not be employed unless the run is important—then the catcher can call for it if he anticipates a steal or hit-and-run or thinks that he can pick off a runner who is taking too big a lead.

(3) A pitcher who is having control trouble cannot afford to waste a pitch, so a pitch-out should not be used at this time.

(4) With a sacrifice in order, a curve ball pitch-out is good strategy, not only as a clue to the batter's intentions but, since he will lean with the pitch as it curves, the runner might be lured into wandering too far off the bag, making himself an inviting target for a pick-off throw. *A missed sacrifice bunt* is a good indication that a pitch-out should be signalled and the runner picked off.

(5) The pitch-out signal should precede finger signs, rendering them meaningless. It should be an "outside" sign, one that the first and third basemen can read. The coach may start the chain with a voice signal. The baseman should end it with a return signal.

The pick-off throw

A random throw to a base should never be made. The catcher should throw only when he sees a definite chance to get the runner and if he is sure that one of his infielders will be moving toward the base to take the throw. This applies even when a pitch-out has been signalled. A throw with little chance to get the runner is a needless one, and risks an advance by the runner if the ball is mishandled.

If the runner has strayed too far from his base, the catcher should not hesitate to throw him out, even if no play has been prearranged. A bluff throw should be used to drive the runner back to his base when no one is in position to take a throw. A realistic fake will keep the runner honest without risking a wild throw.

Should the runner be hung up between bases the catcher should run toward him, ready to throw if he makes a break in either direction. Here the runner would have such a jump toward either base that the catcher should not throw until he has made the runner commit himself.

TO SECOND BASE—This throw should be used by amateur ballplayers only on very rare occasions. Bluffing the throw or running toward the man on base are wiser moves at this level of play.

TO FIRST BASE—To eliminate the danger of obstructing the throw by a left-hand batter this peg should be sidearm and to the right of the batter. When it is hurled sidearm the ball should be started higher to allow for its usual sinking to the right.

With men on first and second, a throw to first should be made only if that runner is a sure-out, since this is an open invitation for the man on second base to advance to third.

TO THIRD BASE—This throw should be on the inside of the diamond so the third baseman can catch the ball in stride and make the tag with little lost motion. With a right-hander at bat the same technique as is used for the "lefty batter throw to first" situation should be employed—and for a similar reason.

A pick-off throw with a man on third should be automatic when the batter swings and misses, since the runner is most likely to be careless at this time. An arrangement for this play should be made with the third baseman and shortstop so that they will expect a throw whenever the situation arises.

The double steal

This play is usually tried with runners on first and third. Since the man on first invariably makes the initial break, the catcher will generally throw toward second base. The object of the defense must be to prevent a run from scoring—and to get an out, either at second base or home plate.

The catcher's throw should be to the base at second. Then it will get that runner if allowed to go through, yet will be easy to intercept if taken by the cut-off man.

The assignments for this maneuver should be prearranged. Occasionally the pitcher is used for this purpose. Naturally, he should be fully informed of his role when involved in the play and a throw to him should be a hard one and head-high, made to look as much as possible like a throw to second.

The entire procedure is discussed in the section on defensive plays. From the catcher's viewpoint it will be more effective if four basic ideas are kept in mind.

(1) The throw should hit the cut-off man in the chest; then, if not intercepted, it will be a good peg to second.

(2) There are only two possible plays by the catcher—the throw to second *always* preceded by a head and shoulder fake toward third; a full-motion bluff toward second and the throw to third.

(3) Exception—if the runner on third is too far off his base, get him; if the other runner has second made easily, forget him.

(4) Ordinarily, the man on third is the catcher's chief concern. If, however, either of the runners represents the winning run, he is definitely the one on whom to make the play.

FIELDING

Grounders and bunts

All batted balls on the ground should be fielded with both hands, even if the ball has stopped rolling. The glove should be placed in front of a rolling ball to stop it and in front of a stationary ball as a safety factor and to facilitate scooping it up.

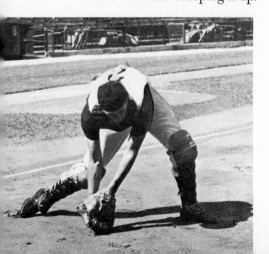

In fielding a batted ball the catcher should try to position himself with his face toward the base at which the play will be made. This keeps the play in front of him and enables him to throw without having to make a blind pivot.

Catcher Fielding a Bunt
(Bob Oldis)

Since he has the entire field in front of him, the catcher should call the play on any bunt or grounder in the home-plate area, directing the throw to the proper base. This is especially so in the case of the pitcher, whose back is to the play.

The catcher's throw to first and third on a ground ball should be on the inside of the diamond—to third, so that the play on the runner will be easier for the third baseman; to first, so as to avoid hitting the runner. In fact, on a ball close to the first base line the catcher should step well into the diamond before throwing to first.

A dropped third strike, on the other hand, should be thrown to the outside of the base when the ball rolls behind the catcher. In this case the first baseman's target should be given in foul territory.

An underhand or sidearm throw (used to save time) is permissible on a play to first or third, but the throw should be overhand on the longer peg to second on which the ball has a tendency to curve or sink if thrown sidearm or underhand.

When the catcher, after fielding the ball, is able to tag the batter out, he should let his infielders know that the force is off and that they must tag the runner if a play is to be made at any base.

On a sacrifice bunt toward third, the catcher should chase the ball and, if the third baseman makes the play, should continue to third and cover the base—but not if the play began with a man on second base, since his responsibility in that case is to cover home. All throws to first base should be backed up by the catcher unless a runner is in scoring position. This, in effect, means following the batter to first on ground balls, at a distance of about forty feet from the base line. When the ball goes through the right side to the outfield, the catcher should cover the bag for a possible pick-off throw from the right fielder after the runner has taken his turn.

A final word of caution for all catchers—never leave home plate unguarded with a runner in scoring position.

Double play by way of home

This play ordinarily arises only with the bases loaded. Almost invariably, it goes home, then to first. In this way the run is cut off and the attempt to complete the double play is made on the batter, who has to recover from his swing and run the full ninety feet to first base, whereas the other runners have started with substantial leads.

In making this play, the catcher should keep his left foot in contact with the plate while awaiting the ball. Then a short step and pivot with the right foot will lead naturally into the throwing stride, which is made with the left foot.

The throw to first should be on the inside of the diamond, away from the batter, who must stay in the three foot lane. With a runner rounding third base and less than two out, a full-motion bluff throw to first should be used before heaving the ball to third to nail that runner.

Tagging the runner

This job is made difficult by its dual nature, wherein the catcher must concentrate on the ball and handle it cleanly, while at the same time setting himself to block and tag the oncoming runner. Fortunately, his equipment affords adequate protection and, by learning certain fundamentals, he can be prepared, in all respects, to perform the task efficiently.

Correct position for receiving the throw finds the catcher to the side of the plate—the third base side on a throw from right field or right center, the first base side (with foot in front of the plate) on a throw from left field or left center, as illustrated in the diagrams.

As he receives the ball, the catcher can either drop to one or both knees and hold the ball in front of the plate where the runner will slide into it, or he can put his left leg in front of the plate and allow the runner to hit his shin guard, making the tag as the man slides into him.

When sufficient experience has been acquired, the catcher may prefer to take all throws on the first base side of the plate. Technique is to expose the plate, square off with the throw, pivot to the left (dropping left foot back while catching the ball)—then the runner cannot elude the tag.

The tag should be made with two hands to lessen the danger of losing the ball as the runner slides in. It is best to hold the ball in the right hand and keep the back of the glove toward the runner. The hands themselves should be close to the ground to prevent a foot from going under the tag; and the ball should be pulled away just as soon as contact has been made with the runner in order to lessen the possibility of losing possession of it.

The catcher may not block the plate unless already in possession of the ball. In fact, an attempt should be made to block the plate only if the play will be close. Wise practice gives the runner a clear view of the

170

plate while remaining in such a position that the man cannot slide straight into home but must hook to reach it. This in no way interferes with the runner, yet it keeps him from having a completely unobstructed path to the plate.

Compliance with the dictates of alert play demands that the catcher follow three basic tactical principles.

(1) Don't reach for the ball too soon if the throw is a good one. Decoy the runner into slowing up by remaining motionless until the ball arrives.
(2) With other men on base, leave your position to intercept a wide throw or bad bounce.
(3) Play the ball, then the runner—you can do nothing until you have that ball in your hands.

Pop-flies

Pop-flies are very difficult to play since they go almost straight up and have tremendous spin, plus a tendency to curve. They are especially tough for the catcher since he must get out from under the bat, locate the ball, and discard his mask before giving chase to it. He should *call for* and take all of those in the home-plate area which cannot be easily handled by the first or third baseman coming in on the ball.

The mask should be whipped off quickly, but not discarded until the ball is sighted. It should be tossed away from the ball so as not to get in the catcher's path. If a long run must be made, the catcher can merely hook the bottom of the mask with his thumb, lift it over his head, and let it slide over his shoulder as he takes off in pursuit of the ball.

When the ball is hit behind him, the catcher, his back to the infield, should get under it so that it looks like it will hit him on the head, then take one step back for the catch. To field a fly hit straight up or in front of home plate, he should still position himself directly under it, but a backward step is not necessary since the natural drift of the ball will be away from him, leaving him in good position for the catch. After the catch, with anyone on base, the ball should be run back to the infield in order to check the runner's advance without the risk involved in a long throw.

The principles behind these methods will be more clearly understood if two factors, based on the laws of physics, are borne in mind.

(1) A pitch thrown on the right side of the plate will be fouled to the catcher's right; one thrown on the left side will be fouled to his left. Thus can the path of the ball be determined just as soon as it leaves the bat.
(2) A pop-fly will always drift toward the infield. The higher the ball is hit, the greater will be the curve.

CATCHING PHILOSOPHY

Morale

The catcher must, in a sense, assume a selfless role since it is the pitcher who should look good—not his receiver. The primary function of the latter is to make the pitcher look good.

The catcher, alone, is in front of the pitcher and is the one to whom the latter will naturally look for help and encouragement. He must be both the pitcher's brains and his eyes. He can see the entire field of play and should pass on anything he sees that will help his battery mate.

The pitcher's confidence should be treated with care. The catcher must guide him over the rough spots as far as both morale and strategy are concerned.

The catcher should adapt himself to the temperament of his pitcher. A significant example of this principle is in the area of working speed. Whether the pitcher is a fast worker or a deliberate one, his preference in tempo should be catered to.

Exceptions to this center on the pitcher's control and the disposition of the batter. A most important aspect of the catcher's influence on his pitcher's working speed is the effect that it has on the latter's control. Slowing the pitcher's pace will often help him regain control. A pause before returning the ball, a few steps toward the mound, straightening the mask and chest protector—these are maneuvers that can slow the tempo of the game and steady a pitcher who is having control trouble.

A conference on the mound (it should always be at that spot) is another effective aid—not only in slowing the tempo and discussing tactics, but in soothing the nerves of a pitcher who finds himself in a tight spot.

As for the hitter and his disposition—if he is nervous and jittery, the catcher should slow his pitcher's working speed. Conversely, for the batter who likes to take his time, the catcher should make his pitcher work fast.

Strategy

Pitching strategy and the most effective ways of coping with the various types of hitters are discussed in detail in the section on pitching. This material should be studied carefully by catchers since they should work in close harmony with their pitchers and, in most cases, call every pitch.

Catching strategy, however, embraces far more than this. Many stratagems of a more general nature, some of them incorporating psychology, are practiced by smart receivers in an attempt to ease the task of the pitcher.

To start with, the catcher should handle the latter part of the pitcher's pre-game warm-up, taking over from the practice catcher when the pitcher is ready to throw at full speed. In this way he will get the feel of the particular pitcher on the particular day and can begin plotting strategy accordingly. He can also begin to exert his influence as a steadying factor, thereby giving his pitcher the little extra confidence that is sometimes necessary to start the game in top form.

There may be a difference between the pitcher's warm-up throws and his pitches from the mound, particularly if, as is so often the case, the warm-up must be taken on flat ground. Whatever the situation, the catcher should discover as soon as possible which pitch is working best on that specific day.

If all the deliveries in a pitcher's repertoire are working properly, the catcher can, of course, call his pitches according to normal operating procedure. If, however, one pitch is working considerably better than the other, that one should be called for when the pitcher is in a tight spot—that is, it is the one the batter should be made to hit. Conversely, if one pitch is not working, the catcher should allow his pitcher to do no more than show it to the batter—it should not be thrown where the batter can hit it solidly.

The catcher should rely heavily on any pitch in which his pitcher has real confidence on a given day. Particularly in the early innings, he should call for the pitch that he thinks the pitcher wants to throw. By setting up the hitter wisely and by making his partner believe in the wisdom of his tactics, the catcher can guide the pitcher tactfully and in a way designed to build confidence in himself—and his catcher.

In considering the tactics to be used on a given batter, the catcher should put himself in the batter's shoes and try to imagine what pitch is anticipated. Then, quite obviously, another one should be called.

There is really no such thing as a set "book" on any hitter. Strategy, while it should be dictated to a great extent by "the book," should be strongly influenced by just what a certain pitcher has on a certain day— as well as any indication which the batter may give as to his intentions on a particular time at bat or pitch.

To state it differently: The catcher cannot always go by "the book"; it is often better to work according to the pitcher's strength rather than the batter's weakness.

A batter will often tip off his intentions by his movements in the batter's box. For instance, he may move closer to the plate when expecting a curve ball or outside pitch; he may "dig in" and appear over-anxious when intending to go for the long ball or when eager to hit the next pitch; or he may move his rear foot away from the plate when he is going for the opposite field. There are several other moves, both with

173

hands and feet, which are made by a great many batters, that can help the catcher anticipate the man's intentions in time to signal for an appropriate pitch.

Although the catcher actually calls the pitches, his battery mate has veto power over those calls. His goal should be to call pitches in the same pattern in which the pitcher is thinking.

Leadership

The catcher is the field general and should direct the play on all batted balls.

His position gives him a full view of the field and allows him to watch all aspects of a play as it develops. He should let all of his teammates know the situation and the play to be made, and if any development dictates a sudden change in tactics, he should make sure that the man (or men) making the play are aware of it.

Another of the catcher's duties in this area is to keep the pitcher informed on the position of base runners while the pitcher is concentrating on the plate.

In short, the complete catcher is, at once, a field general-tactician and psychologist, as well as a hard-working mechanical receiver.

THE FIRST BASEMAN

The first baseman is too often lightly regarded from a defensive standpoint. While it is true that his bat has come to be regarded as more important than his glove, defensive ability on the part of the first baseman will greatly enhance his true value to his team.

The ideal man for this position is tall and rangy and has a good pair of hands. If, in addition, he is agile, alert, and possessed of a strong arm, he is really well-equipped for the job.

It should be understood, however, that regardless of his physical make-up, a first baseman is not stationed at that position merely to serve as a target for the other infielders and to catch their throws. When he has perfected his footwork, acquired the knack of digging low throws out of the dirt, and learned the correct tactical maneuvers, he will be a *ballplayer*—and worthy of his place on the team.

GOOD HANDS

Good hands are, of course, a natural physical attribute. Although awkward or weak ones can be improved in dexterity and strength, it is doubtful if their owner will ever develop into a really good defensive first baseman; hands must be well above average in these qualities at the outset.

The importance of good hands lies in the fact that they are indispensable to maximum effectiveness in catching the many and varied throws that a first baseman is called on to handle in the course of a ball game. They are especially important in pick-ups (a first-sacker should rarely have to step back to receive a low throw) and in ability to field the ball properly when he is endeavoring to use the maximum length of his reach while still keeping his toe on the bag.

"Good hands" is plural. Both should be used to catch the ball whenever possible.

AGILITY

Agility at this position means the ability to go back, forward, and to either side as well as to shift for a throw smoothly and naturally so as to facilitate the making of an easier catch.

There have been big, naturally ungainly men who have become fine first basemen by developing their agility through exercises and mastery of correct techniques.

Agility, then, is not a prerequisite but can be developed, in fact must be developed if a man is to be a top-notch defensive first baseman.

The simplest way in which to develop an agile first baseman, aside from teaching him the correct moves, is to throw at him from a short distance. Over and over again he should be given practice at handling balls thrown at him from every conceivable angle and at every logical trajectory. Familiarity alone will breed both know-how and ability.

MAKING THE PLAYS

Knowledge of correct techniques both lifts first base play out of the realm of the purely mechanical and enables a man to develop his physical attributes to a point of utmost effectiveness. The maneuvers involved are logical, relatively simple, and based on the philosophy of reducing seemingly intricate physical moves to a point where their correct performance will be all but automatic.

175

Position

Proper positioning depends on several variables—the batter, the pitcher, base runners, and game situation. Under normal circumstances the distance that the first baseman plays from the bag should be in accordance with his speed. While he has to station himself sufficiently away from the base to enable the coverage of adequate ground, he should not be so far removed that his natural speed will not allow him ample time to reach the bag and position himself for the throw with a fair degree of ease.

With a runner on first, in most instances, the first-sacker should face the pitcher with his right foot against the inside corner of the base. There are occasions when a position behind the runner is justifiable. These moves will be dealt with in detail when the specific play situations to which they pertain are discussed.

When the bases are empty with two out, the first baseman should play deep and shaded toward the foul line to guard against an extra base hit. This is especially applicable with a left-hander at the plate.

The tight infield alignment is called for when an attempt must be made to cut off a run at the plate. Here the first baseman should play at the edge of the infield grass approximately twenty feet wide of the base. A ball hit to his left in this situation may call for a quick play at the base before the throw to the plate. If so, the runner will have to be tagged out at home, so that an accurate throw is essential (knee-high and slightly to the catcher's left). Experience at making the play should promote the judgment needed to decide on the right move.

Footwork

Probably the most important facet of first base play is the footwork involved in taking the throw. Shifting his feet in the correct fashion will allow the first baseman to handle the ball with a minimum of difficulty and will enable him to save a few feet and a little time in retiring the runner.

Properly, after a quick start, the first baseman will go to the base and place his *left foot* on it. He should then turn to watch the ball and shift as necessary. This implies that, rather than leaving his left foot planted on the bag and fielding the ball as best he can, when he sees on which side of him the ball is coming he will shift toward it, leaving one foot on the bag. In this initial position he will both serve as a target for the throw and be ready to shift whichever way necessary to handle the ball. A contingent benefit is that this will position him in front of the ball and cut down on his tendency to lunge for it, a smooth stretch being far more effective.

Shifting of the feet (and body) should be natural and smooth to facilitate the catching of the ball. On a throw to the left side, a natural jumping motion, replacing the left foot with the right, is correct practice. When the ball comes on the right side of the base the left foot should maintain contact with the bag while the body shifts to the right. Either foot can be used on a throw directly to the base. In any case, the secret lies in the ability to shift naturally in the right direction at the right time.

The actual shift, though a natural jumping motion, is somewhat akin to a waltz-step. It should be practiced repeatedly until it is done automatically and in a smooth manner.

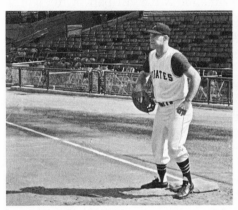

First Baseman in Position to Receive Throw (Rocky Nelson)

First Baseman's Stretch (Rocky Nelson)

First Baseman's Shift to the Right (Rocky Nelson)

First Baseman's Shift to the Left cross-over step for wide throw (Rocky Nelson)

177

Handling throws

Regardless of the footwork required, the first baseman should stretch as far as he can toward the ball, extending his body, as well as his arms to their fullest extent, while still maintaining contact with the bag. This will save valuable time and can often mean the difference between the runner's being safe or out.

Maximum reach is possible for a right-handed first baseman who touches the bag with his right foot and for the left-hander who anchors his left foot. This usage is primarily for a throw straight to the base.

For the longest possible stretch—the toe is the last part of the foot to reach the bag, the heel the first. Then, as the stretch is made, the heel leaves the base and the toe remains anchored to it.

A good stretch, in addition to saving time, also serves to shorten the hop of a throw into the dirt and facilitate its handling. Only occasionally will the hop be so big and difficult to handle that the first baseman must step back into foul territory on one foot to play the bounce, while touching the outside of the bag with the other foot.

Sometimes a very wide throw necessitates the use of a cross-over step and stretch. A right hander will employ this only for throws to his right, touching the base with his right foot, taking a long cross-over step with his left, and back-handing the ball for the catch. A left-hander, conversely, will use this maneuver only on a very wide throw to his left, back-handing the ball after a cross-over step with the right foot, the left one remaining on the bag.

When a throw is really bad, the first baseman should leave the base to get the ball. In this case the runner will be safe, so that the primary concern is to cut off a wild throw and prevent the runner's advancing a base.

A throw into the runner is, needless to say, quite difficult to handle well. There are two facets of this play, each demanding a different technique. A high throw to the left side of the bag, if it is not too wide, can still result in a put-out—but in all probability, the runner will have to be tagged. In this case the first baseman leaps for the ball and tags the runner as he goes by, being careful to hold the ball firmly in his gloved hand as the tag is applied.

A throw into the dirt in the path of the runner is quite another matter. Here a put-out is all but impossible. The aim of the first baseman should be to get the ball and prevent the runner's taking an extra base. A natural tendency to back up on the ball must be resisted since it greatly increases the chances of the ball's hitting the ground and/or the runner, thus becoming unplayable. The first baseman should get in front of the base and the runner. He must play the ball, not let it play him.

178

A throw from the catcher demands still another technique. A target should be given by the first baseman on all throws from the home-plate area. On a dropped third strike he should give the target in foul territory since the ball will, in most cases, roll behind the catcher, thus making a throw to the outside of the base less likely to hit the runner. A bunt or dribbler in front of the plate demands that the target be given in fair territory, where the throw to first will be unobstructed. The target, properly given for this play, is both hands cupped to the side of the first baseman's face. His left foot should be on the inside corner of the bag, his right approximately three feet in fair territory.

Holding the runner

The proper stance with a runner on first is another aspect of position play that must be mastered. The correct station for holding the runner close to the base finds the first baseman facing the pitcher, his *right* foot on the inside corner of the base, slightly crouched and with his gloved hand extended as a target at waist level. From this position he is able to handle throws to either side and tag the runner's foot in the same motion—a sweeping one—by turning to his *right*. Thus, he will be able to make a difficult play with relative ease, while keeping the runner and the diamond in his field of vision.

When returning the ball to the pitcher, an occasional fake throw may catch the runner moving off the base. At the least, it will keep him honest.

There are instances in which it is wise for the first baseman to play two or three steps behind the runner, but still close enough to hold him near the base. A particularly slow runner furnishes one such opportunity.

First Baseman's Position for Holding the Runner

Another is found when the defensive team has a comfortable lead in the late innings. One more such case is encountered when a strong left-hand pull-hitter is at bat, meaning that too much space should not be left through which he can hit the ball.

179

Holding the runner close to the base means that the first baseman will not be able to cover as much ground on a batted ball as he normally does. He should, however, move a few steps into the infield (toward second) with the pitch in order to position himself better to defend against a batted ball.

In moving off the bag after holding a runner, the first baseman should take a step with his left foot, then a long jump into defensive position, facing the batter.

Fielding ground balls

A ground ball to the first baseman, if it is hard hit, should be blocked as long as no quick throw is needed to retire a runner who was already on base. The first baseman is fortunate in that he has only a few feet to go to the bag in order to retire the batter. Thus, he can afford to block the ball rather than try for a quick, clean pick-up. This helps make sure that the ball does not go through him, allowing the runner to make first base safely and possibly advance to second.

On a ground ball hit to the first baseman, he should make the play himself if he possibly can. When he races the runner for the bag, the first baseman should touch the infield side of the base with his left foot. By so doing he all but eliminates the danger of being spiked or of colliding with the runner.

Feeding the pitcher

When the first baseman cannot reach the bag in time to retire the runner himself he will have to throw to the pitcher covering the base in order to get the out. Feeding the pitcher is an intricate maneuver and must be practiced repeatedly until its timing is mastered.

On a ball hit straight to the first baseman or to his left, he should *toss* the ball to the pitcher (not the bag), chest-high and about two steps in front of the base. The chest-high toss will enable the pitcher to catch the ball without looking up or down, then locate the bag.

On most fumbled grounders or balls hit to his right, the first baseman's *throw* should be chest-high, to the bag, since in most such cases the pitcher will have arrived at the base and be waiting for the ball.

The 3-6-3 double play

The 3-6-3 double play—from the first baseman to the shortstop, then back to first, is a very difficult one to execute successfully, and a very pretty thing to watch when it is worked properly. The first baseman has a three-fold task on this play. He must field the ball, make his throw to second, and return to the base to take the shortstop's throw. His throw should be a sidearm, accurate one and he should return to the base, then find the ball.

A left-handed first baseman has a decided advantage over a right-hander on the 3-6-3 double play since he can throw to second without pivoting and can do so merely with a normal step toward that base. Furthermore, as he picks up the ball he is in good position to make a quick underhand or sidearm throw.

First Baseman's Throw on 3-6-3 Double Play (Rocky Nelson)

After fielding the ball, a right-hander generally must pivot to his right, step, and throw. Occasionally he will be called upon to make this play on a ball hit to his left. In this instance, he should pivot to his left for the throw. The rhythm should not be broken on this play—it should be made in one continuous motion.

The first baseman's throw on a double-play attempt should be on the inside of the diamond. This minimizes the danger of the runner's interfering with the play and it is an easier one for the shortstop to handle. Timing, needless to say, is an important factor in making the throw. The ball should go to the shortstop at chest level and the play should be

181

timed so that the ball reaches him about one-half step before he gets to the bag.

The first baseman should always try to return to the base to take the throw. If the ball is hit to his right, he will have trouble getting back in time to make the play, and the pitcher, who should be covering, will probably be in better position to take the throw from the shortstop. Nevertheless, in most instances, this is the first baseman's play.

When the ball is fielded by the first baseman directly over, or close to the base, he should step on the bag to retire the batter and then make his throw to second, making sure to shout to the shortstop that the runner must be tagged, the force having been removed.

Playing bunts

Fielding a bunt with one hand is too uncertain. Rather, the ball should be scooped with both hands and the throw, regardless of the base to which it goes, should be made while straightening up. The pivot for the throw should be on the left foot for a left-handed first baseman, the right foot for a right-hander.

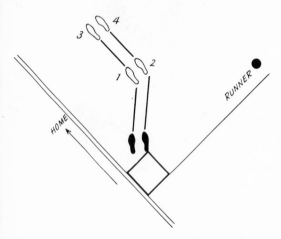

The first baseman will be called upon to play on the base and hold the runner close to it when first base is occupied and the sacrifice bunt is in order. In this case he also has to move off the bag and prepare himself to field the ball if it is bunted toward first.

To charge a bunt properly in this situation, the first two steps should take the first baseman in toward home plate at a 45° angle. The move should be made left-foot first.

When a sacrifice bunt goes toward third or the mound, the first baseman should try to get back to the base to take the throw. After making the put-out he should rush toward third with the ball to prevent a further advance by the runner(s).

ALERTNESS

It is alertness that really sets the good first baseman apart from the mediocre one. A first baseman should always be in a position to help out some place else. This includes correct performance of back-up and cut-off duties, knowing when to go for a ball, and comprehension of the right spot for him in any given circumstance.

Backing up the play

After a runner has passed first, the first baseman is no longer needed at that spot. With this in mind, he should back up any base whenever he can safely leave his position.

Three play situations which call for alertness on the part of the first baseman involve a runner going from first to second.

(1) When a runner makes a break for second base, the first baseman should be sure to let the catcher know about it. Shouting, "there he goes," will alert the catcher to set himself for a quick throw.

(2) With men on first and third, if the runner on first breaks for second, the first baseman should follow that man so that he will be in position to get a quick put-out if a run-down develops. In that way, he will have time to hold the other runner at third or to throw him out at the plate if he tries to score.

(3) If the batter tries for two bases on a hit to left or center field, the first baseman should trail the runner until he is in position to back up second base.

The cut-off play

The first baseman is an important part of a team's cut-off plays. On balls hit to right and center field with a man on second base, the first baseman is the cut-off man. He should station himself about forty-five feet in front of home in a direct line between the thrower and the plate. He should let the ball go through or cut it off according to the catcher's instructions, and, if the throw is going wild, he should rush up to catch the ball before it gets past him. When he lets the ball go through he should feign catching it in order to check the progress of the other runners at least momentarily.

The run-down

Proper handling of this situation is discussed in the section on infield play. Needless to say, a first baseman should know his role no matter where the run-down takes place. If it is between first and second, the first baseman should return to his base as soon as practicable, since the runner should be run toward first by the other infielders involved.

Pop-flies

A smart ballplayer knows that any high pop-fly will drift away from home plate. Realizing this, the first baseman should call for and take any pop-fly to the right side, where he will move in on the ball to make the catch.

The primary requisites of first base play, then, are that a man aspiring to that position concentrate intently on the job, exercise to keep agile, and try to anticipate the play when his team is in the field. Compliance with these requirements will help greatly in making a complete first baseman.

THE SECOND BASEMAN

The second baseman is responsible for a most vital position. His duties are many and varied and include one of baseball's most difficult and most important roles—pivot-man on the double play.

Ideally, a second baseman is fast on his feet, has good hands and an accurate arm, and possesses raw courage to a great degree. The knack of playing second base revolves around a sound knowledge of baseball percentages and the correct tactical maneuvers, the practice of effective mechanical moves, and familiarity with several tricks-of-the-trade designed to make a difficult job a much easier one.

COVERING GROUND

GROUND BALLS. The second baseman should try for every ball hit to the right side. This includes balls which the first baseman may be in a better position to handle. Here, even if he doesn't play the ball directly off the bat, he will be in position to back up the play on balls that get through the first baseman.

On any ball hit to his left which the second baseman can handle, he should be sure to call for it so that the first baseman does not make an unnecessary try for the ball and leave first base uncovered.

A slow roller can be a difficult problem, since the ball must be fielded on the run and thrown while the infielder is off balance. An underhand throw is essential to catch a fast runner, particularly a left-hand batter. A bare-hand scoop and throw is used by many experienced professionals but, until the play is completely mastered, if one hand is to be used, the gloved hand is safer by far. The throw should be made as the player is straightening up and while he is on the run.

The second baseman, because he has a short throw to first, can block the ball on occasion. This is particularly true of hard-hit balls on which there will be even more time to make the play on the batter. Once the ball is fielded, however, it should be played to first with as little lost time as possible.

Getting the jump

Knowledge of two factors—the batter and the pitch that is to be thrown—can enable an infielder to get a good jump on the ball by anticipating the play. A left-hand pull hitter will probably hit to the second baseman's left; a curve ball or change is more likely to be pulled; etc. If he uses such information judiciously, the second baseman can actually be in motion as the ball is hit.

An anticipatory move must not be obvious lest the batter be tipped off as to the pitch. The knack of getting the jump involves starting to move or, at least, to lean as the ball is delivered. Too pronounced a start can catch a man completely out of position if the ball is not hit to the right spot. In mastering this technique an infielder must act with restraint and must practice close observation of both his own pitchers and opposing hitters.

The start for a ground ball should be made quickly, with a slowing of actions as the infielder nears the ball, and an adjustment of his stride so as to receive it on the right hop.

Playing the arc

This means going back in a slight curve on ground balls hit to either side and coming in on the ball to field it. It can be particularly helpful to the second baseman on one of his most difficult plays, the ball hit far to his right, wherein he must field the ball on the run, apply the brakes, and make his throw in the direction opposite that in which he was running. Coming in on the ball in an arc makes the stop-and-throw just that much easier. Playing the arc not only allows for slightly greater effective range; it also makes for continuity of motion—a desirable practice no matter what the play.

Positioning

Generally speaking, with the necessary allowance being made for the game situation, the second baseman can afford to play closer to his base than may seem wise. The base can be shaded in this way for two reasons —he can go to his left more easily than to his right; and more hits go through the middle than through the hole.

Fly balls

In addition to handling flies hit near his normal position, the second baseman must range from behind second base, into the outfield, and over behind first base in foul territory.

He should take flies behind first because, as opposed to the first baseman, he is coming in on the ball. He must be sure to call for the ball. If, on the other hand, he hears an outfielder call for a ball, the second baseman should allow that man to take it, acknowledging the call so as to avoid confusion. Merely shouting "you take it" will let the outfielder know that he has a clear path to the ball.

On any pop-fly that is handled by the shortstop with runners on first and/or second, the second baseman covers the base. On a pop-fly to the first baseman, the second baseman should move toward first, either to help out on the fly if it is too difficult for the first baseman to handle easily, or to cover first base if that baseman has no trouble in playing the ball.

Balls to right field

On a fly ball to right field or right-center, if the ball is over the out-fielder's head, the second baseman should trail him as long as he is going back on the ball. Then, if the ball gets past the outfielder, the second baseman will be in position to act as relay man. If and when the outfielder sets himself to make the catch, the second baseman should return to the infield.

Covering first

In covering first base on a sacrifice, the second baseman should come to the bag from the outfield side of the diamond near the foul line, and should touch the bag with his left foot. This mode of approach will put him in good position to take a throw from the home-plate area as well as helping him avoid a collision with the runner. (The same approach should be used on a pick-off throw to first from the catcher.)

Feeding the pitcher

When the first baseman tries but fails to get a ball fielded by the second baseman, the pitcher must cover first. He will go directly to the bag and anchor thereon awaiting the throw on this play. Consequently, the second baseman's throw should be directly over the bag, chest-high, so that it will be easy to handle whether the pitcher is awaiting the throw or must still reach the bag and plant himself for the catch.

THE DOUBLE PLAY

With a double play in prospect the second baseman should move about two steps in toward home and a step or so closer to second than is normal for the hitter at bat. This saves steps and time in getting to second base to serve as middle-man in the double play, yet will not cut seriously into his fielding range.

With men on first and second, the double play should go by way of second, as it should with men on first and third—unless the runner on third represents the winning run.

The most important rule concerning the double play is "Make sure of the first out." This implies that the fielder should try to take the play himself wherever possible.

Feeding the shortstop

The second baseman should try to be in position to make his throw to second without taking a step. The ball should go to the base (not the shortstop), chest-high. The throw is not a particularly difficult one since the shortstop is moving toward first.

1. An underhand toss should be used on a ball hit toward the base, with the second baseman placing his right foot directly in the path of the ball while fielding it and pulling his glove away when tossing it.

2. The back-hand flip, used for short- and medium-length throws, is the quickest method for the 4-6-3 double play. Rather than pivoting for

Second Baseman Feeding the Shortstop (half-pivot for long throw)   *Second Baseman Feeding the Shortstop (back-hand toss for medium range throw)*   *Second Baseman Feeding the Shortstop (underhand toss for short throw)*

the throw, the second baseman merely tosses the ball with a back-hand motion. It must and should be practiced diligently.

3. A hip pivot to the right should be used on balls to the second baseman's left and on any other play involving a throw of more than fifteen feet. (The pivot should never be to the left—if one to the right is not feasible, the play should be at first.) Here the second baseman pivots quickly to his right and throws with power from a position in which both feet are solidly planted. The speed of the pivot and accuracy of the throw are both important factors.

The tag play

On a ball to his left and slow enough to be fielded in the base line, the runner should be tagged and the play completed at first. If the runner stops to delay the tag he should not be chased. Instead, the throw to first should be made to retire the batter—then the play made on the runner. If the latter runs out of the base line to avoid the tag, he should not be chased—this would defeat a double play. Furthermore, he is automatically out.

Making the pivot

Competence in this area is the main difference between a good second baseman and a mediocre one.

The base should be approached in a direct line with the throw, where possible. This will put the second baseman in good position to take the throw and make the pivot. The approach should be at full speed but the last two steps should be taken slowly, with knees bent for lateral mobility. The pivot should *not* be made on the run—the second baseman should be set for the throw to first.

The pivot should be made in accordance with the path of the runner, who will attempt to break up the double play. If his slide is to the outfield side, the pivot should be made into the diamond; if his approach is to the inside, the pivot should be toward the outfield. If the ball is hard-hit, allowing ample time to complete the play, the pivot can be made directly toward first base.

Another consideration, of course, is the direction of the throw. If the ball is wide in either direction, the pivot will have to be made to the side on which the throw comes.

The second baseman's task is very difficult since he must be concerned with both runner and ball, coming at him from opposite directions. When not in position to anticipate the path of the runner, he should

Second Baseman's Double Play Pivot—Across the Bag
(Bill Mazeroski)

vary the direction of his pivot from time to time so as to make the runner's intentions more difficult to achieve.

TO THE INSIDE. The pivot into the infield can be made with either foot touching the base. If the right foot is used, the step with the left one should be toward a spot about half-way between home and first, and the throw made across the body. When the left foot is used to touch the base, the right one crosses it in a step toward home, and a normal step toward first is made with the left foot for the throw. Both of these methods should carry the second baseman out of the runner's path.

It should be added here that a base runner is permitted to slide only as far out of the base line as he can go while still able to touch the bag with some part of his body. Umpires, however, are very lenient in calling interference on a runner who slides in an attempt to break up a double play.

Second Baseman's Double Play Pivot—Straddle (Bill Mazeroski)

TO THE OUTSIDE.   The second baseman's pivot toward the outfield is made by hitting the outside of the base with the left foot, pushing back on the right, and stepping slightly further toward the outfield on the left foot for the throw.

STRAIGHT AHEAD.   If the runner is not close to second, the pivot can be directly toward first base. The natural method is to hit the side of the base with the right foot and stride toward first for the throw. An

Second Baseman's Double Play Pivot—Jump (Bill Mazeroski)

alternate, and especially safe version is to straddle the bag and drag the right foot across it on the throw. This makes the touching of the base automatic and is, consequently, the recommended method.

If the runner is close when he is straddling the bag, the second baseman can make a fast flip-like throw to first, leaping into the air off his right foot to avoid the slide of the runner.

BACKING OFF.   If the throw is to the left field side of the bag, the second baseman should hop to his right, drag his left foot over the bag, and make his throw from behind the base.

SHORTSTOP BEHIND THE BAG.   When the shortstop goes behind the bag for a ball, the second baseman should plant his left foot against the right field side of the base and face left field. He will then be in a

Second Baseman's Double Play Pivot—Push-back (Bill Mazeroski)

better position to shift for a bad toss, especially one to his right—where the shortstop's throw in this situation is most likely to be. The throw to first will then have to be made after a step back toward the outfield on the right foot.

NO PLAY AT FIRST. No player should ever make an unnecessary throw. When the first out is made but little chance remains of completing the double play—the ball should be held, eliminating the possibility of a bad throw.

A variation of this can be worked with men on first and second. With little chance to complete the double play at first, the second baseman, after making the force at second, should throw to third where a possible put-out can be made on the runner rounding the bag.

THROW FROM THE PITCHER. Ideally the shortstop should handle the pitcher's double-play throw to second. However, with a right-hand pull hitter at bat, the shortstop must play in the hole, so it falls to the second baseman to take the pitcher's throw. Even when the shortstop is able to make the play, the second baseman should be going toward the base to back up the throw.

THE KEY. Whatever method is used, the secret of a powerful and accurate throw is to shift the weight to the right foot before the throwing action starts.

The force play

There are several instances in which the second baseman has to concern himself only with forcing the runner at second. One of these occurs when, with two out and a force possible at second, the play is made to that base. In this case the only problem is catching the ball and touching the base. This play is generally made only on a ground ball to the left side of the infield. In order to make certain of the out, it is recommended that the second baseman take the throw straddling the bag, left foot forward, and drag the right foot across the base when the ball is received. In this way there will be little chance of losing the out for failure to touch the bag while in possession of the ball.

The second baseman should play his base like a first baseman on a sacrifice bunt when the force play is attempted on the lead runner, on a fumble at short or third, and on a ground ball to deep short—in the latter two cases with a man on first and no possibility of completing the double play. In these instances, the play will be a close one so the second baseman must stretch for the ball with one foot anchored on the bag in order to save precious time which might be the difference between the runner's being safe and out.

THE PICK-OFF

With a runner on second base, the second baseman is only of nuisance value. He can fake the runner back toward the bag but is too plainly visible to the man on second to be very effective in picking him off the base. The best time to do this is just before the pitcher delivers the ball to the plate since this might catch the runner leaning the wrong way when the ball is hit and consequently delay his start by a step or two. The second baseman should also keep the runner from taking too big a lead when a definite right-hand pull hitter is at bat and the shortstop must play in the hole. In any of these situations the second baseman must be careful not to be (caught) out of position on a batted ball by moving too far in the direction of the base. Kicking dirt toward second or faking a start in that direction are often sufficient to accomplish the desired purpose.

One instance when the second baseman might possibly be useful in catching the runner off base is after the pitcher has thrown to the shortstop covering second and has failed to pick off the runner. The second baseman should have moved behind the base to back up the play. After the shortstop has returned the ball to the pitcher, he walks in front of the runner and back to his position. The second baseman should then move in to the base from his back-up position and try to pick off the runner as he takes his lead.

The second baseman occasionally covers first base for a pick-off play when a sacrifice is expected. He will be moving toward first to cover that base in this situation and, with the first baseman charging the plate for a bunt, can duck in behind the runner to take a pick-off throw. This can be done on a pitch-out signalled by the catcher. It has even more chance of success if the batter misses a bunt attempt, because here the runner will be leaning toward second or possibly will have taken a few steps in that direction. It is strongly recommended that this pick-off attempt be automatic on a missed bunt.

THE SHORTSTOP

The shortstop position is both a busy and an important one. The ideal man for the job is fast, agile, and possessed of good hands and a strong arm. Almost invariably, good shortstops are aggressive, resourceful ballplayers with sound baseball sense and a well-developed talent for anticipating plays.

A shortstop has much ground to cover and, more than any other player, must field the ball cleanly (because of the long throw to get the runner at first). He is also charged with relaying the catcher's signals (by voice to the infield, by hand signs to the outfield) and with directing strategy on many balls hit to either infield or outfield.

RANGE

The shortstop should try for every ball hit to the left side of the infield. A wide range on his part enables the third baseman to guard the line and the second baseman to protect the hole to a greater degree than would normally be possible. He should call for any medium speed ground ball to his right which he feels he can handle more easily than the third baseman, otherwise the latter will cut in front of him to play it and take advantage of the shorter throw to first which is his.

The play in the hole (far to his right) is the most difficult one for the shortstop. To set himself properly for the long throw he should brake himself on the inside of his right foot; take a short hop on his right foot while straightening up; stride directly toward first; and make a hard, overhand throw with a good follow-through—all of this in one continuous and rapid sequence of motion.

Fly balls

He should take all fly balls in an area running from his normal position, to the mound, to second base, as well as ones behind him, except those called for by an outfielder. His fly-ball range includes ones hit behind the third baseman. The prevailing rule is that a player coming in on it has priority on a fly ball.

Handling the ball

The shortstop must "play the ball" rather than let it play him. He should always move toward it, charging it as fast as possible, slowing his actions as he approaches it, then adjusting his stride to receive the ball on the right hop. He should constantly endeavor to get in front of the ball and set himself for the throw before he fields it.

Because of the length of his throw, speed is of the essence. The shortstop really cannot afford a fumble and must often throw without straightening up, although he should do so when time permits.

Covering second base

It is the shortstop's job to protect second base on bunts and on all batted balls to the right side of the infield. This includes any pop-fly which the second baseman attempts to play.

On a fly ball to left field, the shortstop should follow the outfielder as long as he is going back. If and when he sets himself for the catch, the shortstop returns to second to cover the base. A fly ball or base hit on which the left fielder has the play in front of him calls for the shortstop to go directly to second base. If the ball gets past the outfielder there is still time for the shortstop to get to the outfield to handle a relay. When covering second, if the throw is wide or late the shortstop should leave the base and go to meet the ball.

Since the second baseman has similar duties on fly balls or hits to right field, it is the shortstop's job to cover the bag when the second baseman goes to the outfield and to back him up when he covers the base.

As a general rule, the shortstop should cover second base if the second baseman's duties take him elsewhere.

Specific base-covering assignments are dealt with in sections where the various defensive maneuvers are discussed.

Covering third base

In certain situations it falls to the shortstop to cover third base. One of these is a pop-fly to the third baseman with a man on base. Another is a slow roller which the third baseman must charge—with a runner on first.

On some ball clubs the shortstop is assigned the task of covering third base on certain throws from the outfield, the third baseman backing him up. Specific occasions for such a setup should be decided upon by the coach.

Runner on second

A man on second constitutes a two-fold problem. He must not be allowed too big a lead, and his presence demands proper handling of an attempted pick-off play.

A runner on second and the attention he warrants will reduce, to a certain extent, the shortstop's ground-covering range. To cover as much of his normal territory as possible, the shortstop should take care not to be moving in the direction of the base when the ball is being delivered to the plate by the pitcher.

DISTRACTING THE RUNNER. A runner on second is in perfect position to read the catcher's signals and relay them to the batter. Consequently, it is good practice for the shortstop to drive the runner back to the base just as the catcher prepares to give his signal. This will cause the runner to pay heed to his own safety, thereby diverting his attention from the catcher's signs.

HOLDING THE RUNNER. Without straying too far from his own position, the shortstop should hold the runner close to second base. Preventing a long lead will preclude the extra step or two that can enable the runner to score on a single or advance to third on an infield out.

A feint toward the base, timed to take place just as the pitcher sets himself to deliver the ball to the batter, is the most effective method of accomplishing this purpose. The shortstop should perform his fake without taking an actual step or losing his balance.

GROUNDER TO SHORT. After fielding a grounder, the shortstop should "look the runner back" to second before making his throw to first. If he breaks for third, the play should be at that base.

The runner will try for third on a slow roller or grounder to the shortstop's left. If the ball is fumbled, with no possible play at first, it may be possible to catch the runner taking a wide turn at third. The shortstop should be on the alert for this in such a situation.

SLOW ROLLER TO THIRD. When the third baseman rushes in to field a slow roller, the shortstop should follow the runner to third, where he will be in position to receive a pick-off throw from the third baseman in the event that the latter fumbles and cannot make a play at first.

PICK-OFF WITH THE PITCHER. This is usually a signal play, worked in either of two ways—on a count or by the "daylight method."

When a count is used the shortstop gives the signal. After it is flashed, the pitcher turns toward the plate and counts, one-two, and pivots to throw on three, the shortstop having gone to the bag to take the throw.

The "daylight play" works something like this—the shortstop gives a signal to let the pitcher know that he is going to the base. He then moves in behind the runner and when the pitcher sees daylight between the runner and the shortstop as the latter goes toward the bag, he makes a complete pivot and throws to second.

To make the "count play" effective, the shortstop should approach the runner, fake a move to the bag, then start back to his position as he signals the pitcher. When the pitcher's arm is at rest and he has turned back to face the hitter, the shortstop makes his break for the bag. This is a good method. Experimentation may develop other, even better ones.

Generally speaking, this play should be on a signal so that the pitcher is unlikely to deliver the ball to the plate after the shortstop has gone to second base. Furthermore, the shortstop should make no more than one false start to the bag on any one pitch.

One of the great values in having a good pick-off play lies in the fact that the reputation of having one is often enough to keep the runner close to his base.

PICK-OFF WITH THE CATCHER. Due to the length of the throw, there is relatively little chance of a successful pick-off. The throw from the catcher, however, will keep the runner honest—and may retire him.

If too large a lead by the runner is apparent, this play should be signalled by the catcher, the sign being acknowledged by the short-stop. The latter must be at the base awaiting the catcher's throw when it arrives, yet he cannot make his break too soon lest the runner be alerted. The proper time to go to the base is just as the pitcher delivers the ball to the plate, a pitch-out having been used.

A missed swing by the batter should be construed as an automatic pick-off signal. The shortstop should be prepared for a throw to second to catch the runner. His vulnerability to the pick-off play is greatly increased by the instinctive few steps he almost invariably takes on any swing by the batter.

The sacrifice

The shortstop should cover second for a sacrifice bunt with a man on first. In this situation, little chance exists of completing a double play, and under any circumstances it is the lead runner who should be retired if at all possible. Consequently, the shortstop should play the bag as a first baseman does, stretching for the throw to increase the chance of retiring the runner.

With men on first and second and the sacrifice in order, the shortstop should drive the runner back to the base and hold him there in order to increase the chances of a successful force play at third. After the pitch is delivered, the shortstop should go in to cover the mound which will be left unprotected for a bunt when the pitcher moves over to cover the third base line.

THE DOUBLE PLAY

As in the case of the second baseman, with a double play in prospect the shortstop should move about two steps in toward home and a step or so closer to second than is normal for the hitter at bat. He, too, should remember to "make sure of the first out."

Strategy

Certain basic rules guide the shortstop's approach to the double play.

1. He should make the play at second himself, whenever possible.
2. With men on first and second, a ball so far to his right that he must back-hand it may be thrown to third if this is the easy play.
3. With bases loaded, the double play should go by way of second unless the man on third represents the tying or winning run.
4. With men on first and third, the double play goes by way of second unless the man at third represents the *winning* run.
5. The shortstop, unless he has been deep in the hole for a pull hitter, should cover second on a double-play throw from the pitcher since he will be going toward the base anyhow.
6. If, on a ground ball near first base, the batter is retired before the throw goes to second, the runner must be tagged.

Feeding the second baseman

The shortstop's double-play throw is a difficult one to make properly because of the pivot demanded of the second baseman. It is very important that it be just right. A good one will be chest-high directly at the bag, not at the second baseman.

The throw should be made without straightening up and the glove should be pulled away from the ball so as to give the pivot-man a good view of it. The two-handed scoop or push-throw obscures the second baseman's view of the ball and should be avoided.

Shortstop Feeding the Second Baseman (underhand toss for short throw)

Shortstop Feeding the Second Baseman (side-arm for medium and long throw)

The throw to second can be either underhand or sidearm, the former being used for the short toss on a ball hit near the base. For a longer throw, or on a ball to the shortstop's right on which he must apply the brakes to set himself, a sidearm throw should be used and the ball should be aimed at a spot about one foot on the home plate side of second.

The pivot

The primary considerations in guiding the type and direction of the pivot are the path of the oncoming runner and the location of the throw to the base.

If the throw is wide in either direction, the bag should be crossed on that side. On a good throw directly to the base, the shortstop should make his play according to the path of the runner, going to the outfield side when the runner approaches on the inside of the base line and going to the infield side when the runner comes in on the outside. The distance of the runner from the base permitting, the play can be made directly toward first. In any event, the aim of the shortstop should be to prevent the runner's interfering with his throw to first.

The approach to the base should be made as quickly as possible. As he nears the bag the shortstop should slow down so that the proper adjustment can be made in the stride to facilitate handling the ball. He should speed up again when he sees where the ball is. Ideally he will receive the ball one-half step before he reaches the base.

It would, of course, be preferable to hit the bag with the right foot since only a single step with the left would be required for the throw to first. But, with the runner intent on breaking up the double play, an extra step or short hop is sometimes necessary if he is to be avoided. Other factors, such as the direction of the throw and the position of the shortstop's feet as he gets to the bag, make variations in method imperative. Thus, there is really no set rule for making the double play.

The techniques outlined here should be employed according to the shortstop's physical characteristics and the play situation itself.

TO THE OUTSIDE.   Making the play to the outside necessitates hitting the base with the right foot. The throw should be caught with the right foot on the outside corner of the bag. A step diagonally to the left with the left foot is the next move. If the runner is too close to permit making the throw on this step, a short hop or shuffle-step is made to the left, carrying the shortstop further out of the runner's path. The throw to first is then made as the shortstop lands on his right foot and steps toward first base on his left.

The drag method can also be used when the play is made to the outside. Here the right foot is placed about four inches from the outside corner of the base and is dragged across the bag as the throw is

Shortstop's Double Play Pivot—Outside the Bag (Dick Groat)

made to first. An extra step or hop can also be used if needed to assure avoiding the runner.

TO THE INSIDE. When the shortstop makes the double play by going to the inside of the base, the left foot is the one which establishes contact with the bag. Either the drag or a step can be used, the former

Shortstop's Double Play Pivot—Inside the Bag (Dick Groat)

insuring the force-out at second, the latter carrying the shortstop further away from the bag and out of the runner's path.

When the shortstop steps on the inside corner of the base with his left foot he pushes off diagonally toward home plate, landing on his right foot and making the throw as he steps toward first with his left foot.

If he prefers the drag method and time permits its use, he gets to the bag with his right foot advanced and on the inside of the bag. His left foot stays behind the base and is dragged across it as he steps to throw. A half-pivot to the right on the lead (right) foot and a step slightly in the direction of home plate as the throw to first base is made will help to take the shortstop out of the base runner's path.

STRAIGHT AHEAD. If the runner is still a good distance from second base, the shortstop can afford to follow his natural inclinations and step directly toward first as he makes his throw. This can be done by stepping on the middle of the base with the right foot and throwing as a normal stride is taken with the left foot.

The drag method can also be used here, the shortstop taking the throw while straddling the bag—right foot forward—and dragging his left foot across the top of the base as he stops to throw. When time permits, this is the surest, if not best, way for the shortstop to make the double play.

BEHIND THE BASE. If the shortstop can stay behind the base in making the double play, he will experience very little difficulty with the oncoming runner. However, since he must go to the bag quickly and take the throw while in motion, this is rarely possible. The logical time to use this method is when the shortstop fields a ground ball close to second base and takes the play himself. One step away from the bag he takes a stride with his left foot, releasing the ball on the throw after his foot has made contact with the near side of the base.

Shortstop's Double Play Pivot—Across and Back (Dick Groat)

A variation can be employed in which the shortstop hits the bag with his left foot and backs off toward left field before stepping toward first for the throw.

FIRST-SECOND-FIRST. The shortstop takes the throw on the first-second-first (3-6-3) double play. If the throw is a good one, the best method of making the play is to hit the base with the left foot and step into the diamond to make the return throw. The throw to first should go directly to the bag, as it must be handled by a moving player—either the first baseman or, occasionally, the pitcher—and it should be chest-high.

THE KEY. At the amateur level of play, where arms are not so powerful, the key to a strong, accurate throw is to get the weight on the right foot before the throwing actions are started.

The cut-off play

One of the shortstop's important duties is to serve as cut-off man on certain balls hit to the outfield. He is assigned this task on a single hit with a runner on first base or on a fly ball with runners on first and second. Whether the batter hits to left, center, or right, the shortstop should station himself in a direct line between the outfielder playing the ball and third base—at a point about forty feet in front of the base. The third baseman calls the play, telling the shortstop whether to let the ball go through to the base or to cut it off.

THE SECOND BASE COMBINATION

The second baseman and shortstop are usually thought of as a unit rather than merely as individual ballplayers, and rightfully so. No team can be really successful unless it is strong through the middle, and in its contribution to through-the-middle strength the keystone combination can live up to its name.

Continual practice together is an imperative for the second-short duo. On the double play, in particular, perfect coordination and timing are demanded since any hesitancy, and failure to make the throw just right, will cause the double play to be lost. Thus, they should capitalize on every possible opportunity to acquire complete familiarity with one another's habits and abilities, speed of movement and throwing characteristics. This should be carried to the point where the two men make it a practice always to warm up together, whether it be before an actual ball game or an ordinary practice session.

Covering second

Close cooperation between the keystone pair is essential to a good defense. Each should know what his partner is doing and intends to do at all times.

Who is to cover second on a steal should be decided whenever a runner reaches first base. The shortstop gives the signal for this assignment unless the second baseman is a far more experienced ballplayer.

Hiding his mouth from the opposition with his glove, the one who gives the signal does so by either opening or closing it. An open mouth means that he will cover the base himself—a closed mouth and his partner is assigned the task. Other signals may be used, as long as they clearly convey the right message without revealing it to the opposition.

The importance of properly carrying out this assignment cannot be overestimated. Failure to do so may mean that a throw goes into center field, untouched, allowing a further advance by the runner. At the least it will find the catcher looking vainly for someone to whom to throw while the runner walks into second base.

Several factors determine the base-covering assignment.

THE BATTER. The bearing of the batter on this situation revolves primarily around the direction in which he is most likely to hit the ball.

Ordinarily it is the shortstop's duty to cover second base on a bunt or a steal with a right-field hitter (usually a left-hander) at the plate, on bunts and ground balls fielded by the pitcher, and on all throws from the right side of the infield. The assignment falls to the second baseman when a left-field hitter (usually right-handed) is at bat, except on a sacrifice bunt, in which case second is always covered by the shortstop and first by the second baseman. Needless to say, the bunt is unlikely with two strikes on the batter, so normal assignments prevail.

For a straightaway hitter or one of unknown tendencies, assignments depend on the pitch being thrown. A fast ball is less likely to be pulled than is a curve or change; thus the man charged with signalling the base-covering assignment should consider this in formulating his judgment.

Once the ball is hit, if either man makes an attempt to field it, the other one should cover the base. Regardless of who covers second, his partner should back him up whenever his own responsibilities do not take him elsewhere.

THE PITCHER. The ability of the batter and the type of pitch have a bearing on the direction in which the ball is likely to be hit. These factors should be taken cognizance of by the defensive players in positioning themselves. Where practicable, they should also give consideration to the spot in which the pitcher will try to keep the ball.

The pitcher's stuff on a certain day also enters the picture. If he is particularly fast the batters will have trouble getting around on the ball and will be less likely to pull it. If he is keeping the ball pretty much in one spot, say low and inside to right-handed batters, outside to left-handers, chances are that the ball will be hit to the left side. As the game wears on, the smart ballplayer will observe how the other team is hitting the pitcher and such things as position play and base-covering assignments should be arranged accordingly.

Runner on first

With a runner on first base, both the second baseman and the shortstop should take a step or two toward second after the ball has passed the batter. By so doing they will be in good position to cover the base if the runner attempts a delayed steal.

When the catcher calls for a pitch-out both men can leave their positions with the pitch, the one who is not going to the base to take the throw moving into back-up position.

In taking the catcher's throw on an attempted steal, the man covering second should break quickly and get to the base so that he will present a stationary target and also find less difficulty in shifting for a bad throw. While awaiting the throw he should straddle the bag—facing toward first base and looking toward home. When he receives the ball he should place it between the base and the runner, allowing the latter to tag himself.

Double steal

When the offensive team has runners on first and third, particularly if they are fast men, there is always the possibility of an attempted double steal. If the count on the batter reaches 3-1, or 3-2, this possibility is greatly increased and the second baseman and shortstop should move two steps in, so as to be in better position to combat it.

The second baseman is generally the cut-off man and the shortstop the one who covers second. Since he can see toward third base, the second baseman calls the play.

Both members of the second base combination should remember to give up the run on third if the man on first represents the winning run. This is the one to keep from scoring position.

Further details of the double steal defense can be found in the section on special defensive plays.

The hit-and-run

The hit-and-run is most likely to be attempted with less than two outs, a runner on first base, and the batter ahead of the pitcher in the count. It should never be tried when the offensive team is behind by more than one run.

The second baseman and shortstop should position themselves for the hit-and-run if they suspect that it will be attempted. Normally, the shortstop covers the base with a left-hander at bat and the second baseman does so when the hitter is right-handed.

Going to the base to cover it as the pitcher delivers the ball to the plate will leave too big a gap for the batter to shoot at. The best procedure is to shift a few steps closer to second before the pitch and to wait until the ball is past the batter (or has been hit) to cover the base. If the ball is hit toward either position, the man in question should go for it, relying on his partner to cover the base. The play will be a difficult one at best, but not nearly as tough as it would be if the defensive player has gone to the base and left his position completely unprotected.

When a runner is going from first to second on the hit-and-run or steal and the batter hits the ball in the air, the second baseman and shortstop should fake fielding a ground ball in order to lure the runner on and make a double play possible after the ball has been caught.

The relay

On a fly ball to left field the shortstop is responsible for serving as relay man, if one is needed. The second baseman is charged with this duty when the ball is hit to right field.

On a ball hit to center field, the man who is nearer the base covers it, and the other man is responsible for helping the center fielder or backing up the throw, whichever is needed. However, if one of them has a much stronger arm than the other, he is the one who should serve as relay man.

The relay man should not go too far out from the diamond, bearing in mind that it is the second throw which should be the short (and accurate) one. Several other common-sense rules are germane to the relay man's tactics.

1. The pivot for the throw to a base should always be to the left.
2. If the throw is bouncing, the relay man should let it go through since it will be difficult to handle and unlikely to get the lead runner.
3. If the runner is obviously "in" at second base, the man covering the base should leave it to back up the relay man.

4. If the hit will obviously be no more than a double, the relay man should retreat and cover the bag, while the other one backs him up.

THE THIRD BASEMAN

Third base is rightfully known as the hot corner. Its guardian is so close to the batter and the ball often reaches him so quickly that a good part of the time he is limited to a do-or-die effort to field the ball. The difficulty of the position is compounded by its vulnerability to bunts and slow rollers.

It demands sharp reflexes, quick thinking, sure hands, and a strong arm. Running speed is not essential, but quick reactions and movements are requisites of successful third base play.

The handling of bunts and dribblers necessitates the ability to throw from any position. Hard-hit ground balls often can merely be blocked and require agility in retrieving the ball and making a play on the runner.

Once a ball is hit toward him, the third baseman has little enough time for action and practically none for thought. Consequently, he must be prepared to field the ball on every pitch—and with a definite plan of action in mind.

MECHANICS

Despite the speed with which a ground ball reaches him, a third baseman should try to field the arc, since this will enable him to cover a maximum of ground. This means that he should go back in a slight curve on well-hit balls to either side of him and should move forward to field them. Conversely, on a ball hit directly to him, he should never back up since this would, in effect, allow the ball to play him.

Fielding the arc is not possible on hard-hit balls, except in the form of a dive or lunge diagonally backwards in the direction of the ball. In a sense, this constitutes taking more time in playing the ball.

The third baseman should play in a crouch while awaiting the ball; his hands are near his knees, his weight forward. When the ball is hit on the ground to him, his hands should be very low (scraping the dirt) so that there is no room for the ball to go through.

His throw does not have to be hurried on a cleanly handled ball,

205

but it should be thrown hard. On the many balls that he knocks down or blocks, however, the throw will have to be made quickly.

The third baseman should practice a cross-over step until it becomes second nature to him. This will help him to cover maximum ground. This move, when made with his right foot, is particularly important since most balls hit in his direction will be to his left.

Third Baseman's Cross-over Step on a Ball to His Left

THE PLAYS

Bunts and slow rollers

A slowly hit ball should be charged as quickly as possible. On a bunt the third baseman should be moving toward the plate just as soon as the bat drops.

If at all possible, the ball should be fielded with two hands. When this cannot be done, the surest method, and one which loses little time, is to field the ball on the run and *off the left foot with the gloved hand.* The throw is made while straightening up and with the body still moving forward. The play should be made in this manner whether the ball is to the right, the left, or straight ahead of the third baseman. (The barehand scoop and underhand throw is for professionals.)

Since the batter stands a good chance of beating it out, the ball should be allowed to roll if right on the line. It should be picked up just as

Third Baseman Fielding a Slow Roller

soon as it is in foul territory. Exception: When a runner is on base and will be able to advance while the ball is rolling, it should be picked up to check his progress.

The sacrifice

On those occasions when the sacrifice can be anticipated the third baseman should be alert for a bunt. Often this becomes a certainty by the batter's revealing his intentions, in which case the third baseman should be charging the plate by the time the ball is bunted.

Generally speaking, the third baseman protects the foul line (where the bunt is most likely to go) while the pitcher should be able to handle balls closer to the mound. (In the latter case, the third baseman should give directions to the pitcher.) However, with a slow-footed pitcher on the mound the third baseman should be prepared to field all bunts, even the sacrifice with men on first and second.

With a bunt in order the third baseman's position is about four feet wide of third base and on the edge of the grass. Playing close to the line means that he will be going straight in on the ball when he fields it. It will also facilitate returning to the bag if someone else fields the ball or if the bunt is a fake one.

With a man on second, the third baseman must take care not to leave his position too quickly lest the play be a fake bunt, designed to draw him in, leaving the base unprotected against a steal. In fact, he should return to his base and cover it whenever a bunt goes to someone other than himself, or when he has fielded it and thrown the ball elsewhere.

On the sacrifice with men on first and second, the third baseman should play about two steps from the bag and cover it for a force on the runner, the pitcher being responsible for fielding a bunt in the area near the third base line. If the bunt is hard and gets by the pitcher, the third baseman must field it and make the play at first base. If the batter "hits away" in this situation, the third baseman should break several steps to his left on the swing in order to cover as much of his normal territory as possible.

In taking the throw for the force, the third baseman should play his bag like a first baseman, anchoring one foot and stretching to catch the ball.

With two strikes on the batter, the third baseman can return to his normal position. He should not forget, however, that a poor-hitting pitcher may attempt a sacrifice bunt, even with two strikes.

Pop-flies

The third baseman should take all fly balls between third base and home plate. Since he is going in on the ball he should "run the catcher off" any fly he can handle, always calling for the ball in a loud, clear voice.

By the same token, the shortstop is in better position to play a pop-fly behind the third baseman and should be allowed to do so whenever he calls for the ball.

On a foul fly, if there is a grandstand, fence, or bench in the vicinity of the ball, the proper technique for the third baseman is to go to the barrier as fast as possible. Then he should locate the ball and weave his way back toward the diamond if the ball fails to reach the obstruction.

The double play

The throw to second to start a double play is of the utmost importance if even one man, let alone two, is to be retired. The throw should be chest-high, directly over the base, and timed so that the second baseman will be arriving at the base just as the ball reaches him. In view of the rapidity with which a batted ball reaches him, the third baseman may have to pause before throwing, in order to allow the second baseman to get in position for the play.

With men on first and second, the third baseman's double play should go by way of second base—for speed and ease of execution. The primary exception here is a ball hit near the base, which calls for touching the bag and throwing to first for the second out.

With bases loaded, the third baseman's double play goes home, then to first. Once again there is the exception of a ball hit near the bag, in which case the third baseman should step on the base and then throw home, making sure to let the catcher know that the force is off and that the runner going home must be tagged.

When a left-hand batter hits to third base, a double play is usually out of the question since the second baseman will be in no position to get to the base in time to take the throw. The third baseman should make his throw to first for one sure out rather than risk a throw which cannot be handled at second and will allow both runners to be safe.

If this play occurs with men on first and second, the wisest move is a force at third and a throw to first. Should the ball be to his left, the third baseman may find it easier to get the first out by tagging the runner coming to third.

The cardinal rule: Always make sure of the first out.

Tagging the runner

The third baseman should straddle the base while awaiting a throw from anyone other than the catcher. When the throw is from the catcher, he should take a position at the corner of the bag nearest the pitcher, leaving the base open so that the runner can slide into it with little danger of interference or accidental spiking. At the same time he will be able to go for a wide throw with little difficulty. As he catches the ball he should turn to his left, placing his left foot on the outfield side of the base. He will then be straddling the bag.

The ball should be held in such a position that the runner will slide into it and tag himself. The third baseman should leave the base to go for a wide throw, the ball having priority over the runner. If time still remains he can dive at the runner to make the tag.

Once the ball is applied to the runner it should be removed rapidly to eliminate the danger of its being jarred loose by the contact.

The cut-off play

The third baseman serves as the cut-off man on a fly ball to left field with a runner on third or a single with a man on second. This is a good practice since there is very little chance to get the runner at third and since the third baseman is much closer to the cut-off spot than is the first baseman.

The cut-off position is in a direct line between the left fielder and home at a spot about half-way between third base and the plate. The catcher will give instructions and the third baseman should act accordingly.

Back-up and base-covering duties

With men on base, the third baseman should back up the pitcher on all throws from the first baseman. He should also be alert to back up an overthrow of second base from right field on a single with no one on base, or a fly ball with a man on first. Another back-up role occurs when the shortstop covers third base, some teams using this setup on certain balls hit to the outfield.

When both the shortstop and second baseman go for a fly ball with no one on base, it is the third baseman's job to cover second. If this play occurs with a runner on first base, the third baseman should once again cover second, but should make his intentions known to the catcher and tell the latter to cover third.

Needless to say, with a man on second or one at third, the third baseman must remain at his own base when not in cut-off position.

TACTICS

A good third baseman is, of necessity, an aggressive ballplayer. His basic philosophy should be to take any ball that he can get. Unless the shortstop calls for a ground ball the third baseman should cut in front of him and field the ball if he can, since his throw is a shorter one and has a better chance of retiring the runner.

To help guide his actions and enable him to gain the advantage of an extra step where possible, the third baseman should watch the hitter —not the pitcher. This will give him a better jump on the ball as well as aiding in the early detection of a bunt.

There are several tactical maneuvers which should be adopted by the third baseman which pertain to situations that find a runner or runners on specific bases.

(1) When the opposition has a runner on second base, the third baseman should take a step toward third after the ball passes the batter, so as to be in position to cover the base on a steal. At the same time he should be wary of a fake bunt, which will draw him in toward the plate and leave the base open for a steal.

(2) With a runner on third, a missed swing by the batter is an automatic signal for a pick-off throw from the catcher. The runner has a tendency to take a step or two when the batter swings and, thus, may fall victim to a pick-off throw. If the throw does not succeed in getting an out at third, at least it will keep the runner honest.

(3) A runner on third base should not be allowed to take too long a lead—he should be feinted back if he appears to be getting too big a jump on the pitcher.

(4) When the third baseman fields a ground ball with a man on third base or a man on second base, with no force play possible, he should "look the runner back" to his base before making his throw to first for the out.

(5) The "men on first and third" situation presents a different problem when a medium speed ground ball (one not hard enough to assure a good

chance at a double play) is hit to the infield. If the runner on third breaks for the plate and a play is made on him, he will often try to get caught in a run-down and jockey around until the other runners advance to second and third. In order to prevent this, the third baseman should follow the runner home so that he will be in position to take a throw from the catcher and make a quick tag on the runner—getting the out in time to prevent a further advance by the other base runner. If the ball is hit to the third baseman himself and the runner makes a break for home, the play should definitely be made on him.

(6) In those situations where the third baseman covers his base on throws from the outfield, if the throw is wide or late and there is no chance to get the runner coming to third, the proper procedure for him is to rush to the ball and catch it on the fly for a possible play at first or second.

(7) The third baseman must be prepared to take proper action on an appeal play. He should watch each runner rounding the base on his way home and should check the men tagging up to score after a fly ball is caught. If a runner misses the base, or leaves it too soon on a fly ball which is caught, the third baseman should call for the ball, step on the base, and call the umpire's attention to the violation. Alertness on the appeal plays can save a team occasional runs, especially where third base is involved.

One other important tactic pertaining to positioning should be observed by the third baseman. With two out, he should guard the foul line in an effort to prevent an extra base hit. He should station himself deep and to the right of his regular position so that there is less chance of a batted ball's getting between him and the line and going through for extra bases.

THE OUTFIELDERS

There has long been a theory on the part of the casual observer that outfielders should pay their way into the ball park. Despite the fact that the occasional eye-catching feats of a particularly brilliant outfielder tend, at times, to dispel this belief, the impression still seems to prevail that an outfielder is merely a bat-wielding brute who must take his place in the field since, by convention, nine men are stationed at various points around the diamond when the other team is at bat.

As we go down the ladder in the various classes of baseball, too often we find that coaches and even players themselves consider the outfielders as excess baggage and the three positions as posts which must be filled by men who are not good enough to make the team as an infielder, pitcher, or catcher.

That this is a completely erroneous impression will be claimed by all outfielders and attested to by the vast majority of pitchers. As a matter of well-proven fact, a good outfield is a very important essential in the success of any team.

Generally speaking, the center-fielder is the best outfielder of the three and must cover the most territory. The right-fielder should have a particularly strong arm for the long throw to third when he fields a base hit with a runner on first. A left-hander will best fit into right field since his most difficult throws will be on balls hit to his left. Conversely, a right-handed thrower should play left field since his most difficult throws will be on balls hit to his right.

Individually speaking, natural outfielding ability, that is, speed, sure hands, and a good arm, is an important factor in the making of an outfielder; but certain skills which can be developed, such as getting the jump on the ball, position play, judgment, quick and accurate throwing, and correct maneuvers are almost equally important and will unquestionably make for more effective play on the part of any outfielder. To this must be added the important duty of the outfielder to help out his teammates at all times by backing up both the infielders and the other outfielders whenever he can, and by calling the play for a fellow outfielder who is concentrating on the ball.

Conditioning hints

While going through his regular pre-season conditioning routine an outfielder should "shadow box" while doing his running, simulating the chasing of a fly ball while conditioning his legs.

At all stages of the season he should use his arm as an outfielder's, not a pitcher's. The two positions require vastly different throws and trying to combine them invites arm trouble.

Preparing for the play

One of the most difficult problems encountered by some outfielders is their lack of activity. This leads to impatience—which must be resisted. An outfielder should learn to wait—calm, yet alert—fully prepared in mind and body to make the correct play, properly.

An outfielder should always figure the next ball will be hit to him and should be prepared to make the play when he does field the ball.

The direction and strength of the wind should be checked at the start of every inning since it can greatly affect the flight of any ball which is hit in the air.

An outfielder should know his pitcher, as well as the hitter. The pitcher's speed and his use of various deliveries, when known to the outfielders, can be a big help in allowing them to station themselves properly before the pitch. The shortstop and the second baseman can relay the catcher's signals so that the outfielder will have an even better idea of where the ball might be hit.

Position before the pitch is very important to an outfielder and any information which will help him gain an extra step or two on the ball can well mean the difference between a hit and an out.

Furthermore, the speed of any base runner or runners should be taken into consideration so that the right play will be made when the ball is hit to the outfield. Not only will his speed give an indication as to the runner's daring and his probable intentions, it will also be a guide as to where a throw will go, either to catch a runner or to keep him from taking an extra base.

Making the catch

When going toward a ball to catch it, an outfielder should run on his toes. Running on the heels will make the ball seem to jump and dance.

To play a ball directly in front of him, the outfielder can start on either foot. If it is to the right and in front of him, starting with a cross-over step on the left foot will enable him to get a better jump on the ball; if it is to the left and in front of him he should start with his right foot. When the ball is hit behind him and to the right, the proper start is made with the right foot, and if it is to the left and behind him he should get off on his left foot.

Outfielder Going Back
on a Fly to His Left

Outfielder Going Back
on a Fly to His Right

In going for a ball hit away from him, the outfielder will find his task made easier if he runs to the spot where he thinks the ball is going to land and waits for it. This will enable him to be in good position for the catch merely by shifting a few feet according to the exact location of the ball.

The actual catch should be made facing directly toward the ball if that is at all possible. This involves the safety factor and makes for greater vision and maneuverability.

An outfielder should try to make all catches in throwing position since a fraction of a second gained or lost can be of tremendous importance in heading off a runner. This is one more reason why two hands should be used in making the catch. Using two hands will allow the outfielder to have his throwing hand on the ball just as soon as he catches it. It is a good idea to put these ideas into practice even with the bases empty since constant use will develop these moves into well-ingrained habits.

With men on base, the ball should be played closer to the throwing side so that the throw can be made in a hurry. If a long throw is needed to head off a runner and it is at all possible, the outfielder should position himself to make the catch while moving in on the ball in order to get extra power into the throw.

A batted ball hit in the air to either left or right field, if it curves, will always curve toward the foul line. This seems to be a rarely discussed fact and one which can be of great importance in enabling an outfielder to handle fly balls. This fact is covered by the laws of physics and thus is an irrefutable one. The words "if it curves" have been added to make allowance for the occasional strong wind which can affect the flight of any batted ball.

The problem posed by the sun can also enter the picture in the making of the catch. Sun-glasses are a great help but are not always available. Whether or not sun-glasses are used, the eyes should be shielded with the glove—the bare hand is of little help because it is too small. If the ball is high and in the sun, once it is located the outfielder should glance toward the ground, then back at the ball. This will help eliminate the danger of losing the ball in the sun.

Position play

An outfielder should shift according to the count and the situation. Outfielding is not a stationary job; the situation varies with each pitch, so that in order to be properly positioned the outfielder should move occasionally. For example, when the batter is ahead in the count, he should play the hitter to pull; with a big lead he should play a little deeper; and so forth. He can also shift according to whether a fast ball or curve has been called for by the catcher, remembering that the slower the pitch, the more likely the batter is to pull the ball.

With two strikes on the batter the outfielders should move away from pull positions since the hitter will be guarding the plate and merely trying to get a piece of the ball, rather than taking a full cut which would mean a greater likelihood of his pulling the ball.

The outfield should play deep early in the game when a single won't hurt. This cuts down the possibility of an extra base hit and means keeping runners from scoring position. This also applies late in the game when the defensive team has a substantial lead.

The depth of the infield also should influence the position play of the outfield. When the infield plays in to cut off an important run at the plate, particularly late in the game, the outfielders will do well to play closer to the infield since a fly ball will allow the run to score easily and since they will be in position to field an ordinary single quickly and make a throw home which may cut off the run.

With a left-hander at bat, the left-fielder should move closer to the infield as well as to his left, and with a right-hander at the plate, the right-fielder should move in a few steps as well as to his right. This is occasioned by the fact that a hitter's power lies primarily in pulling the ball. A ball hit to the opposite field is far less likely to go for distance than one that is pulled.

Outfield alignment,
right-handed batter

Outfield alignment,
left-handed batter

In amateur ball there is a tendency for outfielders to play deeper than is warranted by the power of the batters they encounter. Playing a shallower position will allow the cutting off of many bloop hits. Since, at this level of play, the Texas Leaguer type hit is far more prevalent than is the long clout, playing shallow is a calculated risk in which the percentages would seem to favor the defensive team.

Playing the fence

Fields which are enclosed by a fence present problems of their own to the outfielders. If they are not accustomed to playing in a certain ball park, the outfielders should try to become familiar with it before the game starts. Distances from their normal positions to the fence at all parts of the field should be noted and each one of the trio should throw a ball against different parts of the fence in his particular territory to familiarize himself with the way in which a ball will rebound from it.

To catch a fly ball hit over his head and in the vicinity of the fence, an outfielder should try to avoid charging directly at the spot where the ball will land. Rather, he should run to the fence and then along it to the spot where he will field the ball. This greatly reduces the danger of crashing into the fence and risking possible injury.

If it appears obvious to the outfielder that he will be unable to catch the ball and that it will hit the fence, he should position himself facing the fence, ready to play the rebound.

When to make the play

An outfielder should call for all fly balls that he intends to handle if there is any doubt whatsoever as to who will make the play—and he should call out loud and clear so that there is no mistaking his intentions. Once he calls for the ball he should take it unless shouted off by a man in better position to call the play.

"I've got it" is the conventional call for the ball and it should be answered by the other player(s) near the play. "Take it" will suffice since this cannot be confused with the original call. The answering player then should get in position to back up the man who is preparing to catch the ball.

A fly ball that can be handled by either an infielder or an outfielder should be taken by the outfielder. He is coming in on the ball and is in much better position to call the play as well as to catch the ball. This is especially so with runners on base when a throw might be needed to keep one of them from advancing.

As a general rule, the center-fielder should handle any ball that he can get. Furthermore, if two outfielders call for a ball, the center-fielder should take it. Using this rule as a guide will help greatly in avoiding confusion and the reasoning behind it is quite apparent: The center-fielder is usually the best of the three outfielders and he generally plays deeper and has the play more in front of him than the other two. However, with men on base, the man with the stronger arm should be allowed to make the play on a ball which is between two outfielders and the other man should call the play.

Fielding ground balls

It is good practice for outfielders to work out in the field as often as possible in order to learn how to handle ground balls more effectively. Clean handling will prevent many an extra base and possible run.

Generally speaking, the ball should be played so that if a clean pick-up is missed it will be blocked by the outfielder's body—and in such a way that it will bounce in front of him.

When his team is leading by more than one run, an outfielder should play safe on ground balls by blocking them. In this situation a quick return to the infield is not imperative and blocking the ball will keep it from getting through for extra bases.

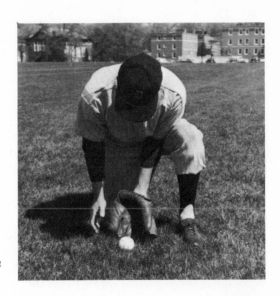

Outfielder Blocking a Ground Ball

When a game is being played in a ball park with a rough outfield, it might be well to block all ground balls, regardless of the situation.

An outfielder should charge all ground balls, even those he intends to block. Once again, this can prevent the runner from taking an extra base and might, in some cases, mean an out at the plate rather than a run.

Making the throw

In dealing with the problem of coping with base runners, a good rule to be followed by all outfielders is: "Always throw ahead of the runner." For example, a throw to second base when the runner has already arrived at, or is just about to reach, that base, will allow him to advance to third quite easily. Throwing ahead of the runner (to third) will keep him on second base.

A ball handled by the outfield should be returned to the infield im-

217

Outfielder Throwing After a Catch (Pete Reiser)

mediately—that is where the play will be and an outfielder can do nothing with the ball but look at it. On most long balls the second baseman or shortstop will come out to assist and if there is no specific base to which the ball must go, it should be thrown to one of them. Short fly balls, just as soon as they are caught, should be run into the infield and the outfielder who has the ball should be ready to throw it if the runner tries to advance.

With a relay needed, the outfielder's throw should be the long one. It should go directly to the relay man, chest-high. Remembering the rule that the second throw should be the short one will insure much more accuracy in the important throw to get the runner.

When throwing the ball home or to a specific base, the outfielder should use the cut-off man as his target and should throw directly to him, head-high. Then, the ball will be in the correct position to be cut off or, if the cut-off man lets it go through, it will be a perfect throw to the catcher or baseman.

The throw to home should arrive on one bounce, making the ball much easier to handle for the catcher. The same practice should be followed on throws to third base from right field and right center. Throws from left and center to second or third, on the other hand, should reach those bases on the fly.

Ordinarily, outfielders can set up a double play by throwing to second on a single. Even if it allows another runner to advance, the throw to second will hold the batter at first, thereby creating a double-play situation. This should always be done if the runner to be held at first represents the tying or winning run.

With the bases loaded in a close game, the outfield should throw the ball home on a single since more than one runner will be trying to score and since a cut-off man will be in position to handle the ball if a quick throw to another base is needed.

A General Theory

The percentage of runners thrown out at home plate is very small. Unless the run is very important or the chance of catching the runner at the plate is very good, it is usually preferable to keep another runner from advancing to scoring position, at the expense of allowing a run to score.

Backing up the play

The outfielders should make themselves part of the game even when the ball is in the infield. One of them should be in position to back up any throw from one infielder to another, and this includes throws from the catcher and the pitcher on bunts and pick-offs.

It is a good idea, if a prearranged play is being used, to flash the signal to the outfield so that they can be ready to move into position to back up the play.

As for specific assignments: The right-fielder should back up first base on all bunts and pick-offs. He should back up second base on all throws from the left side of the infield.

The center-fielder should back up second base on all bunts and plays at that bag.

The left-fielder should back up second base on all plays from the right side of the infield and should back up third on all bunts and pick-offs at that base.

The carrying out of these assignments will insure a team against losing many bases on overthrows. It is part of the principle that outfielding is not a stationary job.

The outfielders should be moving into position so that they are a part of every play, and they should start moving just as soon as they anticipate what the play will be.

A word of caution is needed at this point. The outfielders should not leave their positions to back up a base on a steal or sacrifice until after the ball has passed the batter, lest he swing at it and hit the ball to the spot that has just been vacated.

The foul fly

A special situation of which the left- and right-fielder should be aware arises when the batter hits a long *foul* fly with either the tying or winning run on third base late in the game. If there are less than two out, the ball should not be caught since this would allow the runner to score after the catch.

A Cardinal Rule

Regardless of the other factors that may affect the situation, one cardinal rule which must be kept in mind by an outfielder at all times is—keep the tying or winning run as far from home as possible.

3

OFFENSE

BATTING–THE PHYSICAL ASPECT

FUNDAMENTALS

Successful hitting, to state the case as briefly as possible, revolves around the development of certain skills. The good batsman is always ready to hit, gets his wrists in fast, and keeps his arms away from his body. He attempts to swing only at strikes, to watch the ball hit the bat, to meet the ball ahead of the plate, and he does not swing so hard that he loses body balance.

It is simple enough to list the qualities that make for successful hitting. The problem is how an individual can best acquire those qualities and apply them to his own needs. This section will try to delineate the answers to this many-faceted problem.

The art of hitting can be divided into certain basic fundamentals such as the stance, the stride, hitting actions, the swing, and the follow-through. The average ballplayer must strive for a batting style that will combine these essentials in the way that is best suited to his own capabilities if he is to be a successful hitter.

Types of hitters

Every ballplayer who walks up to the plate with a bat on his shoulders falls into one of three general categories. Basically speaking, he is either a pull hitter, a straightaway hitter, or an opposite-field hitter. These broad classifications may be further refined by individual characteristics, but they are the first groupings to which we should look in analyzing batting techniques.

THE PULL HITTER. Most long-ball hitters, those with real power, are essentially pull hitters. This type is the free-swinger who hits most balls to his respective field—that is, left field for a right-hand batter, right field for a left-hander. He does so because he meets the ball well out in front of the plate with very rapid acceleration of his bat at the point of contact. A slugger of this kind will strike out more often than the straightaway or opposite-field hitter—but he is the man most likely to break up a ball game with one swing of his bat.

THE STRAIGHTAWAY HITTER. The straightaway hitter is the batsman who hits the ball where it is pitched. He pulls an inside pitch, drives a down-the-middle pitch through the center of the diamond, and hits an outside pitch to the opposite field. This type is also known as a spray hitter; he sprays his hits to all fields. He has good bat control and is generally the most reliable kind of hitter. Needless to say, he makes it difficult for the opposition to set their defense for him.

THE OPPOSITE-FIELD HITTER. The opposite-field hitter waits longer before starting his swing and contents himself with just meeting the ball. Because he delays his swing he gets a better look at the pitch and, as a result, seldom strikes out. However, since he slices the ball and rarely gets full wrist-action into his swing he is not a power hitter except on relatively infrequent occasions.

The bat

The tools of his trade are of great importance to any player, and this, of course, applies to the batter and his bat. He should use one that he can handle in such a way that it becomes almost a part of him. Length and weight will vary according to the physical characteristics of the batter as well as to occasional variable factors such as the weather and the pitcher. The important consideration is bat control. The bat should be one that can be handled easily. It should enable a player to cope as effectively as possible with any kind of pitch or pitcher that he may be called upon to face.

WOOD, SIZE, AND FEEL. Good bats are made of either ash or hickory and the concensus of learned opinion seems to be that wood of the straight-grain type is most conducive to power hitting. In addition, it is advisable to select a bat with a knot or two in the wood of the hitting surface. This generally means that the bat is strong and, as the ballplayers say, "has a lot of meat" in it.

The majority of bats used by Major Leaguers vary in weight from thirty-two to thirty-eight ounces and in length from thirty-four to thirty-six inches, generally running approximately one ounce to the inch.

Recently there has been a trend to light bats, even on the part of mature and powerful professionals. Their belief is that a light bat allows them greater control and lends itself to faster hand-action and a better wrist-snap. However, no young ballplayer should be so influenced by a Big League star that he will try to use the same size bat despite entirely different physical capabilities of his own. Rather, he should seek a bat that feels comfortable and will assure him of easy handling and good bat control. In short, the bat should not be so heavy that it swings the player and, at the same time, should not be so light that it cannot be easily controlled.

The size of the bat handle is best determined by individual preference. A thin handle, which can be made even more so by shaving and sanding, is usually preferred by the free-swinging type of hitter who feels that a bat of this kind gives him better wrist-snap and faster hand-action. On the other hand, a thick handle is often preferred by both straightaway and opposite-field hitters since it allows them better bat control. Thick handle or thin, it is definitely advisable to use a bat with a thick barrel or, in other words, a large hitting surface.

Certain variables can influence proper bat weight. For example, an exceptionally fast pitcher demands the use of a lighter bat. On a particularly hot day or at a time when a player is below par physically, he should also switch to a lighter bat. John Mize was a great natural hitter and a serious student of the batting art. He followed a practice of cutting down the weight of his bat progressively as the weather became hotter. Mize also used a heavier-than-normal bat during spring training, feeling that this is a deterrent to the tendency to over-swing that besets most ballplayers at that stage of the season.

BAT CARE. Any man who cherishes his base hits will treat his bat with loving care. Several simple protective methods will enable him to lengthen its life and insure its resiliency. Helpful hints for proper bat care are—

(1) When in use, the bat should be held with its label up. This corresponds with the grain of the wood and will help prevent splitting.
(2) Rubbing the bat with a bone or bottle will help prevent chipping.
(3) Occasional application of a light coat of oil maintains proper condition of the wood.
(4) A bat should not be tossed around indiscriminately since this makes it prone to chips, knicks, and dents.
(5) Bats should be stored in a dry place and wiped dry when they become wet.
(6) When he finds the right bat, a player should keep it for his own exclusive use.

The approach

The role of the batter is not limited to performance in the batter's box. To be of maximum value to his team and to help himself to better performance he should function as a combination coach, groundskeeper, morale-builder, and alert observer.

THE BATTER AS A COACH. A batter's duties take concrete form when he goes to the on-deck circle, awaiting his turn at the plate. He should offer encouragement and help to the man at bat, informing him of any shift in alignment of the defense or a tell-tale move that might be detected on the part of the pitcher or catcher, and by letting him know when to run in case of a dropped third strike or an accidental dribbler.

A runner trying to score should always be coached by the man awaiting his turn at bat. Prior to this, any loose bat or mask that may be in the runner's path should be removed. Then, it is the duty of the man on deck to let the runner know whether to slide or stay up when he crosses the plate. The performance of this task should be mandatory. It can mean not only the difference between a run and an out, but—more important— it may prevent a sprained ankle or broken leg for the runner.

This coaching role should be shared by the hitter, whose duty it is to coach base runners on pitched balls that get away from the catcher, using hand signals to let them know whether to stay put or, in the event that the ball rolls far enough away from the catcher, to advance to the next base.

MAKING PREPARATIONS. The batter can also help himself by his activities while waiting to bat. When on deck he should endeavor to get the timing of the pitches being delivered to the man at bat, even going so far as to stride with them and take an imaginary swing as the ball comes toward the plate.

When leading off an inning, or against a new pitcher who has just entered the game, the batter is in an even better position to familiarize himself with the timing of the pitcher's delivery and the speed of the pitches.

While waiting to hit, a smart batter is observant of the pitcher's stuff at that particular stage of the game, as well as of his operating methods. Even as he enters the box, the batter should be watchful for changes in the positioning of the defense. As he prepares to take his position facing the pitcher, he should remove excess dirt from his spikes; dry his hands thoroughly with rosin, using dirt when no rosin bag is available; and should be swinging either a weighted bat or two extra ones (in absence of a weighted club) for the dual purpose of making his own bat seem lighter and more easy to handle, and of loosening his shoulder and arm muscles.

TAKING SIGNALS. A further important preliminary duty is the taking of signs. Offensive signals, usually given by the third base coach, are the subject of constant scrutiny by the defensive team and any indication that one has been given or received should be avoided. The hitter should look to the coach for a signal—first, as he steps into the batter's box and then, immediately after a pitch has been received by the catcher. In order to confuse the opposition, he should take several additional glances at the coach. In this way he makes it difficult for enemy players to detect the giving of a sign, or to steal the signals.

The grip

THE DIFFERENT TYPES. Batting grips, like types of hitters, fall into three distinct categories. Here, the classifications are end, choke, and

226

End Grip   *Modified Grip*   *Choke Grip*
          (Note Knuckles-on-Down Alignment)

medium-choke grip. Free-swingers generally grip the bat at the very end, their theory being that the greater length of a bat gripped this way gives them added leverage.

The medium-choke style is used by men who desire a greater degree of bat control and who are primarily line drive hitters. It is also resorted to by some end-grippers after the pitcher gets two strikes on them.

Choke hitters hold the bat as much as six inches from the end and by so doing achieve a greater degree of bat control. They are usually place hitters who merely try to get a piece of the ball and, as a rule, are the most difficult ones to strike out.

A few hitters grip the bat with their hands apart. Ty Cobb and Honus Wagner spread their hands on the bat. This method provides good bat control and is conducive to a level swing. In fact, some hitters who employ a conventional grip resort to the hands-apart method during spring training and retain it until satisfied that their swings are level enough to attain good results.

HOLDING THE BAT. Whereas differences exist among ballplayers in the position of their hands relative to the end of the bat, there is great uniformity in the grip itself.

The bat should be held forward in the hands. That is, it should be gripped primarily by the fingers—not seated well back in the palms. This will provide better "feel," which makes for greater responsiveness and quicker reactions to a pitched ball. The fingers of the front hand should be in control as the swing is started, ready to pull the bat through its arc of forward motion.

Establishing contact with a rapidly moving pitched ball and reversing its direction with any degree of authority requires great force-of-resistance on the part of the bat and this, in turn, demands a firm grip. While the initial grip should be firm, it should not be so tight as to cause tension that will impair proper coordination and a fluid swing. It is as the hitting stroke begins that the grip should tighten, reaching a point where it is very firm at the moment of impact with the ball.

AVOIDING TENSION. If too tense while awaiting the pitch, the batter will lose coordination and his hitting will suffer. Furthermore, there will be a marked increase in his tendency to go for bad balls. As stated above, a prematurely tight grip on the bat causes increased tension. For this reason, it is suggested that the batter open and close his top hand before the pitcher delivers the ball, assuring himself of a loose initial grip and an attendant reduction in tension.

CHECKING THE SWING. A perplexing problem for a ballplayer is how to check his swing completely once it has been started. The need for this arises when the batsman decides that the pitch is not to his liking or has fooled him, and can be quite difficult to accomplish. John Mize, to cite him once more, recommends extra pressure applied by the top hand as a great boon to checking a swing that has already been started. Mize's exceptional ability to wait for "his pitch" can attest to the effectiveness of the method which he suggests.

THE PROPER GRIP. Most professionals employ the "knuckles-on-down" grip in holding the bat and its use is strongly recommended, for two important reasons. First, it relaxes the hands and secondly, it assures the proper rolling of the wrists that makes for a fluid, whip-like swing and a good follow-through. As a matter of fact, a batter will find it practically impossible to swing without a proper roll of his wrists and good follow-through if he uses this grip. The term, "knuckles-on-down," means that the knuckles are aligned in such a way that they form a straight line, the second and third knuckles being so aligned that the backs of the two hands come together to form a flat surface. Both bat control and power are improved when this method is employed.

COCKING THE WRISTS. More will be said later concerning the importance of cocking the wrists. At this point, it is sufficient to state that the wrists should be cocked in readiness for the pitch. This is imperative if no motion is to be lost in starting the swing and whipping the bat into the ball.

THE HANDS. The hands should be held comfortably away from the body before and during the swing—before the swing so that the batter is ready for the pitch and will be able to get his bat into motion with no hitch or delay; during the swing so that it will not be "choked," but will have the necessary degree of freedom and fluidity. When a batter holds his hands too close to his body he can be overpowered by a good fast ball. To cite an example of the way in which a truly great hitter treats this phase of batting, Stan Musial holds his hands more than one foot away from his body before starting his swing. His is an extreme case, but most good hitters follow this practice to a considerable extent.

228

A final word pertaining to the grip and the hands—good hitters almost invariably have "quiet hands," that is, regardless of their preliminary motions and body movements, the hands are held as still as possible just before the start of the hitting stroke and until the swing is actually begun. Conformance to this policy means that there will be little of the lost motion that delays the hitting actions and none of the counter-movements that disrupt the fluidity of the swing.

The stance

It has often been said, and rightfully so, that a ballplayer hits with his legs. This maxim is usually meant to imply that a man's batting ability is generally no better than the condition of his legs—and they must be in shape if he is to perform at his best with the bat.

This idea should be made to include the batter's stance—the position of his feet and the distribution of his weight thereon as he faces the pitcher. Any flaw or imbalance in the batsman's initial stance, no matter how slight, is magnified progressively through the successive steps of his pattern of action as he swings at the ball and can seriously impede his attempts to hit with any degree of effectiveness and power. It is for this reason that serious consideration should be given to the stance and every effort made to follow the principles that will make it a well-balanced one, conducive to good and efficient form.

THE MAIN ESSENTIAL. Two words constitute the key to the best stance for a given ballplayer. They are "be comfortable." A wide variety of stances can be found among the game's better hitters, yet they all have something in common. While allowing for individual differences in physique and mechanical ability, the stances adopted by good hitters are ones which insure good balance and allow for a feeling of comfort and ease at the plate. Unless he is successful with it (and this is rare), a batter should discard any stance with which he does not feel completely comfortable. For best results when he goes into action with the bat, a ballplayer should prepare for the pitch by assuming a stance that will find him physically relaxed, yet mentally alert.

THE THREE TYPES. There are three basic types of stance used by ballplayers universally and with little regard to their other batting characteristics—the open, the normal, and the closed stance.

The open stance is one in which the batter's rear foot is closer to the plate than is his front one. He stands almost facing the pitcher, a fact that enables him to get a better look at the ball. The open stance hitter has a decided tendency to meet the ball well out in front of the plate and is usually particularly strong on inside pitches.

The so-called normal stance is one in which the batter's feet are in an almost parallel line, with his front hip and shoulder facing the pitcher. The majority of Major Leaguers use a normal stance.

The closed stance is one in which the front foot is closer to the plate than the rear one. Here, the batter must watch the pitcher by looking over his front shoulder.

VISION AND THE STANCE. No matter what stance a batter finds most to his liking, it should be one that affords him a maximum view of the pitcher. In this respect, it can prove helpful to alter the stance according to whether the pitcher is right- or left-handed. It may prove beneficial to a left-hand batter to open his stance slightly when facing a left-hand pitcher and to close it when opposed by a right-hander. By the same token, a right-hand batter may find his vision is greater when he opens his stance against a right-hand pitcher and closes it slightly when a southpaw is on the mound.

POSITION IN THE BATTER'S BOX. Position in the batter's box has two facets—distance from the plate which is determined primarily by personal preference; and position behind, even with, or in front of the plate, this being dictated by the characteristics of the pitcher as well as the individual taste of the batter.

In regard to the second facet mentioned above, the personal preference of the batter depends primarily on whether he desires to meet the ball before it breaks, in which case he stands forward of the plate, or wishes to have more time to judge the flight of the ball, in which case he stands behind the plate.

The type of pitcher faced on a given day can, of course, have a strong bearing on the position which the batter takes in the box. If the pitcher is particularly fast, a hitter will probably get best results by standing as far in back of the plate as the lines of the batter's box allow. If the pitcher specializes in slow or breaking stuff, a position forward of the plate will quite possibly be most effective. Most good hitters stand at the rear of the batter's box on the assumption that the slight fraction of a second gained thereby will enable them to have greater success in judging the flight of the ball and meeting it solidly.

As indicated, no one position in the batter's box is used by all good hitters alike, individual style and preference being the chief determinant in this respect. They run to wide extremes, ranging from that of the great Rogers Hornsby, who stood at the outside, rear corner of the box, as far from the plate as possible, and stepped into the ball; to that of the former National League star, Rube Bressler, who stood well forward of the plate, with his rear foot on the inside line of the batter's box, and met the ball in a flat-footed manner with practically no stride.

For general purposes, however, it is recommended that the batter stand back of the plate and far enough away from it that the fat part of the bat is directly over the middle of the plate. This will enable him to to get "good wood" on an inside pitch simply by shifting slightly, while at the same time allowing him to protect the outside corner by stepping into the ball. He should never have to *reach for a strike*. Guarding the plate in this manner is advocated because the batter should be able to hit the ball with the fat part of his bat on a pitch thrown over any part of the plate and should be able to do so with a natural and completely unhampered swing.

THE IMPORTANCE OF BALANCE. As the batter assumes his stance in readiness to hit, with his attention focused on the pitcher, his hips and shoulders should be level and his weight evenly distributed. The importance of good balance cannot be overestimated and it should be maintained throughout the entire swing. Consistently good hitting demands a level swing and, in order to achieve one, the hitting stroke must be preceded by a level stance and accompanied by good over-all equilibrium. Each phase of the batter's pattern of action leads to the next and there is a definite carry-over of habits, both good and bad, from one phase to the next.

For this reason, a moderately wide initial stance is recommended. Most good hitters use a fairly wide spread of the feet since it makes for good balance, helps maintain the hips and shoulders on a level plane, and promotes a smooth shifting of the body weight into the swing. Because it gives rise to these desirable qualities in a batter's form it is fortunate, and perhaps coincidental, that a moderately wide stance is almost invariably a comfortable one.

CENTERING THE WEIGHT. Ty Cobb, smartest and possibly greatest of all ballplayers, was of the opinion that slightly more weight should be placed on the front foot than on the back one. He believed that this makes for good balance. In addition, and of almost equal importance, it greatly reduces the tendency to pull away from the curve ball. Finally, placing slightly more weight on the front foot serves as a strong deterrent to lunging, overstriding, and uppercutting.

The batter's feet should be firmly planted and relatively flat on the ground when he assumes his stance at the plate and his weight should be centered mostly on the front part of the feet, not in an exaggerated manner, but comfortably and in a way that promotes a quick, smooth stride and shifting of the weight into the swing. The importance of keeping the weight forward, on the balls of the feet, cannot be stressed too strongly. It is conducive to alertness and quick reactions and is absolutely essential to good hitting. Ted Williams, greatest of modern hitters, has stated flatly that a man who stands on his heels when he bats has no business playing baseball.

THE KNEES. The fact that good hitters are invariably intent in purpose, yet basically relaxed, is a theme that recurs regularly in this study of the batting art. The batsman's intentness should start with his approach to the plate. He should focus his eyes on the pitcher all the while he is awaiting the pitch but should, at the same time, be loose—with his arms relaxed and his knees flexed. The flexure of the knees need not be pronounced but it should definitely be present to some degree in order to prevent tension which is so detrimental to successful hitting.

THE ARMS AND THE STANCE. The position of the arms is an important facet of the stance. That they should be comfortably away from the body has already been acknowledged. The fact that they should be flexed, but fairly straight, should also be stressed. The front arm is the guiding one, both in "pushing" the bat into hitting position and in "pulling" it through the batting stroke. The hands should be held in a high position (at chest level or above) at all times during the initial stance in order to adjust properly to the height of the pitch. This principle revolves around the fact that it is easier to drop the bat in order to hit low balls than it is to raise it into position to hit high pitches.

CORRECTING THE STANCE. The important consideration in this particular fundamental of batting is not the stance itself, but how the batter reacts from his stance. Our discussion has advanced ideas which, if put into practice, will lead to proper reaction from the stance. If, after adapting these principles, a batter finds that he cannot hit certain pitches, an adjustment is necessary. The corrective measures which may be needed can be determined by surveying the results achieved by the batting style employed. Observation and advice by an experienced coach or ballplayer is the best source of help for the batter who needs corrective therapy but, in absence of it, he can often take the proper steps himself. If, for example, the batter finds that he is "getting around" too far ahead of the ball, he can rectify the situation by closing his stance. If he is not "getting around" on the ball quickly enough, an opening of the stance may help overcome the difficulty. After analysis of his trouble, experimentation will show him the amount of alteration that is needed in his stance.

The eyes

In all probability, the very first words of instruction that any youngster receives when taking up a sport are, "Keep your eye on the ball." This advice can be applied universally and is especially pertinent to baseball in general and batting in particular. Establishing contact between the bat and a ball thrown with great velocity and occasional changes in course and speed is difficult at best and, unless the batter concentrates with great intensity on the ball, his best efforts will go for naught—no matter how perfect his form.

The ball should be picked up visually just as soon as the pitcher grasps it in his throwing hand—even before his wind-up begins. This means that the batter should concentrate on the ball from the time he first assumes his stance facing the pitcher and regardless of what motions he goes through preliminary to taking his swing.

An experienced pitcher will, in most cases, keep the ball well hidden until its actual release from his hand. Consequently, eyeing the ball during the entire wind-up will often prove difficult for the batter. Nevertheless, he should make an effort to do so and definitely must pick up the ball as soon as it comes into view.

THE IMPORTANCE OF A QUIET HEAD. A "quiet head" is the term used by ballplayers to describe the stillness of that part of the anatomy which is necessary to insure the steady, even look at the ball that is such a vital part of good hitting. The head will invariably move on a vertical plane with the stride, since the stride has the effect of lowering the entire body slightly as the front foot moves ahead and the weight is shifted forward. On the horizontal plane, however, the eyes should remain fixed. At all times—while idling, on the slight twist to the rear, during the stride, with the hitting stroke, and on through the completion of the forward body pivot and well into the follow-through—the head should be steady and the eyes focused intently on the ball. A relatively familiar picture on sports pages is the one which shows an expert golfer with his eyes still fixed on the spot where the ball lay, long after it has been hit. This practice is one which ballplayers can borrow with great profit. As applied to baseball, the batter's eyes should remain fixed on the spot where ball and bat have met, until he is well into his follow-through and almost ready to take off for first base. Maintaining a "quiet head" is the first step in effecting this good habit.

SIGHTING THE BALL—THE DOUBLE LOOK. The importance of visually picking up the ball at the earliest possible instant is quite obvious. The initial glimpse of it should come while it is still in the pitcher's hand and might be called the first (or quick) look. Equally vital to good hitting

233

is what we shall call the second (or long) look. This is the good look that the batter should take as the ball approaches the hitting zone. It should occur immediately after the stride and just before the hitting stroke begins. Although it must, needless to say, be an almost instantaneous act, it is that important glimpse of the ball during which the batter must judge its line of flight and decide on any split-second adjustment in bat elevation that is necessary in order to meet the ball solidly and with a level swing. The fleeting pause that immediately precedes the swing of the bat is of great significance to accomplished batsmen and it is made doubly so by the opportunity it affords for the essential second look.

FOLLOWING THE BALL—THE SINE QUA NON. There are some really fine hitters who maintain that they can actually see the ball hit the bat. Whether or not this claim is literally true, it does emphasize the point that their eyes follow the ball just as closely as possible during its entire flight to the plate.

Too often a batter will follow the ball as it starts toward him and then lose sight of it because he allows his stride, swing, and body pivot to cause his head to turn and his eyes to wander. Nothing can be more ruinous to good hitting. The last few feet of the ball's flight are the ones in which it curves or changes course and it is here that the second look takes on its importance.

Thus, it seems quite logical that the batter should make it a practice to follow the ball carefully all the way from the pitcher's hand to the plate and should make a determined effort to watch the ball hit the bat. The longer the batter looks at the ball before his bat makes contact with it, the less chance there is of his being fooled by the pitch.

Good hitters go so far as to follow bad balls all the way to the catcher's glove, so highly do they esteem the principle of watching the ball during its entire flight. This practice serves a two-fold purpose. It is a form of self-discipline by which a man acquires a good habit and, in addition, it means that he will be prepared to hit the ball in the event that it should catch part of the plate with a quick last-second break or curve.

The necessity of following the pitch all the way to the bat simply cannot be overemphasized. It is quite possibly the most important fundamental in the entire study of batting. No man can be a consistently good hitter unless he practices it religiously.

The stride

As in most other phases of hitting, the stride varies according to the physical characteristics and the personal preference of each batter. Through experimentation, every ballplayer can find the stride that will give him the most satisfactory results—this is the one which should be used.

There are accomplished batsmen who take fairly long strides; there are others who use practically none—and with good results in each case. For example, two-time National League batting champion, Ernie Lombardi, employed a wide stance and took no stride at all; Hall-of-Famer, Mel Ott, lifted his front foot in exaggerated fashion and took his stride much like a pitcher does in delivering the ball. These two extremes were, however, exceptional cases.

The important factors to be considered by a player seeking the proper stride for his personal use are the maintaining of good balance and the taking of the stride in such a way that he feels completely natural and comfortable. With this in mind, it should be emphasized that it is more than mere coincidence that very few, if any, really good hitters use an exaggerated stride.

ITS PURPOSE. When a batter strides he is, quite obviously, shifting his weight into the pitch. Good hitters accomplish this in a manner that does not interfere with a smooth, level swing.

Careful analysis of successful hitting styles shows quite conclusively that the real purpose of the stride is to force the batter's weight to be centered on his rear foot and to keep it there until the hitting stroke is started. Further study demonstrates that, in order to hit with any measure of power and authority, it is absolutely imperative that the batter's body weight stay behind the swing. When this practice is scrupulously followed, the needed resistance against the swinging force of the bat will have been provided.

HOW IT IS DONE. Our discussion thus far has indicated rather emphatically that the stride, in order to achieve its purpose with any degree of effectiveness, must be well controlled. This quality is invariably present in the batting styles of the game's finest hitters, regardless of the wide disparity found in the exact manner and length of stride used.

While no one style is properly suited to all hitters, it is strongly recommended that an exaggerated stride be avoided. The ideal stride, one which is conducive to good balance, is a short one. To set an arbitrary figure, let us say that it should be anywhere from four to eighteen inches in length, with practically all hitters being able to find the stride best-suited to their own needs within those limits.

The stride is made off the inside of the rear foot, and the striding foot should move into position in sliding fashion, rather than in a pronounced step. Literally sliding the foot is practically impossible because this will cause the spikes to catch in the ground. What actually should be used might be called a "modified sliding-step."

In order to assure the most effective shifting of the weight into the pitch, the batter's rear knee should be bent slightly and the swing, itself, should be against a firm front leg.

Taking the stride in this fashion and keeping it short, with as little forward movement of the head and body as possible, means steady vision and little loss of motion. It will also allow the batter to maintain balance throughout the entire swing and actually enable him to adjust his timing after the pitch is on its way to the plate.

STEP TO HIT. Authorities on batting give strong emphasis to the three words that head this section. Accomplished batsmen most definitely "step *to* hit," as opposed to the weak stickers who "step *and* hit." This really means that good hitters shift their balance and body weight in the direction of the ball—stepping in on an outside pitch, stepping straight ahead on a pitch directly over the plate, and pulling slightly away from an inside pitch. It also implies that the bat is actually swung against the stride, a fact that gives purpose to the previously mentioned principle of swinging against a firm front leg.

For the inexperienced ballplayer, a sound rule to follow is to step toward the pitcher to hit. This will, in most instances, assure his stepping into the ball with his full weight behind the swing. Slight adjustments can be made for inside and outside pitches, with the principle to follow being—the closer the pitch, the shorter the stride and the quicker the hitting actions. When experience has made him a good judge of a pitched ball, the batter can discard the generalized theory of stepping toward the pitcher and take his stride in accordance with the line-of-flight of the ball. Until that time, the more rudimentary method is advocated as sound practice.

TIMING THE STRIDE. The physical action of striding should start at the exact time that the batter sees the ball leaving the pitcher's hand. Ideally executed, it will commence no sooner than at this instant. At the same time, the batter must never wait to see where the ball is going before beginning his stride. Intricate though the element of timing involved here may sound, this exact pattern of movement is essential if the ball is to be hit with real authority.

The "double look" has been described in the section entitled "The Eyes" and is closely allied to all phases of hitting including this one. As it pertains to the stride, the "double look" is applied as follows: there should be a split-second wait immediately following the completion of the stride and backswing, and just before the hitting stroke begins. This minute pause should occur while the weight is on the rear foot. This manner of execution will help to eliminate the damaging tendency to guess at the pitch, which is too often present. In addition, since the level of the batter's eyes is lowered by the stride, this split-second wait gives him the "second look" at the pitch which allows for the necessary adjustment of the eyes to the line of flight of the ball.

As the step is taken with the striding foot, the weight should shift forward, with the hips, shoulders, and head remaining as nearly level as possible and the eyes concentrating directly on the ball. This leads the way to the sought-after level swing. At the same time, the hands should be moving away from the stride as it is started, putting them in good position to move forward into the swing with the shifting of the weight. The time factor returns with the admonition that transferring the weight too soon means that arm-power alone will be behind the swing, the force that can be provided by the legs and body being almost completely wasted. This tendency is most pronounced on the curve ball and change-of-pace and must be guarded against on these slow pitches in particular.

One more advantage of the minutely delayed stride is that it provides great help to the batter in learning to step into or away from the ball properly.

OVERSTRIDING. Probably the chief fault to be found in inexperienced ballplayers is the tendency to overstride. It can be disastrous to any man's batting form and the results achieved thereby because it lowers the arms, shoulders, and eyes; slows up the swing; robs the hitting stroke of power; and impedes the start for first base once the ball has been hit.

The batter who overstrides is easy prey for a smart pitcher, who will have little trouble in upsetting his timing. Furthermore, and as intimated above, even when he does connect solidly the batter will not get good results since his power will have been dissipated in the stride rather than concentrated in the swing.

Overstriding is a fault which must be avoided if a man is to be a good hitter and the best method of accomplishing this is to abide by the principle with which this section was begun—a good hitter does not use an exaggerated stride.

Hitting actions

The "hitting actions" are almost inseparable from the swing and there is much overlapping between the two categories. However, a slight differentiation should be made between them. The hitting actions are those mechanical moves which occur between the stride and the hitting swing, serving as a connecting link between the two.

THE PRELIMINARIES. The techniques and maneuvers described thus far form the basis for the hitting actions. To them should be added three more ideas that are called for to give a more solid foundation to the hitting stroke in coping with certain pitches.

The batter's front shoulder should remain facing the pitcher until the swing is started. This will aid him in hitting the curve ball and outside pitches since it serves as a deterrent to pulling away from the pitch. In addition, it will prevent the loss of power that results from getting out too far ahead of the ball (shifting the body weight too soon).

The theory behind holding the bat in a high position has already been covered. This is a means of being well prepared to handle high pitches. To make it easier for the batter to hit balls on the inside of the plate, a quick turn of the hips (slightly before the swing) is advocated.

THE BACKSWING. Even before the bat is moved back into hitting position the wrists should be cocked. This is one of the most essential fundamentals in the art of hitting. By cocking his wrists, the batter is actually getting ready to hit. This move should be made as the pitcher prepares to deliver the ball. A delay in doing so will find the batter unprepared to meet a fast pitch.

Good hitters almost literally push the bat back into hitting position. The front hand and fingers must be in control as the bat is pushed back as far as possible while still permitting a feeling of comfort. Care must be exercised not to "wrap the bat around the neck," but to push it back in a plane that is parallel to a line drawn from the pitcher's mound to home plate.

The hip pivot, which is of great importance, should, in reality, be a two-way affair. In the backswing this move is not pronounced but, in order to insure the good pivot that leads the way into the hitting swing, the hips must pivot backward slightly. This shifts the weight to the rear foot and is the action which results in the necessary opposite reaction—the forward pivot of the hips.

The end of the backswing is the point at which the vital split-second wait (for the second look) takes place. At this stage of his batting form the hitter should have completed the stride and should have his weight centered on his rear foot. The bat should be at right angles to the shoulders (not parallel to them)—in other words, it should remain fairly erect and its end should never be permitted to droop as far down as the shoulders themselves—and pressure should be felt on the front forearm at the end of the backswing, almost as though it were a signal to move forward into the hitting stroke.

THE START OF THE SWING. Rotary hip-action is absolutely essential to a good swing and actually starts the forward shift of the weight and the movement of the shoulders and arms. It is the key link in the chain of action that extends from the start to the finish of the swing. Rotation of the hips not only starts the movement of the shoulders and "pulls" the weight into the swing properly so that the ball is met with full power; it also leads the body through the continuous flow of motion which has its ultimate conclusion in a good follow-through.

When the hitting stroke is begun, the weight, which has been centered on the rear foot (the "back-pivot heel"), is shifted to the entire foot so that it will be resting equally on both feet when the ball is met by the bat. Care should be exercised to avoid hitting with the weight on the heels— remember Ted Williams' words on this subject.

THE HITTING ZONE AND MAXIMUM POWER. The hitting zone refers to that area where each batter can meet the ball with best results. The proper hitting zone in relation to the position of the hands at the moment of impact is behind the center of the body. The oft-repeated advice that the ball should be met in front of the plate might lead to some confusion now that the other statement has been advanced. In order to clarify the matter in his mind, the reader must take into account the fact that the stride and the rotation of the hips precede the hitting stroke in such a way that, due to the partial completion of the body pivot, the ball can be met in front of the plate while the hands are still behind the center of the body.

One of the most important batting fundamentals is hitting just after the stride. Intentionally or not, every good hitter puts this into practice. In order to facilitate the performance of this essential, the batter should allow his arms to lag slightly behind his stride. When this is done, the ball will be met a slight fraction of a second after the stride—not with it. The lagging of the arms also permits adjustments in timing the pitch to be made at the very last instant and enables the hitter to capitalize fully on his wrist-snap for obtaining maximum power. When bat meets ball a split-second after the stride, all of the power generated by the shift of body weight will go into the swing and will not be wasted on the stride alone. This is another way of saying that the full power of the entire batting action should reach its peak at the exact instant of impact with the ball.

The ability to keep the wrists cocked until the hands reach the center of the body is not only important in imparting power to the swing, it is a technique that demands a great deal of practice—so much so, that it might be considered an art in itself.

In addition to remaining cocked in this manner, the wrists should be held back in the hitting zone as long as possible. The combination of these two principles helps to assure maximum power both by delaying the wrist-snap so that it occurs at the moment of impact with the ball and by making the batter increase the speed of the snap in order to get around on the ball while it is still in front of the plate.

Another necessary feature of good batting form is the holding back of the weight until the last possible moment so that its shifting takes place at the very instant that bat meets ball. The firm front leg against which the stride is made will keep the weight from shifting too soon and, at the same time, will help prevent the head from turning before the ball is hit.

This really amounts to saying that the secret of power-hitting is for the batter to get his weight behind the swing, while delaying as long as he can before committing himself.

The swing

The climax in batting is, quite obviously, reached when bat meets ball. Our discussion of fundamentals has been aimed at helping the hitter to contact the ball with the most telling possible effect. Thus far we have endeavored to establish a sound base for the hitting stroke or swing. Now we are ready to take up the important business of hitting the ball.

STARTING THE HITTING STROKE. At this point the hands have moved away from the body. They are in a raised position. If they have been held high in the first place they will have to be raised less now that the swing is about to start. This eliminates waste motion and saves precious time in the sequence of rapid physical actions needed to meet a ball hurled at great speed.

The bat, which has been pushed back into hitting position, should be "pulled" forward in order to start the swing properly. This technique, coincidentally, makes for "live hands," a must in adjusting quickly to the line of flight of the ball, and its speed. It is the forward hand which should pull the bat across the body. This method serves to delay the uncocking of the wrists far more effectively than does a swing or push-motion.

As the bat moves forward, the hands should be literally whipped into the swing. To help in achieving this, the batter should visualize himself swinging a rope the same length as his bat—with a weight tied to the end of it. The motion which is needed to swing the weighted rope is similar to the one that will best whip the bat into the oncoming pitch. The fat part of the bat coincides with the weight at the end of the rope in this imagined situation.

THE LEVEL SWING. The ideal swing is a level one, that is, the bat should move forward in an arc which is parallel to the ground. The position of the hands at the start of the hitting stroke can be adjusted according to the height of the pitch so that the sweep of the bat will be parallel to the ground whether the ball comes in high, low, or belt-high. The ball can be contacted with a level bat and level wrists and with the weight evenly distributed on each foot at the moment of impact.

The hips and shoulders, which were level during the original stance and at the start of the stride, should continue so during the swing. As the bat moves out across the plate the front arm should be held firm and should be straightening out until it is perfectly straight at the moment

240

of impact with the ball. It is when the arms have reached this position that the swing is at its point of maximum power. The roll of the wrists should take place at this time and carry this chain of action through to its eventual conclusion.

In order to achieve a level swing, the rear elbow should be pointed down and held fairly close to the body at the start of the hitting stroke. This refers to the right arm of a right-handed batter and the left arm of a left-hander. A study of good hitters will demonstrate conclusively that all begin the swing with the rear elbow pointed down.

Ted Williams should be quoted again at this point. This great perfectionist states, "The ideal swing is a level swing but I don't worry about this too much because, if the other fundamentals are right, the swing will be almost perfectly level. On pitches which are higher than the belt buckle, I have the feeling that I'm hitting down on the ball slightly. On pitches that are below the belt buckle, I have the feeling that I'm hitting up.

I think of it as though I were a woodsman cutting down a tree and chopping the classic 'V' in the trunk of the tree.

On the high pitches in the strike zone you seem to be hitting down and as a result you hit the ball on a line. On low pitches in the strike zone, if you think of your swing as though you were cutting up in the 'V,' the result is to hit the ball on a line.

Perhaps it would be well to enter a word of caution here. Don't try to 'golf' the low pitches. And, don't try to pound the high pitches down into the dirt. Just remember the woodsman's 'V.' "

ROLLING THE WRISTS. The swing should come down and across the plate, leveling out before it meets the ball. The wrists are rolled as the ball is met, insuring good wrist-snap and the proper follow-through.

Rolling the wrists is essential to a good swing. In order to achieve the correct roll of the wrists, the bat should be held with the second and third knuckles aligned ("knuckles-on-down") as described in the section on the grip. When this method is employed it will be practically impossible to swing the bat without rolling the wrists.

As previously stated, the wrist-snap should take place at the exact moment of impact with the ball if it is to be hit with real power.

MEETING THE BALL. The ball should be hit well out in front of the batter and when it is in his strike zone. When a batsman does this, the ball will not always be over the plate at the point where it is met by the bat. However, it should be contacted at a point in which its course will carry it over the plate between the knees and the shoulders. This is particularly true of a breaking ball which must pass over just one corner of the plate in order to be a strike and which might well have curved outside of the strike zone by the time it passes the plate.

The batter should not try to overpower the ball. Rather, he should concentrate on meeting it squarely. The lively baseball in use today will go for great distances when "hit on the nose" and if it is met solidly, extra-base hits will take care of themselves. In fact, the home run swing is usually seen only when the batter misses the ball. It is bad in itself, since over-swinging makes the batter turn his head and drop his shoulder, both damaging the batting swing.

The follow-through

Batting does not end with the act of hitting the ball. It must reach a more natural conclusion than the impact of bat and ball if maximum results are to be achieved. Thus, we come to the follow-through, which is the culmination, the last of the fundamentals which pertain directly to the art of hitting a baseball.

THE BASIC PRINCIPLE. Like the idea of keeping one's eye on the ball, the principle of following-through is instilled in would-be athletes from the time of their first introduction to sports. It applies in every form of athletic endeavor as well as to each individual phase of the various games. It is particularly important to batting, where failure to follow through properly can almost completely nullify the good effect that has been achieved by putting into practice the fundamentals which have been covered thus far.

Even a stationary object cannot be driven very far or with any appreciable degree of force and speed if the propelling implement is stopped in flight at the point of contact. If said object is a rapidly moving body which meets an implement that ceases its contrary movement on contact between the two, the rapid movement of the former will be only partially checked when the two meet. Such is the case when a pitched ball is hit by a bat. Before the flight of the ball can be reversed, a very powerful resisting force must be encountered and this force cannot be sufficiently strong unless the bat continues right on "through the ball" in its hitting arc. In a sense, it is comparable to a pitch that is bunted as opposed to one that is hit with a full sweep of the bat.

This application of physical laws gives validity to the principle that a good follow-through is absolutely essential to attaining maximum power in hitting the ball.

COMPLETION OF THE SWING. The forward pivot of the hips has started the hitting stroke. It is a rotary motion which must be allowed to go through to its proper conclusion if good hitting is to become a matter of course. One of the things gained by a full follow-through is a complete hip pivot. At the end of his swing the batter's rear shoulder and hip will have come around to a point where they are facing toward the pitcher whenever the follow-through has been a good one.

A really good follow-through has another important feature. Not only will the batter's rear hip and shoulder have swung around to a point where they are facing the infield; the body weight will also be leaning in the direction in which the ball has been hit, following the ball and giving it extra, added push, as it were.

Ideally, the bat should complete its arc of motion at a spot that coincides with the middle of the hitter's back. When the bat terminates its stroke in this position—in the middle of the back, from both a horizontal and vertical standpoint—it indicates that the swing has been a fairly level one and full enough to assure almost absolute power for that particular batter when he meets the ball well.

Becoming a base runner

The primary concern of the batter is to hit the ball safely. Yet, when he has driven it into fair territory his responsibilities do not cease. Nor should he dismiss them with the attitude that his duties call for him merely to start running. On the contrary, the batter becomes a base runner as soon as he hits a fair ball and then must consider his actions from the viewpoint of a base runner, a specialized category in itself.

Adoption of correct base-running techniques is just as important, if not more so, for the trip to first base from home plate as it is in the remainder of the circuit around the bases. It is covered in detail in the section on base-running.

Clarification

The elements of batting that have been discussed encompass basic essentials and are, needless to say, of the utmost importance to any ballplayer who would be a better hitter. They are, moreover, so closely related that they should be thought of in their entirety—as one continuous flow of motion.

Timing, in its over-all aspect, is the most vital element in batting. As it pertains to the synchronization of the various phases of the batter's pattern of action it can be an intricate business. Because an attempt has been made to break down batting form into its integral segments, some confusion may have arisen on the part of the reader—and understandably so. However, the realization that each of these fundamental parts of hitting takes place in a tiny fraction of a second and that there is not only a strong connection, but a definite overlapping of them in sequence, may tend to clarify the situation.

243

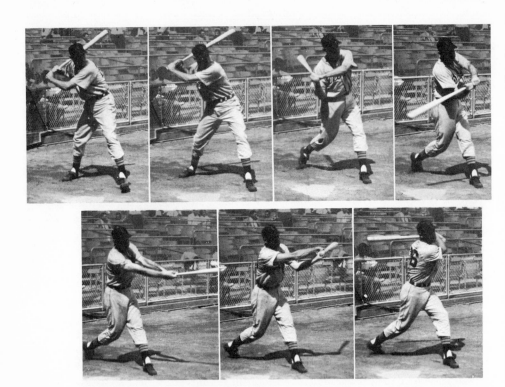

Good Batting Form, Right-handed (Harvey Kuenn)

Good Batting Form,
Left-handed

The therapeutic method

Both individually and as a continuous whole, the physical moves previously described are correct ones, practiced by Major Leaguers almost without exception. These mechanics comprise the most effective method of hitting a baseball well—and with consistency.

Unfortunately, not all ballplayers are able to develop the hoped-for knack of meeting the ball well, even when a conscientious effort is made to master correct techniques.

The aim of the "Therapeutic Method" is to eliminate, in semi-automatic fashion, those flaws most prevalent in the batting forms of men who fail to achieve their own maximum hitting effectiveness.

This method prevents the development of basic flaws by eliminating their causes. Therefore, it is advocated not only as a means of therapy, but as a positive measure in teaching the art of batting—particularly to young and inexperienced players.

THE TECHNIQUE. The philosophy behind the therapeutic method revolves around the position of the hands while awaiting the pitch, and the importance of rotary hip action in giving impetus to the swing.

The bat is held close to or just touching the shoulder, but with the hands away from the body. The entire pattern of action is started by a hip pivot. Everything then turns together smoothly and the bat follows quite naturally in a level, compact swing. As the bat moves out over the plate the wrists should be whipped right through the ball.

The efficiency of this style arises from the elimination of extraneous movements, particularly of the hands, and the preclusion of the incorrect shifting of the body weight.

CORRECTIVE ACTION. The therapeutic effects of the swing are:

1. Elimination of hand-hitching
2. Reduction of the tendency to overstride
3. The cutting down of head movement
4. Prevention of pulling away from the ball
5. Curbing of the premature shifting of the body weight

POSITIVE RESULTS. This method of batting enables a player to effect several positive achievements.

1. The meeting of the ball "out in front," but with the hands behind the center of the body.
2. Getting the body behind the swing.
3. Promotion of a good follow-through.

THE STRIKE ZONE

A theme that keeps running through this study of the art of hitting is that the batter should offer only at good pitches and that he should make a determined attempt to hit the ball in the strike zone. This philosophy is motivated by the belief that no batter should help the pitcher and make that man's task any easier than it is. Percentages definitely favor the pitcher as long as he stays ahead in the count (even the best hitters connect safely only about once in every three times at bat). For that reason the batter must avoid giving the pitcher any extra advantage. One of the principal ways in which a batsman can safeguard his own interests is to know the strike zone and realize fully its importance in the game of baseball.

The reasoning behind it

A thorough understanding of the reasons for which the dimensions of the strike zone have been so defined should help all ballplayers to appreciate its significance.

The founding fathers of baseball were sound in their reasoning when they outlined the limits of the zone through which a ball must pass to be considered a strike. A ball which passes over the plate within this area is far more easy for the average batter to hit than is one which fails to enter it as it goes by him.

Home plate is seventeen inches wide. Any pitched ball which passes over the plate at a point which is above the batter's knees and below his shoulders when he assumes his normal stance is considered to be a strike.

The strike zone is interpreted by umpires to be three dimensional and this fact should be realized by all ballplayers. It is not merely a flat-space area seventeen inches wide and extending vertically from the batter's shoulders to his knees. It also has depth and, if extended to its extreme limits in all directions, forms a five-sided column of space which can be measured in cubic inches. It is shaped much like a pentagonal box-kite.

Every cubic inch of that space is in the strike zone, and, figuratively speaking, belongs to the pitcher. In order to throw a strike he has to make the ball merely touch any part of this space. The batter must protect all parts of that solid area—top, bottom, side, front, and back.

Ted Williams' theory

If it seems that a great deal of stress is placed on the opinions voiced by Ted Williams, it must be confessed that that impression is correct. Williams was the finest hitter of the modern era and, more important to this discussion, one of the keenest students of the art of batting that the game has ever known. His studies have been exhaustive in nature and carried out with astute observation and keen insight. Great natural hitter though he was, his approach to batting is scientific in method and attention to detail. Ted Williams' theory on the significance of the strike zone is well worth passing along. To paraphrase his exact words:

Get a good ball to hit. In order to pick out a good ball to hit you've got to learn your strike zone.

Reducing to mathematics the zone into which the pitcher must throw the ball for a strike, it measures approximately 4¼ square feet (allowing seventeen inches for the width of the plate, three feet for the distance from the batter's knees to his shoulders).

If the hitter develops the habit of swinging at balls that are only two inches above, below, outside, or inside his normal strike zone he enlarges the target which the pitcher must hit by two inches all around. Instead of a 4¼ square foot target, the pitcher now has one of almost six square feet at which to shoot—an increase of 37 per cent in target size. Give a good pitcher an advantage like that and he'll make a monkey out of you.

Master your *own* strike zone. It's something you've got to keep working at and it's the one thing you've got which keeps the pitcher "honest." He has to get the ball into your strike zone or he's going to give you a base on balls.

Knowing the strike zone

Rogers Hornsby is considered by most baseball men to have been the greatest of all right-handed batters. His philosophy regarding his art was brief and to the point: "The secret of good hitting is hitting only good balls."

This probably constitutes oversimplification but it does give weight to the importance of knowing the strike zone and selecting a good pitch to hit.

A batter who offers at bad balls is only helping the pitcher. Many smart moundsmen operate on the theory that the simplest way to retire the hitter is to make him go for bad balls. The batter who does so is actually falling into a trap.

In the case of pitchers who are wild, swinging at a bad ball eliminates the advantage that can be gained from their lack of control. A base on balls not only provides the offensive team with a base runner, it often harms the pitcher's confidence in his control and makes him throw "fat" pitches that greatly simplify the batter's task. And—to repeat for emphasis—a bad ball is much more difficult to hit well than is a pitch in the strike zone.

247

Experience and practice are the best teachers for a batter endeavoring to learn his strike zone. One concrete method of acquiring this knowledge is to stand at "the strings" (see section on drills) when a pitcher is throwing at them. In the absence of "strings," an ambitious batter can take a position "at the plate" while the pitcher is warming up and have the catcher serve as an umpire, calling balls and strikes. Needless to say, the batter should not swing at the ball. Merely standing in his normal hitting position will give him excellent practice in judging a pitched ball.

One qualification is needed. A batter should know his own strike zone —some strikes are not in his strike zone. Only when he has two strikes on him must he swing at any strike.

Perhaps the main cause of swinging at bad balls is tension on the part of the batter. The overanxious hitter is a source of comfort to a smart pitcher. When he finds himself in this state, the batter can help to alleviate the situation by stepping out of the batter's box and taking more time in getting ready to hit. He should bear in mind that, if patient but always prepared for it, he will get "his pitch" in three out of four times at bat.

POWER

Every ballplayer has the yearning to be a power hitter, the big man in his team's attack, the slugger who can clear the bases with one mighty swing of his bat. Unfortunately, nature has endowed very few of us with the ability to deliver the long ball with any great degree of consistency. That too few players realize this fact is also unfortunate because, in their desire to wield the big stick, they attempt to knock the cover off the ball and thereby sacrifice base hits—and power.

This is not meant to discourage aspiring ballplayers by giving them the impression that only a Mickey Mantle can hit the long ball. A look at Major League home run statistics will dispel this belief. What it is intended to convey is the idea that each man should realize his own capabilities and limitations and handle himself accordingly. Mantle has great natural power, but he knows that swinging too hard will impair his hitting and, consequently, he goes for the long ball intentionally, only upon occasion. The average ballplayer should do likewise, contenting himself with good over-all hitting performance and the occasional long ball which will come quite naturally to the man who meets the ball well.

The lively ball

The jack-rabbit baseball in use today has actually been a detriment to hitting in general. The fact that even weak hitters can pound the ball out of the park has given all of them the urge to be home run sluggers. As a result, home run production has increased but batting consistency has declined sharply. In their attempts to overpower the ball, present-day hitters are robbing themselves of both good timing and a smooth, level swing.

Today's ball may not differ in specifications from the one that has been in use for the last thirty years. However, improvements in the manufacturing process have unquestionably added to its resiliency. Furthermore, bats seem to be greatly improved in quality and driving power. This combination has placed an emphasis on the long ball and made it much more prevalent in the modern game.

The most important fact that batters should realize is that they do not have to overpower the ball to hit for distance. Stan Musial, for example, met the ball with a smooth, rhythmical swing. He did not try to tear the cover off of it. As a result, Musial hit for consistently high averages and, at the same time, amassed a goodly share of extra base blows.

It can be emphatically stated that the lively ball will go for greater distances when "hit on the nose." If the batter merely concentrates on meeting the ball squarely, the extra base hits will take care of themselves and his batting average should show a definite improvement.

Providing power

The premise has been advanced that meeting the ball well is the main causative factor in achieving power with the bat. This statement is, to all intents and purposes, irrefutable. For a fuller appreciation of the techniques by which the desired result is attained, however, further investigation and a more detailed break-down are required.

While meeting the ball squarely should be a batter's primary goal, that alone is not sufficient to provide maximum power for him. The speed with which the bat is brought forward is at least the second most important element in hitting for distance. This is, in reality, another way of saying that maximum driving power is brought about by quick action of the arms and hips and is dependent upon rapid acceleration of the swing of the bat at the moment of impact.

The batter's body balance is too often upset by a hard, forceful swing. This means that poor timing results from most attempts to overpower the ball. The vast majority of good hitters use a moderately hard swing, one which is smooth and basically level and which features good, quick wrist-action. They believe in letting the bat do some of the work and try to achieve the feeling of having put about 90 per cent of the shoulder and arm strength and a full 100 per cent of the wrists into the hitting stroke. The addition of the follow-through and body-lean, which should ensue, will place the entire weight behind the swing.

All of this signifies that the correct adaptation of the fundamentals discussed heretofore and the use of a slight degree of moderation in their application will enable any ballplayer to hit with the power that will most closely approach his own individual maximum.

Hitting line drives

The line drive is the optimum in batting. The hitter who can deliver this type of blow consistently is the one most feared by pitchers. Although many home runs have considerable loft, the big sluggers are primarily line drive hitters. Their solid liners are the most frequent producers of base hits and their especially well-hit balls have sufficient carry to clear the fences.

When the ball is hit solidly (that is, contacted in its center by the fat part of the bat) with a level swing and good follow-through, the result will be a low-trajectory ball (line drive).

Ty Cobb, in discussing batting in general and the desirability of hitting line drives in particular, said, "Don't slug at full speed; learn to meet them firmly and you will be surprised at the results."

What Cobb is saying is that rapping out line drives greatly increases the chances of hitting safely and that the best way to do this is to concentrate on meeting the ball squarely.

Timing and power

No matter how far or in what direction this book leads, it seems that it is impossible to get away from the element of timing. Every fundamental of batting involves it and, at the same time, is dependent upon it. In the over-all picture, power-hitting revolves almost entirely around it. The various techniques suggested as aids to the batter have, as their ultimate purpose, the improvement of his timing. On those occasions when it reaches the point of perfection, batting power almost naturally follows.

Good timing comes through practice and with experience. Discussing the ingredients which contribute to it encompasses almost all of the fundamentals discussed this far. For example, in order to synchronize the wrist-snap and the shift of body weight with requisite precision, the wrists should remain cocked until the hands reach the center of the body as the bat is brought forward in its hitting arc.

In a well-timed swing, the bat meets the ball in front of the plate as the weight is transferred to the front foot. The hitting swing reaches its zenith with the complete transfer of weight, while the wrist-snap at the moment of impact can be likened to a sudden explosion of energy.

A word of caution—the hitting zone should be the same for all pitches, fast or slow, in order to insure good timing. This means that adjustment in stride and swing must be made in such a way that the point of impact will always be in the same area relative to the plate and, once again, reaffirms the importance of the principle that the batter should step *to* hit.

Uppercutting—pro and con

Some hitters intentionally swing with a slight uppercut for the purpose of giving loft and carry to a batted ball. While it is true that their method occasionally bears fruit, the fact remains that this imposes a handicap on them as far as consistency is concerned. A pitched ball is much easier to hit solidly when the swing is level. Furthermore, the uppercut swinger will usually have trouble with anything other than a low pitch, hitting the high ones straight into the air. When this breed of hitter does drive out a high pitch with authority it is generally because he has altered his style and has met the ball with a level swing. And this example, of course, is not concerned with an uppercut stroke at all.

Line drives are still the most desirable commodity for a batter and they are best achieved by a swing that is slightly down, if not completely level. This practice (downswing) should be avoided on low pitches—the hitter should remember Ted Williams and his woodsman's "V" and try to meet a high pitch with a slight downswing. When this is done, the swing will be essentially level and line drives will be the result.

The wrists and power

While the arms, shoulders, hips, and legs all give force to the swing, it is the wrist-snap which produces the real driving power and propels the ball with speed and for distance.

Rolling the wrists is of paramount importance in imparting this desired snap to its fullest degree. Properly executed, the wrists roll as the ball is hit. After the ball leaves the bat, the roll of the wrists goes on as a continuation of the swing. The antithesis of this is the sweep-hitter whose stiff-armed hitting stroke does not utilize the wrists and, consequently, deprives itself of much power. To draw a comparison—a sweep-hitter swings at the ball instead of hitting at it as does the man who rolls his wrists properly, and a great difference results in both the distance of the batted ball and the speed with which it leaves the bat.

Some hitters follow through with only one hand on the bat. Bill Skowron, for one, removes his top hand from the bat as it comes around to the completion of its swing. This leads to the conclusion that batting power is attained primarily in the first half of the swing, being generated in the main by the front arm and receiving a big boost in driving force from the wrist-snap. It must be noted, however, that even batters who finish the swing with only one hand on the bat follow through properly in order to achieve maximum driving power.

The bat and power

There has long been a rather widespread belief in the idea that the size of a bat, both its length and weight, has a strong bearing on the driving power of the man who wields it; the feeling is that the larger the bat, the greater the distance the ball will travel when hit.

It is true to a certain extent, that a longer and heavier bat will enable a hitter to drive the ball further—contingent on his ability to control that bat. Unfortunately, it is extremely unlikely that any but the strongest batsmen can handle an extra-large bat with adequate control. Thus, the big stick frequently makes perfect timing impossible to all but a small minority of ballplayers.

Most long-ball hitters hold the bat at the very end. The extra length afforded by the end grip provides more leverage by enlarging the arc in which the bat moves and this, of course, makes for greater driving power. It also means that for every movement of the bat handle there is proportionately greater movement of the hitting surface, making complete bat control more difficult to effect.

In order to gain added leverage, some outstanding hitters have resorted to tucking the little finger of the lower hand under the knob of the bat. Lou Gehrig and Jimmy Foxx, both all-time greats, were two who used this method to increase the length of their bats and gain that added leverage.

On the other hand, bat control is really more essential than is the size of the bat. Even the fabulous Babe Ruth, although he ordinarily employed the end grip, would occasionally work his hands up the handle when the pitcher got two strikes on him.

The trend today is definitely to lighter bats. Present-day ballplayers seem to feel that a smaller bat, one which can be handled easily, lends itself not only to good bat control, but to the rapid acceleration of the swing and the forceful wrist-snap which are the main ingredients of power hitting.

PULLING THE BALL

Most long-ball specialists are primarily pull hitters. There are two perfectly good reasons why this is true.

First, a pull hitter meets the ball well out in front of the plate, driving his bat forward very rapidly and with a pronounced wrist-snap in order to do so. Right there, he has performed two of the essentials which make for power-hitting.

Secondly, the physical construction of ball parks is such that the fences close to the foul lines are generally far shorter than they are in center field and its bordering areas. While the straightaway hitter keeps the defenses spread, allowing a greater number of base hits to fall safely, many of his hardest blows can be caught and merely go for long outs.

If he hopes to clear the fences for home runs the batter, quite obviously, will have much greater chances of success when he pulls the ball. As a consequence, young ballplayers who give evidence of developing good power are both encouraged and taught to pull the ball.

Basic theory

Most ballplayers are natural opposite-field hitters. This stems from an innate fear of the ball and the resultant instinctive urge for self-protection. Following this line of reasoning, a youngster will step into a slow pitch and is likely to pull the ball. Fast deliveries, however, bring out his self-protective instincts and find him with a tendency to see where the pitch is going before he even thinks of swinging at it. Therefore, his batting stroke is a more or less defensive gesture and, combined with the delay in his actions, will cause him to hit to the opposite field, if at all.

Acquiring the knack

The problem, then, is learning how to pull the ball. Some young ballplayers, through experience and the growth of confidence which often follows, develop the ability to pull the ball without specialized coaching. Others must work hard at it. Practice and experience are the first step in overcoming fear of the ball and gaining confidence. A player simply cannot get too much of them. In addition, other more mechanical means can be employed to help a man acquire the knack of pulling the ball.

All hitters are more likely to pull an inside pitch than one which is on the outside of the plate. For that reason it is suggested that a man who has difficulty in pulling the ball should stand close to the plate, thereby making almost any ball in the strike zone an inside pitch. As a matter of fact, a batter should never have to reach for a strike in order to hit it, whether he desires to pull the ball or not.

An open stance is another device which facilitates pulling the ball. Open-stance batters are almost invariably pull hitters because they naturally meet the ball well in front of the plate. Furthermore, they are usually low-ball hitters who particularly like inside pitching. By the same token, it is advisable for would-be hitters to develop a preference for low and inside pitching.

Additional measures which can be of help are a slight bending at the waist—but not at the knees; and the use of the knuckles-on-down grip which both speeds the wrist-snap and increases its strength.

A definite pull hitter will drive a wide pitch through the box and will often have trouble keeping an inside one in fair territory. In batting practice, where the pitching is not as fast as it is in game competition, inside pitches should almost invariably be pulled foul. Then game-time is likely to find a well-hit ball travelling in the desired direction.

ADVANCING THE RUNNER

Theoretically, every ball should be hit where it is pitched. There are times, however, when it is desirable to place-hit to a general area so as to increase greatly the chances of advancing the runner to scoring position. In practically all cases, this involves hitting the ball to right field and it takes two forms: the hit-and-run, in which it is imperative to hit the ball; and hitting behind the runner, in which case the element of compulsion is eliminated but the ball should be driven toward right field when it is hit.

The hit-and-run

The hit-and-run is a do-or-die type of play. In it, the runner takes off for second base with the pitcher's initial motion toward home plate, just as he does on a steal. The batter must hit the ball in order to protect the runner and should try to hit toward right field so as to improve the runner's chances of reaching scoring position safely.

WHY AND WHEN IT IS USED. Probably the primary objective of the hit-and-run as it is practiced in professional baseball is to decrease the possibilities of a double play. The idea behind this conviction is that a ball hit between the first and second baseman is more difficult to turn into a double play because of the long and usually awkward throw involved in retiring the lead runner. The fact that the runner is well on his way to second base when the ball is fielded is possibly an even more important consideration. Furthermore, when the ball goes through to the outfield the runner will more than likely be able to advance to third base with little trouble.

The hit-and-run is mainly for right-handed batters, since a left-hander usually hits toward right field and is more difficult to double at first base because of the better start he gets after hitting the ball.

Occasionally it is best to hit toward the shortstop position. Naturally, this is dependent on who will cover second base. In order to determine this beforehand, the batter should notice the positions of the shortstop and second baseman relative to the bag. The man who is playing closer to it will almost invariably cover the base. Another and even surer method of determining this, is for the batter to take a pitch and have the runner bluff a steal of second. The man who is to cover will usually fall into the trap and start for the base.

It takes an accomplished batsman to execute the hit-and-run in theoretically correct fashion. For that reason, an inexperienced batter should merely hit away, the important consideration being the prevention of a double play.

The play should not be used by a long-ball hitter who stands a good chance of moving the runner into scoring position whenever he meets the ball well. Furthermore, in order to keep the opposition from setting its defenses for the hit-and-run, it should not be subject to overuse. In addition, it is a poor maneuver with a runner on second and/or third since he is already in scoring position.

With protection of the runner of vital importance, there will be times when the hitter should throw his bat at the ball in order to safeguard the man on base. When the defensive team is prepared for the hit-and-run, for instance, they will often resort to a pitch-out in order to foil the play. Here, the batter must endeavor to protect the runner at all costs.

As a general rule, the average batter should merely try to meet the ball and hit it on the ground when the hit-and-run is being attempted. Especially, with a two-ball, no-strike count the batter should hit away since the pitcher is in the hole and will often come in with a "fat" pitch.

HOW IT IS DONE. The points above should not discourage the average ballplayer from acquiring the knack of hitting-to-right. It is a skill which can be of tremendous value to both a player and his team, and is well worth mastering.

Obviously, much practice is needed to become adept at it. Luke Appling, two-time American League batting champion, was one of the game's truly great hit-and-run men. Accomplished as he was, Appling never ceased working to perfect his artistry. In batting practice he would have the catcher call out at irregular intervals, "There he goes," after the pitch was on its way to the plate and would then attempt to hit the ball to right field no matter where it was pitched. The average ballplayer need not go quite that far but he should regularly practice driving the ball to right field if he desires to become a finished hit-and-run man.

There are several methods by which a right-handed batter can hit to right field. All should be tried until the proper one is arrived at. Then, that particular way of doing it should be practiced to the point of perfection. These various techniques can be summarized as follows:

1. Align the *third* knuckles: This prevents a complete roll of the wrists and makes pulling the ball very difficult.

2. Spread the hands: This should not be done so noticeably that it tips off the opposition as to the batter's intentions. Spreading the hands makes for a push-type swing which almost naturally will send the ball to right field.

3. Move the right foot back several inches and stride toward right field: For purposes of masking his intentions the batter should move his right foot as the pitcher is about to release the ball, not any sooner. This method permits a relatively normal swing which more or less aims the ball toward right field, the direction in which the body weight will be moving.

4. Keep the hands ahead of the bat on the swing: This is actually a relatively safe method of swinging late. Because of the position of the bat behind the hands, the ball cannot be pulled but will be hit behind the plate which, combined with the angle of the bat when it meets the ball, will cause it to go toward the opposite field.

5. Keeping the right elbow close to the body on the swing: This is another method of meeting the ball with the hands ahead of the bat, thereby bringing it into the pitch late, thus causing it to go toward the opposite field.

Any one of the above techniques can help the batter to accomplish his purpose.

These tactics should occasionally be varied if the defensive team gives a good indication as to who will cover second base. It might be best to hit toward the shortstop position at times, particularly with a left-hander at bat, in which case the shortstop is most likely to cover the base. A left-hander can use any of the above methods to hit to the opposite field when the opposition indicates that the shortstop will cover second base on the hit-and-run.

TWO VARIATIONS. The bunt-and-run and the run-and-hit are two variations on the hit-and-run theme which do not alter the original to a great extent and which can prove of value to a player seeking to advance a teammate to scoring position with less risk than is involved in the hit-and-run.

1. The Bunt-and-Run: This is a version of the sacrifice in which the runner does not wait until the ball is on the ground before starting for second base. As on the hit-and-run, he breaks with the pitch and the batter must meet the ball in order to afford him the necessary protection. In this case, however, the batter bunts the ball rather than hitting it with a full swing. The bunt should go toward third base. When the third baseman comes in to field the ball he leaves his base unprotected. Then, if the runner has succeeded in getting a good jump on the ball, he will probably be able to reach third.

An alert shortstop can hamper this play by covering third base. Outside of the Major Leagues, however, there are very few shortstops who are able to anticipate it. Furthermore, the play is made to order for a left-handed batter, since the shortstop will almost invariably cover second base with a lefty at bat, leaving third wide open when the third baseman fields the bunt.

While the bunt must be a good one in order to draw the third baseman in, the play stands a better chance in the matter of protecting the runner, since the batter will have less trouble in bunting the ball than in hitting it with a full swing.

2. The Run-and-Hit: This is a play in which the runner breaks for second with the pitch and the batter swings at the ball at his own discretion. It should be attempted only with a 3-1 or 3-2 count. In this play the batter swings at a strike in order to protect the runner (and himself on 3-2) but passes up this pitch if it is a ball since this gives him a base on balls and allows the runner to advance automatically. It is attempted quite often with less than two out and almost invariably with two out, in which case it is a perfectly natural maneuver.

Hitting behind the runner

This play differs from the hit-and-run in that it involves only the batter as far as actual execution is concerned. Then, too, no element of compulsion is present. What is implicit here is the desirability, at certain times, of driving the ball toward right field with men on base.

The object is to advance the runner to second base by hitting the ball on the ground toward the opening between first and second, this gap being larger than usual with the first baseman holding the runner close to the base. In most cases, when the ball is hit in the desired direction, the second baseman will have to field it, going to his left to do so. This means that a double play will be very difficult to effect. If hit hard, many of these balls roll through to the outfield for base hits, allowing the runner to reach third with little trouble.

This play is strictly a no-out maneuver. It is generally attempted only with a man on first base. It is, however, a good move with a runner on second base since it can move him to third where, with one out, he will have at least two opportunities to score. Even with runners on both first and second, the use of this play can be justified since, as previously mentioned, a double play is unlikely on a ball hit to the second baseman's left. Then, with men now on first and third, the first baseman will probably play on the base with the runner and, of course, the man on third will be easier to bring home than he was when on second base.

The batter is not compelled to swing at one particular ball and can, in fact, wait for an outside pitch, which is more easily hit toward right field. He should, however, hit away with a count of two balls and no strikes, when the pitcher is likely to come in with a fat pitch, or when he has two strikes charged against him and must guard the plate.

As for mechanical techniques involved—the batter should be concerned mainly with just meeting the ball, preferably by bringing his arms down so as to increase his chance of hitting the ball on the ground.

Any of the methods described under the hit-and-run can serve the batter's purpose in hitting behind the runner. An idea which should be added at this point is that the nearer to the plate the batter makes his hitting zone (that is, not out in front as it ordinarily is) the easier it will be for him to place the ball toward right field.

BATTING FAULTS AND THEIR REMEDIES

Every ballplayer should have a two-fold goal as far as his batting is concerned. He should strive to hit as well as his physical capabilities allow and he should try to avoid slumps. The former can be achieved, the latter is a more difficult proposition.

Slumps

Even the best of hitters fall into occasional batting slumps which, fortunately, are usually of a temporary nature. They seem to be inevitable and are generally caused by acquiring one or more bad habits in unwitting fashion. When in the throes of a slump, the smart ballplayer will turn to a coach or teammate for assistance. This disinterested observer can often detect a fault which has inexplicably arisen to impair the batter's best efforts. In most cases, the batter is completely unaware of its existence and is conscious only of the fact that something is causing a decline in his hitting. Once discovered, the underlying cause of a slump can be eliminated by application of the proper therapy.

The psychological effects of a slump often prove more damaging than the causative fault itself. A batter beset by such a lapse should realize that it happens to the best, that discouragement in the face of it can be his worst stumbling block, and that he should, at all times, keep swinging naturally with the assurance that sooner or later the base hits will start dropping in for him.

More specifically, when his batting suffers a temporary decline a ballplayer should observe three "don'ts": don't keep the bat on your shoulder, don't lean with the pitch, and don't swing at the pitcher's motion rather than at the ball itself. Furthermore, and probably even more important, the batter should try to hit every ball back at the pitcher until he starts to meet them well once more. He will not actually accomplish this, but merely trying to do so will make him follow the ball closely and will help him to meet it solidly.

Basic faults

The bad habits which cause occasional slumps are the same common faults which keep some ballplayers from achieving maximum results from their natural hitting ability.

As a general rule, men who are poor hitters should make an extra effort to follow the ball closely and to lay off bad balls. They should also concentrate on learning to meet the curve ball squarely and, all else failing, might try hitting to the opposite field until they are watching the ball closely and meeting it well.

The most common, definable batting faults are listed below with suggested remedies for rectifying them.

OVERSTRIDING. This is one of the most prevalent and damaging of bad habits. The batter who overstrides loses balance, wastes power, and will have serious difficulty in adjusting his timing to pitches of varying speeds. The best remedy for this fault is to widen the stance and to put more weight on the front foot. This will greatly reduce the tendency to overstride which plagues so many hitters.

LUNGING. Lunging at the ball is a common fault which seems to be a perfectly natural move on the part of some hitters. It is an exaggerated form of overstriding in which the body weight shifts suddenly and awkwardly, rather than smoothly and with equilibrium. It can be eliminated to a considerable extent by employing a slight inward (to the rear) turn of the body as the pitcher is about to release the ball. This is especially applicable to slow and breaking pitches on which the tendency to lunge is at its height.

FOOT-IN-THE-BUCKET. Fear of the ball is probably the main contributing factor to the habit of pulling away from the pitch. The best suggestion which can be offered to overcome it is for the batter to step toward the pitcher to hit. Where it persists, the foot-in-the-bucket can be compensated for to some degree by the batter's shifting his weight to the front foot with his stride, thereby getting the full weight of his body into the swing by means of his hip pivot.

HITCHING. A hitch in the swing is caused by a movement of the hands and/or arms just as the pitcher is releasing the ball. It not only hampers a smooth swing, but makes it difficult for the batter to get his bat around on fast pitches. The important asset of "quiet hands" is missing here. Holding the bat so that it just barely touches the outer part of the shoulder will lessen the inclination to hitch. The most effective remedy for over-coming this fault, however, is for the batter to raise his rear elbow. This will not only reduce the tendency to hitch, it will make it almost physi-cally impossible to do so.

LIFTING THE REAR FOOT. Lifting the rear foot destroys balance and both delays and upsets the smooth shifting of the weight into the pitch. This fault can be eliminated by placing more weight on the rear foot.

UPPERCUTTING. Long ball hitters often uppercut intentionally, hop-ing to give the ball added loft and distance. This is, however, a bad practice when it reaches the point of becoming a habit. The uppercutter is strictly a low-ball hitter and can be expected to hit high pitching straight up, into the air.

The first thing that an uppercut swinger should do to overcome this fault is to widen his stance, giving him better balance and more even distribution of his weight. He should also open his stance. This will shift the center of his body weight forward, greatly reducing the tendency to uppercut.

Employing the "knuckles-on-down" grip not only makes for proper rolling of the wrists and follow-through but, in the case of the upper-cutter, it helps him in achieving a more level swing.

Carrying the hips and shoulders on a level plane and placing more weight on the front foot are additional aids in eliminating the uppercut swing. Furthermore, if a conscious effort is made to complete the follow-through with the bat in the middle of the back it will be a pretty good indication that the swing has been a fairly level one.

CHOPPING. Chopping is the direct counterpart to uppercutting. While it is less natural as a movement and, therefore, less prevalent in practice, it is equally damaging to good hitting. In order to overcome this habit, the batter should raise his front shoulder until it is level with the rear one and should place more weight on his rear foot.

OVER-PULLING THE BALL. When the batter pulls practically every pitch into foul territory it means that he is hitting with the stride. This causes a serious loss of power. It can be remedied by closing the stance and by consciously observing the slight pause at the end of the backswing and stride. Additional help may be provided by employing the slight inward body-twist which has been suggested previously and by taking care to delay the uncocking of the wrists until the swing reaches the center of the body.

GETTING AROUND TOO LATE. The batter who consistently swings late is quite possibly the victim of a hand-hitch. Other factors, such as slow reflexes or faulty position, can enter the picture. As a general rule, this handicap can be alleviated by opening the stance and by having the bat well back, in position to hit—with the wrists cocked—as the pitcher goes into his motion.

HEAD-TURNING. The eyes should remain fixed on the ball until it is met by the bat. When the batter turns his head too soon he loses sight of the ball and will have difficulty in meeting it solidly, if at all.

This is probably the most damaging habit that a batter can acquire. To overcome it, he should have his front shoulder facing the pitcher until the ball is well on its way to the plate; he should "keep his chin behind the ball"; and he should practice place-hitting or hitting the ball where it is pitched.

SWEEPING THE BAT. A batter who swings in a sweeping motion gets no benefit from a wrist-snap and will look very bad against tight pitches. This type of batter can overcome his fault by the full utilization of his wrists. In order to achieve this he should align his second and third knuckles (the knuckles-on-down grip), should be sure that his wrists are cocked before the pitch, and should make a determined effort to roll his wrists on his swing. Carrying the bat in a high position also seems to have good effect in curbing the habit of sweeping the bat.

CHANGE-UP TROUBLE. This affliction can be described as inability to hit the change-of-pace. The change-up is most bothersome to a batter who overstrides or lunges. Thus, in order to be better prepared to hit it, he should employ a slight inward turn of the hips as the pitcher is releasing the ball.

As a further aid in overcoming difficulty in hitting the change-of-pace the batter should try to hit to the opposite field and, above all, he should just try to meet the ball rather than attempting to overpower it.

CURVE BALL TROUBLE. For quick reference, the best method of overcoming difficulty in hitting the curve ball is to follow the pitch closely right to the bat and try to hit the ball with the rotation.

This topic is discussed in detail in a later section entitled "Hitting the Curve Ball."

BUNTING

The present-day trend toward emphasis on the long ball and the big inning has caused the art of bunting to be sadly neglected. Even experienced professionals are, in a great many cases, mediocre, if not poor bunters. In their defense it can be said that the lively ball and highly resilient bats make it rather difficult to lay down a really good bunt, particularly when the opposing team expects it and the pitcher throws practically nothing but high fast balls while the first and third basemen charge the plate. This does not alter the fact, however, that practice (and more practice) is the best means of attaining proficiency in the ability to bunt.

The sacrifice

The first principle to be observed in the proper execution of the sacrifice bunt is that the word "sacrifice" should be taken literally—that the batter should give himself up.

As the pitcher is about to deliver the ball the batter swings around by stepping forward with his rear foot and should be facing the pitcher with feet squared, and body bent slightly at the waist and knees. When this play is in order, it is more important to get the ball on the ground than to disguise the bunt.

The sacrifice is best executed when the batter's weight is on the balls of his feet and slightly forward. While swinging around into the squared-away position the bat should be *pushed* forward until it is well out in front of the body, with the arms fully extended: The batter should await the pitch with his bat held stationary *just below the shoulders.* By carrying his bat at the upper strike-zone level the batter will automatically know what pitches to pass up and which ones to bunt. A high ball is difficult to bunt well and any pitch which comes toward the batter above his bat should be allowed to pass—it will be a ball. A pitch below his bat is the one to bunt since it will be pushed downward into the dirt by the batter's effort to contact it.

Sacrifice Bunt

The upper hand should slide toward the fat part of the bat and should come to rest with the fingers behind the bat at a point slightly more than half-way to the end, or about even with the label. The upper hand should be loose, the other one tight, and the bat should be guided by the lower hand.

The height of the bat should, to a great extent, be adjusted by raising or lowering the body from the waist and knees—the less arm motion, the better the bunt in most instances.

The actual bunt should be performed in a manner similar to that used in catching the ball. That is, the bat should give with the pitch. In short, the ball should do the work.

When the sacrifice is signalled, the batter is given the prerogative of picking his own pitch. It does not necessarily have to be a strike but should be one that is in a location that makes it buntable. When he is called upon to sacrifice, the batter should never take a strike.

The biggest hazard in executing the sacrifice is the danger of bunting the ball in the air. If the batter lays off the high pitch (at which he would have to bunt upward) and waits until the ball is on the ground before starting for first base he will greatly lessen the possibilities of bunting a pop-fly.

Generally speaking, to succeed in his purpose of advancing the runner the batter must bunt the ball close to either foul line—one that goes toward the pitcher is tailor-made for a force out at second and a possible double play.

More specifically, with a runner on first base the ball should be bunted toward first since the first baseman will be holding the bag against the runner, leaving him in relatively poor position to field the ball in time to make a force play at second.

With a man on second base or men on first and second, the bunt should go toward third. This often causes the third baseman to field the ball, leaving his base uncovered against the runner advancing from second. Care must be exercised, however, to get the ball past the pitcher, forcing the third baseman to field it.

These tactics should be carried out only when the man at bat is an accomplished bunter. Because of the desirability of successfully advancing the runner, the inexpert bunter should facilitate his task by bunting the ball where it is easiest for him to do so on any given pitch.

The bona fide expert can employ a different technique. A really adept bunter can give more consideration to masking his intentions and can afford to attempt his sacrifice without squaring around. In operation, this maneuver is performed in the following manner: With feet remaining in normal hitting position, the batter pivots at the hips as the pitcher delivers the ball; his trunk and knees are bent moderately and his weight is centered on his front foot; the fat end of the bat is pointed toward the pitcher; the bottom hand stays close to the waist, the top one grips the bat lightly—near the label; the bat should give with the ball as it is contacted.

This method should be attempted only after the "safe" way has been thoroughly mastered. Until that time, it is more important to get the ball on the ground than it is to conceal one's intentions from the opposition.

The squeeze

The "safe squeeze" is performed in much the same manner as the sacrifice, with the batter picking his own pitch. The important thing is making the bunt a really good one on which the runner will be able to score from third.

The "suicide squeeze" involves compulsion. The runner breaks for home on a certain pitch and the batter must bunt the ball—on the ground.

Technique for the suicide squeeze differs slightly. The batter delays his square-around move until the pitcher is about to release the ball lest the latter detect the play, change tactics, and throw an unbuntable pitch. Furthermore, the batter should square around by moving his front foot back until it is parallel with his rear foot. In this way he will slightly delay the catcher's efforts to get at the runner should the bunt be missed.

For safety purposes the suicide squeeze bunt should be aimed directly at the pitcher and, to repeat for emphasis, the ball simply must be bunted on the ground.

Bunting for a hit

There are two principal methods of bunting for a hit—the drag and the push. The drag bunt is executed by sliding the upper hand up the bat and using the lower one for a fulcrum as the front foot is moved toward home plate. The bat is dropped (lowered) by the upper hand. The ball should be met behind the body and from a slightly crouched stance.

Drag Bunt

Push Bunt (Bill Mazeroski)

In the push bunt the arms are fully extended and the ball is pushed toward the opposite field.

In either case the batter should not step back with his rear foot. He should move his front foot toward the plate and shift his weight onto it. In addition, he should actually be running toward first base by the time the bat meets the ball.

A right-handed batter can either push the ball toward first or drag it down the third base line while a left-hander pushes a bunt toward third base and drags one in the direction of first base. A bunt aimed toward third should roll along the base line; one toward first should be directed at a spot between the first and second baseman and out of the pitcher's reach.

LEFT-HANDED BATTER. The drag bunt is used when the pitcher is a poor fielder; against a left-hander who falls toward third on his follow-through; or when the first baseman plays very deep. It should be a soft hit, out of the pitcher's reach, made while the batter is taking a cross-over step toward first. In order to direct the ball to the right side, the top hand should roll as the ball is contacted.

The push bunt, most effective against a slow-moving pitcher and a third baseman who plays deep, is also executed while a cross-over step is being taken toward first. The hands should be well away from the body with the bat angled toward third base.

RIGHT-HANDED BATTER. The same considerations apply in selecting the bunt to be used. The fat end of the bat should be pointed at the pitcher for the drag bunt and the ball should roll close to the third base line.

A right-hander's push bunt is executed like a sacrifice except that the bat is pushed rather than allowed to give with the ball. The hands and elbows should be away from the body, with the fat part of the bat facing first base. The push bunt toward first can occasionally be worked with better chances of success when it is preceded by a fake toward third.

As far as the tactical aspects of bunting for a hit are concerned, it is a play which should not be used indiscriminately. It is for experts— men who have mastered the technique of bunting. Moreover, it is an ability which is well worth the time and trouble needed to acquire it. The good bunter will beat out a number of hits over the course of a season and, of equal importance, he will keep the defense on edge and will cause the third baseman to play closer to the plate, thereby cutting down on his fielding range.

This play is not a smart move with two outs and the team at bat trailing by more than one run, with two exceptions: if the batter is a good base stealer, or a long-ball hitter is the next man at bat; or when there

265

is a runner on third base and the first and third basemen are playing deep.

The fake bunt

There are three variations of the fake bunt, all of which can prove of great value to a batter and his team.

A rarely used, but potentially damaging offensive weapon which is based on the sacrifice is known in baseball circles as the "bastard play." In it, the batter squares around as if to bunt but hits the ball with a fairly full, chop-like swing. The idea is to lure the shortstop to second base to cover it against the runner and the second baseman to first to cover it on the batter. The ball is then hit to one of the spots which has been vacated, usually toward shortstop for a right-hand batter and toward second for a left-hander. The fake must be convincing in order to draw the infielders out of position. If properly executed, this play requires no more than an ordinary ground ball hit in the general direction of one of the vacant spots in order to be successful. It is a particularly effective maneuver when worked with men on first and second and the sacrifice in order.

Another version of the fake bunt is the one in which the batter squares around to decoy the third baseman into charging the plate for a bunt, then "rams the ball down his throat." Both this and the first play must be practiced numerous times before a player attains proficiency in their execution. Once perfected, they can be turned into devastating offensive weapons.

The third type of fake bunt does not involve hitting the ball. It is intended solely to pull the defense, especially the third baseman, out of position. The batter squares around as if to bunt but lets the pitch go by. There are two occasions when this move is of particular value— when the batter is taking a pitch, or when a runner is attempting to steal third. In the first case, the step or two closer to the plate which the third baseman may play when he is wary of a bunt will allow just that much more chance of driving a hit past him. On the steal of third, if the third baseman moves in to protect his territory against a bunt he will leave the base uncovered against the advancing runner.

BATTING DRILLS

Batting skill, for most ballplayers, is acquired gradually. A purposeful, systematic approach to the problem is the best means of developing hitting ability to its fullest extent. Carefully planned practice adds interest to the daily routine and, when the ultimate goal of improved performance is achieved, baseball will prove an enjoyable, as well as challenging experience.

Exercises

Pre-season conditioning should not only be calculated to improve a batter's eye and his timing; it should also be designed to attune his bodily movements to the proper performance of basic fundamentals.

The series of pivot exercises described below will accomplish this, while at the same time developing the balance which is closely related to timing.

1. Assume a normal batting stance, place the hands on the hips, pivot at the hips as though swinging the body into a pitch. Go back and forth in this motion until the hip pivot seems natural and the trunk feels loose.

2. Using the heels as pivots and with the arms hanging limply at the sides, pivot to the rear, shifting the weight to the back heel; pivot forward with the weight resting on the whole of both feet as the body returns to its normal position; continue the forward movement until the weight is on the front heel which then becomes the pivot point; continue forward until the complete follow-through position is reached. This should be a back-and-forth motion with no stop.

Repeat this set of actions several times, making a determined effort to keep the head and eyes in a stationary position.

3. Go through the same routine several times with a split-second stop between its various phases.

4. Perform the same series of movements, this time with a bat; first step-by-step, then as a continuous pattern of action. Repeat several times and *keep that head still!*

5. Practice the still-head drill: The batter swings a bat, with a strong light (the sun, when outdoors) at his back. A coach or player then places his foot on the shadow of the batter's head. The object is to take a full cut with the "head remaining underfoot." This should be repeated many times—until the head remains still consistently—and should be continued throughout the season.

Drills

Ballplayers should make it a rule to get themselves thoroughly loosened up before swinging a bat with full force. A series of simple bending and stretching exercises (a minute or two is sufficient) will help prevent muscular pulls and strains and will prepare a batter for the hardest of swings. This rule is particularly applicable to pre-season practice when the muscles are not well conditioned and to cold days when they are slow in loosening up.

The basic fundamentals of batting should be worked on as separate entities, then put together as a whole. Practice in front of a mirror at home, and on the field, with a teammate or coach to observe and make suggestions, is highly recommended.

1. Swing a bat as often as possible. Visualizing a pitcher throwing at you, go through a normal swing over and over again to strengthen the hands and wrists and to develop good form.

2. When bad weather prevents outdoor work and a gym is available, have a fellow player pitch to you, using a tennis ball to eliminate the possibilities of damage to buildings and fixtures. A half-dozen swings at a ball thrown slowly and you should be ready to hit fast pitches. This indoor batting practice is highly recommended in pre-season training sessions. By the time outdoor workouts are held you should be ready to hit at full speed.

3. When on the ball field, practice the start to first. Do it as it has been described on these pages and be sure to include the rounding of first base. This should be performed numerous times until correct habits become second nature.

4. Many ball clubs have strings set up to outline the strike zone for the use of pitchers who are working to perfect their control. Take the opportunity to learn your strike zone by assuming a normal batting stance at the strings when a pitcher is working with them. If no strings are available, stand "at the plate" when a pitcher is warming up and have the catcher call balls and strikes. Incidentally, this will prove helpful to the pitcher as well as to the batter.

5. Play "pepper" with other ballplayers whenever the opportunity presents itself. This is a good conditioner for all hands and is of especial value to the batter. It makes for improved bunting and place-hitting, while at the same time impressing on the batter the necessity of keeping his eye on the ball and meeting it squarely. A visit to a Major League park before game-time will demonstrate the importance with which Big Leaguers view the game of pepper.

Batting Practice

Batting practice should never be a haphazard affair. It is serious business and should be treated as such. It is discussed in detail in the section on coaching.

At various times during the season ballplayers should take the time to work on the different skills that come under the general heading,

"Batting." During regular workouts a batter should practice hitting to right field, selecting random pitches for the purpose. Bunts—sacrifice, squeeze, and for a hit—should be worked into practice sessions. (Bunting practice can be held in lieu of batting practice during indoor workouts.) The fake bunt and its variation, the "bastard play," are other maneuvers which should be tried. Finally, if troubled by a particular pitch, the batter should enlist the aid of his batting practice pitcher and have that man feed him a good sampling of the pitch on which he is weakest.

BATTING–THE MENTAL ASPECT

ATTITUDE

The theory of hitting can be reduced to its most basic element by simplification. It involves merely meeting the ball with the bat and driving it to a spot where it can be neither caught nor retrieved by a fielder and thrown to first base before the batter can reach that goal. In short, batting resolves to that brief, pointed, and now legendary epigram of Willie Keeler's when he said, "Hit 'em where they ain't."

Even this almost facetious definition, however, demands study from a tactical standpoint when it is realized that the so-called zones of safety for batted balls vary with the batter, the opposing pitcher, the physical characteristics of the ball park, and the game situation which prevails at a given moment.

It has been established, thus far, that batting ability is at least partly an inherent talent and that it is comprised of batting eye, coordination of muscle, and the correct performance of certain basic fundamentals.

Unfortunately, in its entirety batting is not quite so simple. One more very important piece must be fitted into place to complete the picture—the mental aspect.

Above and beyond the purely mechanical there is a wide field to which the batter may attain and where he may develop powers quite beyond those to which nature has seemingly limited him. The mental phase of batting is the element that enables a man to make the most of his ability. Proper utilization of his talents allows a ballplayer to rise above the status of being a mere mechanical workman. The successful player is the one who numbers among his assets a combination of energy, perseverance, aggressiveness, ambition, know-how, and confidence.

It is the aim of this section to convey the means needed to develop those qualities.

The right frame of mind

The good competitor is a man who can rise to the occasion and come through with a base hit when the ball game is at stake. He is not necessarily a nerveless character, always cool and calm. As a matter of fact, in many cases he is keyed up and fired with determination, yet he is always able to turn this emotional pitch into an intentness of purpose that enables him to be relatively relaxed until he explodes with a burst of concentrated energy as he swings at the ball.

Enos Slaughter, one of the greatest of competitors, was the living personification of this—a pleasant, reserved individual, outwardly calm and relaxed even in the heat of a ball game, yet a veritable dynamo, motivated by an intense singleness of purpose when he went into action.

A real competitor, such as Slaughter, goes up to the plate to hit. Except on those rather infrequent occasions when the "take" sign is in effect, he is mentally geared to hit every pitch. He is not afraid to "stand in there" with determination and confidence.

As it pertains to batting, a tremendous asset is possessed by the ballplayer who has learned not to hurry. "Two o'clock hitter" is the term used to describe a man who hits line drives in batting practice but pops up in the game. The real difference is the pressure placed on an individual by game-competition. A "two o'clock hitter" is one who tightens under that pressure, while the real ballplayer is the one who, figuratively speaking, takes it easy and relies on his form.

A ballplayer who is under too much tension to perform well at the plate should step out of the batter's box occasionally and make himself take more time. One of the benefits of slowing his pace and relaxing is that it reduces the tendency to go for bad balls. Anxiety is the chief cause of this serious fault, so the batter should take his time in the realization that he will eventually get "his pitch" and that patience and calmness will better assure him of being prepared for that pitch when it comes.

The really good hitter approaches the plate in a frame of mind in which he does not care who is pitching or what is thrown. This man knows that all he must do is meet the ball when it crosses the plate and he feels that he has the ability to do just that.

Inexperienced batters tend to exaggerate the pitcher's ability and to underestimate their own. Naturally, this is particularly so "in the clutch." To nullify this tendency the batter should realize that the pitcher, too, has emotions and that with runners in scoring position it is the pitcher who is in trouble. The batter most emphatically should adopt that at-

270

titude and should remember that as long as he swings he is dangerous.

A batter should keep his chin up and "hang in there" at all times. Obviously, that is the best way for him to overcome the psychological effects of occasional setbacks. Yet, paradoxically, a certain amount of discouragement can be beneficial. Needless to say, a ballplayer should not allow himself to become too discouraged over mistakes but, nevertheless, a mistake can often prove the most valuable lesson that a player can have.

Aspiring hitters are usually subjected to much theorizing and instruction. Although both can be of great help to them and should not be ignored, they should, somehow, try to stand at the plate in readiness to hit—free in both mind and body. Thus, perhaps the best attitude for the batter to adopt is one in which he does not permit the situation to become too big for him. Why should he get rattled? No more is expected of him than that he go up to the plate and do his best. If he will bear that in mind he can rest assured that those base hits will eventually fall in for him.

Fear of the ball

Respect, if not fear, for hard-thrown balls exists in all players. In one sense, the difference between good and bad hitters lies in the degree of fear of the ball with which they are afflicted. A Ted Williams or a Stan Musial, although he has respect for an exceptionally fast pitcher, has practically no fear of the ball and, for this reason, among others, is never the target of an intentional duster. On the other hand, a .200 hitter is gun-shy to a certain extent and is more prone to intimidation by close, fast pitches.

There is little reason for any large measure of fear existing to plague batters. Any man with average eyesight and reflexes should have no difficulty in avoiding a ball thrown at him. Furthermore, protective helmets, mandatory in most leagues, are readily available and reasonably priced. They can help greatly in allaying a man's fear of a pitched ball. While a helmet or protective cap is no guarantee against being hit, it does eliminate most of the danger of serious injury and, as a result, can provide relative peace of mind for all but the most timid of batters.

The batter who needs reassurance concerning his fear of the ball should be made to realize that correct methods can reduce to a minimum the danger of his being hit.

There are several principles which, if practiced faithfully, will enable any batter to go to the plate with little worry over the possibility of being hit by a pitched ball:

1. A close pitch is easy to duck if the batter follows it carefully. It is the ball he loses sight of that can be dangerous.

2. Turning one's head greatly increases the danger of being hit.
3. The batter should not move his *rear* foot to avoid a pitch.
4. The correct method is to move his front foot back, at the same time keeping his eye on the ball. Incidentally, this also helps guard against being caught unawares by a sudden, sharp-breaking curve.
5. All else failing, as a last resort the batter should hit the dirt in order to keep from being hit by the ball.

The incidence of use of an intentional duster or bean-ball is greatly exaggerated. There are many fine pitchers who go through an entire career without once resorting to this practice. The immortal Walter Johnson and the great Bob Feller are two conspicuous examples. In many cases, a brush-back pitch, high and tight—designed to keep the batter from digging in at the plate—is the worst offense of which a pitcher can honestly be accused.

Dusters are thrown primarily by pitchers who are being hit really hard and, even then, serious doubt can be voiced as to malicious intent. Most bean-ball incidents or feuds are sparked by an unintentional wild pitch that sails in close to the batter's head. If deliberate use of a duster is suspected, the practice could be eliminated immediately by an order from the manager or coach for the pitchers to throw at each other.

There are good hitters who are perfectly willing to stand at the plate and defy the pitcher to throw at them. They know that concentrated attention on the ball makes it all but impossible for them to be hit.

Shyness

Shyness on the part of a batter can be defined as the kind of uncertainty that is the middle ground between outright fear and the air of assurance displayed by all good hitters.

Shyness is occasioned primarily by a lack of familiarity that can cause timidity even in a man whose over-all courage cannot be questioned.

The obvious remedy is practice and experience to such an extent that this lack of familiarity disappears, and uncertainty along with it. The whole matter can be disposed of by emphatically stating that experience, by teaching a man what he can do, eliminates shyness and promotes the confidence that is needed to capitalize fully on his physical ability.

Confidence

With this topic we come to the most important element in the mental aspect of batting. While in itself it may not give rise to good hitting, confidence is most certainly a distinguishing characteristic of the game's better batsmen.

The spirit that wins ball games is built on confidence. Perhaps that statement and some of the platitudes included in this section sound like excerpts from a pep-talk. So much the better, for the importance of confidence to a hitter cannot be overestimated. The need for it must be impressed on any ballplayer who aspires to good hitting.

Every batter wishes he could hit—this is hope. Confidence is a much stronger word—it is faith. Indeed, no manager desires the presence on his club of a ballplayer who does not believe in himself, feeling, with justification, that if a man doubts his ability to do a certain thing, chances are that he cannot.

Another way of stating the matter is to assert that confidence, in a very real sense, is the capacity to make the most of one's ability. The fact that a ballplayer should be aware of his limitations and be guided by them has been previously advanced. However, even more emphasis should be placed on the idea that faith in his capabilities is the spur that is needed to capitalize fully on them. Confidence, then, is the mental tonic that can lift batting performance above the level of mediocrity.

George Sisler is one of baseball's true immortals. Twice he batted over .400 and his record of 257 hits in one season is a mark that may never be broken. Sisler, a real student of the art of hitting, is neither a vain nor conceited man. Yet, consider what he said, in all sincerity, about the importance of confidence to a batter. In discussing his phenomenal success over a period of years and the reasons for it, George Sisler remarked, "At times I actually felt sorry for the pitcher when I came to bat. I could hit anything he had. I knew it and he knew it. That's the real explanation for any success I may have achieved."

The old principle that a man can swim better with the tide than against it applies here, this time in the form of the mental tide which is built up through confidence. The assurance which it provides is an important part of the proper frame of mind for a ballplayer. Relaxation at the plate, another vital asset, is based primarily on this all-important factor.

The next phase of the mental aspect of batting to be discussed is determination. It is very closely related to confidence, each of the traits having a strong effect on the other. In concluding this section and starting the next, let it be said that real determination is vital in batting. It is built through confidence which, in turn, stems from practice, desire, and ability.

Determination

Determination to make good is the catalytic agent that motivates all of the desirable mental qualities which enable a man's physical assets to bear fruit. As it pertains to batting, it is an indispensable attribute.

Quite possibly the greatest ballplayer who ever lived was Ty Cobb. The number of records credited to him gives cold, statistical evidence to his phenomenal ability. Yet, perhaps his greatest value lay in his capacity to upset the opposition by taking advantage of every conceivable opening and, in many cases, by creating those openings himself. Cobb possessed good natural gifts, but not those of a super-star. Cobb's greatness came from his mental approach to the game, the burning desire to excel that drove him to the pinnacle of his profession.

Thus, Ty Cobb is the proper authority on whom to call for testimony as to the stress that should be placed on determination as a salient point in the mental phase of batting.

Cobb attributed his remarkable accomplishments primarily to purely mental qualities, putting special emphasis on his determination to succeed at all costs. It was his belief that he was a normal .320 hitter and that his .367 lifetime average, or a difference of almost fifty points in his batting percentage, was due to one thing—his tremendous determination.

Al Simmons, a devastating right-handed batter and, himself, a member of baseball's Hall of Fame, credited much of his success to this burning desire to excel. Speaking of his development into one of the game's most feared hitters, Simmons said, "I developed a contempt for pitchers." Ty Cobb called this the best short definition of batting ability ever spoken, adding that, in his opinion, the most important factors pertaining thereto are concentration and determination.

As previously stated, the good competitor is the ballplayer who can arise to the occasion and come through with a base hit in the clutch. One of the reasons for this faculty is sheer determination—especially against good pitching. That bears repetition: A good hitter's determination is at its height against good pitching.

Needless to say, a player's physical equipment, his natural ability, is the first thing that catches the eye of a Major League scout. If it is not present, the candidate will not merit a second look. More important to our consideration of this phase of batting, however, is the fact that a scout looks for more than mere mechanical skill. Attitude is a vital factor to a scout. He pays close attention to the determination to succeed, the willingness to strive for success, demonstrated by a ballplayer. They are the keys which give a scout an insight into just how much a man will be able to make of his natural talents.

In the final analysis it would seem that determination can be defined as consistent courage or guts, which is actually earnest, courageous, aggressive good sportsmanship.

274

TACTICS

Regardless of how well he has mastered correct batting techniques and no matter what his ability as a hitter may be, a ballplayer can get even better results at the plate if he is a smart hitter—one who is observant, takes advantage of every opportunity to gain an edge on the pitcher, and employs the tactics and tricks of the trade which will enable him to accomplish his dual purpose of helping himself to better performance and his team to greater success.

Throughout the text, numerous references have been made to tactical maneuvers pertaining to batting. Even in a discussion of fundamentals which are basically physical in nature, batting strategy is inevitably involved as the various ramifications of the mechanics of hitting arise. The two are closely interrelated and, consequently, many sound policies of the batting game have been explained. There are, however, several other purely tactical elements which definitely should be mentioned: these will teach inexperienced ballplayers how many smart batsmen gain the advantage over the pitcher, thereby becoming successful hitters.

On being prepared

It is assumed that the batter will follow the policy, laid down as being elementary and vital right at the outset, of being physically relaxed—yet mentally alert as he faces the pitcher. But what of the pitcher, himself, and the consideration which must be given his operational methods?

A batter should always be set for the *fast ball*. Despite the fact that there are definite situations in which a pitcher will usually rely on a certain delivery and in which that pitch can be looked for with some degree of certainty, "guess hitting," which is covered in more detail in the next section, is very risky business and should be discouraged right from the start. Good hitters rarely resort to it—they set themselves to be able to cope with a fast pitch. Then, rather than concentrating on where the ball is going, they endeavor merely to meet it squarely.

Because of the great speed with which a pitched ball reaches the plate (it usually covers the sixty feet in less than ½ second), a fast ball will be past the batter before he is set to swing, unless he is ready for it. Furthermore, adjustments in timing can be made which will enable the batter to handle the curve ball, change-of-pace, or other such pitch, all of which are slower than the fast ball. This entails the second look, or slight pause after the stride, that has been emphasized as vitally important in the section on fundamentals. Thus, if he is always set for the fast one, the batter will be ready for any type of pitch.

275

A high, tight fast ball is one of the most difficult pitches to meet solidly. If the batter has trouble with this type of pitch he should adopt a slightly crouched stance and pass up the high ones—the pitcher will have to come down to him.

A slight crouch serves another purpose which is beneficial to the batter. It brings his strike zone a little lower and, at the same time, makes it slightly smaller, giving the pitcher less room in which to maneuver as well as a smaller target at which to shoot in order to throw strikes. Possibly even more important, a slight crouch brings the batter's eye level down—nearer the strike zone—affording him a much better look at the ball.

When to take

The obvious answer to the question of when to hit would seem to be any time a batter takes his position at the plate. If a batter could be sure of hitting safely a majority of times, that answer could be accepted and further discussion would be superfluous. There are, however, certain situations when percentage play (the law of averages) dictates that the batter should take a strike. It is generally good practice to make the pitcher throw a strike under the following conditions:

1. When the batter's team is losing by more than two runs in the late innings (the seventh, eight, and ninth): In this situation every out, in fact every pitch, counts and the batter should not be too anxious to swing. Getting on base is the important consideration and as long as the pitcher throws "balls" the batter stays alive.

2. When the preceding batter has walked or been hit by a pitched ball: Here the pitcher might have hit a wild streak or may become upset by his momentary loss of control, so the batter should not help him by offering at the first pitch or, especially, a bad ball.

3. If the batter is the lead-off man in an inning or when a new pitcher takes the mound: This gives the hitter a chance to look over the pitcher's stuff and to prevent him from being in the enviable position of having gotten one out with one pitch.

4. When the preceding batter has been retired on one pitch: The batter should try to avoid making the pitcher's task an easy one. On the contrary, the opposing hurler should be made to work hard. He should never be allowed to get two outs on two pitches.

5. A pitcher with overpowering stuff should be made to throw as many pitches as possible in the hopes that the physical effort involved will take its inevitable toll and that he will lose some of his stuff and be easier to hit in the late innings. This practice should be applied against any pitcher on a hot day when there is a strong possibility that

the enervating effect of the high temperature will cause him to "run out of gas."

The batter who takes a strike should "play out the string." In other words, until the pitcher throws a strike the batter should continue his policy of taking the next pitch. This is what is meant by the term "take a strike."

Needless to say, the batsman should not let the pitcher know when he is taking a pitch. Doing so will allow him to groove one for an automatic strike. With respect to this idea, faking a bunt on a first-pitch take is a good move—and it may draw the infield in a step or two.

Naturally, these tactics should be varied occasionally to keep the other team guessing. There are times when a pitcher who is plagued by a wild streak will ease up to get the ball over the plate. When he "lays the ball in there" in this fashion it is an invitation for the batter to hit. As a general policy, however, taking a pitch under the circumstances outlined above is sound baseball.

When to hit

There are times when the batter should attempt to hit the first good strike. One of these occasions is when he comes to bat with a runner in scoring position and the run involved is an important one, i.e., it will increase a lead, make or break a tie, or reduce the opposing team's margin to a point where the score will be close. Exceptions to this are when the count is three balls and no strikes; and when first base is open (only second, or second and third, is occupied), in which case a walk will not prove too damaging and the pitcher will be careful not to throw a "fat" pitch.

A batter should not take strikes when he is "up there to hit." This does not mean that he should swing at anything the pitcher throws plateward, but it does signify that when runners are in scoring position or his team has the opposing pitcher on the ropes, he should "be a hitter" and offer at any pitch that is to his liking and in the strike zone. Quite obviously, no batter ever got a base hit with his bat on his shoulder and under these circumstances he should take a strike only if the pitcher has been exceptionally wild or one of the "take" situations applies.

Occasionally a batter will get the green light from his manager or coach to "hit the cripple" (the three ball, no strike pitch) but only when he is a good hitter and a strong possibility to deliver a long ball and his team has runners in scoring position, or when the hit-and-run has been signalled.

With two strikes on him, the batter should swing at any pitch that looks like a strike. A good philosophy for any ballplayer to adopt is, "If the ball is close enough to argue about, it's close enough to hit."

How to hit

The manner in which the batter swings at the ball is subject to occasional alteration in accordance with the game situation. To cite one instance, with the infield playing in to cut off a run at the plate, the batter should not try to overpower the ball but should concentrate on merely meeting it solidly. The advantage in this case lies in the possibility of hitting the ball through or over the infield rather than in driving it beyond the reach of the outfielders. An old baseball adage has it that when the infielders are in tight positions, a .200 hitter automatically becomes a .500 hitter and an ordinary ground ball will, in many cases, go through the infield for a hit.

When the batter has two strikes he should be "guarding the plate." In other words, he must concede something to the pitcher, who has him at a disadvantage. Power should be sacrificed and emphasis placed on meeting the ball, rather than knocking it out of the park. Many good hitters go so far as to shorten their grip when these circumstances prevail.

There are, conversely, definite occasions when the batter should attempt to hit for distance. For example, it is desirable to go for the long ball when the bases are empty, and there are two out—here, unless the batter can reach scoring position it might possibly take two additional hits to score him. For a similar reason an attempt should be made to drive a man home from first when he is the only base runner with two out. It is also sound baseball, in some cases, to swing for an extra base hit with runners on first and second and the opposition leading by more than two runs. A long ball under these conditions makes it possible to score both runs. It also eliminates the possibility of a force play at second base, while on the other hand a single will score only one run and at the same time set up a double play with less than two out.

A specific example of batting tactics was covered in detail under the section "Hitting Behind the Runner." This is the case wherein the batter should try to drive the ball on the ground between first and second. Something that was not touched upon, however, is the role of the batter on a steal of second base. When this play is prearranged, the batter can help the runner by standing deep in the batter's box and by swinging at the ball (and missing it) so as to interfere slightly with the smooth continuity of the catcher's throw to second. Inexperienced players who cannot afford to waste too many strikes can limit this maneuver solely to those times when the pitcher throws a strike.

The batter should step out of the box when he tends to be over-anxious; this will reduce the tension under which he finds himself, and cut down on his tendency to go for bad balls. This should also be done against a pitcher who takes an excessive amount of time between deliveries; the aim is to prevent tension from mounting for the batter and possibly to cause some degree of impatience, if not over-anxiety, on the part of the pitcher. One other time when the batter should step out is when he has hit a foul ball with a man on base. This is done to assure the runner of a good opportunity to return to his base and also to give him a chance to catch his breath and to survey the situation anew. One word of caution is in order: When the batter steps out of the box he should make sure to request time out from the umpire, since the umpire alone is empowered by the rules to call time.

With a runner on base, stepping out when the pitcher is in the middle of his motion or just after he breaks his set position may cause him to balk.

GUESS HITTING

The batter who attempts to guess what pitch is coming next is playing right into the hands of a smart mound artist. The pitcher *knows* what he is throwing; the batter can only guess. An experienced hurler, merely by varying his operating methods, will take full advantage of this and have the batter completely at his mercy. If the batter is lucky enough to overcome these odds and guess correctly, he *might* succeed in hitting safely. If he does not get the pitch he is expecting he will look very foolish, indeed.

Baseball's better hitters do not try to outguess the pitcher. They are always prepared for the fast ball and concentrate primarily on getting good wood on the ball, making the necessary adjustments in timing only after they see that the ball is an intermediate-speed or slow pitch.

Looking for the logical pitch

Without succumbing to the pitfalls of guess hitting, a batter can safely look for a certain type of pitch in any of several specific situations. In other words, he can expect to be pitched to in the way that is most advantageous for the opposing moundsman.

It should be clearly understood that guess hitting is not advocated. The batter should be prepared for any kind of pitch. There are times, however, when a pitcher can reasonably be expected to rely on a certain delivery—the logical pitch in a given situation, as it were.

For example, with the double play in prospect or with the infield playing in close to cut off a run at the plate, the batter can look for low pitching, particularly curve balls, since the pitcher will undoubtedly try to make him hit the ball into the dirt.

Other instances which can be cited are: with the sacrifice in order the batter can reasonably expect high, fast balls which are the most difficult ones to bunt successfully; then, too, when the pitcher is unusually wild with one kind of pitch, the batter can expect to be fed another kind the great majority of times.

This is related to the case of the pitcher who has one particularly good delivery but is mediocre with his other pitches. Hoyt Wilhelm, the great relief pitcher, fits into this category. Wilhelm has a baffling knuckle ball, which is his "out-pitch." His fast one, only fair at best, is used as a waste-ball, rarely thrown over the plate and used just often enough to let the batter know that it exists. Some pitchers will resort to this strategy on certain days when one of their deliveries might not be working well. Under these circumstances, the batter can logically look for the "money pitch" on most occasions, particularly when the pitcher is behind in the count.

Physical characteristics of the ball park also have a bearing on the situation. If, for example, the right-field fence is very short, a left-handed batter will, in all probability, get very few inside pitches. (However, he should not crowd the plate in exaggerated fashion, looking for an outside pitch, lest the pitcher deal him one in close and find him relatively helpless against it.) When both fences are short, the batter will probably see very few slow pitches since they are the easiest ones to pull. And, on dark days or in the twilight hours, when visibility is poor, a pitcher with a good fast ball can be expected to rely mainly on that pitch.

A smart pitcher will continually try to set up the batter for certain deliveries, and the latter must guard himself against falling into these traps. For instance, the pitcher will shoot for the outside corner a couple of times and, if he notices the batter moving closer to the plate to protect the outside of it, he will "bust one in on his fists." Or, to cite another practice of some of the better moundsmen, when the pitcher gets a count of two strikes and no balls on the hitter he will often brush him back with a high, close fast ball (or try to get him to go for a bad ball, usually high and tight) and then come in with a curve ball, low and away.

Finally, when the game situation is a tight one, with the pitcher in the hole, the batter can logically expect to get the hurler's best, or "clutch" pitch. Most pitchers operate on the principle that when in a jam they should pitch to their own strength.

These are some of the situations in which observation of the pitcher's habits, plus common sense, can give the batter a pretty good indication as to the type of pitch for which he should be prepared.

Watching the pitcher constantly—learning what he throws, how he throws, and when he throws it—will help the batter to react, not guess.

Positive guessing

As a general rule, first-ball hitters are weak on the curve ball and they lie in wait, ready to pounce on the first fast one they see. They assume that most pitchers try to get ahead of the batter with a quick strike, usually a fast ball. Furthermore, they are loath to let the pitcher get them in the hole where he can go to work on them with his curve ball.

On the other hand, straightaway and opposite-field hitters usually anticipate the intermediate and slow pitches (curve ball and change-of-pace) and, because of the type of swing they favor, seem to enjoy better success against this kind of pitch.

When they guess right, batters who fall into these categories stand a good chance of hitting safely. Conversely, when their surmise is incorrect they fare poorly. Wise hitters who follow this pattern greatly improve their prospects by adopting a method which might be called "positive guessing." In other words, they anticipate a certain pitch and swing at the ball only if they get that particular pitch. As opposed to this, batters who rely on pure conjecture commit themselves to swinging at any ball, but in a fashion that is geared to meet one type of pitch. Then, if their guess-work is wrong, their timing is badly off and their base hits will be few and far between.

This form of positive guessing has a variation which is occasionally practiced by good hitters when the pitcher falls behind in the count. A typical case in point would be that of a batter who likes a pitch in a certain spot, say, on the inside corner about crotch-high. With a count of two balls and no strikes, for example, he can set himself to swing at a pitch in his strong zone. Then, if he gets that pitch he hits away. If not, he passes it up. This is the method that is quite often used when the hitter gets the green-light from his manager to hit the cripple.

Although guess hitting is frowned upon as ill-advised by most experienced baseball men, it does exist and will unquestionably continue to do so as long as the gambling instinct is present in any ballplayer. In this respect, it should be mentioned that, in many cases, it is the catcher against whom the guessing is done. He is, after all, the man who gives the signals, the brains of the battery to a good extent. Some receivers fall into set patterns in their calling of pitches and are predictable enough to furnish the batter with a good indication of the probable pitch. There are catchers, for instance, who will rarely call for a fast ball under certain circumstances. At times this habit is so pronounced that a team can anticipate the pitch when a certain catcher works with a certain pitcher, but will abandon the idea when a different catcher is behind the plate for the same pitcher.

Reading the pitch

"Reading the pitch (or pitcher)" is the term used to describe the ability of sharp-eyed coaches to detect, from a tell-tale mannerism on the part of the pitcher, what he is about to throw. It also covers the stealing of the catcher's signals by either a coach or base runner. This field of operation is more a matter of observation than of sheer guessing.

The reading of pitches by the batter himself is risky business since it is based on partial knowledge at best. It should not be encouraged. A smart coach can be far more successful at this practice. On the other hand, occasionally a pitcher is so overpowering that even foreknowledge of his offerings is of little avail to the batter. In his early days, Bob Feller is said to have telegraphed his pitches but, nevertheless, he mowed down enemy hitters with monotonous regularity—even when they knew what was coming.

Some players refuse to accept this information, preferring to hit completely on their own. There is actually some justification for this: an element of danger is involved. A pitcher who suspects that he is being read can resort to a last-minute switch. Furthermore, a coach can make a mistake. And a fast ball headed for the batter can be a real source of peril when he is waiting for it to curve.

It would seem that a runner on second base could be a great help in picking off the catcher's signals and relaying the information to the batter. This idea can be largely discounted, however, because a good catcher will use alternate sets of signals with a man on second base.

The catcher can, at times, be a source of visual information to an alert ball club. Some receivers have a tendency to move closer to the plate when a curve or change-up is coming. Others may turn the right foot to the outside when a curve is being thrown, or widen the stance for a fast ball. The glove, too, can be an indicator: it is often held flat for the fast ball and pointed down for the curve.

A smart batter will take advantage of every piece of information in his possession, but trying to outguess the pitcher should definitely not be adopted as a regular practice by him.

Guessing—a final appraisal

A smart batter cannot observe pitching over a period of years without a pretty good idea of what some pitchers are going to do under certain circumstances. Occasions arise when guessing becomes almost a certainty. Experience, familiarity with a pitcher, and a knowledge of how he operates in a given situation can, at times, give a batter an insight into his probable working method so that the next pitch can be sensed with a good degree of accuracy. In such a case the batter would be foolish if he did not take advantage of his knowledge. What it amounts to is that every batter who uses his eyes is guilty of guessing or, in this situation, what could more accurately be termed "observation."

Then, there are some good hitters who go by the policy that, "I want my mind on the ball and nothing else. I want to feel that I can hit it no matter what happens. If the pitcher is trying to outguess me he's wasting his time because I don't guess." The batter who follows this policy is definitely playing his percentages wisely. As long as he refrains from guessing, the probability of guessing wrong will be eliminated.

Honus Wagner was one of baseball's all-time greats. He was an exceptionally fine batsman whose views on guessing are interesting. Wagner once said, "Outguessing the pitcher is a tough proposition. Once in a while I might have figured that a curve ball was about due, or maybe a fast one. But not often, because I was no mind-reader. My main job was not to hypnotize the pitcher but to hit the ball. So, most generally, I tried to be ready for whatever might come. That is the only safe rule in the long run."

HITTING THE CURVE BALL

The curve ball is more troublesome to most hitters than is the fast ball and quite naturally so, since a change in the course of the ball's flight is obviously quite difficult to contend with when the batter is attempting to get good wood on it. That the mound fraternity seems to be in accord with this contention is evidenced by the widely accepted pitching maxim, "When in doubt, curve him."

Nevertheless, regardless of how sharp it is, the curve ball is slower than the fast ball, and thus can be hit well by any ballplayer endowed simply with ordinary coordination, eyesight, and intelligence.

"Curve ball-itis" has, in the case of more than a few batters, reached the point of being a full-fledged phobia. Because of this and the fact that coping with it is, in many respects, a psychological matter, it is being dealt with as part of the mental phase of hitting. Irrespective of what category it should fall in, the fact remains that hitting the curve ball with consistency demands some thought as well as coordinated physical activity. Needless to say, in terms of response the mental and physical aspects are closely related, perhaps more so than in any other facet of the game.

There are two primary reasons why ballplayers experience undue difficulty in handling the curve. First, because there is a strong tendency to pull away from it, a tendency to which many batters succumb. Second, there is the fact that too many hitters do not follow the ball closely all the way to the bat. If these two habits are nonexistent, practically any batter should be able to hit the curve ball.

At just what point it is best to try to meet the ball has long been the subject of conjecture. That is, will the batter get best results if he tries to hit the ball before, during, or after it breaks? The best suggestion that can be offered is that each player should experiment by shifting his position in the batter's box until he finds the method that best suits his own style. Incidentally, it should be added that the best curve ball hitters try to meet the ball during or after the break.

The batter should try to hit to the opposite field a curve ball that is breaking away from him; if it is breaking in to him he should attempt to drive it back through the pitcher's box—if he does so, in all probability he will pull the ball. In other words, and quite logically, the batter should try to hit the curve ball with the rotation. In addition to this, if the batter places more weight on his front foot he will lessen the tendency to pull away from the ball. (Closing his stance and sighting the ball over his front shoulder will also help.) Obeying these principles will demand that the batter follow the ball closely and will aid him greatly in trying to meet it solidly.

A smart pitcher rarely telegraphs his pitches but, generally speaking, it is very difficult to cover up the curve ball entirely. Some of the telltale signs which usually indicate that the curve ball is coming can be listed as follows: when the pitcher's free leg goes higher than usual; if his wrist bends inward noticeably; and if his arm is bent at the elbow in pronounced fashion.

The following ideas may prove helpful in telling a batter what type of curve ball to anticipate: A pitcher who throws from the same side (right-handed batter vs. right-handed pitcher) is more likely to throw his curve three-quarters overhand or sidearm, figuring on making it break away from the hitter. (The batter should try not to pull away from a sidearmer's deliveries.) One who throws from the opposite side (righty vs. lefty) will probably try to throw his curve ball over the top, in other words straight overhand, in order to make the ball break down rather than in to the batter.

Two of the basic fundamentals of batting will help a player to spot the curve ball more easily. They are (1) trying to watch the ball meet the bat and (2) observing the split-second pause and hitting just after the stride. Both should be practiced religiously to improve a batter's performance in general and his hitting the curve ball in particular.

The off-pitches

The fast ball, curve, and change-of-pace are the basic pitches. The batter who can hit those three consistently will be able to cope with almost any pitcher. However, mention should be made of the so-called off-pitches which are employed by a great many moundsmen.

The one which is most prevalent in use today is the slider. Often called a "nickle curve," the slider is, more accurately, a variation on the fast ball. By gripping the ball off center and delivering it with a normal fast ball motion or by applying a slight last-minute twist to the ball the pitcher can make it move sharply to the side in sliding fashion rather than break in the pronounced manner of the curve. The value of the slider lies in the fact that it is almost as swift as the fast ball and approaches the plate looking very much like that pitch. Since it is difficult to detect because of its similarity to the fast ball, there are no particular measures which can be taken to hit any one particular slider. It is especially tough to contact after its break. If a batter has great trouble with the slider, one means of overcoming his difficulty is to move forward in the box and/or to concentrate on meeting the ball instead of worrying about where it is going.

The knuckle ball is another pitch that is in rather wide use. There are two varieties of this delivery. When thrown slowly or at half-speed the knuckler dances in such a way that it is often called a "flutter ball." When thrown hard it acts like a "dry-spitter," dropping very sharply as it nears the plate. The knuckler is unpredictable and, consequently, difficult to meet solidly. It occasionally baffles pitcher, catcher, and batter alike. Most pitchers who employ this delivery rely very heavily on it and are generally lacking in the fast ball department. Thus, when facing a knuckle-baller, the batter should be concerned primarily with that pitch. The suggested means for combatting it is to stand forward in the box, cut down on the swing, and concentrate merely on meeting the ball. The batter most definitely should not try to overpower the knuckler. "Hit the ball in the same way that it is pitched," is the watchword here.

The other off-pitches, such as the fork ball, screw ball, palm ball, and so forth, are used only occasionally, even by pitchers who throw them; thus, they can be passed over here without elaboration.

The sinker will not be considered here because the way in which the term is used is somewhat misleading. The sinker is actually a fast ball which, for some pitchers, moves down and in, rather than taking off. In order to avoid added confusion, the batter should not consider it a separate pitch but should treat it as a fast ball.

The change-of-pace is one of the basic pitches and has been covered

285

in the section on batting weaknesses. However, an additional idea which may prove helpful to batters who are bothered by slow stuff was advanced by Bobby Avila, American League batting champion in 1954, who had always been troubled by slow pitching. In his championship year he adopted a method of coping with the "junk balls" which was very fruitful for him. He used a light bat against slow pitchers. This enabled him to wait until the very last moment before committing himself, since he was able to whip the light bat into the ball with an especially fast swing.

PINCH-HITTING

A man who is called upon to pinch-hit fills a difficult role at best. He must come off the bench cold and in what is generally a tight spot. There is, consequently, more cause for his having to contend with a certain amount of tension. Thus, to some extent, his problem is mental rather than physical.

Major League clubs can afford to carry men whose talents are specialized even in this relatively limited field. There are, for instance, pinch-hitters who excel at leading off an inning; ones who are particularly adept at scoring a runner from third with a long fly ball; and those who can be counted upon to move a runner from second to third when there are no outs. The big responsibility lies with the manager, who must select the right man for the right spot, giving consideration to how each man hits against the kind of pitcher who is working and what the team will have in reserve for an even bigger situation which might arise.

Outside of the Big Leagues reserve strength is often questionable and the problem, therefore, more acute. The manager or coach will use the best man available at the time to serve as a pinch-hitter and, consequently, more of the weight falls on the shoulders of that player.

When a player is tapped for pinch-hitting duty he must, first of all, try to be as loose as possible, both physically and mentally. All hitters should swing a weighted bat or several bats in preparation for going to the plate. This is particularly important for a pinch-hitter who has been sitting down for most of the game. He should swing the weighted club until his shoulder and arm muscles feel free and supple, then he will be ready physically.

The pinch-hitter should consider just what kind of hit will best serve his team's purposes and then act accordingly. If the game is close and a runner must be moved into scoring position, a ground ball to the right side may do the trick. When a long ball is needed the pinch-hitter should swing for distance. Any one of the techniques discussed earlier might be the one to employ in order to do his team the most good. Nevertheless, it need hardly be said that a clean base hit will go a long way toward providing the desired results.

Because he comes into a game cold, a pinch-hitter should have to contend with fewer restrictions than a player who is taking his regular turn at bat. Being called upon to take a "fat" pitch for a strike is a particularly bad thing for him to have to do and the only time that this is called for is when the pitcher is exceptionally wild and waiting him out seems like good strategy.

One thing which the pinch-hitter should bear in mind is the necessity of reporting to the umpire before taking his position at the plate. This is a regularly observed custom and, although no penalty will be imposed on the batter himself, his team is liable to a fine in organized baseball and certain other leagues.

A pinch-hitter should try to be relaxed, both mentally and physically, and should not let the situation seem too big for him; he should be well aware of the fact that the most that can reasonably be expected of him is that he just do the very best he can.

BASE-RUNNING

Base-running has important factors other than sheer speed of foot. In fact, many fine base runners are men who lack exceptional speed but who excel on the base paths because of alertness, good judgment, and thorough knowledge of sound technique and baseball percentage as it applies to any given situation.

A base runner can look to a coach for advice and instructions before a play starts but, once he is in motion, he must depend on his own judgment and knowledge of proper base-running practices 90 per cent of the time.

Three basic principles

Good base-running revolves around three basic principles:

(a) *Know the importance of your run.* All moves by a ballplayer when on the base paths must be guided by this principle. He must be fully aware of exactly how much the run he represents means to his team and should base his actions almost entirely on this consideration. Of course, if the other team gives him an extra base he should take advantage of it. But, generally speaking, a base runner should take chances only when his run is an important one and then only to get into proper scoring position.

(b) *Always watch the runner ahead of you.* Too often, this relatively obvious principle is neglected. A ballplayer can do little but hurt his team by breaking up a rally if he does not pay heed to the actions of any of his teammates who may be ahead of him on the base paths. When two runners find themselves caught on the same base, you can be sure that the trailing runner has been guilty of a very serious error of omission.

(c) *Touch every base.* That's what they are there for.

The start

Needless to say, getting off to a good start is highly important for any runner in any branch of athletics. This most certainly applies to baseball in general, and base runners in particular. Every ballplayer should go all-out on the first three steps and run on his toes at all times to achieve maximum speed at the earliest possible instant.

A batter can save himself a valuable fraction of a second in getting to first base by getting a good start from home plate; in this way he can beat out infield hits that would otherwise merely be outs.

A right-handed batter should take his first step with his right foot after his follow-through. At this point, his right foot will actually be in better position for the initial step, since his weight will have shifted to the left one.

A left-handed batter should start with his rear foot (the left one). This will be a cross-over step and will give him a real jump since his weight, due to his follow-through, will already be going toward first base.

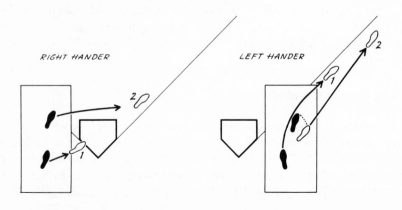

Approaching the base

The manner of approach to any base should be determined by the same principles that guide a runner nearing first base. When running directly to a base, the runner should touch the middle of it. This applies particularly to first base, of course, since there is no need to worry about over-running the bag. He should, at the same time, endeavor to contact the base without altering his normal stride. Jumping for it when he nears the base will actually cause the runner to lose time in his race with the ball.

When rounding a base, the runner should touch and pivot against the corner of the bag nearest the mound. He should swing wide as he gets to within about twenty feet of the base and should hit it without breaking stride, using either foot, although the left one is preferable. Swinging wide before reaching the bag will enable the runner to be moving directly toward the next base as he rounds the one he is nearing, thereby eliminating the need to take several extra steps in order to continue on to the next base.

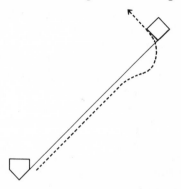

Taking signals

Generally speaking, no offensive play should be attempted unless the coach or manager signals for or gives approval of it.

A runner should return to his base to get the signal which is usually given immediately after the pitch. When he does not get the signal, the runner should call time. Halting play to tie his shoe is one method of doing this.

Both the batter and the runner(s) should adopt the habit of taking an occasional look at the coach *after* the signal has been given. This can often prevent the other club from guessing that a signal has been given.

Strategy

To repeat one of the basic principles of base-running: A runner should try for an extra base when he represents the tying or winning run. It is senseless to gamble when the run is not an important one.

Ordinarily, the time to take chances is with one out. With no outs a team should play it safe, since there are usually at least three chances to get the runner around the bases to the plate. With two outs a team should also play safe lest it kill its possibilities of scoring at all.

Guides to action

As long as the ball is in front of the runner and within his field of vision, he is on his own. In all other cases, he should look to the coach for guidance and should do so before he arrives at a base so that he will allow sufficient time to take the proper course of action.

Of course, it is not possible to look for a coach when going in to second base, and here, of necessity, the runner is on his own. When breaking from first base the runner should look for a batted ball as it is fielded, not only to guide his actions if he continues on his way around the bases, but to prevent his being doubled up on a line drive or fly ball on which he could otherwise return safely to his base. When he sees that the outfielder must play a grounder far to his glove-side, an alert runner will go for an extra base.

When the throw is behind him, the runner should watch the hands and eyes of the infielder who is awaiting the throw. The slide should be made to the side of the base away from the ball and, in this case, the fielder's hands and eyes are the best guide to use. If the baseman reaches toward the runner for the ball, the slide should be straight into the base, making the catch more difficult. This also applies on a force play, when the runner should get to the base as directly and quickly as possible.

Tagging up

When on first or second, a runner would do well to tag up on any routine fly ball to the outfield with no outs. In many cases he will be able to advance after the catch. If, however, the fly is a short one, no advance will be possible, so the runner should go half-way.

In any case where it is doubtful that the ball will be caught, the runner should go half-way—until the ball is either caught or falls safe. When a fly ball is hit with one out the runner should always go half-way.

Needless to say, with two outs the runner should be moving on any batted ball.

When on third base the runner should tag up on any ball hit in the air, even a line drive which looks like an obvious base hit. This will save valuable time and enable the runner to score if the ball is caught. If it falls in for a base hit he will have no trouble scoring anyhow.

This move back to third on any ball hit in the air should become an automatic and immediate reaction on the part of any ballplayer who would become a sound base runner. The very instant the ball is hit in the air the runner should instinctively return to third base.

Foiling the double play

With a double play in prospect the runner on first base should slide into second in such a way that he will interfere with the throw to first base.

The rules of the game state that the runner should slide so that some part of him is within reaching distance of the bag. Allowing approximately three feet on either side of the base will permit the runner to break up the double play while remaining within the bounds of legality.

To break up a double-play attempt, the runner should use a hard slide, with his knees at a 45-degree angle, and should endeavor, if possible, to hook the striding foot of the defensive player.

Every ballplayer, when considering such tactics, should always bear in mind that he should play the game as hard as he can but should, at all times, stay within the rules. He should never play dirty baseball and intentionally injure an opponent.

One special play which arises with the double-play setup comes on a ground ball hit to the second baseman, on which there is a possibility of tagging the runner for the first out. The man on first base should never run into the tag on this play. If the second baseman comes at him in an attempt to make the tag, the runner should hold up and make the second baseman chase him, delaying the tag (if not avoiding it completely) long enough to prevent a double play. In fact, the runner should hold up just as soon as it is apparent that this play can be made.

First-and-third tactics

When a team has runners on first and third (or the bases loaded) with less than two out, there is always the possibility that the defensive club will try for a double play by way of second base. For this reason the runner on third should notice if the left side of the infield is playing back and, in effect, giving up a run.

As a matter of fact, any time a runner reaches third base he should observe the position of the infield to see if they are conceding him a run on a ground ball.

If, on the other hand, the infield is playing in to cut off the run at the plate, the runner on third must wait for the ball to go through the infield before attempting to score, except, of course, when the bases are loaded and he will be forced at the plate. When the infield plays in close position with runners on first and third, the man on first should take advantage of being lightly regarded by the defense and should steal second, thereby placing two runners in scoring position.

With men on first and third and the runner on first representing an important run, he must be careful not to take too big a lead and be caught off base. The defensive team will be looking for just such an opportunity—they will be concentrating on the important run and paying little attention to the other runner.

In the first-and-third situation, the runner on third should attempt to score on a ground ball in almost every case where one is hit. The main idea here is to prevent a double play. Even if the throw does not go home, the runner breaking for the plate may succeed in diverting the infielder's attention just enough to prevent the completion of a double play—and will have scored a run in the bargain. In the case where the play is made on the runner at home, he should pull up and get caught in a run-down and try to permit the other runners to advance to second and third. He should jockey around sufficiently to put two runners in scoring position and, as a final maneuver to delay the tag, should run or even dive out of the base line at the very last moment. In nine cases out of ten, the defensive player making the tag will follow the runner or instinctively lunge at him, allowing more time for the other runners to advance to scoring position.

The exception to this practice arises when the ball is hit too slowly for the defense to complete a double play. In this case they will be playing for one out and will probably go for the runner at home. A similar instance is the medium speed or slow ground ball with men on first and second. With no chance to complete a double play, the pivot man may try to catch the runner taking a wide turn at third after the force has been made at second. In either case the lead runner must be careful of attempts to catch him napping.

Trying to score

The time to take chances is with one out. For this reason, among others, it is recommended that with a runner on third, or runners on second and third, and one out, the man on third should try to score on a ground ball to the infield (excluding the pitcher). Unless the infield is playing in to cut off the run at the plate, this gamble is easily worthwhile since it takes clean handling of the ball and a perfect throw to retire the runner trying to score. Over the course of a season the percentages are with the offensive team and many more runners should score than will be thrown out at the plate.

Men on first and second

When a team has runners on first and second, the man on first base can afford to take a comfortably large lead, particularly if the pitcher gets behind the batter and cannot afford to waste a pitch-out.

In the case where the run at first is more important than the one at second, the defensive team will be playing the man at first at the expense of the other runner, so caution must be exercised by the runner at first. If, by any chance, a pick-off throw is made by the catcher to first base, the runner at second should be alert for an opportunity to steal third —he can probably make it since here, again, unusually good throws and clean ball handling will be needed to get him.

Bases loaded

Needless to say, the bases-loaded situation means that all runners must get a good jump and go all-out to beat the throw on any ground ball hit to the infield. For this reason they should take substantial leads and ordinarily can afford to do so. They must, at the same time, be very careful not to get caught off base. This would be almost inexcusable since it would break up what is the definite prospect of a big inning.

The two-out, run-and-hit situation in which the runners break with the pitch must be handled with care. The proper time for this is, of course, on the 3-2 count with the batter swinging at his own discretion. On this maneuver the runner at third should not break for the plate since doing so will interfere with the batter's swing. The other runners should merely jog lest a smart catcher make a throw which catches one of them rounding the bag after a base on balls.

Safety rules

Any man who crosses the plate with a run should, just as soon as he scores, assume a position which will enable him to coach any other runner who may be trying to score on the same play. He should let him know whether to slide or stay up as he comes in to home plate. This simple move can mean the difference between a run and an out and, even more important, may well prevent an injury to the runner by keeping him from sliding unnecessarily or hesitating due to indecision.

It is also a good idea for the lead runner to pick up a loose bat or mask if it will be the way and cause possible injury to the oncoming base runner.

On being doubled off base

One of the pitfalls of which a base runner must be most wary is getting doubled off base on a line drive. The only times when this can be justified are when he is off with the pitch on a hit-and-run play and the batter hits a line drive to one of the infielders, and when the first baseman has been holding the runner close to his base and catches a line drive hit directly over the bag. In all other cases the runner should be able to return to his base safely. There is no rule compelling him to be further from his base than the nearest infielder and he should make it a practice not to break for the next base until the ball is on the ground or through the infield.

A runner should never allow himself to be doubled up on a line drive or fly ball to the outfield, no matter how miraculous the catch or throw by the defensive player.

On being picked off base

Any man who reaches base immediately becomes a very important and valuable commodity, both as a potential run and, in the team aspect of base-running, in upsetting the pitcher. He should be fully cognizant of this fact and must never allow himself to be picked off base. The runner guilty of this crime breaks up a potential big inning and might well cost his team the ball game.

The run-down

When caught in a run-down a ballplayer rarely escapes safely. For that reason his main objective should be to delay the put-out as long as possible to allow any other base runner(s) to advance. He does so by running back and forth between the bases, changing direction just as soon as the ball leaves the hand of any pursuing infielder. He should try to work toward the more advanced base and in a last attempt to delay the tag should run or dive out of the base line.

A maneuver which may succeed against an unsuspecting defense and which, if it works, will not only avert a put-out, but will also advance the runner, goes as follows:

The runner, caught in a run-down, changes directions just as an infielder throws the ball and, instead of continuing to jockey around, rushes just as fast as he can at the man who has just thrown the ball. He endeavors to make physical contact with that defensive player. If he succeeds, a defensive player not in possession of the ball will have blocked the base line. The umpire must call interference on the play and the runner(s) may advance to the next base. This play can be worked successfully, particularly in amateur competition, if timed perfectly.

Taking a lead

When a player becomes a base runner, his job is to advance as quickly and easily as possible around the bases until he scores a run for his team. Any move that will make his task easier should be both studied and perfected.

One of the methods by which a runner can help himself is to master the correct technique of taking a lead, a maneuver that varies according to the base involved and the game situation. Needless to say, the runner who takes a proper lead greatly enhances his possibilities of getting a good jump on the ball and, of course, of eventually scoring a run.

THE LEAD OFF FIRST. The pitcher's move to first is the major factor in determining a safe, as well as sufficient, lead. Against a left-hander, especially one with a good pick-off move, a small lead is a necessary precaution. Naturally, greater liberties may be taken with a right-hander on the mound.

To set an arbitrary figure, a lead of four steps would seem ideal. This allows for two steps and a slide. As stated previously, this will depend on the pitcher. In some cases a bigger lead will be possible but it is strongly recommended that two steps and a slide be used. This will prove substantial—and safe.

The runner, in taking his lead, should keep on his toes with his weight well balanced. A modified crouch with the arms slightly extended to the side will help maintain good balance and allow the runner to move quickly in either direction. When the pitcher makes a pick-off throw, a slide should be used where necessary to get back safely.

One rule which should be scrupulously observed by a base runner is never to cross his legs when taking a lead. Once he does so he can be caught flat-footed by a pick-off throw. Backing off the base until the full lead has been reached is a good method of avoiding the tangled feet which can cause the runner to be caught off base.

The pitcher's feet and knees should be closely observed for the tip-off on a throw to first to pick off the runner. When a right-hander lifts his *rear heel* as his initial move he is definitely going to first base with the ball.

The so-called secondary lead is of great importance. This is the lead which the runner can take on the pitcher's motion. In order to assure the runner of a good start on a batted ball, a moving secondary lead of two or three steps should be taken. However, it should be taken at only half-speed and never in such a way that the runner will be retired on a pick-

Base-running—the Take-off

off throw from the catcher. Safety for a move in either direction is the keynote here.

In making a break for second base the runner should start by pivoting on his right foot. The first step is then a cross-over with the left foot. This means that almost a full step is gained in comparison with starting by a step on the right foot—and every step is important in making the next base safely.

GOING FROM FIRST TO THIRD. Going from first to third on a single is a move which should be thought about and practiced until a player is thoroughly prepared to take full advantage of the opportunity to do so when it arises.

The runner (and coaches) should be aware of the exact position of the outfielders and the throwing ability of each of them. The latter includes tendency to charge the ball, to field it cleanly, to get it away fast, and the actual strength of their arms. They should also take full cognizance of how hard the ball is hit.

With two outs the runner should be absolutely sure that he can make third before attempting to do so. With one out he can afford to take a chance. With no outs the attempt to reach third may be worth the gamble since it might set up a big inning.

THE LEAD OFF SECOND. Taking a lead off second differs markedly from the one off first for two reasons. First of all, at second a runner is not held close to the bag as he is at first base; secondly, the catcher's pickoff throw is a long one, consequently less danger exists of being caught off base on a throw by the catcher.

For this reason a big lead is not necessary at second base even though a longer one is possible than at first. As a matter of fact, a really big lead at second should be discouraged. There is little sense in drawing a pickoff throw or in being lured into a trap for a well-timed play by the pitcher and shortstop.

The runner at second should not venture further from the base in taking his lead than the shortstop or second baseman, whichever one is closer to the bag. A lead of about four steps is recommended. A bigger one is not needed since the runner can get fifteen to twenty feet on the pitcher's motion—and this is a moving lead, not a stop-and-go one.

The runner on second should make a ball hit to the shortstop go through before breaking for third. If, however, the ball is hit to his left he can set out for third as there is very little possibility of his being thrown out on such a ball.

THE LEAD OFF THIRD.   The first rule to be observed by a runner at third is that he should take his lead in foul territory. A runner who fails to follow this rule betrays evidence of poor coaching and inexperience. The reason for taking a lead in foul territory is to eliminate the possibility of the runner's being hit by a batted ball in fair ground. This would, of course, result in his being declared out.

In returning to base the runner should move into fair territory so as to obstruct the vision of both the catcher and the third baseman should a pick-off throw be attempted.

Principle number two is that the runner at third should return to his base and tag up on any ball hit in the air. The reason for this has been dis-

The Lead Off Third

Returning to Third

Tagging up

cussed previously, so suffice it to say here that the importance of an *immediate* and instinctive return to the base cannot be overemphasized.

When tagging up on a fly ball, the runner should shift his weight to the advanced foot before the actual start. The first step is then taken with the rear foot (in this case, the left one), allowing him to get a much better jump on the ball—it saves almost a full step. The runner is allowed to leave his base just as soon as the ball comes into contact with any part of the fielder.

Ordinarily a big lead can be taken at third base. There is more danger of a pick-off throw from the catcher than from the pitcher and, with this in mind, the runner should see just how much lead he can get on the pitcher's motion. He should, however, avoid taking such a big lead that he will have to start back toward third before the catcher actually has possession of the ball since this can cause him to lose an opportunity to score on a passed ball.

Faking a steal of home can occasionally disconcert the pitcher and impair his effectiveness. On this maneuver the false start should be made just as the pitcher reaches the top of his wind-up, in hopes that his concentration on the pitch to the batter will be upset.

Sliding

The purpose of the slide is threefold: it can enable a runner to avoid being tagged and to reach base safely in many cases where he would otherwise be put out; it is a very effective brake for a runner who must stop at a base—far more so than an erect stop; and it can serve to prevent a possible collision between the runner and an infielder.

THEORY. Sliding should be practiced diligently by all ballplayers. Properly done, it is one of the most useful (and necessary) skills that a player can acquire. Improperly done, it can result in serious injury.

A good slide is actually a form of controlled falling in which it is of the utmost importance to have the muscles relaxed. In order to provide maximum safety from leg injuries, a ballplayer should fall backward as he hits the dirt. The slide should be made on the most well-padded part of the anatomy—the buttocks. In addition, the front foot should be raised off the ground to eliminate the danger of having the spikes catch in the dirt, and the runner should be limp as he hits the bag.

PHILOSOPHY. When in doubt, or on any play that will be even reasonably close, the runner should slide. He cannot err by doing so, one important factor in his favor being that the braking effect of a slide will eliminate the need to slow down before reaching the base, something which must be done if he goes in standing up. And, needless to say, a slightly earlier arrival at the base will result.

Once the runner makes up his mind to slide he should do so. There should never be the least bit of hesitation in the slide itself—hesitation or changing one's mind at the last second being the chief cause of injury to a sliding runner.

DIRECTION. A runner should look to the coach for a slide or stay up signal. A good coach will also indicate the side to which the slide should be made. At second base, where there is no coach, the runner must take his cue from the infielder who covers the bag.

The slide should be to the side opposite that on which the ball is coming. The position of the fielder's hands and eyes serve as a guide to the runner for judging the direction of the throw. When the fielder reaches directly toward the runner the slide should be straight into the bag in an attempt to interfere with the throw. This applies also to a force play.

THE SLIDES

There are three basic slides, each of which should be practiced and mastered—and on both sides of the body for slides to either side of the base. They are all feet-first slides. The head-first slide should be discouraged since it not only allows for very little deception but also greatly increases the danger of injury—to head, face, and hands.

As a further precautionary note, when sliding the runner should do so in a way which will find his face turned away from the throw. Furthermore, since there is a strong tendency to put the hands down on the ground, giving rise to cuts and scrapes, the sliding runner should make sure to carry his hands well off the ground. Picking up a handful of pebbles or dirt each time he gets on base will help a runner to rid himself of this tendency. The hands and arms can also be used to protect the head and face—often a wise move.

THE BENT-LEG SLIDE. The bent-leg slide is usually made straight in to the bag. It serves as an effective brake and also enables a man to spring up and keep going.

The take-off can be made on either foot. When the slide is made straight in to the bag, either side can be used; the choice depends on whichever is easier for the player involved. As he starts his slide the

299

The Bent-Leg Slide

runner should fall back on his buttocks, tucking one foot under his body with his knee bent at approximately a right angle. The advanced foot should be kept in the air so that the spikes won't catch in the dirt, and the leg should be practically straight. The body weight should be back on the buttocks—not on the knee.

If the runner desires to stop at the base into which he is sliding, his forward foot should go over the bag, which is then hooked with the rear foot.

In the case of an overthrow or mishandled ball the runner might want to continue on to the next base. If so, he should hit the bag with his front foot, at the same time pushing up with the leg that is tucked under him. His momentum, plus the added push, will enable him to spring up and get away quite easily.

The bent-leg slide can also be used to elude the tag. Here, the slide is made slightly to the side of the base, the lead foot hooking the nearest corner of the bag as the body continues on to the side away from the throw.

Primarily, however, the bent-leg slide is the one which should be used when the runner intends to go straight in to the base.

THE HOOK SLIDE. When a runner is attempting to avoid being tagged, he generally uses the hook slide. It can enable a runner to establish contact with the base while, at the same time, falling away from the tag with his body. The hook slide should be mastered on both sides so that the runner will always be able to slide away from the ball.

In making this slide the runner should take off on his left foot for a slide to the left and with his right foot for a slide to the right. He should go straight in to the bag, contacting the middle of the front part of it with the left foot when sliding to the right and the right foot when sliding to the left. The other foot should be held off the ground and goes to the side of the base. The momentum of the slide will cause the body to hook around to the side of the base.

300

The Hook Slide

In short, the hook slide should be straight in to the base until contact with the bag is established—then the body falls away from the tag. This method enables the runner to save valuable time in reaching his objective. Too often, ballplayers fall away from the base before actually contacting it. This means that the runner will have travelled an extra two or three feet before arriving at the base—often the difference between being safe and out.

The whip slide is a variation of the hook slide and is used to avoid the tag when the baseman is waiting with the ball. It starts like the hook slide but the runner slides further to the side of the base, kicking his legs away from the base as he hits the ground. He reaches for the base with the nearer arm and as the baseman tries to tag him he whips his arm back and away, turning his body in. At the same time he reaches for and touches the base with his other arm. The baseman must follow the slide and the runner gives him only his arm or hand as a target for the tag.

THE FEET-FIRST SLIDE. This is a straight-in slide used to get back to the base on a pick-off throw or when the runner is in danger of being doubled up. Although not advisable, the head-first slide can also be used in this situation—anything to get back safely.

On a straight-in slide, the runner should concentrate on watching the base. Conversely, on a slide designed primarily to avoid being tagged, he should concentrate on the baseman's hands.

TWO SPECIAL SLIDES. The double-play slide (the slide to break up a double play) has been described in a previous section, yet some of its salient points could bear repetition.

In breaking up a double play the runner must slide in such a way that some part of his body is within reaching distance of the base. The most effective method to use is a hard straight-in slide with the knees bent at a 45-degree angle. If possible, contact should be made with the striding foot of the defensive player.

Sliding in to first base is another special slide. The runner should slide

301

in to first base only when it will mean avoiding a collision on a close play, or when the throw pulls the first baseman off the bag toward home plate so that he must try to tag the runner. A slide will often enable the runner to avoid being tagged and to reach first base safely.

OFFENSIVE PLAYS

The steal

Running teams are usually successful ones—going, in many cases, on the theory that, when the other team can be made to throw the ball, there exists the possibility of an error which will enable the runner to advance. Indiscriminate base-running, however, can be of little value to anyone but the defensive team. The steal, in particular, must be judiciously employed.

The value of the steal lies in the fact that it gives the offensive team something for nothing—the advance of a runner without sacrificing an out—and can help them to a run which would not have scored had it been left entirely to batting power. As a corollary, an indirect advantage accrues from the disconcerting effect that the threat of a steal often has on the pitcher.

FACTORS AFFECTING ITS USE. Generally speaking, the steal should be attempted only when it involves an important run, and then almost never to win a game—only to get a runner into scoring position. For instance, it should not be used, unless it is a gift, when—

1. A team is more than two runs behind.
2. The opposing pitcher is having control trouble.
3. A runner is on second with two outs (he's already in scoring position).

Needless to say, use of the steal is precluded by a slow base runner. With the right man on base, its use must still be tempered by the ability of the man at bat. For example—

1. With a good hitter at the plate a steal of third or home should not be risked.
2. With two outs and a weak hitter at bat, a steal is unwise since an unsuccessful one means a poor batsman will lead off in the next inning.

302

3. With two outs and a good hitter up, a steal of second is a good move since it can put a runner in position to score on a base hit.
4. A steal of second is more likely to succeed with a left-hander at bat (he obstructs the catcher's throw, to a certain extent).

The count on the batter should be given consideration. The steal is more logical when the pitcher is behind and cannot risk a pitch-out. Whether behind or not, if the pitcher can be expected to throw a curve the steal will have more chance of success due to the slightly slower speed of and relative difficulty in handling the curve ball.

In the vast majority of cases the steal will be signalled by the coach. Very rarely should the player be on his own and then only when he is a smart and experienced base runner.

GETTING THE JUMP. Bases are stolen on the pitcher—not the catcher. Predictably rhythmical pitchers are the easiest ones on whom to steal. They work in a cadence in which the rhythm is almost identical on every delivery to either the batter or the base. A smart base runner will watch the pitcher closely to learn his rhythmic pattern and will attempt to steal "on a count." In other words, where the pitcher's delivery forms a five-count rhythmic cadence, the runner will go when the count reaches "four." If by any chance a pick-off throw is made to the base, the runner should keep going and try to reach his objective.

When the count method cannot be employed the pitcher's knees and feet can provide tell-tale signs as to his intentions. Almost invariably, a right-hander will lift his right heel as the initial move in throwing to first. A left-hander, needless to say, is far more deceptive and difficult to steal against.

Clues which indicate pretty definitely that the pitcher is delivering to the plate are—dropping his rear shoulder, raising his front elbow, bending his rear knee, and, especially, the raising of his front heel.

Combining these two methods—counting and tip-offs—where possible, will provide an almost perfect way in which to get a good jump on the ball; this is the secret to successful base-stealing.

THE BATTER'S ROLE. The batter can aid materially in effecting a successful steal.

When this play has been signalled, the batter should move to the rear of the batter's box and should swing to miss the ball, especially if it is in the strike zone. These are both devices intended to disconcert the catcher. Swinging to miss, of course, is out of the question with two strikes on the batter. Nor is it necessary when the pitch is wild enough to cause the catcher difficulty in handling it and making his throw.

The batter can be of considerable help to a teammate who is trying to steal third, merely by bluffing a bunt. This may draw the third baseman plateward, leaving his base unguarded against the steal.

On a steal of home the batter serves a useful purpose by crowding the plate and remaining in position until the last possible instant. He may be able to swing at the ball, missing it intentionally. If so, the swing should be an easy and high one. Needless to say, it cannot be risked if the runner is too close.

STEALING THIRD. Any discussion of base-stealing pertains primarily to the steal of second base. A steal of third is relatively rare, despite the fact that it is more easily accomplished than a steal of second. The fact that the runner can get a much bigger lead and jump on the pitcher is offset by the fact that he is already in scoring position and need not risk an out by attempting to steal third.

A steal of third is best done with one out and a right-hander at bat. This will put the runner in position to score on a ground ball, fly to the outfield, error, or squeeze play. Ordinarily, an attempted steal of third with no outs is bad policy, as three chances remain to bring him in from scoring position. It is really bad baseball to try a steal of third with a left-hander at bat since, in this case, the catcher has a clear view of third and an unobstructed throw to that base.

A PRECAUTION. When a runner has had to return to his base several times because foul balls have nullified a steal, the play should be called off since the repeated efforts will have a tiring effect on him.

STEALING HOME. A steal of home is a foolish play at best because of the many safer ways in which a runner can score from third. It is most logically tried with two outs, a weak right-hand batter at the plate, and after at least one fake has been made to lull the pitcher into a sense of false security. Needless to say, its chances of success are directly proportionate to the length of the pitcher's wind-up.

THE DELAYED STEAL. The delayed steal is a play which should be attempted only by an exceptionally fast man. It is worked after the catcher has received the pitch and should be tried only if the runner has noticed laxness by the catcher (lobbing the ball back to the pitcher) or carelessness on the part of the second baseman and shortstop (failure to move toward the bag after the pitch). If properly timed by the runner, he will take off just as the catcher starts his throw to the pitcher. The pitcher then must catch the ball, pivot, and throw while the infielder who covers must come from a deep position to make the play—all aspects of the situation combining to improve the runner's chances of reaching second safely.

A delayed steal of third base is a rare occurrence. A good lead must be gained on the pitcher's motion and the break for third should come just as soon as it seems that the runner has succeeded in drawing a throw to second from the catcher. It can be worked only against a catcher who likes to throw and will not hesitate to fire the ball to second base. The delayed steal of second can also capitalize on luring the catcher into throwing behind the runner (to first base).

THE DOUBLE STEAL. A double steal of third and home does not make sense since two runners are in scoring position, a normal double-play situation does not exist, and it is a very risky undertaking.

The primary aim of a double steal of second and third is to eliminate the possibility of a double play and to advance a second runner to scoring position. Most propitious time for its use is when the offensive team is no more than two runs behind and there is one out. It is merely a steal of third with the man on first following. Thus, conditions pertaining to the steal of third apply here.

It is the men-on-first-and-third situation with which we are primarily concerned when discussing the double steal. It can be justified under two sets of circumstances: with two out, when no more than two runs behind, and with a good hitter at bat—the objective being to advance a second runner to scoring position—scoring the man on third is only a secondary aim; with one out, when no more than two runs behind, and with a weak hitter at bat, the objective being to prevent a double play and possibly to score a run on the steal itself. It is worked as follows:

The man on first breaks for second on the pitch and if the throw goes through to the base he pulls up short and gets caught in a run-down. The man on third waits until the ball is over the pitcher's head before making his break for home, having moved out into the base line to obstruct the catcher's view of third base. If executed perfectly, this play can result in one run scored and a runner on second base. An alternative, when the throw is cut off, is to have the runner on third hold his base and the other runner continue on to second. This, of course, puts one more runner in scoring position, even though it is not literally a double steal.

THE TRIPLE STEAL. This play is comparable in all respects to the steal of home except that, with two other men on base, it is an even more foolish venture.

THE FORCED BALK. With a poor hitter at bat, men on first and third, and an inexperienced pitcher on the mound this play may succeed. In it, the runner on first should start for second as soon as the pitcher looks away from him. The object is to induce a balk on the part of the pitcher, something that will happen if he takes action without first stepping off the rubber.

A variation may be attempted if a batter walks with a runner on third. He should jog to first and start for second if the pitcher looks the other way.

This play is best employed with less than two outs so that if the pitcher does not balk a put-out will not end the inning with men on base.

The sacrifice

The only purpose of the sacrifice is to advance a runner by sacrificing an out. The batter should give himself up, concentrating solely on getting the bunt down and in the right location. An attempt to mask his intentions will detract from the batter's ability to bunt well. Furthermore, the defensive team, especially in amateur competition, is more likely to lose its composure when it knows that a bunt is coming.

Bunting technique is described in the section on batting.

THE PITCH. When the sacrifice is on, the batter picks his own pitch, selecting one that is "buntable." To qualify thusly it does not necessarily have to be a strike. However, if it is a strike and the batter does not try to bunt it, he has committed a serious error.

THE PLACE. Ideally, a sacrifice should go toward third and be hard enough to make the third baseman field it, leaving his base open. But, unless the bunter is really accomplished, for safety's sake he should bunt the ball where it is pitched.

If he is capable of placing his bunts well the batter should do so according to the game situation. To negate somewhat the first sentence above—with a runner on first base a bunt toward first can be effective against a right-handed first baseman. He will have been holding the runner and will be in relatively poor position for a throw to second. Of course, this will eliminate the possibility of the runner's advancing to an unguarded third base.

Ordinarily a bunt toward third is desirable with a runner on second base. However, with men on first and second and a force out possible, the relative fielding ability of first baseman and pitcher should be considered. The bunt should go toward third if the pitcher is the poorer glove-man, toward first if the first baseman is more inept, with the additional qualification that the play at third is easier for a left-hand pitcher.

The distance of defensive players from home plate at the time of the play is another factor in determining the wisest target for the sacrifice bunt.

THE TIME. The philosophy behind a sacrifice makes it an advisable, if not mandatory, maneuver at times. It is definitely a wise move in certain situations.

1. In the late innings of a tight game, especially with no outs and a runner on first or men on first and second.

2. With a weak hitter at bat, followed by a strong hitter. A pitcher, when not a good hitter, should sacrifice even with one out to eliminate the double-play possibility and to give himself a rest if he bunts successfully.

3. As a surprise play—with one out and a good hitter coming up next.

4. With a man on second, no outs, the score close, and in the late innings. The runner can then score on a fly, error, or short hit.

5. In a close game, with no outs and men on first and second, even with a good hitter at bat. Having two runners in scoring position makes the loss of the out worthwhile, good hitter not withstanding.

6. In a close game with men on first and third, no outs—especially if the man on first is the winning run. At worst, the offensive team should wind up with men on second and third, one out and, if the bunt is well placed, the man on third can score.

THE RUNNER. The runner should be able to advance unless the bunt is a really poor one. He must, however, exercise caution in one respect— making sure that the bunt is on the ground before breaking for the next base. He should not allow himself to be doubled up if the bunt is popped into the air or picked off by the catcher if the bunt is missed completely.

After taking his lead, the runner should advance an additional few steps in a secondary lead as the pitcher delivers the ball. He should then hold up and delay his break for the next base until sure that the ball is on the ground.

Patience is demanded of both batter and runner. Neither should commit himself too soon and both should remember that it is preferable to advance to second via a walk.

THE BUNT-AND-RUN. This play can be very effective and can be a judicious substitute for the hit-and-run. Here, as in the hit-and-run, the runner breaks with the pitch. The batter, rather than swinging, lays down a sacrifice bunt. The runner should be able to reach third base if the bunt is a good one, particularly if the third baseman must field it. The runner must exercise caution, however, lest a smart third baseman throw to second and catch him rounding that base.

The squeeze play

When properly executed, the squeeze play not only scores a run, it also can have a demoralizing effect on the defensive team. But, it cannot be used indiscriminately and it is potentially dangerous since any indication that it is being employed will bring an unbuntable pitch and an easy out.

THE TIME. The proper time to try the squeeze is in the late innings of a close game, and with *one* out. There is little sense in gambling for the run (and the risk is great on a squeeze) unless it is an important one.

Moreover, with no outs there are three chances to score the runner from third.

THE BUNTER. The man at bat on a squeeze play must be a good bunter, since he absolutely has to get the ball on the ground in fair territory. As stated in the section on batting, technique for the squeeze bunt involves moving the front foot back in squaring around, so as to allow slightly more time to bunt, to delay the catcher, and to increase the chances of causing interference by the catcher.

THE SUICIDE SQUEEZE. This is an all-out gamble to score a run. The runner breaks for the plate and the batter must bunt the ball no matter where it is pitched. The runner and the batter must wait until the pitcher is in the act of throwing to the plate before making their moves. The batter has one main concern—to bunt the ball in fair territory, on the ground.

THE DOUBLE SQUEEZE. This is merely a suicide squeeze with runners on second and third. The runner from second breaks with the pitch, rounds third, and continues home on the throw to first.

THE SAFE SQUEEZE. As on the sacrifice, the batter picks his own pitch and the runner does not break for home until the ball is on the ground (in this case, in the right spot to allow him to score). The batter should not square around too soon and—of utmost importance—the bunt must be well placed. Obviously the batter must be an excellent bunter. The surprise element and the minimizing of the possibility of losing the runner are factors contributing to the advantages offered by the safe squeeze. The sacrifice with men on first and third is a version of the safe squeeze.

TWO-OUT SQUEEZE. With an outstanding bunter at bat, a drag-bunt squeeze with two out may prove successful, depending entirely on the unexpectedness of the play and the ability of the batter to bunt safely for a hit. It is a variation of the safe squeeze.

The hit-and-run

The hit-and-run can be a devastating weapon, effective in advancing runners as well as discouraging to the opposition. Upon it is based the attack of a so-called running team.

PHILOSOPHY. The hit-and-run is based on the idea that the runner moving toward second will draw either the shortstop or second baseman away from his normal position. Obviously, it is intended to advance the runner possibly two bases, rather than one.

Probably more important as an aim is the elimination of a possible double play on a ground ball. In this case, not only will a double play be avoided, but a runner will advance to scoring position.

THE TIME. The hit-and-run should be used only when a run is needed and with an experienced player at bat. It is always a good play when the pitcher is behind the batter and must throw a strike.

This is particularly so on the 3-1 pitch, wherein a fourth ball does not have to be hit by the batter, a safe advance to second being automatic.

The hit-and-run is often sound policy with a weak hitter at bat—a man who is more than likely to hit a double-play ball; but it is not good policy when more than one run behind or with two outs.

THE BATTER. The runner must be protected, therefore a good hit-and-run man is one who is capable of "getting a piece of the ball" on a given pitch. Preferably he has sufficient bat control to hit to the spot vacated by the man moving to cover second on an apparent steal. Generally, he should be adept at hitting behind the runner (to right field) in order to enhance a team's chances of moving the runner from first to third.

The batter should be alert in detecting a player's edging over to cover second base. Usually the second baseman takes it for a right-hand batter, the shortstop for a lefty. The batter should use this to guide his actions. When the covering infielder cannot be detected in time, it is always safe to hit to right field (behind the runner).

THE RUNNER. The runner should break for second base just as soon as the pitcher is going to the plate with the ball—just as he would on a straight steal. When he has taken a few steps and after the ball has been hit, the runner should look for it to make sure that it is not a fly ball which will be caught and on which he could be doubled up at first base.

THE BUNT-AND-RUN. This play really belongs in the category of the sacrifice, where it has been discussed. It is a relatively safe maneuver with a good bunter at bat.

THE RUN-AND-HIT. For a team devoid of good hit-and-run men but which desires to play a running game, the run-and-hit is a most effective weapon. "Starting the runner" involves his breaking for second on the pitch. The batter, however, swings only if it is a strike. This provides two options—a steal if the pitch is a ball, the hit-and-run if it is a strike.

The run-and-hit is particularly effective with the count at 3-2. If the pitch is a strike the batter has a good ball to hit; a ball and the runner advances automatically.

STRATEGY. For most effective results this play calls for a fast man at first base and a right-field hitter at the plate.

It can be used with men on first and second but, in this case, is not likely to open a hole at either short or second.

The hit-and-run should not be used with a slow man on base and a fast one at bat. A slow base runner stands little chance of stealing second if the batter fails to hit the ball; a fast man at bat is unlikely to hit into a double play. Thus, under these circumstances, it is both unwise and unnecessary to employ the hit-and-run.

A long-ball hitter or a man who hits sharp line drives should not be required to swing at a certain pitch since this will greatly reduce his chances of hitting the ball solidly. The hit-and-run should not be employed with such a man at bat.

It is bad policy to hit-and-run with men on first and third, no outs, and a 3-2 count on the batter for the following reasons: there are three chances to score the man from third; a line drive or strike-out can result in a double play, choking off a possible rally; and since the runner on third will score anyhow on a ground-ball double play.

THE BASE COACHES

The first- and third-base coaches play an important role in the success of any team. Theirs is a demanding role in that they must concentrate fully on their tasks, keeping one jump ahead of the play and being prepared to make split-second decisions as various situations arise.

Whether this role is filled by a manager, coach, or player its duties and responsibilities should be thoroughly understood by any man who occupies a coaching box.

The basic rule

As a first consideration, the coaches must never assume that a runner will do the right thing—they must always give him instructions.

Every offensive play and possibility should be clear in the mind of the coach so that he can properly instruct the runner. It is imperative that he be aware at all times of the inning, the outs, the score, the count, the speed of the runner, the ability of the next hitter, and the habits of the defensive players.

The two coaches

The first-base coach has jurisdiction over the batter just as soon as he becomes a base runner and should encourage as well as guide him as he comes to first. Once the runner passes first base his attention must be focused ahead of him and he becomes the responsibility of the third-base coach. However, this should not prevent the first-base coach from shouting warnings or advice as they may be needed.

The third-base coach is the more important of the two, both in that he is the one who usually gives the signals for offensive plays, and insofar as the direction of base-line traffic is concerned. After the runner has reached scoring position it is the third-base coach who must attempt to guide him safely in to home plate with a run.

Advising the man on base

About 90 per cent of the help that a coach can give the runner comes before the ball is hit. It includes the location of the ball; the number of outs; the alignment of the defense; any offensive play which has been signalled; when to play safe; the throwing ability of the outfielders; when to tag up or go half-way; the pick-off move of the pitcher; the catcher's throwing ability; what to do on a ground ball; the danger of a line drive; and any other information pertinent to the game situation.

To inform the runner of these things the coach should move as close to him as possible between pitches. This helps the runner understand the coach's advice and prevents the opposition's overhearing what might prove to be valuable information to them.

Guiding the man in motion

Once in motion, the runner is, for the most part, on his own. However, the coach must be depended upon almost entirely when the ball is outside the runner's field of vision. Regardless of the situation, any encouragement or instructions which the coach may give can be of assistance to the runner.

An oncoming runner should be advised as to whether to keep going, take his turn and stop, or stay right on the bag. He should also be urged on if the play will be close—a coach should bear in mind that a runner does not always go all-out and must be reminded to do so when the occasion demands it.

Signalling the runner

Rotating the arms in a clock-wise motion is a signal to the runner to keep going to the next base. The coach should step toward the base line when giving this signal so that there will be no doubt as to his intent.

When the coach holds one hand in the air, palm toward the runner, and points to the next base with his other hand he is indicating that the runner should round the base and hold up, remaining alert for the possibility of advancing an extra base.

311

Coaching Signals—Take Your Turn (round the base)

Coaching Signals—Stop

Coaching Signals—Slide

312

In order to stop the runner, the coach should hold both hands in the air, palms toward the runner, and, if the play dictates that the runner should stay right on the base, the coach should point to it.

The third-base coach should signal a runner whether to slide or stay up. Occasionally the first-base coach may be called upon to do so but this is a relatively rare occurrence.

In order to stop the runner, the coach holds both hands in the air, palms toward the runner. To indicate the necessity of sliding, the coach should extend his arms toward the ground, palms down, much as an umpire does in calling a runner safe. Holding the hands toward either side of the base will let the runner know to which side the slide should be made.

As the runner approaches third base, the coach should move up the line toward home plate so as to be able to advise the runner at the last possible second. This, of course, is applicable only when there will be no play at third base.

Whom to watch

With a man on base the coach should pay little attention to the pitch but should keep his eye on any infielder who might sneak in behind the runner for a pick-off attempt.

With one exception, it is the baseman moving toward the base to take a throw who will tip off a throw to the base. Only at first, with the first baseman holding the runner close to the base, is it the pitcher who should be watched for a pick-off attempt.

Tagging up

The coach should see that a runner who has tagged up on a fly ball gets a good start just as soon as the ball is touched by a fielder. He should watch the ball and give the runner a signal to go just as soon as the ball comes into contact with the fielder. With no outs, it is good percentage baseball to have a runner on first or second tag up on a medium-deep fly ball, a possible exception being one hit to center field, where the throw to second is short.

When there is one out or if it appears doubtful that the ball will be caught, a runner at either first or second should go half-way. With two outs, of course, all runners should be moving just as soon as the ball is hit.

A runner at third base should instinctively and immediately tag up on any ball hit in the air. This will save him valuable time in trying to score on a caught fly ball. If the ball falls in for a hit, even if it is a sharp line drive, he can still score easily. The coach should remind any runner who reaches third to tag up on a ball hit in the air; this move should become automatic and instantaneous.

A special play which presents interesting possibilities is the foul fly, hit with runners on first and third. Both runners should tag up and just as soon as the ball is caught they should both bluff a break for the next base. If this maneuver draws a throw it will enable at least one of them to advance. In this case a throw to second base could enable the runner on third to score; a throw to the plate will permit the runner on first to move to second, thereby placing two runners in scoring position. This play is certainly worth a try if the occasion for it arises.

Avoiding the double play

On only two occasions is it excusable for a runner to be doubled up on a ball hit in the air: (1) a line drive to the infield on a hit-and-run play; (2) a line drive which the first baseman catches directly over the bag with a runner on that base.

In all other instances there is no need for the runner to be further from the base than the nearest infielder. The coach should alert the runner to the danger of being doubled up on a line drive and should have him headed back to the base as soon as the play seems apparent. The runner should not leave for the next base until the ball is on the ground or has gone through the infield.

A runner should *never* be doubled up on a *fly ball;* it is the coach's duty to see that he is properly alerted at all times.

Avoiding a gift out

The coach should not allow a runner to run right into a tag on a ground ball to an infielder. The runner should be warned of this ahead of time so that he does not blunder into this situation.

For example, on a grounder to the second baseman with a man on first, when a tag of the runner is attempted, he should stop and make the second baseman chase him. Delaying the tag in this way will often eliminate the possibility of a double play.

The pick-off

A runner who is picked off base breaks up a potential big inning. This should never happen and, to a great extent, it is the coach's responsibility. The coach should keep the runner informed at all times and should prevent him from wandering so far off base that he is easy prey for a pick-off throw.

Specific coaching duties

The runner is, of course, the key individual when he is on the base paths, but the coach can exert a strong influence on his actions. There are several specific responsibilities which can help in this respect.

FIRST BASE

1. Do not allow the runner to take his lead until the pitcher is on the mound, ready to pitch.
2. Watch for a predictable rhythm in the pitcher's motion and inform the runner if a cadence can be "counted." It can help him get a real jump on the ball.
3. With a sacrifice in order, watch the second baseman lest he sneak behind the runner for a pick-off throw.
4. Advise a runner on second only if a fielder sneaks behind him. In all other cases, a conflict with the advice from the third-base coach should not be chanced.
5. Advise a runner on first of the game situation and any signals given.

THIRD BASE

1. Inform a runner on second of the number of outs; whether to tag up or go half-way on a fly ball; remind him to make the ball go through the left side of the infield before advancing; to run full speed if forced on a ground ball; whether to "play it safe" or to take a chance; and how much room the shortstop is allowing him.
2. As a runner rounds third on his way home the coach should let him know whether to run hard or take his time.
3. Once the runner passes third base the coach should concentrate on the succeeding runner(s).
4. The coach should be alert for a throw intended to catch a runner who has taken his turn at third.
5. The coach should remind a runner at third of the number of outs; to tag up on any ball hit in the air; whether or not the infield is playing in to cut off a run at the plate; to stay outside the base line; to be alert (and not moving back to third) on passed balls; and should tell him (verbally) of any signal which may have been given.

Signals

The signal for an offensive play is usually given by the third-base coach. This is invariably so when the manager or head coach fills that role. Where the manager remains on the bench he occasionally gives direct signals himself, but generally relays them through the third-base coach.

On some ball clubs the third-base coach gives signals to a left-hand batter, the first base coach to a right-hander. Usually, however, the third-base coach gives all of the signals.

OFFENSE

THE PLAYS. Signals are generally used for five offensive maneuvers. They are the take and the hit-away for the batter; and the sacrifice, steal, and hit-and-run for both runner(s) and batter. For purposes of simplicity the hit-and-run and squeeze can be covered by the same signal.

TYPES OF SIGNALS. The signals used should be simple and should be conveyed by a natural movement or gesture on the part of the coach. They can be given by one gesture, a series of moves, or by elimination of one of the series of moves. In addition, they can be indicated by a key which precedes or follows the sign.

It is advisable to have an answering signal from both batter and runner(s). This helps avoid confusion and can eliminate costly mix-ups in attempted plays.

BY THE BATTER. A team with a good hit-and-run man often allows him to give his own signal for the play. It should be arranged with the three men who precede him in the batting order and demands an answering signal.

DUAL PURPOSE SIGNS. The run-and-hit, where employed, is a combination play. It has the effect of a hit-and-run when the batter swings at the ball and is a steal when he takes the pitch. Some ball clubs use this in lieu of the hit-and-run when that play is signalled; others have a special sign for it. It is particularly useful with a 3-1 or 3-2 count since a fourth ball will achieve the desired result with no risk of an out.

Many teams use the same signal for both hit-and-run and suicide squeeze. The safe squeeze, on the other hand, can be indicated by using the sacrifice sign.

CONCEALING SIGNALS. The manager or coach who gives his signals from the bench is invariably subjected to close scrutiny by the opposition. Consequently, an oft-used practice is to have one of the players on the bench give signs at the manager's bidding. Then the opposing team must discover who gives the signals before they can begin to decipher them.

The danger of a club's having its signals stolen is ever present. Some teams go so far as to have certain players on the bench concentrate on the coaches, batter, and runner(s) during an entire game to accomplish this purpose. The hit-and-run sign is the only one in which professional clubs are really interested and knowledge of it by the defense can paralyze a team's attack. For this reason, an alternate set of signals should be resorted to when the least suspicion of stolen signals is aroused.

SAMPLE SIGNALS. There are, of course, innumerable gestures and combinations thereof which can be used as offensive signals. Assuming that they are to be given by the third-base coach, the following sets of signals will serve as examples of three commonly used methods of giving

316

signs. Each is combined with a key and resorts to occasional use of a verbal signal. Answering signs should be arranged for hitter and runner(s) alike.

ONE GESTURE

Key—walk toward the hitter when giving the signal
Sacrifice—right hand to cap
Steal—right hand to letters
Hit-and-Run—right hand to belt
Take-Off (cancel)—left hand to same spot
Take—both hands to cap
Hit Away—skin to skin
Answer—batter: step into box left foot first; runner: skin to cloth

SERIES

Key—hands on knees after giving signal
Sacrifice—touch cap, letters, and pants—in that order
Steal—touch letters, pants, and cap—in that order
Hit-and-Run—touch pants, cap, and letters—in that order
Take-Off—rub hands together
Take—remove cap
Hit Away—verbal: "get yourself a hit"
Answer—batter: run hand up bat; runner: tip cap

ELIMINATION

Key—cup hands to mouth and shout at batter or runner
General Signal—touch cap, face, letters, and belt—going down
Sacrifice—don't touch face
Steal—don't touch letters
Hit-and-Run—don't touch belt
Take-Off—rub upward
Take—verbal: "look it over"
Hit Away—hands on knees
Answer—batter and runner both hitch pants

4

ADDENDA

BASEBALL TACTICS IN ACTION

The practical application of many of the ideas presented in this book can, perhaps, best be shown by the analysis of an actual game.

The third game of the 1956 World Series between the Dodgers and Yankees has been chosen to serve as an illustration of many of the points emphasized in the text. That this particular contest was played several years ago and that it was not a particularly memorable one are inconsequential. Important is the fact that this was an interesting game from a tactical standpoint and that it serves admirably to demonstrate how Major League ballplayers practice sound techniques and tactics.

The clubs held pre-game meetings in which they reviewed the capabilities and habits of their opponents, both individually and collectively. The strength, weakness, and tactics of each hitter; the speed and daring of each man when on base; the fielding and throwing ability of each player; the operating methods of the rival pitchers; the characteristics of the ball park; the prevailing weather conditions; and over-all team strategy were carefully discussed.

The game was played at Yankee Stadium on October 6, 1956. It was a sunny, rather cool day as the game started, with a moderate wind blowing in from right field. Playing conditions were good.

The line-ups:

BROOKLYN	NEW YORK
Gilliam, lf	Bauer, rf
Reese, ss	Collins, 1b
Snider, cf	Mantle, cf
Robinson, 3b	Berra, c
Hodges, 1b	Slaughter, lf
Furillo, rf	Martin, 2b
Campanella, c	McDougald, ss
Neal, 2b	Carey, 3b
Craig, p	Ford, p

FIRST INNING

Whitey Ford, a left-hander, was the Yankee pitcher. He has a good fast ball and a very fine curve which he controls exceptionally well.

321

Dodgers:

Gilliam, after taking a strike, was thrown out by Carey.

° ° Gilliam, leading off, was playing the percentages by taking a strike.

Reese struck out after running the count to 3-2.

° ° Ford's first five pitches were fast ball, curve, fast ball, curve, and fast ball, in that order. On the 3-2 pitch he used the same rhythmical motion but hesitated at the top of his wind-up, throwing Reese's timing off sufficiently to enable him to slip a fast ball past Reese for the third strike.

Snider struck out on a bad ball.

° ° Ford was making his task easier by staying ahead of the hitters.

Roger Craig, a tall right-hander with a sinking fast ball and fair curve, was the Dodger pitcher. He occasionally deals sidearm to right-hand batters.

Yankees:

Bauer took a strike, then flied deep to Furillo on a curve ball.

° ° Bauer followed the ball well, hitting the curve with the rotation (to right field).

Collins flied to Snider on a 3-1 pitch.

° ° The outfield was playing deep since they could afford to give up a single early in the game.

Mantle beat out a bunt to the right side.

° ° Mantle caught the infielders playing back and layed down a perfect drag bunt, just out of Craig's reach and too soft to allow Neal to make a play at first.

Berra took two balls and a strike before grounding to Neal.

° ° Hodges tried for the ball but returned to cover the base when Neal, who had the easier play, called for the ball.

SCORE—New York 0, Brooklyn 0

SECOND INNING

Dodgers:

Robinson walked on five pitches.

Hodges singled to deep short.

° ° McDougald, seeing that he had no chance to retire the batter, tried for a force at second but Robinson, running with the pitch on a 3-1 count, run-and-hit situation, beat the throw.

Furillo took a strike, then flied to Bauer, Robinson advancing to third after the catch.

° ° With no outs Robinson tagged up and went to third after the catch. He was now in position to score on a fly ball to the outfield. Bauer's throw went to second to keep Hodges from advancing to scoring position.

Campanella flied to Bauer, Robinson scoring after the catch.

° ° Once again the throw went to second to keep Hodges from scoring position.

Neal fouled out to Berra.

° ° Berra played the ball to allow for drift back toward the infield. Ford went toward the ball to give advice and encouragement to Berra.

322

Yankees:

Slaughter flied to Gilliam.

°° Gilliam was wearing sun-glasses but was prepared to shield his eyes with his glove if the ball got into the sun. He played the ball to curve toward the foul line.

Martin hit a home run into the left-field seats.

°° Martin met a curve ball well out in front of him and his normal swing enabled him to hit it out of the park since he met the ball squarely.

McDougald walked on a 3-2 pitch.

°° Craig was being extra careful after the home run and lost the hitter.

Carey struck out.

°° There was little danger of a steal, with the pitcher due up next, but Campanella, like all good catchers, caught each pitch prepared to throw out the runner.

Ford struck out on a curve ball.

°° Craig took advantage of his "out-man" and went right to work on the pitcher.

score—New York 1, Brooklyn 1

THIRD INNING

Dodgers:

Craig singled to right field.

Gilliam hit into a double play, Martin to McDougald to Collins.

°° Gilliam fouled off two bunt attempts, both high fast balls, Ford making it as difficult as possible. Martin and McDougald moved in a couple of steps and were in perfect position to execute a quick double play.

Reese singled to center.

°° The pitch was a high fast ball, almost a waste-pitch, since Ford had a count of two strikes and one ball on the batter.

Snider fanned on three pitches.

°° Ford got ahead of the batter and made him chase a wide curve ball.

Yankees:

Bauer struck out.

°° Craig was following the book by concentrating on his curve ball to Bauer.

Collins grounded out, Hodges to Craig.

°° Craig broke for first as soon as he saw that the ball was hit to the right side. Since the ball was hit to Hodges' left, Craig took the throw running parallel with the foul line. The throw from Hodges was a good one—chest-high and reaching Craig two steps before he hit the base.

Mantle popped out to Campanella.

°° Craig got ahead of the batter and made him go for a bad ball. Campanella positioned himself with his back to the infield to allow for the drift of the ball. He discarded his mask by tossing it away from the direction in which he was running.

score—New York 1, Brooklyn 1

323

ADDENDA

Dodgers:

Robinson was thrown out by Carey.

** The Dodgers had been taking a strike but suddenly changed tactics. Robinson swung at the first pitch and hit it sharply, Carey making a great play to retire him.

Hodges grounded out, Carey to Collins.

** Carey did not hesitate but fired the ball to first to retire the runner.

Furillo was called out on strikes after fouling off two pitches.

** Ford had Furillo looking for the curve ball and whipped over a quick fast ball for a called third strike.

Yankees:

Berra flied to Neal in short right field.

** Furillo came in to make the catch and was in better position to do so but, since Neal was calling for the ball and concentrating on it, Furillo let him take it, rather than risk a collision.

Slaughter singled to left.

** Slaughter worked the count to 3-2, then hit the ball where it was pitched, driving an outside pitch to left field. Reese tried for the ball and was out of position so Neal covered second.

Martin hit into a double play, Craig to Reese to Hodges.

** The hit-and-run was on but Martin hit the ball sharply to Craig and there was time for a double play. Craig turned quickly but threw deliberately—but hard—to Reese, chest-high and a half-step to the left of second base. Hodges' long stretch for the ball helped complete the double play.

SCORE—New York 1, Brooklyn 1

Dodgers:

Campanella singled to left.

** Ford got two strikes with curve balls, then tried to sneak in a fast one. Campanella concentrated on just meeting the ball and got a base hit. Slaughter blocked the ball in left field, playing it safe to insure that the ball did not get through and allow Campanella to reach scoring position.

Neal struck out on a 2-2 curve ball.

** Carey had been playing in to guard against a possible sacrifice bunt but moved back to normal position when the count reached two strikes.

Craig missed a sacrifice attempt and Campanella was thrown out, Berra to McDougald.

** Campanella failed to wait until the ball was on the ground before taking off for second and was an easy out. Possibly this was a bunt-and-run.

Craig grounded out, Martin to Collins.

Yankees:

McDougald singled on the first pitch.

Carey struck out, swinging.

** The Yankees evidently were playing for a big inning and had Carey hit away rather than sacrifice. Craig, ahead of the hitter, got Carey to fan on a high fast ball.

Ford hit into a double play, Neal to Reese to Hodges.

** Ford squared around as if to bunt, hoping to draw the infielders out of position, but took a full swing, hitting an easy double-play ball to Neal.

SCORE—New York 1, Brooklyn 1

SIXTH INNING

The skies had become cloudy and the sun was no longer a problem.

Dodgers:

Gilliam popped to Martin.

** Martin called for the ball in loud, clear tones.

Reese tripled to right center.

** Martin went out to handle the relay, McDougald was in cut-off position, and Ford backed up third.

Snider flied to Mantle, Reese scoring after the catch.

** The infield was in close to cut off the run at the plate. Reese tagged up as soon as the ball was hit in the air and shifted his weight forward, ready to break for the plate. In short, he lost as little time as possible in scoring this big run.

Robinson grounded out, Carey to Collins.

** With two out Carey was guarding the third base line to reduce the possibility of an extra-base hit.

Yankees:

Bauer took a strike, then singled to left.

** As lead-off man, Bauer was taking a strike with his team behind in the late innings.

Collins flied to Snider on the first pitch.

** Bauer went half-way on the fly to center, returning to first after the catch. The Yankees did not sacrifice, playing for more than one run with their power coming up.

Mantle popped to Hodges on a 2-0 pitch.

** With the tying run on base, the Yankees had their best hitter, Mantle, hit away, even with a count of two balls, no strikes, figuring this to be their best scoring chance. Possibly anticipating this, Craig was careful not to throw a "fat" pitch. In fact, Mantle went for a bad ball and popped it up, neglecting to wait for "his pitch."

Berra singled, Bauer stopping at second.

** Craig got ahead of Berra, two strikes and no balls, but came in with too good a pitch, Berra singling cleanly. With two out and Brooklyn leading, Bauer played safe, stopping at second. Furillo threw ahead of the runner (to third), the throw being cut off by Reese.

Slaughter hit a home run into the right-field stands, scoring Bauer and Berra ahead of him.

** Slaughter worked the count to 3-1 and, with the "hit away" sign on, set

325

himself to swing if he got his pitch. He did, a belt-high fast ball on the inside corner. Circumstances decreed that he go for the long ball and, as a result, the Yankees, who had been losing 2-1, now enjoyed a two-run lead late in the game, meaning that Brooklyn would have to play conservative baseball in an attempt to keep their chances alive.

Martin flied to Snider on the first pitch.

** Snider ran to where he thought the ball would go and was waiting for it when it came down. He was ready to adjust his position according to the exact location of the ball.

SCORE—New York 4, Brooklyn 2

SEVENTH INNING

Dodgers:

Hodges walked on five pitches.

Furillo singled off Ford's glove. Hodges advanced to second on the hit and continued on to third when Martin bobbled the ball.

** Ford uses a large glove and it enabled him to block the ball and keep it from going through to the outfield. The ball was deflected toward Martin. He fumbled it and was unable to retrieve it in time to prevent Hodges from moving to third.

Campanella's fly was taken by McDougald in short left field.

** McDougald ran the ball back to the infield after the catch. This was wise. Without risking what was really an unnecessary throw (since there was no definite play to be made) it prevented the runners from advancing.

Neal grounded to Carey who, in his anxiety to make a play at the plate, bobbled the ball and then threw poorly to Berra. Hodges scored, Furillo reached second, and Neal was safe at first.

** Hodges was correct in breaking for the plate since, if he drew a throw, it would eliminate the possibility of a double play and, if the throw did beat him home, he could pull up and get caught in a run-down, giving the other two runners a chance to reach scoring position.

Carey's decision to make the play at home was a poor one at best. Hodges' run was relatively unimportant because, even if he had scored, the Yankees still would have been leading. If possible, the tying run should have been kept from scoring position and, in this case, a double play might have resulted, ending the inning then and there. Even a play at first seemed more justified, particularly after the fumble, since the out was a relatively sure one and would have left the Yankees still in commanding position.

The complexion of the game had suddenly changed. Brooklyn had the tying and winning runs on base with only one out.

Jackson batted for Craig and flied to Slaughter.

** Slaughter's throw went to third but was intercepted by McDougald who was in cut-off position. With one out Furillo and Neal had gone half-way. They returned to their bases after the catch.

Gilliam grounded to McDougald. Neal was forced at second, McDougald making the play himself.

** McDougald correctly made the easiest possible play for the third out, a big one in this inning.

Clem Labine, a right-hander with a good sinking fast ball and an excellent curve took over the pitching duties for Brooklyn.

Yankees:

McDougald grounded to Reese on a 3-2 pitch.

** Reese charged the ball and played it cleanly. As a good shortstop should, Reese played the ball rather than letting it play him.

Carey took a third strike.

Ford, too, was called out on strikes.

** Labine did not waste time with the Number 8 and Number 9 hitters. He got ahead of them both and came in with his best pitch, the curve ball. The result was two strike-outs and Brooklyn was still in the ball game.

SCORE—New York 4, Brooklyn 3

EIGHTH INNING

Dodgers:

Reese took a strike, then grounded to McDougald.

** Brooklyn, behind in the late innings, was taking a strike. Perhaps aware of this, Ford was getting ahead of the hitters.

Snider was called out on strikes.

** Ford got two quick strikes with a curve, then a fast ball. He had been getting Snider out with his curve ball and, sensing that Snider would be looking for that pitch, he set him up perfectly for the fast ball which he whipped over for a called third strike. Snider was fooled completely, since he made the mistake of guessing, "curve ball." The batter who is always set for the fast ball is ready to hit anything since he can always adjust his timing to the other pitches which are invariably slower than the fast one:

Robinson singled to left.

** The count went to 3-2 and Robinson fouled off several pitches before hitting a single. With two strikes he was guarding the plate and merely trying to meet the ball. Slaughter got the ball back to the infield quickly, making his throw to second base. McDougald, alert to rush out to left field if the ball got through Slaughter, returned to second base to take the throw, Martin backing him up.

Hodges flied to Mantle.

** Ford had been giving Hodges practically nothing but curve balls. He suddenly switched to his fast ball. It was a good pitch and Hodges went for it but was unable to get good wood on the ball, lifting a harmless fly to Mantle in center.

Yankees:

Bauer flied to Snider.

Collins grounded to Neal and was safe on the latter's wild throw to first.

** Neal, possibly over-anxious, made a hurried throw which arrived before Hodges had reached the base and was fully set for it. It went wild but was retrieved by Campanella before Collins could advance to second. Campanella had followed the batter to first and was in perfect position to retrieve the overthrow.

Mantle popped to Neal.

** Labine got ahead of Mantle with two quick strikes, the second called. He then made Mantle hit his (Labine's) pitch, a good curve ball under the hands.

Berra doubled to right center, scoring Collins.

** Labine threw five consecutive curve balls, all strikes, four of which Berra fouled off. Quite logically, he then tried to sneak over a fast ball but Berra was ready for it. His solid double gave the Yankees an insurance run.

Slaughter was purposely passed.

** This was good policy for several reasons: Slaughter had been particularly hot that day; he is a left-hand batter and Martin, who followed him, bats right-handed; and, above all, it set up a force play at any base.

Martin flied to Gilliam.

** The Yankees were swinging at the first ball in this inning, figuring that Labine's control was good and that he was getting the first pitch over for a strike. Perhaps Labine was guessing with them and not making the first pitch too good. At any rate, the Yankees were not doing much with the first ball.

SCORE—New York 5, Brooklyn 3

NINTH INNING

Dodgers:

Furillo doubled to right center but was out trying to stretch it into a triple, Bauer to Martin to Carey.

** Furillo's attempt to stretch his hit into a triple cannot very well be justified. With no outs and his team losing in the ninth inning, his main job should have been keeping his team's chances alive. He definitely should have been playing safe. Furthermore, at second base he was already in scoring position and, in addition, his run meant nothing at the time because, even if he had scored, Brooklyn would still have been trailing by a run.

Campanella was called out on strikes.

** Ford was getting the big outs with his best pitch, a well-controlled curve. In short, when the chips were down he was pitching to his own strength.

Neal grounded out, Carey to Collins.

** Collins hustled to the bag, found it with his left foot, and was prepared to shift in any direction according to the location of the throw.

FINAL SCORE—New York 5, Brooklyn 3

By playing sound baseball throughout the game and by capitalizing fully on their opportunities the Yankees had won their "must" game.

A discussion of baseball tactics as employed by the two teams in the World Series of 1956 should certainly include mention of an incident which occurred in the fourth game. It serves as a good example of Big-League thinking at its best.

Jackie Robinson was on first base with one out in the second inning and Sandy Amoros was the batter. Brooklyn attempted a hit-and-run play and Robinson was more than half-way to second when Amoros hit the ball. Amoros' effort was a foul fly close to the first base stands. Billy Martin, the Yankee second baseman, was thinking every inch of the way. He faked fielding a ground ball. To complete the subterfuge Gil Mc-Dougald, the shortstop, ran toward second base as though he were going to take the throw for a force-out and possible double play. Robinson was taken in by the ruse and continued to run hard for second. In the meantime, Collins caught the ball, Sturdivant, the pitcher, covered first base, and Robinson was out by the proverbial mile. Unfortunately for the Yankees, Collins threw wild and Robinson was able to return to first safely. Regardless of the eventual outcome of the play, this was a wonderful demonstration of the smart, quick-thinking play which marks a real professional.

RULES INTERPRETATION

A thorough knowledge of the rules is too often neglected, even by professionals, and it cannot help but improve one's play, both from an individual and team standpoint, to be completely familiar with them.

Baseball's rules are the most intricate of any sport's and continual study is necessary if they are to be mastered.

The following discussion of the interpretation of certain rules is not designed to be comprehensive. Rather, it covers several relatively common situations which can arise in a ball game and are too often misunderstood by players and fans alike.

1. Appeal Plays: The meaning of this term implies that certain violations of the rules must be called to the attention of the umpires before a decision can be made on them. Appeal plays are three in number, and every team, when in the field, should be alert for these rules infractions so that full advantage will be taken of every opportunity to get an out.

(a) Failure to touch a base: When an opposing base runner fails to touch a base, the ball should be retrieved and the base in question touched by a defensive player in possession of the ball. If, by any chance, the ball is hit over a fence, lost, or goes out of play in like manner, the pitcher should throw the ball to the appropriate base after he has received a new ball from the umpire and taken his position on the rubber—and before delivering a pitch to the next batter.

(b) Leaving a base too soon: If a runner leaves his base before a fly ball comes into contact with a fielder who is in the act of catching it, the ball should be thrown to that base. When the base has been

329

touched by a defensive player in possession of the ball, the runner should be declared out.

(c) Batting out of order: This violation is a tricky one and can become quite involved. It should not be called until after the batter becomes a base runner—but it must be reported to the umpire before a pitch is delivered to the next batter. It is the original batter, not the one who batted out of turn, who is declared out. Unless the violator causes a definite disadvantage to the defensive team it is wise to refrain from appealing to the umpire. Should the other team fail to realize its mistake and repeat it later in the game when the scoring of runs may be involved, the defensive club will then be able to take advantage of this infraction of the rules.

It must be remembered that the umpire is powerless to rule on these plays unless they are appealed to him.

2. The ball is dead and no further play is possible in the following cases:

(a) The batter is hit by a pitched ball—base runners may advance only if forced to the next base.

(b) A balk is called—base runners are entitled to advance one base; the count on the batter remains the same.

(c) A ball is batted illegally (the batter hits it while not completely in the batter's box)—the batter is declared out; base runners may not advance.

(d) A foul ball is not legally caught—the ball is dead until the pitcher takes his position on the mound with the ball.

(e) Interference is called on a player—if on a runner, he is declared out; if on a defensive player, the runner is awarded the next base.

(f) A batted ball hits a runner—he is declared out and the batter is awarded first base and credited with a hit.

(g) A batted ball hits an umpire before passing a fielder other than the pitcher.

(h) The ball touches a spectator.

3. A ball is judged foul or fair by its position relative to the foul line, not by where a fielder is when he touches it. A ground ball is considered fair if it passes first or third base in fair territory or if, before reaching the base, it rolls dead in fair territory. A ball hit in the air is fair or foul according to its position when it lands beyond first or third base, when it is touched by a fielder, or when it leaves the ball park by clearing a fence.

4. The infield fly rule: The batter is declared out when he hits a *fair* fly ball which, in the judgement of the umpire, can be handled by an *infielder* when first and second, or first, second, and third bases are occupied with *less* than two out. Base runners may advance at their own

risk. The infield fly should be called by the umpire as soon as possible after the ball is hit. To play safe, defensive players should treat this as an ordinary fly ball.

5. If two runners are on the same base, possession of it belongs to the man who originally occupied it. The other runner may be tagged out if he fails to return safely to his original base. Base runners should be fully aware of this rule to avoid being caught in an accidental double play. Defensive players can play safe by tagging both runners.

6. If the ball hits an umpire after having passed a fielder, other than the pitcher, it is in play. Base runners should move as they would on an ordinary batted ball and the defense should treat the play in the same fashion, retrieving the ball as quickly as possible.

7. A base runner must run around a defensive player who is in the act of fielding a batted ball. In this situation, any contact between runner and fielder will result in the runner's being declared out for interference.

8. A fielder who is not in possession of the ball may not block a runner in the latter's attempt to reach a base. In this case, interference should be called on the defensive player and the runner is awarded the base to which he was advancing.

9. On a batted ball handled by the catcher the batter must run in the three-foot lane which is marked off from a point half-way between home and first, to that base. This also applies to bunts and batted balls fielded by the pitcher in the home-plate area. Actually, it applies on all plays at first base but there seems to be little inclination on the part of the runner to wander out of the three-foot lane on plays other than those cited. A runner who is hit by a thrown ball on such a play shall be declared out for interference if he is not in the three-foot lane when hit by the ball or if he obstructs the first baseman, causing the latter to drop the throw.

10. The dropped third strike rule: A batter may run on a dropped third strike as long as first base is unoccupied. With two out, he may run even with first base occupied. The batter should be alert for a dropped third strike and should not allow himself to be tagged by the catcher in this situation, remembering that as long as he can make the other team throw the ball there exists the possibility of an error.

11. The balk rule: A balk shall be called by the umpires; the ball becomes dead, and runners are allowed to advance one base in the following situations:

    (a) The pitcher makes any motion which can be construed as a move to deliver the ball to the batter or to throw to first base without completing the throw. He can, however, fake a throw to either second base or third, when occupied.

    (b) If he does not step toward the base in making a throw to it. A left-hander is allowed considerable leeway in throwing to first base, his move being considered within the rules if he steps toward a point at least half-way between home and first.

(c) If he delivers the ball to the plate while his pivot foot is not in contact with the rubber. He can, however, throw to or fake toward any base when not on the rubber.

(d) If he pitches while not facing the batter.

(e) If he makes a motion to pitch while not in position on the rubber.

(f) If the pitcher holds the ball so long as to delay the game unnecessarily.

(g) If he takes his position on the mound while not in possession of the ball.

(h) If he moves his arm, shoulder, knee, hip, or body in such a way as to indicate that he is pitching the ball to the plate without doing so. This applies also to a move toward first base.

(i) If he makes any motion to pitch while not in possession of the ball.

(j) If he takes either hand off the ball after coming to his stop and does not deliver the ball.

(k) If he throws to an unoccupied base.

(l) If the pitcher drops the ball while on the mound and ready to pitch.

(m) If the pitcher does not come to a *complete stop* after taking his stretch and before delivering the ball to the plate.

The pitcher may step off the rubber and call time without being guilty of a balk, but he must be careful to do so without making any motion toward home plate or first base, moves which might be considered as intending to deceive the batter or runner.

12. A balk is called on the catcher if he steps out of the catcher's box before the ball is delivered by the pitcher. This pertains primarily to the intentional pass, and the catcher must take care to delay his stepping outside the confines of the catcher's box until the ball is on its way to the plate.

HUSTLE

1. Hustle is being at the right place at the right time. It is making the right play at all times. It is helping your team by helping yourself.
2. Hustle is bearing down all the way—and bearing down twice as hard when the going gets tough.
3. Hustle is playing with your head as well as with your arms and legs. It is in the doing; it is action, not mere words.
4. Hustle is taking advantage of every opening. It makes its own breaks.

5. Hustle is what separates the men from the boys, the big leaguer from the busher. It is the one ingredient, above all others, that wins ball games.
6. Be a big leaguer in everything you do—hustle all the way.

Always Know

1. The score
2. The outs
3. The inning

Realize

You should play to win, but be willing to accept defeat gracefully, profit from today's mistakes, and go out and win tomorrow's game.

Remember

No team ever walked to victory.

Above All

Baseball is a team game—help one another at all times.

INDEX

INDEX